Fragmented Lives, Assembled Parts

FRAGMENTED LIVES

ASSEMBLED PARTS

Culture, Capitalism, and Conquest

at the U.S.-Mexico Border

Alejandro Lugo

UNIVERSITY OF TEXAS PRESS ᘓᘔ AUSTIN

Requests for permission to reproduce material from this
work should be sent to:
    Permissions
    University of Texas Press
    P.O. Box 7819
    Austin, TX 78713-7819
    www.utexas.edu/utpress/about/bpermission.html

♾ The paper used in this book meets the minimum
requirements of ANSI/NISO Z39.48-1992 (R1997)
(Permanence of Paper).

Library of Congress Cataloging-in-Publication Data
Lugo, Alejandro, 1962–
Fragmented lives, assembled parts : culture, capitalism,
and conquest at the U.S.-Mexico border / Alejandro Lugo.
— 1st ed.
        p.   cm.
Includes bibliographical references and index.
ISBN 978-0-292-71766-4 (cloth : alk. paper) —
ISBN 978-0-292-71767-1 (pbk. : alk. paper)
1. Offshore assembly industry—Employees—Mexico—
Ciudad Juárez.   2. Ciudad Juárez (Mexico)—Social
conditions.   I. Title.
HD8039.O332M61584   2008
331.700972'16—dc22
                                    2007044626

Para todas y todos los trabajadores de maquiladora, y especialmente con gratitud profunda para aquellos y aquellas que me ayudaron tanto y que con mucha paciencia han esperado este proyecto.

In a call for justice for all the working-class women of Juárez who have been killed; and in special memory of Claudia Ivette González, who disappeared and was never seen again after she was sent back home by a maquiladora guard who did not let her in because she arrived two minutes late for work.

En memoria de mi prima Toña, a single mother of two little girls, who died as a result of an accident that occurred while riding a bus on her way to work at a maquiladora.

In memory of Dra. Guillermina Valdés-Villalva, pioneer of border studies and women's rights in Ciudad Juárez.

Para mi amigo y colega César Silva Montes— ex–maquiladora worker, activist, scholar.

Para don José Cazares—ex-bracero, ex–street vendor, ex–maquiladora worker— *y en memoria de doña Lola.*

Para mi mamá, Vicenta Juárez Viuda de Lugo, the last survivor of the 1940s generation of Juárez migrants in my family; *y en memoria de mi papá,* Federico Lugo Rivera, bracero and migrant farmworker.

Si hay una cosa en la tierra
Más importante que Dios:
Y es que nadie escupa sangre
Pa' que otro viva mejor.

If there is one thing on earth
More important than God;
It's that nobody should cough up blood
So that somebody else can live better.

— Atahualpa Yupanqui

CONTENTS

ACKNOWLEDGMENTS

IT HAS BEEN a very long time since I started this book project. As we all know, all academic work is a collaboration, particularly in the case of an ethnography based on anthropological fieldwork. Without the women and men who generously offered their time for the fieldwork interviews and conversations that highly inform this historical and ethnographic study of postcolonial working-class border life in late-twentieth-century Ciudad Juárez, this book would not have been possible. I will always be indebted to many people in Juárez, especially Sergio de Z., Lencho (Shibata), Rosy S., Julia, Rafa B., Martín, Juan C. S., Alfredo, Paty, Jorge de Nayarit, Chela, Susana (*por los compadres*), Chuy (*el mejor futbolista*), Socorrito, Lola, Araceli, Rosita, Elio, Alma S., Chapo M. P., Chelito, the late Lola S., *el señor ex-sociólogo* and *la señora Estela.* Thanks for all your support and particularly your patience: *Espero que mis descripciones de la vida en las maquiladoras no los desilusionen.*

I would also like to thank Lili and Lupe, two of my sisters who have always defended my anthropology. Muchas gracias también to my three older sisters, who, as young adolescents, started working in the maquiladora assembly line in the early seventies, when I was still in grade school in Juárez: Cruz, Luz Elena, and Rosa María—*gracias por lo que ayudaron a nuestros padres y a sus hermanos menores.* It took me years to understand and see that I myself benefited from patriarchy, both at home and in the larger society. And it took me just as long to suspect that even the relatives of maquiladora workers do not understand or know what kind of life their loved ones live inside the factories nor the kinds of uncertainties they experience on their way to or from work. I hope this book makes a positive difference in this regard.

In the academic arena, I will always be grateful to those who provided me with the anthropological training that eventually led to this book: in particular, Renato Rosaldo, Jane Collier, George Collier, Sylvia Yanagisako, Aihwa Ong, Maria Lepowsky, Florencia Mallon, Ann Stoler, Robert Brightman, Emiko Ohnuki-Tierney, Frank Salomon, Pamela Bunte, and especially Bradley Blake, who introduced me to the discipline. In addition, ever since I completed my doctoral research, the following colleagues, friends, and students kindly reminded me, through their good spirits, about my responsibility to carry this ethnographic and historical project to completion and turn it into a book: Martha González-Cortez, Miguel Díaz-Barriga, Cheryl Howard, Cheryl Martin, Chuck Ambler, Emma Pérez, Kathy Staudt, Elea Aguirre, Zulma Méndez, Charles Cuauhtémoc Chase-Venegas, Sylvia Peregrino, Jorge Balderas Domínguez, Nancy Abelmann, Bill Kelleher, Alma Gottlieb, Janet Keller, Steve Leigh, Brenda Farnell, Arlene Torres, Charles Varela, Cynthia Radding, Joyce Tolliver, Angharad Valdivia, Cameron McCarthy, Adrian Burgos, Anne Martínez, Wanda Pillow, Larry Parker, Brian Montes, Gabriel Cortez, Arisve Esquivel, Angélica Rivera, Alyssa García, Kevin Karpiak, Walter Little, Judith Zurita Noguera, Rogelio Santiago Salud, Sarah Scheiderich, Aidé Acosta, So Jin Park, Jennifer Shoaff, Daniel Gutiérrez, Sujey Vega, Alison Goebel, and M. J. Walker.

I would also like to thank the following cohort comrades for always being there for me: Susana Sawyer, Bill Maurer, Diane Nelson, Kaushik Ghosh, Lynn Meish, and especially Lourdes Giordani. I am also grateful to Neil Foley, Matt García, Joseph Bastien, Akhil Gupta, and particularly Lynn Stephen for their special support. It has been a privilege to be in the company, even if at a distance, of the following *compañeros* and *compañeras* in the human sciences who have struggled as much as I have to better understand Ciudad Juárez: Víctor Ortiz, María Patricia Fernández-Kelly, Devon Peña, Lourdes Portillo, Susan Christopherson, Gay Young, Rosa Linda Fregoso, Alicia Castellanos, Sarah Hill, Eduardo Barrera, Melissa Wright, Patricia Ravelo, Pablo Vila, Socorro Tabuenca, Alfredo Limas, Kathy Staudt (again), and Leslie Salzinger.

The final version of my manuscript presented here would not have been possible without the time and effort put into it by two reviewers: one anonymous and the other one, María Patricia Fernández-Kelly, who wrote the first anthropological ethnography in English describing what maquiladora women, such as my older sisters, had gone through on the global assembly line in Ciudad Juárez. Both reviewers contributed substantially, through their useful suggestions and constructive criticisms, to making this book precisely what I imagined it to be from the beginning.

Claudia Rivers, Head of Special Collections at the University of Texas at El

Paso, and Rick Hendricks, in charge of "Prenuptial Investigations" at the New Mexico State University Library in Las Cruces, provided me with their time and resources even when I showed up without advance notice.

I am forever grateful to my wife, Martina, and to our two daughters, Elena and Rosalía, for all they had to endure while I was working on this project. And a very sincere "thank you" to an extraordinary editorial team at UT Press: Lynne Chapman, for overseeing the manuscript with so much care; Theresa May, Assistant Director and Editor-in-Chief, for giving me this opportunity and for her endless and friendly patience with me; and Nancy Warrington, an outstanding copyeditor, for her rigor and her commitment to the book.

Needless to say, in spite of the support and inspiration of all the individuals mentioned above, I am ultimately responsible for any errors.

My anthropological fieldwork for this book was funded by Ibero-American Studies at the University of Wisconsin in 1987, by the Center of Latin American Studies at Stanford University in 1989, and by a Stanford Dissertation Fieldwork Fellowship in 1990–1991. While writing my dissertation, I lived in El Paso from 1992 to 1995. Since then, I have visited the region every summer (except the summer of 1998) and during key holidays, including Holy Week, Mexico's independence day, Catholic saints' celebrations (such as San Lorenzo and La Virgen de Guadalupe), and several Christmas breaks. Throughout the 1990s and into the present, I consulted newspapers, took additional "fieldwork" notes, and remained in touch with key friends/informants. Throughout most of the last decade, a period in which I have tried to trace general developments regarding maquiladora life (and death) at the border, my archival work and research stints were financially supported by University of Illinois research and travel funds and by the Illinois Program for Research in the Humanities during 2000–2001.

Fragmented Lives, Assembled Parts

The rose/*La rosa*. "Roses are the Mexican's favorite flower. I think, how symbolic—thorns and all" (Anzaldúa 1999, 113).

ONE

Introduction

The scope of the modern European expansion which began in the fifteenth century far exceeded that of any previous "world" conquest. During the 1500s and 1600s it proceeded to enmesh in its web of domination the natives of the Americas, Africa, southern Asia, and the islands of the South Seas . . . As in the wake of other conquests, there were many different trends and counter-trends with respect to the acceptance and rejection of what the conquerors offered as a new and superior way of life. . . . In most cases, after the native peoples were subjugated, strong sentiment grew up in the conquering nation regarding the injustice of the original conquest . . . but only a segment of the dominant nation was influenced by such sentiments. In contrast in every country stood those generally classed as practical people who remained dominated by the old urge for conquest, but now expressed in new terms, such as political integration and cultural assimilation.   —EDWARD H. SPICER, *CYCLES OF CONQUEST*

If we knew the sixteenth century better . . . we would no longer discuss globalization as though it were a new, recent situation. . . . Right from the Renaissance, Western expansion has continuously spawned hybrids all over the globe, along with reactions of rejection. . . . Planetwide mestizo phenomena thus seem closely linked to the harbingers of economic globalization that began in the second half of the sixteenth century, a century which, whether viewed from Europe, America, or Asia, was the Iberian century *par excellence*, just as our own has become the American century. This glance backward is merely another way of discussing the present . . .
          —SERGE GRUZINSKI, *THE MESTIZO MIND*

CIUDAD JUÁREZ, CHIHUAHUA, Mexico, founded in 1659 and with a current population of approximately 1.3 million people, is both the oldest colonial settlement along the U.S.-Mexico border (Arreola and Curtis 1993) and one of the largest industrialized border cities, not only in the Americas but in the world. Of major importance is the fact that many of the sociocultural markers of empire (including names of ethnic groups, missions, urban settlements, and rivers, for instance), as well as the unequal social relations that produced these markers, have persisted, with minor alterations, for more than four hundred years—at least since the conquest of the area by the Spaniards in 1598. Furthermore, several of the colonial identities that emerged from the conquests of northern New Spain, particularly from the conquest of southern New Mexico (where Paso del Norte—present-day Ciudad Juárez—was located), inevitably became intertwined with the social, material, and cultural relations of economic globalization during the last four decades.

This book juxtaposes the social and human consequences of global industrial capitalism in the late twentieth century with those of the early imperial conquest of Mexico's northern frontier during the sixteenth and seventeenth centuries in order to document, both ethnographically and through historical analysis, the "urge for conquest, expressed in new terms," that has culminated in the material and cultural subjugation, or present conquest, of economically vulnerable populations in the U.S.-Mexico border region.

I conducted ethnographic research (participant observation) inside multinational assembly plants, or maquiladoras or maquilas (as the workers often call them), and on the streets and in the neighborhoods of Ciudad Juárez in the mid- to late 1980s, during 1990–1991, and intermittently throughout the 1990s. This ethnographic material on everyday life under late capitalism complements my interpretive analysis of a rich but selective historiography and literary work that allowed me to explore the articulation of the conquests of Mexico and New Mexico in the sixteenth century. In this process, I (1) weigh the varying late-twentieth-century labor practices of industrial-capitalist agents of the American empire (mainly multinational corporations) against sixteenth-century military strategies of conquest on the part of the Spaniards (both Crown and Catholic Church officials—missionaries, military men, and chroniclers); (2) compare the Spaniards' material and discursive techniques of control and physical exploitation with the symbolic forms of domination deployed through twentieth-century academic discourses and disciplinary practices of American or U.S.-trained historians and anthropologists; and (3) examine writings by local Juárez/El Paso intellectual and ethnographic voices of subalterns, including maquiladora workers.

These three major juxtapositions, which make up (not necessarily in a linear way) the main body of this book, lead, eventually, to the following argument: that the continuing social-economic-political domination of the Mexican masses, particularly the indigenous poor and the mostly mestizo working- and lower-middle classes, is a sociohistorical product of the politics of conquest of two global empires: the Spanish Empire (1521–1810) and the American Empire (1848–present), which are currently operating almost simultaneously as a doubly heavy "iron cage" (to invoke Max Weber) on the shoulders of Mexican subalterns, not only in Mexico but in the United States as well.

In consequence (at least for the historically and politically important case of Ciudad Juárez at the turn of the twenty-first century), the conditions for general class mobilization against capitalism and other forms of conquest are not occurring, precisely because class mobilization itself is constantly being *unmade*—culturally, politically, and economically—at both the global level and that of everyday life. I am not arguing here, of course, that workers do not rebel or organize; they do (see Peña 1997). But in most instances, either the state apparatus represses them or the mobilization is relatively temporary (see Castellanos 1981). I hope to show that this uneven but effective assault on the workers, this *unmaking*, is complicated by the complex nature of its constitution: it is a power matrix made up of gender, class, and color hierarchies and "border inspections" of all kinds—all of which have a culture and a history in the particular politics of global capitalism in Ciudad Juárez and in the specific politics of imperial conquest in the region.

Ultimately, by deciphering this power matrix throughout the chapters that follow, I hope to disentangle, at least analytically, the "web of domination" associated by Edward Spicer with "modern European expansion" since the sixteenth century, and by Serge Gruzinski with "Western expansion" since the Renaissance. Through these juxtapositions, I argue that Mexico, as a colonized society both historically and into the present, is a product of the uneven combination of the Iberian century and the American century, as Gruzinski defined them. These historical and political forces are clearly manifested in the postcolonial border metropolis of Ciudad Juárez, Chihuahua, Mexico—the focus of this ethnographic study.

As an anthropological study of contemporary Mexico, this monograph comparatively complements, both geographically and chronologically, some of the major historical and anthropological studies of Mexican society, especially Eric Wolf's *Sons of the Shaking Earth* (1959), Octavio Paz's *Labyrinth of Solitude* (1961), Ruth Behar's *Translated Woman* (1993), Ana María Alonso's *Thread of Blood* (1995), Guillermo Bonfil Batalla's *México Profundo* (1996), Claudio Lomnitz's *Deep Mexico, Silent Mexico* (2001), and Lynn Stephen's *Zapata Lives!* (2002).

Two decades ago, explicit debates on urban working classes in the social scientific literature of northern Mexico were rare. Today there are several excellent and useful sociological, historical, and ethnographic studies about different aspects of this region's working classes, including, but not limited to, descriptions of working-class neighborhoods, social and ecological environments, the informal economy, and working-class women in particular, as well as specific studies of "working-class formation" (Arreola and Curtis 1993; Behar 1993; Bustamante

1983; Carrillo and Hernandez 1985; Fernández-Kelly 1983; García 1981; Hart 1998; Heyman 1991; Hill 2003; Iglesias 1985; Kopinak 1996; Orozco Orozco 1992; Peña 1997; Ruiz and Tiano 1987; Sklair 1989; Staudt 1998; Stoddard 1987; Taylor and Hickey 2001; Tiano 1994; Young 1986; among others). The present book contributes to this vast and rich literature, not only with ethnographic material collected in the late 1980s and early 1990s among male and female factory workers (see also Salzinger 2003)—as well as its analysis of print media representations and depictions of border life and death throughout the 1990s and into the present (see also Fregoso 2003)—but also with an explicit cultural analysis of working-class life under the shadow of its early colonial past.

It is precisely the analytical juxtaposition of the colonial and postcolonial realities of Paso del Norte/Ciudad Juárez, and their consequences for the continuing politics of conquest against border subalterns, that distinguishes this book from previous monographs about this desert metropolis, including the following foundational texts: Oscar Martínez's (1978) *Border Boom Town: Ciudad Juárez since 1848*; Alicia Castellanos's (1981) *Ciudad Juárez: La vida fronteriza*; María Patricia Fernández-Kelly's (1983) *For We Are Sold, I and My People*; Armando B. Chávez's (1991) *Historia de Ciudad Juárez, Chihuahua*; Devon G. Peña's (1997) *Terror of the Machine*; Kathleen Staudt's (1998) *Free Trade? Informal Economies at the U.S.-Mexico Border*; Mario Lugo's (1998) *Detén mis trémulas manos*; Pablo Vila's (2000) *Crossing Borders, Reinforcing Borders*; Sergio González Rodríguez's (2002) *Huesos en el desierto*; Jorge Balderas Domínguez's (2002) *Mujeres, antros y estigmas en la noche juarense*; and Leslie Salzinger's (2003) *Genders in Production* (in addition to the interdisciplinary ethnographic essays in Pablo Vila's [2003] edited collection, *Ethnography at the Border*, which in itself amounts to a productive collaborative monograph on the Paso del Norte region).

With the exception of Armando Chávez's historical study of Juárez and W. H. Timmons's (1990) historical study of El Paso, none of these key monographs (either historical, anthropological, sociological, or geographical) explores the sixteenth and early seventeenth centuries, and neither Chávez nor Timmons examines the impact of the early colonial encounters on the postcolonial subjecthood and subjectivities of underprivileged communities in late-twentieth-century Ciudad Juárez.

With regard to the vast literature on border crossings—perhaps the most theoretically exciting interdisciplinary body of work produced since the mid-1980s (for instance, Anzaldúa 1987; R. Rosaldo 1993; Flores 1993; Limón 1994; Morales 1996; Vélez-Ibáñez 1996, 2004; Michaelsen and Johnson 1997; Saldívar 1997; Bonilla et al. 1998; Jackson 1998; Maciel and Herrera-Sobek 1998; Aldama 2001; Staudt and Coronado 2002; de Genova and Ramos-Zayas 2003; Fregoso 2003; Bejarano 2005)—this book contributes complementary ethnographic material on "border inspections" and a cultural analysis of late industrial capitalism, as well as focusing primarily on the Mexican side of the border (see also Fregoso 2003 and Staudt and Coronado 2002), including an examination of the latter's discursive "invention" in the sixteenth century. Most of these studies have prioritized the plight of Mexican Americans and other Latinos on U.S. soil. For the most part, they ignore the Mexican side of the crossing in the context of its early colonial history (Arreola and Curtis 1993 and Jackson 1998 are exceptions).

These resources on northern Mexico, border issues, and feminist preoccupations of working-class women have influenced the key theoretical questions I raise herein. In several ways, this study attempts to engage directly and indirectly with these rich, heterogeneous traditions—all in order to better understand the working classes in the twenty-first century as products of the changing modern nation-state in the contexts of monarchy, transnationalism, and power (Foucault 1978). I can only hope that this study about Paso del Norte/Ciudad Juárez offers the next generation of politically committed scholars exactly what I want to give: a reminder that in manufacturing (and assembling) capitalist societies, working-class life, particularly as it was constituted in its everydayness during England's nineteenth century (see Thompson 1966), has not improved for many of the rank and file carrying out the working day around the world, even at the turn of the twenty-first century. In fact, in many places such as Ciudad Juárez, for many of the workers inhabiting these industrial, historical, and cultural borderlands—especially young women—life *and* death have gotten worse.

Organization of the Book

The ethnographic and historical materials in this book are necessarily presented in a nonlinear manner covering two seemingly unrelated historical moments organized into two major sections: (1) the original conquests of Mexico and southern New Mexico in the sixteenth and early seventeenth centuries and (2) the economic and cultural conquest of the U.S.-Mexico borderlands in the late twentieth century. *Fragmented Lives, Assembled Parts* also includes a theoretical treatise (Chapter 9), which is empirically substantiated with specific materials in Part I, the historical chapters (2 and 3), and in Part II, the ethnographically grounded chapters (4–8). The book closes with an epilogue on the killings of women and young girls in Ciudad Juárez.

The two chapters in Part I, Sixteenth-Century Conquests (1521–1598) and Their Postcolonial Border Legacies, attempt to delineate specific historical processes that gave "official" identity to the region under study during the encounter between local indigenous communities and the Spaniards in the sixteenth century in both central New Spain and in what became New Mexico, and during the encounter with the Americans under the new imperialism in the nineteenth century (though the latter period is dealt with only briefly).

Chapter 2, "The Invention of Borderlands Geography: What Do Aztlán and

Tenochtitlán Have to Do with Ciudad Juárez/*Paso del Norte?*" traces the political and economic processes that gave names (and thus initial Western identity) to the territories we currently call Mexico and New Mexico. The chapter does not take for granted any of these critical inventions of conquest. The chapter moves in time (chronology) and space (geography) from the invention of "Mexico," the "Aztecs," and "Nueva/New Mexico" as cultural categories, to the invention and naming of the "Río Bravo," "Rio Grande," "Paso del Norte," "Aztlán," and lastly "Ciudad Juárez," a phrase coined in the late nineteenth century. I attempt to uncover the political and economic layers that gave cultural form to the late-twentieth-century space we call today the U.S-Mexico (Chihuahua–New Mexico–Texas) border region: the Paso del Norte region, which includes Ciudad Juárez, Mexico; El Paso, Texas; and Las Cruces, New Mexico.

I believe it is important to understand the historical and cultural processes through which the border region has been imagined as part of a larger entity, such as New Spain, Mexico, the American Southwest, New Mexico, Texas, Chihuahua, and lastly, Aztlán. The latter so-called mythical place of origin of the Aztecs, and its broader cultural legacy, is the analytical and political epitome of the chapter due to its continuous historical and political importance, especially for Mexicans and Chicanos/as (politicized Mexican Americans) on the U.S. side of the border, though I revisit Aztlán in the context of the Spaniards' appropriation of its "mythical reality." One of the major goals of this chapter is to show how the two conquests of Mexico and of New Mexico in the sixteenth century gave identity not only to "a place" as we know it today, but also to the politics of conquest of the Mexican masses in both central and northern Mexico—a politics of domination that too many, even today, cannot escape or transcend (see Spicer 1962).

Chapter 3, "The Problem of Color in Mexico and on the U.S.-Mexican Border: Precolonial, Colonial, and Postcolonial Subjectivities," attempts to historicize and problematize the social geography of the Mesoamerican and Southwest regions, not through naming, but through a specific cultural practice of coloring individuals according to peoples' different shades of skin color (see also Chapter 6). I argue here that the discourse on color was *heterogeneously* maintained from the time of conquest through the colonial period, from independence to the Mexican Revolution, and from the revolution era to late capitalism under the maquiladoras of Ciudad Juárez. This chapter presents the reader with the historical and cultural contexts, dominated by hierarchies of color, within which to better understand a relatively "silent" aspect of the everyday life not only of maquiladora workers but of the Mexican population in general.

By interrogating the category of "the postcolonial," the chapter also challenges both the Latin American and the non–Latin American(ist) postcolonial reader, as well as the literature on *mestizaje,* by calling for the analysis of a new term, *colorismo,* particularly given the many ways "Mexican identity" can be questioned when issues of color are raised. Lastly, this chapter examines the problem of racism in Mexico *within* the so-called mestizo population—a political problem so far largely ignored. The sociohistorical treatment given here underscores the question of color constituting social inequalities in Mexico, especially as these will be manifested and depicted ethnographically in the subsequent chapters on culture, class, and gender (Chapters 4–8).

In Part II, "Culture, Class, and Gender in Late-Twentieth-Century Ciudad Juárez," five chapters explore industrial life inside and outside the factories as lived by women, men, and this anthropologist. Each chapter, by describing social life within an industrial/assembling setting, documents how cultural practices are produced, reproduced, and transformed, as well as how class experience is made while class mobilization is unmade—all through the everyday actions of individual human beings struggling to live a decent life under late industrial capitalism. Through these five chapters, the reader should capture what it meant to live as a factory worker in the late twentieth century on the U.S.-Mexico border.

Chapter 4, "Maquiladoras, Gender, and Culture Change," introduces the initial ethnographic research questions I raised about cultural change in gender relations, particularly during the mid-1980s, and my early ethnographic findings with respect to hiring practices of several transnational corporations, job-searching techniques used by unemployed men and women looking for maquiladora work, and the general effect these strategies for survival under global capitalism had on the local gendered labor market and on gender relations among workers in the new industrial border city.

Chapter 5, "The Political Economy of Tropes, Culture, and Masculinity Inside an Electronics Factory," focuses on the problem of "culture," both its production and its reproduction, in particular industrial contexts. It examines the cultural notion of "laziness," not only in a historical context (starting with the colonial relation between "Indians" and Spaniards), but in the equally global, though more complicated, circumstances of the international division of labor under late capitalism in the late 1980s. The chapter specifically documents through ethnographic detail how working-class language is incorporated into the production of microcircuits for computers, and how, in the process, the localized ideology of *machismo* (exalted manliness or masculinity) is reproduced through a transformed notion of laziness articulated in the term *barra,* which denotes both "lazy" and the name of a tool used in production. It is also in this chapter that a systematic concept of culture is utilized (following Boas, Sahlins, and R. Rosaldo) to examine additional ethnographic material. I argue that our academic imaginings about culture (and class) do not exist and, in fact, have not existed outside "structure and agency." I try to maintain this argument while at the same time applying, to appropriate situations throughout the book, Renato Rosaldo's notion of "cultural borderlands."

Chapter 6, "Border Inspections: Inspecting the Working-Class Life of Maquiladora Workers on the U.S.-Mexico Border," tells stories of defiance and failure on the part of working-class people in Ciudad Juárez. It also suggests that the analytical strength of "border crossings" as a theoretical tool can be ethnographically enriched in an empirically substantial manner by recognizing that most border crossings are constituted by "inspection stations" that inspect and monitor what goes in and out in the name of class, gender, race, and nation. The chapter explores (and attempts to explain) the pervasiveness of border inspections under late industrial capitalism inside an automobile type of maquiladora and beyond, and calls explicitly for a new analytical tool, border inspections, to be added to the current metaphor of border crossings. While it is true that there are multiple borders, the chapter tries to demonstrate that too many of them cannot be crossed, especially if the crosser is an underprivileged, working-class person.

Chapter 7, "Culture, Class, and Union Politics: The Daily Struggle for Chairs inside a Sewing Factory in the Larger Context of the Working Day," examines, through the exposition of selected notes from the (battle)field, the unstable way in which "structure and agency" disarticulate or rupture from each other, causing cultural change or transformation in the life of sewing-factory workers. In this particular garment factory, the workers were not assigned a chair in which to sit. They had to negotiate a different chair every morning at 6:00 AM. The problem at the everyday level was that not all negotiators were equal. In fact, due to the changes in the structure of the labor force since the 1980s, the negotiators tended to be unequal: men negotiating against women, teenage women negotiating against men in their twenties, and shy newcomers from the south of Mexico negotiating against experienced and "aggressive" workers from the working-class neighborhoods of Juárez.

In this process of negotiation and occasional confrontation, cultural forms of respect toward others were practically and immediately discarded from workers' cultural baggage, especially when they were told by the supervisor that they must start working at 6:00 AM, and not later. The determination needed to keep their chair transforms itself into aggressiveness not only on the shop floor but also outside the workplace, where the workers must struggle to lead a new life characterized by being at the right place and "on time." Thus, in trying to keep the job and the quota fulfilled, sewing-factory workers, men and women, had to transform their subjectivities and, inevitably, their cultural and class consciousness (shifting from respecting co-workers to competing with them). Unfortunately, the simultaneous reproduction of working-class subjecthood did not transform itself into a working-class consciousness—that is, into political mobilization that could lead to independent union organizing. In fact, it unmade it, and the union itself contributed, along with the multinational corporation, to the latter effect: the unmaking of the Mexican working class.

In Chapter 8, "Women, Men, and 'Gender' in Feminist Anthropology: Lessons from Northern Mexico's Maquiladoras," I bring together material from the three previous chapters to show the challenges for feminist anthropologists, particularly to critics of Michelle Z. Rosaldo, when studying both men and women systematically. Thus, in trying to "rescue" Rosaldo's early work on gender, I hope to bring together, theoretically and empirically, two major aspects of cultural life in late-twentieth-century northern Mexico: class and gender and their implications for our understanding of working-class women and men at the border. The latter ethnographic project would not be possible, however, without Devon G. Peña's practical advice:

> Future research on workplace politics might focus on determining whether there are in fact any significant gender-based differences among maquila workers. My own limited account here suggests that there are some differences, but whether these are attributable entirely to gender or to other factors as well (such as seniority) is something I am not prepared to resolve at this point. Students of maquila workplace politics would do well to design future survey and ethnographic research projects with this problem in mind: it is important that we select equal numbers of male and female respondents in future studies. To continue to ignore male workers is to risk misunderstanding and misrepresenting the nature of the shifting construction of gender in maquila workplace politics. (1997, 261–262)

This analysis of gender and class (also see Salzinger 2003) acquires an even denser texture by situating the class and gender experiences of factory workers in the larger predicament of color and race inspections dealt with in Chapters 3 and 6.

In the concluding section, "Alternating Imaginings," readers will find my final arguments regarding theories of culture, history, class, and the state. Chapter 9, "Reimagining Culture and Power against Late Industrial Capitalism and Other Forms of Conquest through Border Theory and Analysis," systematically presents a critical reexamination of our academic imaginings of "borderlands" within cultural anthropology, border studies, and studies of the state and beyond—all in the context of capitalism and empire—through what Edward Said (2002, 9) called an "extremely productive tension" of the combined theoretical work of Antonio Gramsci and Michel Foucault.

Chapter 9 ultimately demonstrates that the changing contexts of the nation-state and the unchanging nature of introductory industrial capitalism as a new form of conquest throughout the past century reflect (and are reflected in) uneasy conceptions of class and changing conceptions of culture (from "shared cultural patterns" to "fragmented cultural borderlands" in the life of working-class people, for example) within the academy. The book closes with an epilogue on the tragic consequences of the overlapping conquests affecting Ciudad Juárez today: the brutal killings of economically vulnerable women and girls that began in the late 1990s and continue today.

As a whole, the chapters in *Fragmented Lives, Assembled Parts* propose analytical shifts in the theoretical conceptualization about the border working classes of Ciudad Juárez—from border "crossings" to border "inspections" (Chapter 6); from cultural production to cultural reproduction (Chapters 4 and 5) and cultural transformation (Chapter 7); from a feminist focus on either women or men to a feminist focus on "gender" (which must include both women and men; Chapter 8); from a centralized focus on the conquest of Mexico to a focus on the conquests of both Mexico and New Mexico, especially regarding the northern borderlands (Chapter 2); and, lastly, from a discussion of *mestizaje* to a discussion of *colorismo* among Mexican people (Chapter 3)—all with the purpose of acquiring a critical understanding of the complex constitution of the unmaking of the Mexican working classes and their mobilization, an unmaking derived from multiple forms of conquest, including the brutal assassination of working-class women.

This ethnographic study is based on actual fieldwork research in distinct sub-industries of the maquiladora mode of production in Ciudad Juárez—electronic, garment, and automotive (from finding a job, to being trained in it, and eventually to performing it). The immersion of the ethnographer in the everyday life of factory workers, from the time they get up in the morning to the time they get back home in the afternoon or evening, was vitally important, especially given the inevitable yet unplanned constructive critique of multinational corporations that is produced by such a "witnessing ethnography."

The methodology consisted mainly of getting jobs as an assembly-line worker in three different factories (I explain in the pertinent chapters the specificities of how I was hired); walking, riding, and driving the streets and avenues of Ciudad Juárez; and residing in three geographically dispersed working-class neighborhoods, where I lived in rooms (*cuartos*) and/or apartments I rented. I attended several birthday parties; religious celebrations; rock, *ranchera,* and *norteña* music concerts; and family gatherings, and I witnessed children's games in their neighborhoods. More than three dozen informal and formal taped interviews were conducted (about labor and migration histories, personal views on the maquilas, the border economy, and border social life in general) with men and women of all ages, from sixteen to sixty years of age, and who worked in several factories of Ciudad Juárez. The taped interviews lasted between two and four hours each, and most were carried out in people's own homes and some in open spaces, such as front yards, back yards, and parks. The daily newspapers, contemporary and historical, were a major source for the recording and collecting of everyday happenings in the larger Ciudad Juárez area.

Gender inequalities, hierarchies of color or class, and (unequal) regional and international divisions all intermittently land on the workers' shoulders, both as gendered subjects and as human beings. My observations, my experiences in the factories, and my personal and political preoccupations have led me to denounce, in writing and in public, certain working, living, and dying conditions that should not have existed in the late twentieth century but that continue into the present.

I hope this book contributes effectively to a much-needed attempt to "recapture" the concept of culture in its relation to class, gender, color, and race and vice versa. I also hope it provides a convincing critique of transnational corporations—a critique that might lead to the official recognition, legitimation, and viability of attempts by maquiladora workers to demand better *working and living conditions* for the twenty-first century.

I

Sixteenth-Century Conquests (1521–1598)
and Their Postcolonial Border Legacies

TWO

The Invention of Borderlands Geography
What Do Aztlán and Tenochtitlán Have to
Do with Ciudad Juárez/Paso del Norte?

I do not offer a competing historical theory, since it should be clear that I am not talking about what "actually happened." Yet what I am talking about—indigenous schemes of cosmological proportions—may even be more significant historically.

—MARSHALL SAHLINS, *ISLANDS OF HISTORY*

IN DECEMBER 1993 and January 1994, a political debate emerged in the Mexican newspapers about whether or not the term "México" should be institutionalized as the official name of the country. The initial discussion of this matter occurred at the Chamber of Deputies in Mexico City, where it was acknowledged that "in no article of the constitution is the official name of this country clearly established; it is interchangeably called Mexican United States [Estados Unidos Mexicanos], Mexican Republic [República Mexicana], or simply México" (*Diario de Juárez*, 1993, 4A). The headlines in national and local newspapers read as follows: "México: a consulta su nombre" [Mexico: its name to be researched]; "México, ¿en busca de nombre?" [Mexico, in search of its name?]; and "Nombre del país: preguntas sin respuesta" [Name of the country: questions without answers]. Early in 1994, due to the media's focus on the implementation of the North American Free Trade Agreement (NAFTA) and on the Chiapas rebellion on January 1, the debate on Mexico's name disappeared. When Carlos Salinas de Gortari, president of Mexico during that time, was asked his opinion on the subject, he said, "Mexico will keep on being called Mexico" (*Diario de Juárez*, 1994, 4A).

But why was the country named "Mexico," anyway? Is it just a problem of semantics, or is it a problem of history, or, more important, is it a problem of power and the politics of naming, as Benedict Anderson (1991) argues regarding the nationalist problematic? Let us consider the following generally unknown moments of encounter in what became New Spain, one in the north and one in the south:

It has been recorded that when the early Spaniards encountered the valley dwellers of the Gila and Salt rivers, they asked many questions of them. The usual Indian reply was *pi-nyi-match*, or "I don't know." From this, the Spaniards took to calling them "Pima." The name by which they indicate themselves is *ah-kee-mult-o-o-tom*, meaning "River People. (Dutton 1983, 203; italics in original)

When the Spaniards discovered this land, their leader asked the Indians how it was called; as they did not understand him, they said *uic athan*, which means, "what do you say or what do you speak, that we do not understand you." And then the Spaniards ordered it set down that it be called *Yucatan* . . . (Antonio de Ciudad Real, 1588, cited in Clendinnen 1987, vi)

These two cases of hegemonic naming, one relating to a particular people here named "the Pima" in what is today called the American Southwest and the other relating to an area of land we now call the "Yucatán Peninsula," constitute socio-historical processes of conquest that led, in situ, to specific productions of ethnic identity (the Pima) and place (the Yucatán).

In *Imagined Communities* (1991), Benedict Anderson warned those scholars who write about (and live under) the nation-state against the nationalist imaginings and the social-political conjunctures legitimizing "official" historical pasts of nations and empires. In particular, he provides historical materials about what's in a name and why such a name exists (i.e., "English," "Indonesia," "Dutch") throughout the chapters of his provocative book about the emergence of nationalism in the late eighteenth century. It is astonishing, however, that in spite of Anderson's discussion of the centrality of the Latin American independence movements for the emergence of nationalism in the nineteenth century, very little is said in *Imagined Communities* about Mexico (Lomnitz 2001). Even with regard to the colonial period, scant analysis was devoted to New Spain and its politics of naming. For instance, for the sixteenth century and beyond, Anderson wrote:

New York, Nueva Leon, Nouvelle Orleans, Nova Lisboa, Nieuw Amsterdam. Already in the sixteenth century Europeans had begun the strange habit of naming remote places, first in the Americas and Africa, later in Asia, Australia, and Oceania, as "new" versions of (thereby) "old" toponyms in their lands of origin. . . . What is startling in the American namings of the sixteenth to the eighteenth centuries is that "new" and "old" were understood synchronically, coexisting within homogeneous, empty time. Vizcaya is there *alongside* Nueva Vizcaya, New London *alongside* London: an idiom of sibling competition rather than of inheritance. (1991, 187)

In this context, I find it imperative to note that Anderson's statement about cases such as Nueva Vizcaya, which bordered New Mexico to the north, does not help answer the following questions: How do we explain the emergence, within the same continent (and not across the Atlantic), of both New Mexico and Mexico in the sixteenth century? What specific cultural visions were given political and military impetus to move "north" during the same period (which covered at least two conquests—that of Mexico in 1521 and that of New Mexico in 1598)? What were some particular historical consequences of these cultural visions, especially with regard to the naming and labeling of regions, peoples, and places? How were cultural identities and historical places produced during these vital moments of invention at what became the U.S.-Mexico border in the nineteenth century? In other words (to paraphrase Sahlins 1981, 1985): What is the social content of the historical metaphors and the mythical realities charac-terizing the colonizers and the colonized of northern New Spain in the sixteenth century?

In this chapter I hope to answer these historically relevant questions through an exposé of the ways in which the "myth of Aztlán" in the 1500s led to the social invention of the physical geography of what became northern Mexico. Specifi-cally, I discuss the naming of Nueva México itself and, within this province, the naming of one of its main rivers (Río del Norte [currently called Río Bravo in Mexico, Rio Grande in the United States]), one of its main missions (Paso del Norte [current Ciudad Juárez]), and the naming of the original inhabitants of the El Paso–Ciudad Juárez area: the so-called Mansos. To understand the emergence of "Nueva México," however, I briefly examine the naming of Mexico (as in both "Ciudad de México" [Mexico City], which replaced "Tenochtitlán," and "el Valle de México" [the Valley of Mexico]) in the context of the 1519–1524 conquest of Mexico (Tenochtitlán). The culturo-historical process of the European naming of this region of central Mexico is then juxtaposed with the 1598 conquest of New Mexico (*la conquista de la Nueva México*). The analyses of these two regions of New Spain are mainly based on two key documents, in addition to other rele-vant literature, of the respective eras: Hernán Cortés's *Letters from Mexico* (1986 edition of *Cartas de relación* translated by Anthony Pagden) and Pérez de Villa-grá's epic poem about New Mexico: *Historia de la Nueva México* (1992 edition). In what follows, I demonstrate that the conquest of New Mexico was intimately connected with the conquest of Mexico, both through concrete kin relations (Hernán Cortés and Juan de Oñate were affinal relatives) and through specific cultural visions surrounding their search for wealth: on the one hand, finding Tenochtitlán and inventing *la ciudad de México*, and on the other, searching for the mythical land of origin of the Aztecs, Aztlán; that is, the hope for *otra ciudad de México*—"another [wealthy] Mexico city"—a strategic plan that resulted in the invention of what came to be known as "Nueva México" (or "New Mexico" in its English translation).

The historical and political significance of reexamining both the conquest of New Mexico at the (border) crossing at Paso del Norte (current Ciudad Juárez) and its colonial embedment with the conquest of Tenochtitlán and the Spaniards' movement toward the "north" in the sixteenth century is inevitably tied to the need for a better understanding of the historical and present geopolitics of both Mexico and the United States. In this regard, Howard Cline noted, "The northern movement of the Spanish frontier of New Spain provides a dynamic element in Mexican colonial history equal in historical significance to the later Western movement in the history of the United States" (1972, 21). Similarly, but with regard to the historical importance of the conquest of New Mexico beyond its region, Miguel Encinias, Alfred Rodríguez, and Joseph P. Sánchez properly argued that "the salient themes and facts regarding the founding of New Mexico in 1598, an event tantamount to the founding of Jamestown, Virginia, in 1607, is as much a part of the United States's national story as it is that of Mexico's" (1992, xxv).[1]

This chapter has two main purposes: first, it attempts to map out a colonial geography of conquest that acquired shape and political meaning as various Spanish military and missionary men "traveled" from the Gulf Coast to Tenochtitlán, and from Tenochtitlán to Paso del Norte in the sixteenth century. Interestingly, the streets, the neighborhoods, the industrial parks, and the places of recreation in current Ciudad Juárez were given meaning and a sense of place by the working classes as they tailored their everyday practices to the needs of global capital in the late twentieth century. Likewise, these same workers, for similar economic needs of capital, gave particular cultural meaning to the social geography of the shop floor, the cafeteria, and the restrooms inside multinational assembly plants (see Part II of this book).

Second, related to the first but perhaps of more practical importance at the turn of the twenty-first century, this chapter will demonstrate that the political consequences of certain culturo-historical metaphors associated with imagined physical territories, such as Aztlán and Nueva México, inevitably depend on who is using these metaphors as weapons: the weak or the strong? My utopian hope about the reality of these kinds of metaphors for the twenty-first century is framed by the practical recognition that as long as minority groups within nation-states and colonial empires (such as Chicanos and Chicanas in twentieth-century United States and the Mansos in sixteenth-century New Spain) remain politically, economically, and militarily weak, their dreams and possibilities about belonging to a territorial country they themselves make will remain (and have remained) at best a spiritual reality. Either way, however, such metaphors as Aztlán, Mexico, and New Mexico are not fictive myths or simple "names" with referents to something else that is "more or less real"; rather, they are concrete realities with historical and, ultimately, human significance to those concerned (Sahlins 1981, 1985).

The Naming and Conquest of Mexico: From Tenochtitlán to Mexico City

As I noted earlier, if we want to better understand why Mexico is today called "Mexico," we must examine one of the earliest texts documenting the use and, I argue, the invention, at least in its Spanish pronunciation, of such a European name:[2] Hernán Cortés's *Letters from Mexico* (*Cartas de relación*).

Cortés's first attempt to identify a collectivity of people as an indigenous group occurred immediately after one of the first battles the Spaniards engaged in on Mexican soil, the Battle of Cintla,[3] on March 25, 1519, on the coast of what is today the state of Tabasco. In his First Letter,[4] Cortés documents how, after the fighting, he supposedly addressed two indigenous messengers: "The captain then asked these Indians through his interpreters[5] *who the people were he had been fighting with in the battle;* they replied that they had assembled from eight provinces, and that according to the written records they had, there were in all some forty thousand men, for they were able to count on such a number" (Cortés 1986, 22; my emphasis).[6]

In this initial encounter with an uncertain collectivity of people, Cortés did not perceive a homogeneous political group associated with a particular identity or name. They had just "assembled from eight provinces"; thus, he conceptually fought individuals who could be associated more with Renato Rosaldo's multiply layered bordered subject (1993) than with an ethnically homogeneous entity— in this case, from the present state of Tabasco. Cortés's vision of the "other" at that moment of encounter was associated neither with a specifically strategic place—"Mexico"—nor with an ethnic extension of it, that is, "Mexicans" or "Aztecs"; they were simply "Indians." This is the case in spite of the fact that he was looking for a specific name when he asked the question about who he had been fighting.

As he continued in his conquest, Cortés stayed away from concrete attempts at "group" classifying. For example, he did not identify the people of Cholula or Churultecal as "Tlaxcaltecans." In fact, throughout the First Letter and in the early part of the second, Cortés provided no discourse on Tenochtitlán, or Temixtitan, as he later called it. It is in his Second Letter to the king, written in late 1520, that he tries to identify people and places in linguistic forms we can begin to recognize; he had, however, apologized to Charles V for not knowing the names: "I beg Your Highness to forgive me if I do not . . . give the correct names either of some of the towns and cities, or of their rulers, who have offered themselves in the service of Your Highness as your subjects and vassals" (Cortés 1986, 48–50). We must remember, nonetheless, that by avoiding appropriate names, Cortés was, in a calculating manner, playing down the expeditions that Francisco Hernández de Córdoba and Juan de Grijalva had carried out from Yucatán to Tampico (Linne 1948, 3) and, thus, "the awkward fact that the latter had taken formal possession of the land was quietly ignored" (Elliot 1986, xx).

In spite of these reservations on his strategically "limited" vision of the geography being invented, Cortés tried to articulate for the king how to imagine the "new" lands. In a passage where he is struggling to please the monarch, we read for the first time about a specific place associated with what we call "Mexico":

> Before I begin to describe this great city [Temixtitan] and the others which I mentioned earlier, it seems to me, so that they may be better understood, that I should say something of *Mesyco,* which is Mutezuma's principal domain and the place where this city and the others which I have mentioned are to be found. This province is circular and encompassed by very high and very steep mountains, and the plain is some seventy leagues in circumference: in this plain there are two lakes which cover almost all of it, for a canoe may travel fifty leagues around the edges. One of these lakes is of fresh water and the other, which is the larger, is of salt water. (Cortés 1986, 102; my emphasis)

What Cortés identifies as "Mesyco" has been associated with "Anahuac" ("near the water"), the name given to the regions around the lake system of what became the Valley of Mexico (see map on pp. 136–137 in his *Cartas de relación* [1994], which traces Cortés's travels of conquest).

In examining Cortés's letters, it is evident that there is a specific development in his use of the terminology that led to "Mexico": from "Mesyco" in the First Letter (1519) to "province of Mesico" (p. 148) and "Mesico" (pp. 154, 155) in the Second Letter (1520); and from "province of Mexico and Temixtitan" (pp. 169, 173, 176, 177, 182) in the Third Letter (1522) to "México" (p. 307, with the written accent mark) in the Fourth Letter (1524). By 1524, Cortés had already received from the king, on July 4, 1523, the "Coat of Arms for Mexico City" (González Obregón 1959). That Cortés changed the official name of the indigenous city from "Tenochtitlán" to "Mexico City" is well documented by eminent historian Luis González Obregón:

> Several conquistadors opined that the new city should be established in Coyoacán; others, in Tacuba; still others opined that it should be established in Tetzcoco. Diverse opinions were debated; but the one that was maintained was the one by Cortés, who said: "Since this city in the time of the Indians had been the lady of the other provinces, it must follow that it should remain the same in this time of the Christians, *and since God Our Lord in this city had been offended with sacrifices and other idolatries, so here we should serve and honor His holy name more than in any other place.*" (González Obregón 1959, 23; my translation and emphasis)

Thus, Mexico City was established in Tenochtitlán as a form of religious revenge.

Nevertheless, Cortés ended his Fourth Letter claiming to be in Temixtitan: "From the great city of Temixtitan in New Spain on the fifteenth day of October in the year 1524" (Cortés 1986, 337). This is perhaps one of the first examples, in what came to be the American continent, of "imperialist nostalgia": the feeling of nostalgia for what the imperialists themselves destroyed (see R. Rosaldo 1993, chap. 3). In fact, the continued use of "Tenochtitlán" throughout the 1520s, and indeed the uncritical use of it today by "mestizos" and "European Mexicans" to talk about Mexican roots (see next chapter), can be explained with the same reasoning and critique: imperialist nostalgia.

In the Fifth Letter (1525), besides using the phrase "Mexico City" (p. 366), Cortés privileges the noun "Mexico" by itself (see pp. 387, 393, 406, 407).[7] This last letter is mainly about his expedition to Honduras. Thus, it is from a distance that "Mexico" begins to acquire a metonymic aspect in which a part (the city of Mexico) represents the whole (the whole territory conquered at that time, what officially became "New Spain"). It has not been studied whether the official name after the conquest, New Spain, was able to compete with the term, "Mexico." To be sure, Johann Buschman argued in 1852 that "the Spaniards called Mexico all those provinces subjected to the New Spain Viceroy, even if not all of them belonged previously to the Aztec Empire" (1998, 206). From my discussion at the beginning of this chapter, it is clear that "New Spain" shared a similar cultural and political status as "Estados Unidos Mexicanos" does today. In fact, if we follow Anderson's observation (1991, 50) that before the eighteenth century "España" was in fact "Las Españas," then in the American continent, "New Spain" or "La Nueva España" was not as popular as "Mexico."[8]

Regarding the people's "dominant" language in the territory appropriated by Cortés, Miguel Leon-Portilla noted: "The Nahuatl language, which is also known as Aztec or Mexican, is part of the great Uto-Aztec linguistic family. . . . Written Nahuatl . . . was introduced by the Spanish missionaries soon after the Conquest. With the exception of x, which is pronounced like the English sh, the letters have the same phonetic value as in Spanish" (1992, xlvii). The problem that I find with the explanation of the x from the Latin alphabet, and its possible relation with the term "Mexico" or "Mexican" at the time of the conquest, is that it does not explain the specific development that constituted the hegemonic uses of "Mesyco," "Mesico," then "Mexico" in the mentality of the influential conquistador, especially if it was Cortés, as I am arguing here, who named Tenochtitlán "Mexico City."

To what extent is the term "Mexico" associated with the Mexica people? Two prominent historians, Miguel Leon-Portilla and Francesco Clavigero, the latter a Jesuit historian of the late eighteenth century, argue that the name Mexica "was derived from Mexitli, a term associated with Huitzilopochtli" (Leon-Portilla 1992, 87). Clavigero himself was very specific about the "Mexico"/"Mexica" linguistic connection: "[Mexico is] the place of the god Mexitli or Huitzilopochtli

. . . because of the sanctuary that the *mexicanos* built there for him. The *mexicanos* drop from the composition of the name [Mexitli] the final syllable *tli* and add *co*, . . . [which then turns "Mexico" into] 'the place or temple of the god, Mexitli'" (1945, 233–234). Regarding the "Aztec" element of concern here, prominent historian Vicente Riva Palacio (1888) described the linguistic process through which "Azteca" emerged from "Aztlán": "[The Mexica] were called Aztec because they came from Aztlán: one of the ways the name of a people was given was to drop the last syllable from the name of the town (pueblo) and add *tecatl,* which means person (*persona*). Thus, from Tlaxcallan one gets *tlaxcaltecatl,* from Cholollan *chololtecatl* and from Aztlan *aztecatl* and in plural this becomes *azteca*" (Riva Palacio 1888, 459). The consequent linguistic association between Mexico (a place) and Mexica (a people) is thus understood.

Yet, even if we initially accept Clavigero's argument that Mexico acquired its name by adding the syllable *co* and dropping *tli* from the indigenous "Mexitli" (Clavigero 1945, 233–234), we should immediately question, in the case of "Mexico and Mexico City," who did the more extensive dropping: the Spaniards or the locals?—especially after taking into consideration that "the Raramuri" of Northern Mexico became "the Tarahumara" as a consequence of a similar process, in this case carried out by Fray Juan Fonte in 1600. Mexican historian Zacarías Márquez Terrazas writes about this Spanish invention, a product of a personal, though powerful, whim: "It was first Fonte who mentions the *tarahumares* in his letters. They called each other *raramuri,* using the *r* instead of the *t.* . . . Fonte opted for the initial *t,* since *r* in Spanish, at the beginning of a word, has the sound *rr;* thus, Fonte thought, it was closer to the soft sound of the letter *t,* and thus, created the term *tarahumares*" (1991, 30).

I would argue here, then, that we have historically privileged the term "Mexico" more because of Cortés—an *español* who decided that Tenochtitlán was going to be Mexico City and the area around it (the whole territory) "Mexico" due to the religious significance of the site—than because of the locals' roots or ancestry with the "Mexica" or the "Aztecs." Even the idea that "Mexico" must essentially be associated with "the indigenous" is in itself a Spanish/European invention (also see next chapter). More often than not, the Mexico/indigenous connection works in reverse. For instance, with regard to the term *mexicano* and its preference and persistence today among indigenous peoples living in Puebla and Tlaxcala within the current Mexican nation-state, Jane Hill and K. C. Hill wrote: "The use of the term *mexicano* for the language by Malinche speakers is far more than a casual, uninformed vernacular usage. The usage makes a moral claim about the people's identity and rights to participation in the Mexican state, toward which they feel intense patriotism" (1986, 93). This patriotism has been so persuasive that even today the official "Estados Unidos Mexicanos" cannot compete with the popular "México," and the nationalist *mexicano/a* maintains itself first and foremost against any political attempt, whether by academics, minorities, ethnics, or regionalists, to legitimize (at the national level) identities of difference that would rather speak to the multiculturalism and regionalisms that characterize and have characterized the distinct populations inhabiting the vast land called Mexico.

In what ways are these situations of conquest and power related to what we call today the U.S-Mexico borderlands . . . or to Aztlán?

The Mexico/Nueva México Connection:
The Legacy of Cortés in Paso del Norte

Just before Cortés took Moctezuma prisoner, Moctezuma had given him a daughter. When Cortés arrived at Tenochtitlán, the indigenous ruler treated him as an ambassador/"god" and granted sleeping and eating quarters for the Spaniard, along with certain gifts, human and material: "After having joked and exchanged pleasantries with him and after he had given me some gold jewelry and *one of his daughters and other chiefs' daughters* to some of my company, I told him that I knew what had happened in the city of Nautecal" (Cortés 1986, 88–89; my emphasis).[9] This young woman (Moctezuma's daughter), whom Cortés immediately impregnated, appears in colonial documents as Doña Ana. She was killed, presumably before giving birth, around the same time that her father, Moctezuma, was assassinated (see Martínez 1990, 41–71). Hernán Cortés bedded several women/wives, including two legitimate and at least five illegitimate ones.[10] From the latter encounters, at least three mestizo children were born from different indigenous women: Martín (son of Doña Marina), Leonor (daughter of Doña Isabel, Moctezuma's oldest daughter), and María (daughter of an unknown Aztec princess) (see Conway 1940, 90).

Sometime after the conquest but before 1529, Cortés impregnated Moctezuma's oldest daughter, Tecuichpotzin, who was baptized Isabel. Isabel Moctezuma and Hernán Cortés had Leonor,[11] who later married a wealthy man, Juan de Tolusa, one of the conquistadors of Zacatecas and one of the first Spaniards who discovered and later owned the rich mines of what came to be Nueva Galicia. In Zacatecas, Juan and Leonor had three children: Juan, Isabel, and Leonor (Mecham 1968, 40). Leonor Tolusa, granddaughter of Hernán and Isabel, married Juan de Oñate, founder of Nueva México.

Juan de Oñate was the son of Cristóbal de Oñate, one of Cortés's friends and accountants and also one of Nuño de Guzmán's captains in the 1530s conquest of Nueva Galicia (see Mecham 1968, 22–23; Martínez 1990, 412–415). Lloyd Mecham has briefly delineated the Oñates' own family history of empire: "Cristóbal de Oñate was an hidalgo of illustrious parentage. He was a native of Vitoria, in the Basque province of Alava, and a descendant of López Díaz de Haro, 'Señor de Vizcaya,' chief and captain-general of the Andalucian frontier, and conqueror of the city of Baeza from the Moors in 1227. . . . Cristóbal de Oñate came to New

Spain in 1524. He married Doña Catalina de Salazar, daughter of Gonzalo de Salazar, first factor of real hacienda in New Spain. An issue of this marriage was Juan de Oñate, conquistador of New Mexico" (1968, 22–23).

The founding of New Mexico in 1598, and its sociopolitical ties with the Cortés/Oñate kinship connection, is synthesized by El Paso, Texas, historian W. H. Timmons:

> For more than a decade the viceroy of New Spain searched for a suitable candidate to implement King Philip's plans for New Mexico. Individual fame and fortune were essential ingredients in the selection process, since the Spanish crown had decreed that no royal funds would be forthcoming, and that the candidate himself would have to bear all the costs of the expedition. At length, in 1595 the viceroy awarded the contract to Don Juan de Oñate, whose father made a fortune from the silver mines of Zacatecas, and whose wife was the granddaughter of Cortez and the great-granddaughter of Montezuma [here Timmons plays down the wealth of Oñate's wife]. The contract gave Oñate the title of governor and captain general, while religious duties were assigned to the Franciscans . . . the Oñate enterprise was to be involved in colonization as well as conquest. (1990, 12)

The Oñate expedition left the mining town of Santa Bárbara (southern Chihuahua) in January 1598, and arrived April 30, 1598, at the Río del Norte, at a place later called San Elisario, which is twenty-five miles south of what is today El Paso, Texas. There, Oñate drew the borderline between Nueva Vizcaya and Nueva México. On May 4, 1598, at a site just west of current downtown El Paso, but on the southern bank, the expedition crossed the river to the other side: "Oñate called this operation 'El Paso del Río del Norte'" (Timmons 1990, 14).

The Naming and Conquest of New Mexico:
Historical Consequences of the Mythical Aztlán

Before Juan de Oñate and his people arrived and passed through the area, other Spaniards had traveled through "Nueva México." Some of them were, for the most part, lost (Álvar Núñez Cabeza de Vaca, 1534–1535; Marcos de Niza, 1539; Francisco Vásquez de Coronado, 1540–1542); others were in charge of reconnaissance parties (Francisco Sánchez Chamuscado, 1581, and Antonio de Espejo, 1582); and still others, the last ones before 1598 (Gaspar Castaño de Sosa, 1590–1592, and Francisco Leyva de Bonilla and Antonio Gutiérrez de Humaña, 1593), were involved in unofficial expeditions. The first trespasser, Castaño de Sosa, was arrested, Gutiérrez killed Leyva, and Gutiérrez was in turn killed by Plains inhabitants (see Encinias, Rodríguez, and Sánchez 1992 and Timmons 1990; for a relatively early critique of the geographical ignorance of "conquistadores," see Bancroft 1962).

In 1581 and 1582, Chamuscado and Espejo, respectively, were the first explorers to use the route that followed the two main rivers of Nueva Vizcaya: from Santa Bárbara (Chihuahua, Mexico) up through the Río Conchas, or Río de las Conchas, and then to the Río del Norte. The latter are names actually given to these rivers by Gaspar Pérez de Villagrá, captain, conquistador, colonizer, and chronicler of the Oñate expedition of 1598. In 1610, he published in Spain his *Historia de la Nueva México* (1992), where the conquest of what we call in English New Mexico was first vividly and experientially depicted. His use of the feminine "Nueva México" manifests the most common way of addressing the unknown territory at that time. In fact, this peculiar phrase, "Nueva México," is the only one used in Villagrá's text, one of the first epic poems of the New World.[12]

During the sixteenth century, and mainly because of Cabeza de Vaca's and Niza's mythical stories about the wealthy Seven Cities of Cibola in the "North," it was generally hoped and imagined by conquistadors that they would find a new paradise of gold like Tenochtitlán, which after 1523 officially became Mexico City, or *la ciudad de México*. In the Spanish language, *ciudad,* or "city," is considered a feminine term and is usually accompanied by the feminine article *la,* as in *la ciudad de México* (Mexico City). According to Hubert Bancroft, it was Francisco de Ibarra, founder and governor of Nueva Vizcaya, who first coined the idea of a "new" Mexico—a *nueva México*—in 1563, thirty-five years before Villagrá and Oñate arrived in the territory. Ibarra himself, however, never reached "New Mexico" or even saw it, due to political and military unrest in northern Nueva Vizcaya or, more specifically, around the area of Paquimé in (current) northern Chihuahua (see Mecham 1968, 176–177; also see Figure 2.1, which traces Ibarra's travels). In fact, some argue that Paquimé marks the end of Nueva Vizcaya in that area, west of the Río del Norte, in northwestern Chihuahua. Bancroft wrote about the invention or production of a "new" Mexico in the following way: "It is perhaps worthy of notice . . . that on his return governor Ibarra boasted that he had discovered a 'new Mexico' as well as a new Vizcaya. It is not unlikely that from this circumstance the name New Mexico came to be applied in later years to a country [*sic*] that Don Francisco [de Ibarra] had probably never seen" (1962, 73).[13]

Although it might be difficult to find out why the linguistic transformation from the feminine *Nueva* México to the masculine *Nuevo* México took place, it is possible to hypothesize that the change was due not only to the later recognition or association of "México" with a whole valley (Cortés's earlier "Mesyco" or *el Valle de México*) but also to what Lockhart (1992) called a "back translation" (i.e., from a modern notion of "Mexicano" to a pre-Spanish concept for "Mexica"). In this case, the back translation takes place from the English "New Mexico" to

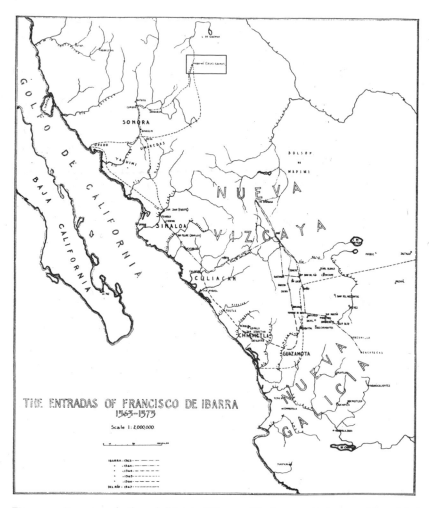

Figure 2.1. Francisco de Ibarra's "Entries." Source: Mecham, 1968, 114–115. (Box added by author.)

the Spanish "Nuevo México," dropping the feminine "Nueva" in the process of translating[14] it back into Spanish. Even before 1598 (see 1587 map by Richard Hakluyt on p. 78 in Burden 1996), European maps drafted by English and French scholars labeled the area in its "Spanish masculine" form: Nuevo México. Considering that these problems of translation have been reproduced from the sixteenth century until the present (see Philip Burden's 1996 *The Mapping of North America* for several examples), we do not have to attend to the vast literature about the northern Spanish borderlands produced since then. It will suffice to present a relatively recent but magisterial example from the latest edition (1992) of Villagrá's epic poem *Historia de la Nueva México, 1610*, translated and edited by Miguel Encinias, Alfred Rodríguez, and Joseph P. Sánchez, and published by the University of New Mexico Press. This is how Villagrá's text begins in this bilingual edition:

Canto Primero

Que declara el argumento de la historia y sitio de la nueva México y noticia que della se tuvo en quanto la antiguilla de los Indios, y de la salida y descendencia de los verdaderos Mexicanos.

Canto I

Which sets forth the outline of the history and the location of *New Mexico*, and the reports had of it in the traditions of the Indians, and of the true origin and descent of the Mexicans. (Encinias, Rodríguez, and Sánchez 1992, 3; my emphasis)

Figure 2.2. Map (from 1660) by Pierre Duval, showing "R. de Nort" flowing from "Nueva México" into "Mer verm e ille" (current Gulf of California). Source: Burden 1996, 454.

Figure 2.3. Section from Giovanni Battista Nicolosi's map (Rome 1660)
that shows "Rio Escondido" (Río del Norte/Rio Grande/Río Bravo) flowing
from "Nuovo Mexico" into gulf of "Nuova Spagna" (Gulf of "New Spain"—
what we call the "Gulf of Mexico"). Source: Burden 1996, 455.

Both introductory statements and the respective names *nueva México* and
New Mexico, as well as the search for the origin of Mexicanos (Aztlán), are pro-
vided with explanatory footnotes by the editors and are also associated with
Ibarra:[15]

[Footnote in Spanish]
Que hayamos podido comprobar, la designación de Nueva *México para esas*
tierras al norte fue primero usado por Francisco de Ibarra, gobernador de
Nueva Vizcaya, tras su entrada por las mismas en 1563.

[Footnote in English]
To our knowledge, the term "*Nuevo* México," used to identify those unknown northern lands, was first employed by Francisco de Ibarra, viceroy
of Nueva Vizcaya, after his exploration of the same in 1563. (Encinias, Rodríguez, and Sánchez 1992, 3; my emphasis)

This dropping of *Nueva* for *Nuevo* as late as 1992 in the process of retrans-
lating from English back to Spanish has specific repercussions on readers' consumption of identity while reading the text. If it is true that most of the literature
on the northern provinces and states of New Spain and pre-1848 Mexico, respectively, has been dominated, historically, by Euro-American enterprises (until recently, Mexican intellectuals and academics had been too preoccupied with the
"Center"—central Mexico), then it is also true that this literature is heavily involved in the active production of identities—a major cultural practice in itself.

Thus, pronunciation in the case of *mexicano* (from "Mexica") and translation
in the case of "*Nueva* México" constitute in themselves hegemonic struggles between production and consumption (and their respective producers and consumers), which in turn provide surplus value or cultural capital about the politics of conquest regarding self and place.

Aztlán and the Spaniards

We must not forget that Oñate and Villagrá reached Nueva México to search for
the origin (the exit and descent) of the "true Mexicanos," "*los verdaderos mexicanos*": Aztlán. It is generally believed that the Spanish travelers were mostly
in search of the Seven Cities of Cíbola or a Quivira. It is hardly acknowledged
that some of them were, more strategically, in search of Aztlán. Mecham has
argued that after the arrival of Cabeza de Vaca from his "trips" throughout the
north in the mid-1530s, Viceroy Mendoza and Hernán Cortés engaged in political disagreements that "culminated in keen rivalry . . . for the exclusive right of
exploring the new lands" (1968, 27). This conflict among the elites was closely
associated with the fact that "Cortés acquired certain Aztec chronicles and maps
which referred to the early home of that people" (ibid., 28). Thus, more than
about confirming a legend or a myth, the expeditions to the "north" that were
looking for the origin of the Aztecs constituted a serious search for more riches
and wealth akin to what the Spaniards had found in Tenochtitlán. In fact, it is
in the context of the rivalry between Mendoza and Hernán Cortés in the 1530s
that the expedition of Nuño de Guzmán (who was accompanied by Cristóbal de
Oñate, Juan de Oñate's father) into Nueva Galicia took place (see Peter Gerhard's
map of "Colonial New Spain, 1519–1786 ["Mexico in 1580"]," in Cline 1972, 68, for
the province of Nueva Galicia, which was located north of "Nueva España").

After Nuño de Guzmán passed the Río Grande de Tololotlán in northern

Nueva Galicia and found a town called Aztatlán, he thought he had discovered Aztlán, the origin of the *mexicanos* (see Mecham [1968, 23] for the exact location of Aztatlán in the current state of Nayarit in northwestern Nueva Galicia). John Chávez explains this encounter: "In 1530, about four hundred miles northwest of Mexico City, the conquistador Nuño de Guzmán encountered a place called Aztatlán, whose name and environment resembled those of the legendary Aztlán. Though the evidence indicated (and still indicates) that Aztatlán and Aztlán were one and the same place, it must have seemed too mundane a location for a land that had been idealized to the point of a paradise on earth" (1989, 56). That Aztatlán and Aztlán are synonymous terms is also confirmed by Miguel Leon-Portilla (1992, 85).

After Francisco de Ibarra extended the European-centered geography of North America in 1563, that is, when he constructed the systematic possibility of discovering a "Nueva México," Aztlán was placed by the Europeans themselves somewhere north of the imaginary province, especially in *Codex Ramírez* (1583–1587) and *Crónica Mexicáyotl* (1597–1598; both cited in Piña 1989, 21–23). In 1652, in his *Crónica miscelánea*, Fray Antonio Tello placed Aztlán north of what is today the U.S. Southwest (Chávez 1989, 62). In 1784, Clavigero (1945, 218) thought that Aztlán was somewhere in northern California. At least until the late eighteenth century, the European imagination placed Aztlán in an unknown territory, especially one that was not only beyond that which they had already acquired but also one that they somehow were most likely to appropriate: from Nueva Galicia in the 1530s, to Nueva Vizcaya in the 1560s, to Nueva México in the 1590s and early 1600s. As Chávez argues, when in 1652 Fray Antonio Tello situates Aztlán north of what we call the American Southwest, it was evident that "the frontiers of the unknown had moved farther north by the mid-seventeenth century" (1989, 62).

Historically and militarily, what appear to be innocent "legends" and "myths" about the origin of the "Aztecs" or the "Seven Cities of Cíbola" were in fact turned by the Spaniards (throughout the postconquest sixteenth century, and in some cases by Americans in the early twentieth century) into political tools, if not weapons, to appropriate someone else's land. For example, parts of what today is considered to be "the Midwest"—Kansas and Nebraska—were "unofficially" explored by the Spaniards Francisco Leyva and Antonio Gutiérrez in 1593 (before Oñate arrived in Nueva México) precisely because of the possibility of finding Aztlán. As Encinias, Rodríguez, and Sánchez explain:

> Leyva and Gutiérrez learned about the plains and were determined to go there in hope that some great civilization similar to the Aztecs existed. After all, they may have reasoned, Vázquez de Coronado, Sánchez Chamuscado, and Espejo probably did not go far enough in the correct direction to find it. Leyva and Gutiérrez headed northeastward into what is now Kansas. They

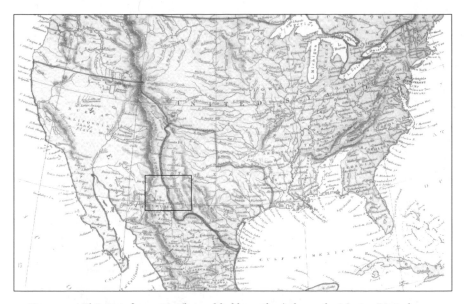

Figure 2.4. This map from 1844 (box added by author) shows the Mexico/United States boundary before the Mexican War of 1846–1848 (what Mexicans call La Guerra de Intervención Norteamericana [The War of North American Intervention]). Source: Portion of map, "North America," scale ca. 1:21,250,000, by the Society for the Diffusion of Useful Knowledge, 1844. London: Chas. Knight & Co. Courtesy of the Map and Geography Library, University of Illinois at Urbana-Champaign.

may have reached as far as the Nebraska plains—farther than any European had heretofore gone into the North American heartland. (1992, xxvii)

But in a conflict between them, Gutiérrez killed Leyva, and "Gutiérrez and his men were ambushed by Plains Indians" (ibid.). One "Mexican Indian," Jusepe, who survived, lived to tell the story—to Oñate in 1598.

It is difficult to identify the historical moment when the active political preoccupation with Aztlán (on the part of the elite) ceased. Perhaps the territorial "consolidation" of New Spain in the late eighteenth century and the imperialist expansion of the United States of America onto northern Mexico in the mid-nineteenth century, as well as Mexico's need for political consolidation after the French invasion of the 1860s, all led to the decrease, if not the demise, of the motive to search for a "new, rich land" in the "north." All these lands (in northern New Spain) had already been taken by Spain or France, or reclaimed by Mexico, or taken over by the United States (see Figure 2.4).

These historical contexts of territorial struggle, in which the "mythical" concept of Aztlán is used (for the most part quite effectively) as a political weapon to acquire desired territory, were repeated again in the late twentieth century (but without much official success or recognition on the part of the established Anglo power structure).

Chicanos/as and Aztlán

In the late 1960s, *a subordinate group* (politicized Mexican Americans who called themselves Chicanos and Chicanas) issued a call to identify and claim their homeland: Aztlán. Before this particular political mobilization (which was part of the civil rights movement led by Martin Luther King, Jr., and César Chávez), the search for Aztlán had been conducted by varied European (usually elitist) groups, with the exception of Moctezuma's subsidized pilgrimage to the "north." Although the military search for Aztlán allowed Spaniards during the sixteenth century to effectively appropriate and invent Nueva Galicia, Nueva Vizcaya, and Nueva México, politically underprivileged Chicanos and Chicanas were not as successful in reappropriating their envisioned Aztlán, no doubt due to their historically, economically, and politically based subordination in the United States of America. The new Aztlán was located in and constituted the U.S. Southwest (see Anzaldúa 1989, 191), where the Aztecas del Norte live. Alurista (the pen name for Alberto Baltazar Urista Heredia), one of the major Chicano activists, argued that Aztlán is somewhere around the Four Corners area (1989, 221). Rudolfo Anaya (1989) claimed that the Pueblo inhabitants of northern New Mexico are the indigenous descendants of the Aztecs, who left the Rio Grande on their pilgrimage to Mexico City. For most Chicanos, however (including this author), Aztlán includes and is beyond geography: "We are Aztlán" (Alurista 1989, 222; for a Chicana feminist critique, see Anzaldúa 1987 and García 1997, among others).

The linguistic evidence supporting the claim that the origin of the Aztlán migrants is the greater Northern Mexico area (which includes the Southwest), as well as recent archaeological discussion about it, is quite compelling. For instance, archaeologist Michael E. Smith has convincingly examined the "dual conception of the cultural origins of the Aztecs, who believed themselves descended from both savage [*sic*] Chichimecs [from the north] and civilized Toltecs" (1996, 41). More importantly for our purposes here, Smith has eloquently argued that (and he should be quoted at length)

> the north-to-south movement of the Aztlan groups is supported by research in historical linguistics. The Nahuatl language, classified in the Nahuan group of the Uto-Aztecan family of languages, is unrelated to most Meso-american native languages. Whereas the other major Mesoamerican language families—Mayan, Oto-Mangueyan, and Mixe-Zoquean—had deep roots going back millennia, Nahuatl was a relatively recent intrusion into

Mesoamerica. The Uto-Aztecan languages originated in northern Mexico or the southwestern United States, and Nahuatl was brought to central Mexico by peoples moving south. Linguists argue over the exact timing of the arrival of Nahuatl speakers in central Mexico, but most agree that this must have occurred sometime after the collapse of Teotihuacan and before the rise of the Aztecs. Since the descendants of the named Aztlan groups were Nahuatl speakers in 1519, it is reasonable to assume that the Aztlan migrants spoke Nahuatl when they first arrived in central Mexico several centuries earlier. Whether they were the initial speakers of Nahuatl in central Mexico is uncertain, but once the Aztlan migrants arrived, the Nahuatl language spread rapidly through both migration and cultural contact. . . . By the time of the Spanish conquest, Nahuatl had spread far beyond its initial stronghold in the fertile valleys of central Mexico. (1996, 41)

If Chicanas and Chicanos were or could have been as powerful as the Spaniards were in their time, today there would be an Aztlán, as there is a New Mexico—a Spanish myth become reality. For the Spaniards, Aztlán and the Seven Cities of Cíbola or Nueva México were converted into actual geographies of conquest and territorial appropriation (just as the geographically awkward "Midwest" exists today for European Americans, for whom it is, of course, culturally, historically, economically, and politically significant). To this extent, I strongly disagree with Encinias, Rodríguez, and Sánchez (1992, xx), who interpret Villagrá's vision "of the legendary coming of the primitive Mexicans (Aztecs)" exclusively as a "fictional passage." For Gaspar Pérez de Villagrá, the chronicler of Oñate's expedition, the origin of the *mexicanos* was somewhere to the "north" of Nueva Vizcaya, in Nueva México, close to a river that they had to cross. It is to the Pass of the River of the North that I now turn.

Río del Norte, Río Bravo, and Rio Grande

The cultural/historical category "Paso del Norte" and its uncertain relationship with such nationalist nomenclature as Río Bravo (as used in Mexico) and Rio Grande (as used in the United States) can be explicated by examining the name of the key river that was to separate Nueva Vizcaya from Nueva México and that later became the major political dividing line between post-1848 Mexico and the United States: the Río del Norte.

There is no doubt, of course, that the Spaniards gave the river such a name. Besides examining how the Spaniards named the crossing, we must address an additional problem, which is that the river has had two additional names, especially since the Mexican War of 1846–1848 (in Mexican historiography, this war is called La Guerra de Intervención Norteamericana, or "the War of North American Intervention"). Mexico calls the river "Río Bravo" and the United States calls it "Rio Grande." Is this difference just another problem of translation or one of confusion or both? Villagrá writes about the moment of arrival at the river, after several drought-plagued days of search:

[Spanish]
Mas la gran providencia, condolida, / Que tanto es mas beloz en socorrernos / Quanto con más firmeza la esperamos, / Al quinto abrió la puerta y fuimos todos, / Alegres, arribando el bravo Río / Del Norte, *por quien todos padezimos / Cuidado y trabajos tan pesados.*

[English]
But the great Providence, pitying, / Which is always more quick in helping us / As we more firmly trust in it, / The fifth day opened us the door / And we all, happily, did come upon the roaring *River / Of the North,* for which we all had undergone / Such care and such enormous toil. (Canto IV, in Encinias, Rodríguez, and Sánchez 1992, 126; my emphasis)

In the original version of Villagrá's text, "bravo" precedes "Río del Norte," and in the 1992 translation of it, "roaring" precedes "River of the North." In a 1990 citation of another translation (1933) of the same passage in Villagrá's poem, however, Timmons, one of the major historians actively writing about El Paso, uncritically cites a translation that drops the adjective *bravo,* which would remind post–mid-nineteenth-century Americans that the river was "Bravo": "Our faith was finally rewarded. That Providence which never deserted us at length crowned our efforts with success! After journeying, as stated, for four days without water, on the morning of the fifth we joyfully viewed in the distance the long sought waters *of the Río del Norte*" (Villagrá in Timmons 1990, 13; my emphasis). Besides this key moment in *Historia de la Nueva México,* Villagrá invokes this roaring and dangerous river in several other passages. One of these will suffice to make this critical point:

[Spanish]
En este medio tiempo, abía salido / El Sargento mayor a toda priessa, / Con tres Pilotos grandes que dezían / Ser en aquella tierra bien cursados, / Por sólo descubrir las turbias aguas / Del caudaloso Río que del Norte / Deciende manso y tanto se embrabece / *Que también* Río bravo *le llamamos. (my emphasis)*

[English]
In the meantime, there had set forth / The Sergeant Major, in great haste, With three famed guides who said they were / Well learned in all that land,

With purpose to seek out the turbid flood / Of that wide stream that from
the north / Flows calm, yet swells so much That we call it the Rio Bravo, too.
(Canto XI, Encinias, Rodríguez, and Sánchez 1992, 98–99)

In Villagrá's text, the phrase "Río Grande" never appears, although it is evident that there is a sense from his poem that he conceptualized the river as
a wide, large stream of water. Perhaps because of this characterization (as opposed to actually labeling it) as a wide stream, in a few eighteenth-century maps,
the river is depicted as "Río Grande del Norte." In fact, "Rio Grande" becomes
quite ubiquitous in the literature produced by nineteenth-century U.S. histo-
riographers, mostly as a result of the Mexican War of 1846–1848. Perhaps with
some irony, in the 1992 edition of Villagrá's book here under consideration, "Rio
Grande" appears only in the sections in English written by the late-twentieth-
century editors, Encinias, Rodríguez, and Sánchez (xxv, xxviii, xxix, xxx, xxxi,
xxxii, xxxiv, xxxv) and never in the voice of the Spaniards (see also Timmons
1990, especially chap. 1).

Using the name "Rio Grande" for both the river that existed between Nueva
Vizcaya and Nueva México during the colonial period of northward expansion
and the one between Texas and Mexico after 1848 on the U.S.-Mexico border
could have been a product of confusion (originally on the part of some Spaniards) as to the location of the Río Grande de Tololotlán (in northern Jalisco),
which used to be close to the dividing line between Nueva Galicia and Nueva
Vizcaya (see map on p. 30 in Mecham 1968). Anything beyond central Mexico
too often is easily considered to be "north"; after all, both Tenochtitlán and
Mexico City were (and continue to be) the dominant center of political, cultural,
and economic power (for instance, see maps by Howard Cline [1972, 167–168],
where "northern" Mexico begins in southern Zacatecas, San Luis Potosí, and
Aguascalientes). Considering the ignorance, vagueness, and blurriness of the
border between Nueva Vizcaya and Nueva México, it is possible that the use of
the phrase "Rio Grande" could have been a historical product of the parallelism
characterizing the two borders during the colonial period: the border between
Nueva Vizcaya and Nueva México and the border between Nueva Galicia and
Nueva Vizcaya (see map on northern New Spain by Gerhard, in Cline 1972).
After all, close to the Galicia/Vizcaya border but north of the Río Grande de Tololotlán, sometimes called "rio grande, because it is one of the largest that runs
through that area" (Clavigero 1945, 70–71), we find the town of Aztatlán (Nuño
de Guzmán's "discovery" of the land of the Aztecs). And is not Aztlán supposed
to be (as implied in Villagrá's poem) somewhere in Nueva México, north (or in
the northern part) of the Río Grande del Norte, or Río Bravo?

The conquest of northern New Spain followed the western route from Guadalajara and Tepic, through the Río Grande de Tololotlán to the beginnings of
Nueva Vizcaya in the town of Chiametla, Sinaloa; then, it went to Zacatecas,

Durango, and into Santa Bárbara, Chihuahua, from where the Oñate expedition started. As it was argued by Mecham in 1927, "The exploration and settlement of Nueva Galicia was a necessary preliminary to the development of Nueva Viz-caya" (1968, 19). Mecham describes the role of the Río Grande de Tololotlán in the formation of Nueva Vizcaya in the following ways:

> The territorial limits of Nueva Vizcaya . . . were . . . but ill-defined . . . [In 1524] with about eighty men, Francisco Cortes marched through Chimal-huacan, or western Jalisco, as far north as the Rio Tololotlan (Rio Grande). There he secured the allegiance of the "queen" of Jalisco, but discovered no Amazon Islands and but little gold. . . . At Tepic, [Nuño de] Guzman [founder of Nueva Galicia] left a garrison; then he crossed the Rio Tololo-tlan on May 29, 1530. He was now on virgin soil, insofar as it had never be-fore been visited by white men. . . . Guzman and his followers then pushed up the coast beyond the Rio San Pedro to Azatlan [Aztatlán] on the Rio Acaponeta. . . . From that place a reconnoitering party under Lope de Sama-niego, in November 1530, effected an entry into the province of Chiametla. . . . Samaniego's expedition constituted the first entry of white men into the region which later became Nueva Vizcaya. (Mecham 1968, 7, 21, 23–24)

Ibarra's contribution to the establishment of Nueva Galicia, even though he was the founder and governor of Nueva Vizcaya, is evident by the following towns "discovered" by him in the former province: Nombre de Dios, Fresnillo, Nieves, Sombrerete, San Martín, Ranchos, Chalchihuites, and Avino.

Thus, the possible use of "Rio Grande" to describe Río del Norte on the part of the Americans in the nineteenth century could be an appropriation of earlier politics of conquest and of naming associated with the uncertainty that accom-panied the establishment of Nueva Galicia and Nueva Vizcaya, or it could be the reproduction of the latter problem when they tried to delineate the borders between Nueva Vizcaya and Nueva México. It seems obvious that in their "con-fusion of tongues" (see Geertz 1973a), the agents of the Spanish Empire tended to repeat their "discoveries" every time they moved to a new area. In this spe-cific case, the double existence of an Aztlán north of Nueva Galicia (Nuño de Guzmán) and north of Nueva México (Villagrá) explains the double existence of a possible Rio Grande, one south of Aztatlán in Nueva Galicia and one in Nueva México on or south of the Pueblos of northern New Mexico. More than a problem about the exact location of Aztlán in the Euro-Mexican imagination, or about the proper name of Río del Norte in the Euro-American mentality, the name "Rio Grande" speaks to power politics of land appropriation that allow geographical spaces to be invented in times when the conquerors (either the Spanish or the Americans) can construct a world in their own image, whether it fits others' reality or not.

It should be noted that throughout the sixteenth and seventeenth centuries, European maps showed the confusion of the "Rio Grande" in the "north." Since the Río Grande de Tololotlán flows west into the Pacific Ocean, many maps unsuccessfully tried to come up with ways of locating the Rio (Grande) del Norte in "North America," flowing into the Gulf of California! (see Pierre Duval's map, drawn in Paris in 1660, reproduced as figure 2.2, p. 27). In fact, according to Philip Burden, in a map drawn by Giovanni Battista Nicolosi in Rome in 1660, "The Rio Grande is for the first time correctly depicted flowing south-east from New Mexico and discharging itself into the Gulf of Mexico" (1996, 455; Figure 2.3). Due to the wars between the European empires, however, Spanish maps were decidedly unclear: "The lack of any great detail [reflected] the official policy of protecting Spanish knowledge of the New World" (Burden 1996, 170; please see Figure 2.3, p. 28).

That "Río Grande del Norte" was used by the Spaniards to describe the crossing into "New Mexico" does not necessarily mean that "Río del Norte" was not the preferred name, especially in relation to either "Rio Grande" or "Río Bravo." That the United States appropriated "Rio Grande" as a strategy to differentiate themselves from the "Mexicans," who preferred "Río Bravo" (which is often and strategically used by Villagrá in his text of 1610), is manifested through the ignorance shown in the tautological meaning given to the term "Rio" when Americans, verbally and in written form, argue that the dividing line between the United States of America and Mexico is "the *Rio Grande river*."[16]

Paso del Norte (Current Ciudad Juárez) and the "Mansos"

Paso del Norte, que lejos te vas quedando, tus divisiones, de mí se están alejando [Paso del Norte, I can hardly see you anymore, your border crossings, I am leaving so far behind]
— MEXICAN SONG MADE POPULAR BY ANTONIO AGUILAR IN THE 1960S

If the dividing line between the Provincias was not always clear, the crossing of Río del Norte was incontestably called "El Paso del Río del Norte." In 1659, however, when the Spaniards established the first colonial institution in the area, a mission in honor of the Virgen de Guadalupe, they dropped "del Río" from the phrase and left it as "El Paso del Norte." The full name of the religious mission is the following: Misión de Nuestra Señora de Guadalupe de los Mansos del Paso del Norte.

The term *paso*, however, more than simply implying the physical crossing of the river, has a religious origin as well, manifested in the word *passo* (note the double *s*; see Aguirre 1993). In the "Acta de Fundación" (Foundation Letter) of the Mission of Nuestra Señora de Guadalupe, *passo*, in the religious sense of living through hardships or maintaining a feeling of endurance and courage against all odds, is used by its founder, Fray García de San Francisco (see Hertzog n.d. and Alcázar de Velasco n.d., UTEP Special Collections).[17]

The mission was established for two reasons: to serve as a resting place midway on the commercial trail between Parral (southern Nueva Viscaya) and Santa Fe (northern Nueva México) and, more importantly, to convert the local inhabitants surrounding that particular pass of the river. Specifically, the Spaniards had a mission to convert indigenous peoples, the so-called Mansos (literally "the tamed"), to Christianity; thus, the name of the mission: . . . Misión . . . de los Mansos del Paso del Norte.

The production of this specific identity, "Manso," tells much more about the European imagination than about the self-identification of the indigenous "group" here being politically invented. *Manso* in Spanish means "tamed." For the most part, the name is taken for granted (see Timmons 1990). Recently, there have been some attempts to historicize it. For example, Mexican historian Zacarías Márquez Terrazas believes that this specific name emerged from the name of a priest, Fray Tomás Manso, who had missionized in the "north" since 1631 (1991, 125). In 1610, however, in referring to "what happened" during the few days after claiming possession of the territory of Nueva México, Villagrá described his first encounter with the locals in 1598 when five Spaniards (including Villagrá) went looking for a good ford to cross the river:

[Spanish]
Y andando embebecidos todos juntos / En busca de buen vado, cuidadosos, / De súbito nos fuimos acercando / A vnos pagizos ranchos, do salieron / Gran cantidad de bárbaros guerreros. / Y por ser aquello pantanoso / Y no poder valernos de las armas, / Assí para los bárbaros nos fuimos / Mostrándonos amigos agradables. / Y como el dar al fin quebranta peñas, / Dándoles de la ropa que tuvimos / Tan mansos los bolvimos y amorosos, / Tanto que quatro dellos se vinieron / Y un lindo vado a todos nos mostraron. (my emphasis)

[English]
And, travelling all together, studiously, / Careful in search for some good ford, / We suddenly did come upon / Some thatched huts from whence there came out / Great numbers of *barbarian warriors*. / And as that place was all marshy / And we could not well use our arms, / We went ahead toward the barbarians / Showing ourselves agreeable friends. / And as giving even breaks rocks, / Giving them of the clothes we had / We made them so *peaceful, friendly,* to us / That four of them did come with us / And showed to us a goodly ford. (Encinias, Rodríguez, and Sánchez 1992, 130; my emphasis)

The critical transformation in the same passage from *bárbaros guerreros* (barbarian warriors) to *mansos y amorosos* (the editors translated this phrase

"peaceful, friendly," but it should be "tamed and loving") is actually an enactment of production of the identity of an indigenous group by and in relation to
the Spaniards.[18] This same historical moment (when the ethnic category Manso
is invented) is described differently in another "unedited" text quoted by Encinias, Rodríguez, and Sánchez (1992, xxviii), who noted that "the well-armed and
European-attired Spaniards contrasted with the almost nude natives, who came
to make peace. 'They had Turkish bows, long hair cut to resemble little Milan
caps, head gear made to hold down the hair and colored with blood or paint.
Their first words were *manxo, manxo, micos, micos,* by which they meant "peaceful ones" and "friends." They make signs of the cross by raising their fingers.'"[19]

It is obvious that "Manso" is a term imposed on the locals by the Spaniards,
the authors of these passages. The Spaniards in the Oñate expedition, like Cortés
during the conquest of Tenochtitlán, carried with them a specific vision of the
world characterized by oppositional dichotomies in which those they encountered were either friends or enemies, friendly or hostile; thus, the rivers they
encountered were either fierce (*bravos*) or tamed (*mansos, amansados*). Villagrá
envisions the streams he was encountering in the same way that he envisioned
the "barbarian warriors" or the "tamed, calm barbarians":

[Spanish]
Por sólo descubrir las turbias aguas / Del Caudaloso Río que del Norte /
Deciende manso *y tanto se* embrabece / *Que también* Río bravo *le llamamos.*

[English]
With purpose to seek out the turbid flood / Of that wide stream that from
the North / Flows *calm,* yet swells [*sic;* I prefer "infuriates"] so much / That
we call it the *Rio Bravo,* too. (Encinias, Rodríguez, and Sánchez 1992, 99; my
emphasis)

In Canto XII, Villagrá describes in "*manso*" terms the captivity of two indigenous men:

[Spanish]
Los dos bien afligidos se quedaron / Y como aquéllos que forzados llevan, /
Mansos de todo punto, ya rendidos / A la fuerza del remo riguroso / Y encen-
dida braveza de crugía, / *Assí,* mansos forzados, les llevamos.

[English]
The two, most afflicted, remained, / And, like those sentenced galley
slaves, / In all points *meek* [again, I prefer "tamed"], surrendered / To toiling at the rigorous oar / And *fiery* harshness of the galleys, / So *meek* prisoners, we bore them off. (Encinias, Rodríguez, and Sánchez 1992, 111; my
emphasis)

Through these oppositions between tamed and wild, even meek and fierce, the Spaniards invented what were to be ethnic categories, following the same oppositional cultural constructs that constituted their imagined world.[20] In this process, those who were not "Mansos" (tamed) or "settled" (the "Pueblo" Indians) were wild, nomads, barbarians, such as the Apaches, whom the Spaniards placed in direct opposition to the more calm Pueblo Indians of the north and in opposition to the Mansos in southern New Mexico. The Apaches of the Paso del Norte region came to be called Sumas during the 1600s, and they were considered to be a species of Apaches mainly because they resisted the missionization and colonization process (see Mecham 1968, 72).[21]

However, in 1680, during the Pueblo Rebellion in northern New Mexico, and in 1684, in the Misión de Guadalupe-Paso del Norte area, the Spaniards were to be proven wrong about their own cultural categorizations. The indigenous peoples inhabiting the Ciudad Juárez/El Paso/Las Cruces region in the late sixteenth and seventeenth centuries, in spite of their peaceful overtures when encountering Spaniards, suffered both physical and psychological exploitation. I have not found indigenous versions of "what actually happened" in the early 1600s in this specific geographic region of what was southern Nueva México, but a document cited by the Juárez native historian Armando Chávez (1991, 119–124) should allow us some access to the Spaniards' brutality against the so-called Mansos.[22] The document cited by Chávez is dated June 20, 1626, and its author is Fray Juan de Santander, who worked under the direction of Fray Alonso de Benavides, Commissioner of the Holy Office and Custodian of the Provinces and Conversions of New Mexico. Santander presented the document to King Philip IV of Spain.

What follows is my own translation of the text that relates to "the Mansos" and how they are presented to the king as a tamed nation, subdued through the malicious use of dogs (see Figure 2.5) by the Spaniards.[23] These Franciscans, Santander and Benavides, are trying to make a case for religious conversion, which would eventually lead to the establishment of a mission in 1659:

> This river [Río del Norte] is inhabited by a nation that we commonly call Mansos [tamed] or Gorretas [caps]; we gave them these names because they fix their hair in such a way that they look as if they are wearing caps; and [we call them Mansos] because they have become aware that our dogs have bitten them a few times when they receive us in war; and when they receive us in peace and mansos [tamed], we tell our dogs "go away" so that they will not bite them. They also prevent themselves from being bitten by our dogs by telling us "go away manso, manso." And because of this, they are commonly known among us by the name of Mansos. . . . They are also of the condition that if they see things going their way, they will do all the bad they can [si ven la suya, hacen todo el mal que pueden], but since they are

Figure 2.5. "Incidents after the surrender of the Aztecs." Source: Leon-Portilla 1992, 143.

not able to do bad things, they all come in peace so that we will give them food. . . . These mansos, since they are at the pass of this river, are unavoidable; and they take us to their own ranches so that we will give food to their women and children, and they also give us what they have of fish and mice. They are a very giving people. Since we have preached to them so much, they now tell me that I should bring them more Religious people who can teach them and who can baptize them. . . . Besides the principle of the conversion of souls . . . it would also assure the two-hundred-league pass while setting a good example for the other nations. This could be accomplished by bringing three or four Religious people, with only fifteen or twenty soldiers. . . . This is already a *mansa* nation very much disposed to its conversion: because whenever we talk to them about God, they listen to us and they very much feel that if they do not become baptized they will go to hell and burn. (Santander, cited in Chávez 1991, 120–123 [original, June 20, 1626]; my own translation)

Eventually, toward the end of the seventeenth century, the Pueblos and the Mansos rebelled, each in their respective areas. Between 1680 and 1682, the Spaniards, who inhabited Santa Fe and the surrounding settlements, were forced by the indigenous peoples on a pilgrimage down to Paso del Norte. With the arrival into the region of dispossessed Spaniards and of some indigenous peoples called Piros and Tiwas, a civil multiethnic community (with the Spaniards at the top of the social/racial hierarchy) was established in the vicinity of the Misión de Guadalupe. This community was made up of five settlements: Paso del Norte, San Lorenzo, Senecú, Ysleta, and Socorro.

In 1684, an indigenous conspiracy against the Spaniards and their allies led Manso, Suma, Piro, and Tigua inhabitants of the Paso del Norte area to an armed rebellion that some historians have called the Great Southwestern Revolt. Due to these acts of resistance on the part of indigenous peoples, the Spaniards soon established a military presidio, or fort, close to Guadalupe Mission. By 1684, all three colonial institutions at the pass—the civil community, the mission, and the presidio—became specifically known as Paso del Norte. The mission was under the jurisdiction of Nueva México, whose capital was Santa Fe, while the presidio was under the jurisdiction of Nueva Vizcaya, whose capital was in Durango. After Mexico's independence from Spain, Paso del Norte belonged to New Mexico. In 1824, however, Paso del Norte became part of (the current state of) Chihuahua, which (along with Durango) "replaced" Nueva Vizcaya (see Altamirano and Villa 1988a, 224–225, 258–259). Thus, from 1684 on, and through the Mexican War in 1846–1848 and until 1888, the place on the south side of the river was generally known as Paso del Norte.

Conclusion

In this chapter, I have tried to map out the complex colonial origins of a particular area on the south bank of the Rio Grande, which in the 1880s began to get urbanized through the arrival of the railroad. In 1888, Paso del Norte was named Ciudad Juárez in honor of Mexico's 1860s president Benito Juárez (see Chávez 1991, 295; Martínez 1978, 19; Timmons 1990, 183). The legacies of the conquests of Mexico and of southern New Mexico are found everywhere throughout the border metropolis. Though of a different kind and still not well documented by historians, the early colonial history of Ciudad Juárez is as profound as that of any city in southern Mexico. As Mexican colonial historian Francisco de Solano noted with regard to the importance of the early colonial period for the present: "The image Mexico has today proceeds in large part from the one that was formed during its three hundred colonial years" (1984, 11; my translation).

Unequivocally, most of the names of places and peoples analyzed in this chapter are still in wide use today. A major street, a large neighborhood, and an industrial park all carry the name Los Aztecas. Rio Grande is the name applied to the river on the American side, whereas Río Bravo is the phrase used by Mexican nationals. While New Mexico is still the official name on the U.S. side of what once was Nueva México, in Mexico they call it Nuevo México. Yet, the New Mexico county bordering Ciudad Juárez at the new "international" Santa Teresa crossing is called Doña Ana County. Interestingly, several Mexican Americans who reside in this New Mexico–Juárez border area use two kinds of car plates:

a New Mexico plate on the back of the car that says "New Mexico USA" ("USA" is used to remind Americans that New Mexico is in fact in the United States of America) and a plate on the front decorated with the colors of the Mexican flag, *verde, blanco y colorado* (green, white, and red).[24]

The foregoing analysis of the Juárez–New Mexico border should remind readers that Ciudad Juárez must be understood (both in the present and in past times) in the larger historical, economic, and political contexts of the Juárez/ New Mexico/El Paso, Texas, region. Thus, the phrase "El Paso" is the official name of the Texas border city that was established on the north bank of the Rio Grande in the 1850s as a military post called "Post Opposite El Paso (del Norte)" (Timmons 1990, 106). "Paso del Norte" is still widely used in some popular songs in honor of the history of Ciudad Juárez; it is the name of the main international bridge to cross into El Paso, Texas, either walking or driving; it is also a common name for restaurants, hotels, and business conferences for maquiladora managers on both sides of the border; finally, it is also the name of an international Latin American Film festival funded by the Mexican federal government that has taken place every summer in Ciudad Juárez since the summer of 1991.

The indigenous peoples the Spaniards called Mansos have mostly disappeared from both sides of the border. Nicholas Houser, however, one of the few scholars conducting ethnographic research among indigenous peoples who reside in the El Paso/Las Cruces/Juárez area, identified a multi-indigenous community descendant from the Mansos. He wrote:

> The Texas [Ysleta del Sur] Pueblo is associated with the nearby Tigua community of Tortugas in Las Cruces, New Mexico. This Indian community is a daughter colony of Ysleta del Sur [which is located south of El Paso]. It evolved some time between 1850 and 1900 from a composite of Tigua, Piro, and Manso Indians and was formally incorporated in 1914. . . . The [Tigua] Ysleta Indians have relatives across the river in Mexico, from the former Piro Pueblo of Senecú near Juárez. . . . The Piro Pueblo of Senecú ceased to exist as an organization around the first decade of the twentieth century. . . . Descendants of both tribes, including the Manso, can still be identified within the El Paso-Paso-Juárez area. (Houser 1979, 336–337)

These indigenous peoples who call themselves "Manso-Piro-Tiwa" are fighting the local government for official recognition as a tribe (see Houser 1979). This vital community of indigenous citizens must be systematically studied in the immediate future, particularly in the broader tri-city/tri-state areas, and in the historical contexts of colonialism, multiculturalism, and late industrial capitalism, which will be examined in Part II of this book.

One of the main purposes of this chapter was to demonstrate that when the historical metaphor of Aztlán (or any metaphor of a physical territory) is used as

Figure 2.6. The "Juan de Oñate Trail" (on the U.S. side of
the river) under the Puente de Córdoba ("Puente Libre")/
International Bridge of the Americas. A tractor-trailer used
to transport merchandise crosses over and above the "Trail."
Photograph by Alejandro Lugo.

a weapon by the strong (the Mexica before the Spaniards or by the Spaniards in
the sixteenth century), its realities do come about: the existence of New Mexico
(a Nueva México) from the late 1500s and up to the present moment. But when
the historical myth of Aztlán is used as a weapon by the weak (Mexican Americans and Chicanos in the late twentieth century [from the 1960s and into the
present]), Aztlán remains a "myth," even in the most sophisticated treatments of
it by many Chicano/a scholars; it does not become a physical reality, as "Mexico,"

"New Mexico," and "America" became during their respective historical moments. My observation for the twenty-first century remains: As long as minorities within nation-states remain politically and economically weak, their myths about a physical territory will remain only a spiritual reality.

The politics of conquest and its impact on the naming of the region where Ciudad Juárez (old Paso del Norte) is located could not have been understood without an analysis of how the political identity of the self and its specific geographical place was constructed during the conquests of Mexico and of New Mexico in the sixteenth century. Similarly, the conquest of New Mexico (and of Paso del Norte in the process) was directly influenced and shaped by the cultural logic, kinship relationships, and politics brought about by the conquest of Mexico-Tenochtitlán (see Figure 2.6). These colonial contexts, and the complex power relations that accompanied them, should be kept in mind when I examine, in the next chapter, the ways in which both Mexico and the U.S.-Mexico borderlands have witnessed the ironies, uncertainties, and contradictions that the problem of color instantiates for the discursive practice of a nationalist ideology, *mestizaje,* in a postcolonial context.

THREE

The Problem of Color in Mexico
and on the U.S.-Mexico Border
Precolonial, Colonial, and Postcolonial Subjectivities

WHAT FOLLOWS IS part of a taped conversation Don Ernesto and I had in the summer of 1991.[1] Originally from Jalisco, Mexico, Don Ernesto has been in Ciudad Juárez for more than forty years.

LUGO: You know what racism is, right?

DON ERNESTO: No, not really, not directly. I've heard that word, that's all.

LUGO: And what do you know about "racism"?

DON ERNESTO: About racism I know *nothing*. [He emphasizes "nothing."]

LUGO: Some people say that there is a lot of racism in the United States and that there is discrimination against Mexicans and blacks, mainly because of their race, that we are supposedly inferior. They think that we are lazy. They don't want to give welfare to us because we are lazy. "They should work," they say. That is a form of racism. Racism can result from skin-color preference; whites would not marry blacks. . . . Don Ernesto, do you think that racism exists in Mexico . . . against specific groups?

DON ERNESTO: Yes, there is racism in Mexico, but it is because of government's self-interest. They always deal with Indians because they want to take advantage of them. They take away from them what they had and do not let them progress. And according to the government, they claim to be helping them to progress. The government blames the mediators [political representatives] for the Indians' loss of land . . . *los indios no tienen la culpa* . . . it is not the Indians' fault.

LUGO: Do you think racism in Mexico occurs because of skin color? Do you think dark-skinned people are discriminated against?

DON ERNESTO: As with the Tarahumaras [Raramuri], the indigenous people of Chihuahua . . . Well, it does not occur because of their skin color . . . in reality it is because of their behavior, their mode of dressing, their [lack of] hygiene . . . that's what it is. I do not see a difference between them and us [Don Ernesto and I, as mestizos/Mexicanos, are supposedly "cleaner": *más higiénicos*]. It is the lack of hygiene. . . . I don't think that is racism. You liberate yourself from them for the same reason [at one time, Don Ernesto allowed several Raramuri to live in his backyard].

Chela is a woman in her midthirties. She was born in Ciudad Juárez and has worked in several maquiladoras intermittently for ten years. The following is taken directly from a three-hour interview.

LUGO: Do you know what racism is?

CHELA: It has never called my attention . . . it means not liking blacks . . . that *güeros* [blonds/whites] do not like blacks. Why not? We are all the same. . . . Just because of their skin color.

LUGO: You hear a lot about racism in the United States.

CHELA: Yes. Not here [in Mexico]. I haven't heard about it here.

LUGO: What about against indigenous peoples?

CHELA: Not really . . .

LUGO: No? People don't talk about racism in Mexico, [is that?] right?

CHELA: Not that I remember.

In a society where privilege and power are the monopoly of the fair-skinned, Esperanza is acutely aware of her dark skin, and of her Indianness. . . . Yet her Indianness is not based in an ethnic identity, but in race/class distinctions that have developed since the European conquest of Mexico and that continue to assert the power of white-skin privilege. (Behar 1993, 8)

Introduction: The Problem with the Nationalist Ideology of *Mestizaje* and the Color-Line Alternative

In his representation of contemporary Mexicans and their nationalism, Jorge Klor de Alva produces a discourse in which "Spanish" hegemony is notably absent. He made the following statement supporting José Emilio Pacheco's reading of *The Broken Spears*: "José Emilio Pacheco, one of Mexico's foremost writers, dared to speak for all Mexicans, Indians, and mestizos, when claiming the book [*The Broken Spears*] was 'a great epic poem of the origins of our nationality.' And he did not hesitate to add that it was a 'classic book and an indispensable work for all Mexicans'" (Klor de Alva 1992, xiii). In very striking dichotomous terms (that is, reducing the multiplicity of colonial encounters to the encounter between "two worlds"), Miguel Leon-Portilla argues that Mexico and Latin America "descended" from the "dramatic union . . . of the encounter between two worlds, the Indian and the Spanish" (Leon-Portilla 1992, xlviii), and he has characterized "the Mexican people of today" as "the living consequence of that violent clash between two worlds" (Leon-Portilla 1992, 176). A much more direct representation of a "promised land" without "Spaniards" is Eric Wolf's depiction of the "Mexico" that emerged after the Virgen de Guadalupe appeared in the imagination not only of those considered "Indian," but most importantly, of those considered "illegitimate offspring of Spanish fathers and Indian mothers": mestizos. Wolf continues:

> Where Spaniard and Indian stood squarely within the law, they [the mestizos] inhabited the interstices and margins of constituted society. These groups acquired influence and wealth in the seventeenth and eighteenth centuries, but were yet barred from social recognition and power by the prevailing economic, social and political order. To them, the Guadalupe myth came to represent not merely the guarantee of their assured place in heaven, but the guarantee of their place in society here and now. On the political plane, the wish for a return to a paradise of early satisfactions of food and warmth, a life without defeat, sickness or death, gave rise to a political wish for a Mexican paradise, in which the illegitimate sons would possess the country, and the irresponsible Spanish overlords . . . would be driven from the land. (1958, 37–38)

Most recently, in spite of his critical and sophisticated take on the production of the discourse on *mestizaje* in the twentieth century, Roger Bartra, in evaluating the work of Ezequiel Chávez, does not go beyond the ideology of the "the melting pot" hypothesis, which I am criticizing here:

> The indigenous sediment endures and, in addition, the "mixed races" form two irrevocably separate groups: one, the "superior *mestizos*," coming from stable families and forming "the resistant nerve of the Mexican spirit"; the others, the "vulgar *mestizos*," never developing an "organic cooperative spirit" because they are descended from "individuals united in a deserted marriage bed of incessant illicit union." The Revolution did, however, accelerate the "melting pot of the centuries," and the result was that these *mestizos* became the unifying symbol of national progress. (Bartra 1992, 93)

The characterization of postindependence and postrevolutionary Mexico as a country of mestizos (either "superior" or "vulgar") has been, for the most part, an assumption, and a very convincing one, at least to those "invisibles" without a culture/race/ethnicity who control it.[2] However, those with a culture and with an ethnic identity distinct from the institutionalized "Mexican," not only the Raramuri, or Tarahumara, of Chihuahua but also non-European or mestizo Mexican Chiapanecos (people from Chiapas) still wondered, as of January 1, 1994—and now for more than a decade—whether "the irresponsible Spanish overlords . . . would be driven from the land" (see Collier 1994; Nash 2001; Stephen 2002).

In this chapter, I make the following propositions. First, I show that in spite of the dominant discourse on *mestizaje,* the "whites" never left Mexico. My major argument here is that the prevalent, though hardly acknowledged, hierarchies of color that pervasively characterize Mexican society question in a definitive manner not only the ideology of *mestizaje* but more specifically the viability of the concept of *mestizaje* used (in academic writing such as the ones noted above) to describe postindependence and postrevolutionary Mexico. Thus, and secondly, I argue that social relations, whether under colonial New Spain or under postcolonial Mexico, have always been partially mediated or ruptured by the problem of color, which, at least in its beginning, had been given different cultural meanings both by the Spaniards and by the local inhabitants. Later, whether through the interventions of the Americans or of the French in the nineteenth century, race and color were constituted differently, according to how Mexicans were described by outsiders. In the early decades of the twentieth century, however, Mexican nationalist leaders (i.e., Lázaro Cárdenas in the 1930s) themselves described the "Indian" problem or solution in race-specific terms, while those in power were depicting themselves in a colorless and raceless narrative. Yet, I show here (see also Chapter 6) that the racially based diversity within the so-called mestizo community has been characterized more by a racialized color than by an ethnic narrative.

Third, with the deployment of prejudicial practices regarding color and race, both in the national and in the global context of Mexico, the peasants and proletariats who migrated north throughout the twentieth century, either to the American Southwest or to Mexican border cities such as Ciudad Juárez, brought with them, along with the need for employment, culturally specific notions of color.[3] Fourth, in the U.S.-Mexico borderlands, and more specifically the El Paso–Ciudad Juárez area, color has not only been applied along gender lines, as had occurred during sixteenth-century encounters of conquest, but has also simultaneously acquired class, racial, and nationalist overtones that relate in very specific ways to the Ciudad Juárez border experience. In consequence, the ethnographic analysis of Ciudad Juárez in this chapter and in Chapter 6 should not be applied, especially carelessly, to the analysis of Chihuahua City, the capital of the state, for instance, or to the analysis of the state of Chihuahua as a whole.[4]

Finally, the main theoretical and empirical proposition of this chapter is that, in the case of Mexico, despite the transformational complexity characterizing the hierarchies of race, class, gender, and nationalist incongruities, the problem of color (in spite of the distinct meaning given to it in different times and places) has remained a constant site of social and political struggle since the time of the conquest. This analysis will, I hope, help to better explain, understand, and contest the tensions, contradictions, ambivalences, tragedies, ironies, and use of force (see Chakrabarty 1992) delineating the uneasy relation that the "Rest" (indigenous peoples of Mexico and northern Mexico as well as the industrial working classes) have had with the superimposed "West" (Spanish Empire and its multiple agents as well as Euro-American corporations) in the Americas.

This focus on the question of color within a so-called mestizo world constitutes not only one way, at least for me, of telling a particular history of the Juárez/El Paso/New Mexico border area in the larger global and colonial contexts of Mexico and the American Southwest, but also a way of exposing a serious social problem (see also Chapter 6) that very few have articulated as something that has to be eradicated along with racism against indigenous and black Mexican people.[5]

The Color and Gender of the Conquest

In the late sixteenth century, Bernal Díaz del Castillo wrote the following description of Moctezuma:

The great Montezuma was about forty years old, of good height, well proportioned, spare and slight, and not very dark, though of the usual Indian complexion. (1956, 224)

Díaz del Castillo's depiction of Cuauhtémoc's color contrasts with the usual characterization of indigenous people in Mexico. He noted that

Guatemuc was very delicate, both in body and features. . . . He was twenty-six, and his complexion was rather lighter than the brown of most Indians. . . . (Díaz del Castillo 1956, 405)

The question that should be raised is not whether Díaz del Castillo accurately identified the "proper" skin pigmentation of the "Aztecs," but rather why he would be so preoccupied with "coloring" the individuals described. There is no doubt that Europeans constructed various categories in relation to themselves not only to make cultural sense of specific encounters but mainly to appropriate, politically and economically, those encountered (see Chapter 2). Since the Spaniards defined themselves as white and superior vis-à-vis their black African slaves, native peoples in the new continent would have to be placed somewhere in the European color continuum ranging from black, red, brunette, and brown to light skin, white, and the latter's extreme, blond. More than a structural classificatory scheme, white and black, or "civilized" and "Indian," represent asymmetrical power relations between colonizer and colonized, or between conqueror and conquered. In the case of Mexico, these incipient inequalities of conquest, both evident and embedded in the coloring of individuals, have never been eradicated from the shifting contours of everyday life; in fact, they have left a legacy that only the naive observer can ignore or simply miss.

These strategies for depicting newly encountered subjects did not occur unilaterally. In *The Broken Spears* (Leon-Portilla 1992), a key document representing the indigenous version of the conquest, we find a certain type of local colorism through which the Spaniards were described. Color adjectives were used by the local inhabitants in at least two episodes: during the first encounters in what became the Gulf coast of "Mexico" and during the massive resistance that led to the expulsion of the Spaniards from Tenochtitlán and which is called "La Noche Triste" (Night of Sorrows). Regarding the former cases, the following was reported to Moctezuma by one of his messengers:

> On their heads they wore red kerchiefs, or bonnets of a fine scarlet color, and some wore large round hats like small comales, which must have been sun shades. They have very light skin, much lighter than ours. They all have long beards, and their hair comes only to their ears. (Leon-Portilla 1992, 17; orig. in *Crónica mexicana* by Tezozomoc, 1598)

In another description of the first encounter, found in Bernardino de Sahagún's *Codex Florentino,* 1585 edition, we find an indigenous concept of color applied to people:

> The strangers' bodies are completely covered, so that only their faces can be seen. Their skin is white, as if it were made of lime. They have yellow hair, though some of them have black. (Leon-Portilla 1992, 30)

It is evident that this notion of color is culturally distinct (specific to material surroundings) from the European one (specific to the human/physical body): the colors applied to individuals by the local inhabitants were much more related to the natural environment (for instance, to the lime used "to paint" their bodies in rituals, such as for war) than to inherent physical attributes—the Spanish concern. One of Moctezuma's main "chiefs," Quetzalaztatzin, "Keeper of the Chalk," was the "official in charge of the colors with which the priests painted their bodies before performing certain rituals" (Leon-Portilla 1992, 31n3). Thus, the categories "white" and "yellow" used in Sahagún's *Codex Florentino* seem to have been associated with certain colors of paint and not so much with physical/ racial attributes. We must interpret in similar terms the following indigenous description of the dead bodies during the major expulsion perpetrated by the infuriated, occupied "Aztecs":[6]

> They loaded the bodies of the Tlaxcaltecas [apart from the people of Tez- coco, the people of Tlaxcala were the Spaniards' main indigenous allies] into canoes and took them out to where the rushes grow. . . . They also threw out the corpses of the women who had been killed in the retreat. The naked bodies of these women were the color of ripe corn, for they had painted themselves with yellow paint. . . . But they laid out the corpses of the Spaniards apart from the others; they lined them up in rows in a sepa- rate place. Their bodies were as white as the new buds of the canestalk, as white as the buds of the maguey. . . . (Leon-Portilla 1992, 88; orig. in *Codex Aubin*, 1576)

This culturally specific notion of color contrasts quite clearly with the meaning given to color found either in Díaz del Castillo's work or in the *Codex Ramírez*, which was written in 1580:

> The prince [of Tezcoco] was astonished to see a man [Cortés] with such white skin and with a beard and with so much courage and majesty, while Cortes, in turn, was astonished by the prince and his brothers—especially by Tecocoltzin, who was as white as any of the Spaniards. (Leon-Portilla 1992, 58)

During and after the fall of Tenochtitlán in 1521, the Spaniards began to make sexual demands on the conquered people in terms of color preference. In fact, Sahagún's "informants" described in color-specific terms how some of the women who were trying to flee the newly conquered areas were harassed by the Spaniards: "The Spanish soldiers were stationed along the roads to search the fleeing inhabitants . . . the Spaniards searched all women without exception: those with light skins, those with dark skins, those with dark bodies" (Leon-Portilla 1992, 118; orig. in *Codex Florentino*). Just as race was strategically gen- dered in nineteenth-century Indonesia when "white" women were introduced into the colonies (Stoler 1991), during the conquest of "Mexico," color was sexually and racially gendered, specifically with regard to women. Indigenous women in conquered (not yet colonized) New Spain were sexually objectified or eroticized through the andro-Spanish conception and categorization of color. This is evident in the following "order" given by Cortés to Cuauhtémoc, through a messenger named Xochitl: "You are to deliver women with light skins, corn, chicken, eggs and tortillas. This is your last chance. The people of Tenochtitlan must choose whether to surrender or to be destroyed" (Leon-Portilla 1992, 139; orig. in Manuscript 22, 1528).

In spite of the conceptual difference representing what we now consider "skin pigmentation," there was a space where the two distinct cultural visions could meet, or at least be mediated: the hierarchical indigenous association of the "sun" not only with lighting but with illuminating/whitening and the consequent association of the Spaniards' lightness of skin color/white paint with the gods. We find this indigenous cultural concept associating the Spaniards with the gods/the sun in two critical texts, Sahagún's *Codex Florentino* and *Codex Ramírez*:

> Motecuhzoma ordered the sacrifice [of captives] because he took the Spaniards to be gods; he believed in them and worshipped them as deities. That is why they were called "Gods who have come from heaven." As for the Negroes, they were called "soiled gods." (Leon-Portilla 1992, 33–34, orig. in *Codex Florentino*, 1585)

> The Indians knelt down and adored them as sons of the Sun, their gods, believing that the time had come of which their dear king . . . had so often spoken. (Leon-Portilla 1992, 58; orig. in *Codex Ramírez*, 1580)

Even though Moctezuma's presumed interpretation of the Spaniards as gods has been seriously questioned by some historians (Guzmán 1989; Pagden 1986) as being Hernán Cortés's justification "of a 'voluntary' submission of Motecucoma, and [of] the 'legal' transfer of his empire . . . to its rightful ruler" (Elliot 1986, xxviii), neither Leon-Portilla (1992) nor Klor de Alva (1992) have responded to the challenge. Nevertheless, the conquest itself seems to have produced an indigenous cultural practice of calling Pedro de Alvarado, one of the main Spanish mercenaries, "the Sun." This honorific term was ironically given to the individual directly responsible for the massacre at the Main Temple, which in turn led to the "Noche Triste." Yet because of his "blond" (color)/"yellow" (painted) hair, he was called "the Sun." As Pagden recently noted, "[Pedro de Alvarado] was said to have been brave but rash, a judgment which the events bear out. He had blond hair, which earned him the name of Tanatiuh ("the Sun")" (Cortés 1986, 473n78). Extracting from *Codex Aubin*, Leon-Portilla documented the state of affairs just before the massacre:

> [Cortés] left the city to meet another force of Spaniards who were marching in this direction. Pedro de Alvarado, called the Sun, was in command during his absence. When the day of the Fiesta arrived, Motecuhzoma said to The Sun: "Please hear me, my lord. We beg your permission to begin the fiesta of our lord." The Sun replied: "Let it begin. We shall be here to watch it." (Leon-Portilla 1992, 80)

There seems to be no doubt in the versions of most historians that "the Sun" took advantage of the ritualized congregation at the Main Temple and tried to exterminate the local inhabitants of Tenochtitlán. For purposes of the problem of color that concerns us here, however, I cannot help but note the reemergence of a different type of "sun," singer Luis Miguel, in the Mexico of the 1980s and 1990s, who is also of Spanish extraction and is conducting a different type of conquest through different means: His mission is to conquer the hearts as well as the money of young (and older) women through his romantic songs. Though born in Puerto Rico, he also arrived in Veracruz, just as Alvarado and Cortés did. As one female fan of Luis Miguel told me, "Since he was raised in Veracruz, he is considered a Mexican from Veracruz." Then I asked her, "Why is he called 'the Sun'?" She responded, "Porque está güerito" (Because he is blond). Luis Miguel, thirty-eight years of age in 2008, has only one sibling, a younger brother who is known in Mexican jet-set circles as "el hermano del Sol [the Sun's brother]." Luis Miguel was also the idol of Salinas de Gortari's daughter, Cecilia Salinas Occelli (Diario de Juárez 4-E, June 2, 1993), to whom he dedicated one of his concerts.

In the summer of 1993, Luis Miguel went to Ciudad Juárez to give what came to be the most-attended concert the city had ever held (between twenty-five and thirty-five thousand people). The local newspapers described Luis Miguel in the following ways (my translations):

Before the concert, which took place on Sunday, July 11, 1993:

For those who have followed his steps since he was a child, Luis Miguel is the Sun and the King. [He has nine LPs to his credit, and was already a musical star at age twelve.] (Diario de Juárez, Semana a Semana, July 9, 1993)

The Sun also rises at night. The King of the stars will appear in the Juárez sky. On Sunday night, the Sun will come out at exactly 8:30; take your sunglasses and be ready to live a unique experience here in our city. (Norte de Ciudad Juárez, Diversión, July 9, 1993)

The stars predict a special night in which not only the Moon cedes its function to the Sun, but also everything is in favor of Aries [Luis Miguel's astrological sign], which promises to disperse its energy all over. They predict temperatures of 101 degrees centigrade and a low of 75. It will be a Sunny day, and in case of rain, the Sun will not be shadowed by it. The bed on which Luis Miguel will sleep is King size, perfect for his stature. Tomorrow night, the Moon will cede its function to the Sun and you cannot miss such a bright spectacle. (Norte de Ciudad Juárez, 4D, July 10, 1993)

The day of the event:

> Everything is ready. Yesterday, under a cloudy sky, "The Sun" arrived in
> Ciudad Juárez in his personal plane at 7:40 PM. Last Friday, he managed to
> break a record of fainted women (250) in Chihuahua City. Today's concert
> is the summer's most anticipated and the most expensive in the history of
> Juárez. (*Diario de Juárez*, 1D, July 11, 1993)

After the event:

> It was all madness! Women, women, and more women! were witness to the
> eclipse provoked by "The Sun" in a concert in which the night and Juárez
> belonged to Luis Miguel. More than twenty-five thousand people gave
> themselves a date at Benito Juárez [soccer] Stadium and sang with the idol
> his hits of yesterday and today. The madness took over his fans when the
> Sun said: 'My Ciudad Juárez. Isn't it amazing, amazing, amazing! referring
> to the large number of people he managed to gather. (Rosario Reyes, *Diario
> de Juárez,* 1D, July 12, 1993)

The question that must be posed with regard to the continued existence of
European or Europeanized Spanish characters in the popular imaginations of
Luis Miguel fans is the following: Does the hegemonic presence of "white" or
light-skinned figures like Luis Miguel, and most Mexican presidents, question
in any way the conventional wisdom that Mexico has been under the control
of mestizos (persons of mixed Spanish and Indian blood), at least since independence days (1810–1821)? While the political and economic identity of most
individuals descended from the miscegenation between "Indians" and "Spaniards" has been transformed into Mexican peasants and Mexican proletariats
(and the latter into some of the emergent middle class), the meaning given to
their skin color has hardly changed; nor has the color of those in power, who
remain "white" or culturally and racially transparent, at least to themselves (see
Chapter 6 on "border inspections").

For the most part, Mexico's political officials and its movie and soap opera
stars, as well as most pop music singers like Luis Miguel, have been white or
light-skinned. As Carlos Morton argued:

> In Mexican television, 95 percent of the models or actors are white Euro-
> peans, giving the absurd impression that the country has no Indians or
> mestizos (those of mixed Indian, black, and European bloods). Magazines
> and movies proclaim the same message: If you're not pretty (white), then
> you must be ugly (brown). (1993, n.p.; also see Chapter 6 herein)

Yet, in spite of recent dominant representations of Mexicans as being "white" in Mexico's major television programs, the stereotype of the Mexican, at least in the United States, has been that of a dark-skinned individual — a historical product of certain political and economic factors, several of which have crystallized in the U.S.-Mexico borderlands.

The Problem of Color in the El Paso–Ciudad Juárez Area

Since the 1880s, underprivileged Mexican male peasants have traveled to the American Southwest to work, first for the transcontinental railroads and later in the agricultural fields, where they harvested cotton, red and green chili peppers, lettuce, onions, and other crops. In urban areas, such as El Paso, Texas, working-class Mexican women have worked as cooks, maids, and laundresses. Throughout the twentieth century, except for the period during the 1930s Depression when 500,000 of them were repatriated, the majority of Mexican migrant workers have lived and worked mainly in the states of California, Arizona, New Mexico, and Texas (in addition to Midwest states such as Illinois and Michigan), as well as in Mexican border cities such as Ciudad Juárez and Tijuana. In 1942, the Bracero Program was instituted by both the Mexican and American governments in order to legally contract Mexican male workers who were again needed to maintain American productivity (mostly in the agricultural sector) during World War II. The Bracero Program was officially terminated in 1964. Since George W. Bush became president in 2000, he has been pushing, unsuccessfully as of early 2008, for a similar program for twenty-first-century waves of working-class Mexican immigrants.

Interestingly, in the early 1950s, an economic project akin to the male-oriented Bracero Program was suggested by white middle-class bourgeois women of El Paso. They insisted on allowing maids from Ciudad Juárez to work legally in El Paso and for "appropriate" wages. As Pauline Dow noted, "The members of this organization [Association for Legalized Domestics] wanted to import maids in the same way Mexican farmworkers were recruited under the Bracero Program" (1987, 13). Even though in 1953 as many as three thousand Mexican maids worked legally and illegally in El Paso, the "Contract-Maid" proposal was rejected (Dow 1987, 15).

Nonetheless, the high influx into the United States of Mexican proletariats and landless peasants continued and, unfortunately, reproduced the racial stereotypes about Mexicans coined in the mid-nineteenth century by such American presidents as Ulysses S. Grant, James K. Polk, and others. In 1919, in a local debate about whether or not the "Mexican" workers should earn the same wages "Anglo-Saxon" laborers earned in the El Paso laundries, an employer made the following statement:

We are confronted with the deep-seated difference in temperament existing between the Anglo-Saxon and mixed Latin races, the difference between the progressiveness, initiativeness and energy of the former and the backwardness of the Mexican. There seems to be no material desire to learn, to understand, to develop and progress. (Dow 1987, 10, citing the *El Paso Herald Post,* November 20, 1919)

There was no critical difference in the way Mexicans on the Juárez side of the border were treated by white U.S. American visitors. In the late 1940s, the American poet William Carlos Williams visited Juárez on a one-day visit and wrote "The Desert Music," a twelve-page poem in which he creatively manifests his emotions and feelings about people's tourist-oriented life at the border; he described the latter, in quite prejudicial terms, in the following:

Why don't these Indians get over this nauseating prattle about their souls and their loves and sing us something for a change? . . . What else, Latins, do you yourselves seek but relief! With the expressionless ding dong you dish up to us of your souls and your loves, which we swallow. Spaniards! (though these are mostly Indians who chase the white bastards through the streets on the Independence Day and try to kill them). (Williams 1954, 280, 283)

Even if this representation by William Carlos Williams is interpreted as an ironic commentary on Euro-American stereotypes about "the other" at the border, the explicit distinction between white Europeans (Spanish) and dark-skinned Indians or Mexicans does not leave room for its own challenge. This dominant narrative about color is so ubiquitous in the Euro-American imagination that even Pauline Dow, who wrote the brief but critical history of maids in El Paso that concerns us here, does not escape the color-based inequality—distinguishing the Mexican maid as being, almost by definition, dark-skinned, specifically in relation to her "white-skinned American" employer—even as she is criticizing it. Regarding Pat Mora's poem about a maid's painful encounter with the problem of color (see Chapter 6 for my analysis of the poem), Dow wrote:

This sentiment reveals the sad and unfair reality that if the maid were a white-skinned American instead of a dark Mexican, she would be a little closer to enjoying the economic and social opportunities enjoyed by the employer. (1987, 32)

Could the employer not be a "white-skinned Mexican," or could the maid herself not be a white-skinned Mexican? Are white-skinned Mexicans in El Paso more privileged than their dark-skinned counterparts?

In the American Southwest and in California, the racialized color problem mediating or rupturing Anglo-Mexican relations led to the production of such tense political moments as the pachuco Zoot-Suit Riots in Los Angeles in the 1940s and to those long-term social forces such as the Chicano movement of the 1960s and 1970s. In both cases, the majority of the non-Anglo participants were working-class people (sometimes children of ex-bracero farmworkers) who found pride in their lived and imagined Mexican communities and cultures, as well as in their culturally and historically specific vision of themselves as being brown vis-à-vis whites (Anglos/gringos/*gabachos*).

In other words, to a large extent, these specific sociopolitical groups in the American Southwest appropriated and/or internalized, for their own community-based interests and purposes, the color-specific categories of race invented by the Europeans. A cultural transformation is indeed evident in that the term "white" is not associated anymore with environmental surroundings, as it was among the inhabitants of Tenochtitlán; in this more recent context, "white" is associated, unfortunately, with biological attributes. At the same time, this pride of being essentially/racially/culturally "Mexican," "Chicano/a," or "Hispanic" has widely been documented and has, fortunately, led to the establishment of Chicano/a Studies and Latino/a Studies programs in some universities in the United States. Thus, the use of race in color-specific terms, being inherently double-edged, can constitute a dangerous game. At times we can use it to our own benefit; many times, however, it can be used against us, whether we are "black," "brown," or "white." (But taking a color-blind position is far from the solution.)

In continental Mexico in the late twentieth century, "Mexican" was, and still is today, particularly in its nationalist sense, a political category associated with the nineteenth-century Mexican state, when "Mexicans" fought against the Americans (1846–1848) and against the French (1862). This same term, however, can still be turned into a racialized cultural category, as used both by outsiders (mainly Americans and Europeans) and by the Mexican tourist industry that serves those "outsiders." Yet, the problem of color in Mexico has also constituted, culturally and politically, a shifting social matrix of power relations in which indigenous and mestizo Mexicans have to cope with European Mexicans and with the hierarchy of color that history has forged on the psychology and culture of state citizenry; this particular power field is especially deleterious to those—the lower classes—who are far from enjoying "the power of white-skin privilege" (Behar 1993, 8), unlike the upper or more privileged classes of Mexico (see Chapter 6 on border inspections).

In such Mexican border cities as Ciudad Juárez, Tijuana, and Mexicali, a new generation of pachuco and *cholo* social groups (see Hernández Palacios and Sandoval 1989) emerged in the late 1970s and early 1980s. These individuals, similar to their counterparts from the American Southwest, also tended to be explicitly proud and outspoken about "La Raza"—their racialized community. Academic research focusing on these specific social groups living on the Mexican side of the border is much needed. For now, it must be noted that in their own ways, these working-class cultural-political groups in northern Mexico have appropriated the Indianness of the pachuco and the Chicano, as well as the Indianness of the Virgen de Guadalupe, precisely to differentiate themselves from the middle- and upper-class Spanish/Europeanized, lighter-skinned Mexicans.[7]

The color of race and gender, however (along with that of class), must not be forgotten. The experience of Chicano novelist Benjamin Alire Sáenz with the problem of "brown" color when he crossed (with his white, blue-eyed Anglo friend, Michael) the "Paso del Norte" international bridge captures the color of race at the border crossing:

> On the way back [from Juárez], the customs officer asked us to declare our citizenship. "U.S. citizen," I said. "U.S. citizen," Michael followed. . . . He looked at me. "Where in the United States were you born?" "In Las Cruces, New Mexico." He looked at me a while longer. "Go ahead," he signaled. I noticed that he didn't ask Michael where he was from. But Michael had *blue eyes;* Michael had *white skin.* Michael didn't have to tell the man in the uniform where he was from. (Sáenz 1992, xvi; my emphasis)

The foregoing application of color to the eyes, apart from the skin, has worked in quite strategic ways with regard to sexual preference and harassment in the maquiladora industry, especially during its beginnings when it focused on hiring mainly women. As Fernández-Kelly documented:

> There were [Mexican] *ingenieros* [engineers] who insisted on having only the prettiest workers under their command. A sort of factory harem mentality had been at work. If you were not attractive, you didn't get hired. She [Sandra] had known a man ("Would you believe this?") who wanted as much female diversity as possible. He had a crew formed of women all of whom had—upon his own request—eyes and hair of a different color. (Fernández-Kelly 1983, 129)

As is evident here, "being attractive" or having "*buena presentación*" (good appearance) is appropriated in ways that maintain a social hierarchy that has been historically, regionally, and politically established as well as silently institutionalized since the time of the conquest, not only in continental Mexico but also in the U.S.-Mexico borderlands. "*Buena presentación*" is requested when attending discos (see Chapter 6), was and sometimes is used as a requirement to be hired in the maquiladoras (nowadays this requirement is mostly applied to secretarial positions), and was also implied as well as demanded by Hernán Cortés during the first encounters ("deliver women with light skins").

Conclusion: Critical Differences and Hegemonic Sameness

Critiques of *mestizaje* as a nationalist ideology are not sufficient, especially if concrete issues about color (beyond race and ethnic "talk") are not addressed. Thus, it must be argued that if it is true that the "whites" never left Mexico, then the term *mestizaje* conceals more than it reveals (to academics) about the national discourse, particularly regarding the social and political hierarchies of color so pervasive among Mexicanos and Mexicanas of all classes on both sides of the border (even if the "Spanish" left, they also left the problem of color behind). I suggest that because of *colorismo*, not *mestizaje*, "colorful" and coloring social relations are found in everyday life and are being mediated, often confrontationally, by insiders and outsiders, locals and foreigners, conquered and conqueror, men and women, employee and employer, "Indians" and "Mexicans," and anthropologist and informant.

In *Translated Woman*, Ruth Behar made it clear that Esperanza's "Indianness is not based in an ethnic identity, but in race/class distinctions that have developed since the European conquest of Mexico and that continue to assert the power of white-skin privilege" (1993, 8). In addition, as we have seen, ethnicity, race, class, and nationalism remain fluid and changing categories, but color rankings have been passively and silently maintained. Yet they have not been systematically addressed by Mexicanists who have written about the U.S.-Mexico border or about Mexican nationalism. It concerns researchers because color hierarchies will not be dismantled if we continue to privilege our own categories, such as "ethnicity" and "race," and continue to use color distinctions only as descriptions of individuals considered ethnic or racial. Instead, we must problematize the category of color itself in order to disentangle it from "*colorismo*," that is, from the sociohistorical and political processes that create it.

Therefore, I suggest here that the many possibilities of the *castas* (castes) during the colonial period speak more to the *problem of colorismo* than to that of *mestizaje*. The multiplicity of racialized equations represented by "*las castas*" attempted to give a name to the human diversity unfolding, as a product of the colonial encounter in Mexico, before the Crown's and the colonizers' eyes. María C. García Sáiz (1989, 24–28) provides the most comprehensive list of the *castas*: criollo, mestizo, mulatto, *zambo, castizo, morisco, albino, ahí te estás, albarazado, barcino, calpamulato, cambujo, coyote, chamizo, chino, cholo, grifo, jenízaro, jíbaro, lobo, no te entiendo, salta-atrás, tente en el aire, torna-atrás, zambaigo*. With the emergence of the Republic in the 1820s (see Menchaca 1993), the *casta* categories stopped functioning (if they ever "functioned"), but the color hierarchies remained, albeit *without a name*.[8]

Issues of coloniality and postcoloniality that attempt to understand, explain, and transform the vexing problems of racism in contemporary multicultural societies are not effectively discussed nor interpreted if we do not transcend the legacy of structuralist, dichotomous thinking. After all, as Andreas Huyssen reminds us: "Dichotomies, which . . . are central to the classical accounts of modernism, have broken down [as] part of the [postmodern, poststructural] shift" (1990, 267). Such a discussion, in fact, would trap us in the inevitable emerging dichotomy of colonial/postcolonial, which ultimately risks conceptualizing the postcolonial condition as essentially distinct from the colonial experience. Regarding the deleterious persuasiveness of color, even Gayatri Spivak makes a critical distinction between the colonial and the postcolonial: "Clearly, if you are poor, black and female, you get it in three ways. If, however, this formulation is moved from the first-world context into the *postcolonial* (which is not identical with the third-world) context, the description 'black' or 'of color' loses persuasive significance. The necessary stratification of colonial subject-constitution in the first phase of capitalist imperialism makes 'color' useless as an emancipatory signifier" (1988, 283; my emphasis). In actuality, Spivak's problem is not so much in the colonial/postcolonial distinction, but rather in the fact that Spivak and most of us "postcolonials" have not problematized at a theoretical level the category of color itself, which in the case of color in Mexico includes an analysis of the precolonial. Apart from the specific politics of empire and imperialism in Asia, Africa, and Latin America, the power relations experienced, reproduced, and even transformed in everyday life remain an issue of just that: power—and its dispersal (see Foucault 1978; Gramsci 1971, 1985; Hall 1986; also see Chapter 9 of this book).

These inequalities, besides particularizing and being particularized in certain racisms, colonialisms, conquests, genderisms, classisms, or nationalisms, simultaneously make up and pervade, in a general sense, all the isms themselves; in the case of Mexico and the U.S.-Mexico borderlands, however, they all fall under the stubborn shadow of the problem of *colorismo*. It is in this highly politicized, theoretical context that a "postcolonial" category or "context" introduced into identity discussions of the "politics of difference" does not necessarily "change," as Homi Bhabha claims, "the very terms of our recognition of the person" (1990, 190), nor does it make "the description . . . 'of color' lose persuasive significance," as Spivak believes (1988, 283). In other words, the late-twentieth-century Mexican world did not necessarily differ substantially from, for example, the color-specific encounters of conquest and colonialism depicted in the body of this chapter. Dipesh Chakrabarty's suggestion about the prison-house of modernity in India applies to issues of postcoloniality in Mexico: "The idea is to write into the history of modernity [coloniality] the ambivalences, contradictions, the use of force, and the tragedies and the ironies that attend it" (1992, 21).

To further clarify this issue, let me pose the following questions: What is the critical difference between the maquiladora engineer who asks for certain female workers along color lines in his assembly line and Hernán Cortés who demanded the presence of "light-skinned women"? Or, what is the critical difference between the nineteenth-century American or French politician who treats all Mexicans in racial terms and the relatively privileged Mexican citizens (see R. Rosaldo's [1993] use of "citizen") who associate indigenous groups with inferior races? Besides the fact that one was a killer and the other is a lover, what is the critical difference between the two conquistadors, early-sixteenth-century Pedro de Alvarado and late-twentieth-century/early-twenty-first-century romantic/ pop singer Luis Miguel?

As has already been implied, the differences speak to the cultural and historical specificities of each political moment. The ubiquitous similarity, however, is the embedment and dispersal of power inequalities in all social relations, from the most mundane and private to the most sacred and public. In spite of the apparent privilege given to historical narratives, historicizing power itself renders it, inescapably, antihistorical, and thus antimodern, anticolonial, and antistructural—in other words, against itself. Perhaps by unveiling this hegemonic process, the nonsovereign subject can genuinely refuse and question any element of sovereignty that crawls and creeps onto our world (for useful rereadings and applications of the colonial/postcolonial dialogue, see Burton 2003; Chakrabarty 2000; Cooper and Stoler 1997; Duncan 2002; Goldberg and Quayson 2002; Gregory 2004; Kelleher 2003; Mallon 1994; Rodríguez 2001; Singh and Schmidt 2000; and Thurner 1997).

If in almost two hundred years (since 1810) Mexican subjects have not explicitly claimed political spaces associated with what we consider a "postcolonial" subjectivity, it is not because they/we have not articulated a "colonized" mentality, but because for too many of them/us, the socioeconomic and political situation has not really changed since the conquest. It is generally known and understood that the powers that be have not been transformed; in fact, they have been reproduced, under the most heterogeneous contexts characterized by *colored* incongruities of race, class, gender, and nationalist identities. This is what the Chiapas Rebellion of 1994 was all about: the attempt to transform the structures of conquest, colonialism, capitalism, and white-skin privilege (Collier 1994, Nash 2001, Stephen 2002).

As the main Juárez newspaper documented in the aftermath of the Chiapas uprising, "In 1993, Mexico paradoxically had fourth place in the world with thirteen persons fitting the 'multimillionaire' category, while 91.9 percent of the population is poor, and of the latter, the indigenous population lives in extreme poverty, [enduring] economic and racial inequality, which in turn is translated into inequality of civil and political rights, to such an extreme degree that on January 1, 1994, it caused an armed rebellion in the southern state of Chiapas" (*Diario de Juárez*, March 13, 1994, 3A; my translation). With any luck, the "postcolonial subjects" produced in the twenty-first century will not take as long to come to this realization: that the debate about the "post" of the postmodern, postcolonial worlds, when examined closely, tends to belong more to the privileged ones (modern and postmodern academics and intellectuals) than to the working-class communities who continue to experience the legacy of the conquest and of colonialism in the "modern" contexts and conditions (analyzed in this book) of late industrial capitalism.

Finally, I am not arguing here that the "postcolonial" category be discarded; instead, my position is that we must acknowledge *both* its privileged status and its much-needed critique of the continued presence and domination of the Modern, of Europe, of Whiteness. The working-class community, such as the factory maquiladora workers with whom I labored and whom I will fully introduce in the following ethnographic section of the book, does not distinguish, and finds no meaning in the distinction, between the colonial and the postcolonial, nor for that matter between the modern and the postmodern. They are still experiencing, at the turn of the twenty-first century, a sense of coloniality (*con raíces en los aztecas, en lo indígena*) and of the conquest (*la conquista*), though highly embedded in modernity (*lo moderno*)—that is, with the hope for a better economic life for them and for their children. It is to the industrial forms of capitalist conquest that are reinforming and reforming these precolonial/colonial/postcolonial conditions that I now turn.

II

*Culture, Class, and Gender in
Late-Twentieth-Century Ciudad Juárez*

Maquiladora women during May Day parade. Photograph by Alejandro Lugo.

Maquiladora men during May Day parade. Photograph by Alejandro Lugo.

Choferes de rutera (Bus drivers) during May Day parade. Photograph by Alejandro Lugo.

Working-class neighborhoods in Ciudad
Juárez. Photograph by Alejandro Lugo.

Author in the field: participant
observation inside a maquiladora.
Photograph by coworker.

An upper-middle-class gated community in Ciudad Juárez. Photograph by Alejandro Lugo.

FOUR

Maquiladoras, Gender, and Culture Change

Postcolonial Developments in the Making of a Border City of Laborers

As was noted in Chapter 2, Paso del Norte was named Ciudad Juárez in 1888. Since the 1848 American occupation of the southwestern borderlands, and particularly since the late nineteenth century, Ciudad Juárez, Chihuahua, has grown according to the needs of its American counterpart, El Paso, Texas. Between 1848 and 1880, many Anglo-Americans, in their search for gold, rested in El Paso, Texas, while on their way to California (Christopherson 1982, 58). The naming of this American border city developed from Franklin in 1849; to Post Opposite El Paso, also in 1849; to El Paso, Texas, in 1852 (Timmons 1990, esp. chap. 5, 105–106 and 111). Contrary to some scholars' beliefs (i.e., Rodríguez and Ward 1992, 20), it must be clarified that El Paso, Texas, proper has always been a distinct urban locality and should not be confused with Paso del Norte.

During the latter part of the nineteenth century, El Paso was a stopping place along the trade route between several cities in the United States. Ciudad Juárez was characterized mainly by an agricultural economy that subsisted by the production of cotton (Christopherson 1982, 61). In 1881, however, a drastic transformation occurred on the Mexican side of the border: the introduction of American investment. As Susan Christopherson (1982, 59) says: "The center of this investment strategy was the development of railroad lines to increase access to Mexico's mineral wealth," especially copper and silver. These railroad lines served mainly the U.S. markets.

Consequently, the labor demand that characterized the economy of the area as it evolved from 1890 to 1910, emphasizing railroads and agriculture as the major sources of employment, meant that the region became a temporary home for thousands of male workers. These men came to the border mainly from the northern Mexican states of Durango and Zacatecas and from southern Chihuahua. But throughout most of the twentieth century, many of these underprivileged men migrated to the American Southwest to work first for the transcontinental railroads and later in the agricultural fields.

In 1942, the Bracero Program (Mexican Labor Program) permitted the legal contracting of Mexican male workers, who were again needed to maintain American productivity (mostly in the agricultural sector) during World War II. Mexico's relationship of dependency with its powerful northern neighbor throughout most of the twentieth century can be described in these words by Christopherson: "During periods of war, Mexico benefited from the demand of labor and raw materials in the United States. During periods of recession or depression, dependence on the United States decreased but at the cost of high unemployment" (1982, 68; also see Fernández-Kelly 1983; Heyman 1991; Kopinak 1996; and Peña 1997).

It is crucial to emphasize that, until 1965, most of the individuals who came to such border localities as Ciudad Juárez and then to the southwestern United States (including southern New Mexico and West Texas) were males—especially fathers and older brothers who were economically responsible for families left behind. This gender specificity, which characterized the labor force until the mid-1960s in Ciudad Juárez, manifested itself first through the main types of jobs available in the area: construction, agricultural farm labor, smelting of iron and steel, meatpacking, baking, and peddling in the streets (Martínez 1978; see also Castellanos 1981). Most women who worked were laundresses, waitresses, cooks in restaurants, or prostitutes. Second, the gender specificity also manifested itself through the Bracero Program, which controlled the flow of braceros (contracted male migrant workers) into the American Southwest. In fact, Christopherson notes that during the period between World War II and 1965, Ciudad Juárez attained tremendous growth due to labor demand from the United States (1982, 143). The population of Ciudad Juárez increased from 48,881 in 1940 to 122,566 in 1950 and to 252,119 in 1960 (Martínez 1978, 158; also see Arreola and Curtis 1993). Most of the migrants were dispossessed peasants who immediately became proletariats in the border city. Since the majority of them worked, at least temporarily, on the American side, Ciudad Juárez ended up becoming a "labor depot" serving mainly the economy of the southwestern United States (Christopherson 1982, 68). This high influx of people eventually stimulated settlement expansion, particularly to the western side of Juárez (ibid., 145). Since the 1960s, all of the industrial parks, in contrast, have been established in the eastern and southern sections of the city (see Figures 4.1–4.3).

1. Omega and Magnaplex	5. Fernández	9. Río Bravo	13. Intermex
2. Los Fuentes	6. Gema	10. Zaragoza	14. Panamericano
3. Bermúdez	7. R. Rivera Lara	11. Salvarcar Zone	15. Salvarcar Park
4. Juárez	8. Los Aztecas	12. Aeropuerto	16. Aerojuárez

Figure 4.1. Industrial zones and parks of Ciudad Juárez. Map originally redesigned by Steve Holland, in consultation with author, from the following source: "Ciudad Juárez, Chihuahua, 1999," Desarrollo Económico de Ciudad Juárez, A.C.

María Patricia Fernández-Kelly (1983, 26) documents that when the Bracero Program was terminated in 1964, 200,000 braceros were suddenly unemployed at the border, while considerable numbers of agricultural workers from southern Mexico continued to migrate to the north. Unemployment rates reached 50 percent and stimulated the implementation (by Mexican officials) of the Border Industrialization Program (BIP) in 1965, which included the Maquiladora (Export Processing Plant) Program. The stated objective of the BIP was to bring jobs to the unemployed men (Fernández-Kelly 1983, 26). However, 80 percent to 90

Figure 4.2. Population of Ciudad Juárez by zones in 1998. Total area: 46,373 acres. Population density: 23/acre. Approximate scale: 1:110,000. Map originally redesigned by Steve Holland, in consultation with author, from the following source: "Ciudad Juárez, Chihuahua, 1999," Desarrollo Económico de Ciudad Juárez, A.C.

percent of the maquiladora employees hired were women who worked in the textile and electronics industries; by the early 1970s, a new female labor force had already been created. In fact, since 1965, women have constituted the majority of the population of Ciudad Juárez; in 1991, there were 712,335 women and 574,399 men (Desarrollo Económico de Ciudad Juárez [hereafter DECJ] 1992). By the late 1990s, statistics show 506,012 women and 505,774 men, totaling 1,011,786 (DECJ 1999).[1] As of 1997, there were seventeen industrial parks, where 201,105 employees were working in approximately 278 assembly plants (DECJ 1999; Figure 4.1).[2]

In 1983, the multinational corporations began to hire men for the assembly line in greater numbers (see also Chapter 5). To understand the nature of the labor force of Ciudad Juárez in the last two decades, we must answer the following two questions: (1) Where did the employed men of Ciudad Juárez work from 1965 to 1982? and (2) Why did men begin to be hired by multinational corporations in the early 1980s? With regard to the first question, once the Border Industrialization Program began in 1965, many of these men started to work in the

	Less than 3 minimum wages		Ecological integration zone
	From 3 to 5 minimum wages		Other uses
	From 5 to 11 minimum wages		Industrial zones
	More than 11 minimum wages		

Figure 4.3. Socioeconomic zones of Ciudad Juárez in 1998. Map originally redesigned by Steve Holland, in consultation with author, from the following source: "Ciudad Juárez, Chihuahua, 1999," Desarrollo Económico de Ciudad Juárez, A.C.

construction of industrial parks as well as in residential building, the latter being a consequence of persistent migration. Fernández-Kelly documents that in 1979, "Among . . . [the men] . . . who were employed, certain occupations were found to be prevalent. In order of importance, these were unskilled construction workers (30 percent), petty clerks (27 percent), general unskilled workers (15 percent), and street vendors (7 percent)" (1983, 56). Furthermore, out of 111 cases that Christopherson studied (1982, 13), 47 percent were "intermittent day workers (in construction or services, for example)." In the year 2000, approximately 40 percent of the close to 230,000 maquiladora workers were men, and approximately 60 percent were women.[3] This growth in the labor sector had its parallels in the urban development and political geography of the city itself, particularly in the last two decades. For instance, in the 1990s, dozens of new working-class neighborhoods on the east and southeast of the metropolis, mostly established through government-subsidized housing, now surrounded the industrial parks built in the 1970s on what used to be agricultural and desert lands (see Figures 4.1–4.3). This newly urbanized vast area is called the New Juárez, El Juárez Nuevo. It is located approximately five to ten miles away from the older downtown areas of El Paso and Juárez.[4]

The second question (why men were hired for the assembly line) was answered early in the 1980s by the late Guillermina Valdés-Villalva (1985), but her answer is hardly ever acknowledged by social science scholars, who for more than a decade after the fact continued to write about Juárez maquiladoras without necessarily incorporating into their analyses the importance of the maquiladora *male* labor force (for important exceptions, see the recent works by Salzinger [2003] and Vila [2003]). Valdés-Villalva, a local pioneering researcher of the topic, noted in 1985 that at the beginning of 1983 it was still possible to argue that 93.8 percent of the labor force was female (1985, 162; also see Chapter 5 herein). As Fernández-Kelly's much-needed ethnography (which richly documented the plight of maquiladora women in *the late 1970s*) was being read widely in academic circles during the 1980s, Valdés-Villalva and other researchers who had been conducting research in Ciudad Juárez in the 1980s were already documenting the presence of both men *and* women on the assembly line (e.g., Catanzarite and Strober 1993; Lugo 1987, 1990). This transformation in the structure of the labor force was a product of the "scarcity" of female labor caused by the high influx of multinational corporations into the area. This influx was stimulated by two interrelated forces: one national, the other global, respectively: (a) a very strong devaluation of the peso during the Mexican crisis of 1983, which cheapened even more the price of local labor (consequent devaluations continue to cheapen it); and (b) the concurrent arrival of the automobile (assembling) industries, which were running away from strong labor unions in the American Midwest. The latter factories initially hired hundreds of men and women for their production lines.

Throughout the 1990s, with close to three hundred plants established in Ciudad Juárez, the maquiladora industry was heavily immersed in the hiring of both women and men, younger and older, or anyone needing a job (though specific factories still discriminated along lines of gender, education, and degree of civility or criminality). With the subsequent multiple devaluations since the early 1980s and the implementation of NAFTA since 1994, these corporations were experiencing different unending heights of surplus value, which, this time, at least since the early 1980s, emanated not just from the plight of working-class women, but also from that of working-class men.

Initial Re-encounters and Arrival

[S]tay away from . . . facile generalizations. . . . Your study should explore the complexity of the matter. . . . Let's stop discussing the maquiladora workforce as if it were monolithic.

— MARÍA PATRICIA FERNÁNDEZ-KELLY,
PERSONAL COMMUNICATION, 1986

In the summer of 1987, when I first carried out anthropological fieldwork among maquiladora men and women in Ciudad Juárez, the phrase "Look for complexity, complexity, complexity" was always in my mind as I tried to capture, at the everyday level, the cultural changes in gender relations that had occurred during the first two decades of the maquiladora industry—that is, from the mid-1960s to the mid-1980s. During the first two weeks of my anthropological arrival in the border city that had been my birthplace and my hometown as a child, I stayed at my older sister's house until I found a small one-room apartment, or *cuarto*, on the southeast periphery of the city. While looking for a place to rent, I visited several industrial parks, such as Bermúdez Park (the largest and oldest maquiladora industrial park, which is located on the northeastern side of the border city), so I could experience the process of getting a job in a maquila. I would leave at 5:30 AM in order to catch the bus, or *rutera*, to get to the industrial parks by 6 AM at the latest. Then I would begin the search for a job. I was amazed to see so many people, young and old, in sporadic groups of two or three persons; it was also common to see loner individuals, men and women, who were looking for jobs from one factory to the next. This is how I began my ethnographic research, by informally interviewing the young men and women who were looking for work in the midst of intensely hot summer days. We would talk while waiting in line for an application, while walking to other factories, and while filling out applications given to us. At that time, I was twenty-five years old.

I visited all forty-two global assembly plants located in Bermúdez Park to see what kinds of factories were there (electric/electronic, textile, and automotive, with the first and last types the most common) and to document the hiring practices faced by entering workers. In particular, my goal was to document what kind of labor force the companies preferred to hire: male or female workers, single or married, or both, relatively young (between sixteen and twenty-five years of age), or those with a specific level of education, either elementary or secondary.

During this time, I realized that I was going to have a problem finding a job, since I did not have one of the necessary requirements: the certificate of elementary education. Since I was born in Ciudad Juárez, I did have a birth certificate. I remembered, however, that those in charge of hiring in maquiladoras often hired people who lacked an education, especially in times of a labor demand, such as in the mid-1980s. I quickly found out that during the summer of 1987, there was a problem of rotation, or worker turnover. Yet, as a researcher, I was still uncertain as to whether or not I was going to find a job. Consequently, my sister, who was working at a maquiladora, talked to her personnel manager about my research. This person then transferred me to another personnel manager who worked for a different factory. This latter individual had been a sociology student when he was younger, and he therefore became very interested in helping me with my project. After all, he told me, the maquiladora where he worked was having a serious problem of rotation; he was hoping that through my research, he would understand why they kept losing so many workers to other maquilas. Apparently, he had not been able to convince the "gringo" general manager that the shop floor conditions needed attention.

Through his generosity and by putting himself somewhat at risk, I was able to carry out participant observation inside the electronics factory, which was an American subsidiary, mostly managed by Anglo-American male executives. I entered as someone recommended by him to work in the assembly line. Nevertheless, I still had to claim, during the job interview, that I had only had a fifth-grade education and that prior to my maquila job, I had worked as a street vendor (these were not necessarily lies: I left for the United States while in the middle of my fifth grade in Mexico, when I was eleven years old; at that time, I had also sold bread in the streets of Juárez, not for survival, but to earn some money as a preteen). I asked Mr. Sociologist, however, that those immediate to me in positions of authority (i.e., supervisor and foreman) not be told about my research project, since I did not want any exclusive treatment (for an elaboration of the everyday experience in this particular factory, please see Chapter 5).

This overall research strategy was effective because I still spoke the slang of the people of Juárez; it was also ethical and legitimate because anybody could recommend a friend or a relative. Having a contact in the maquiladora industry was one of the strategies people used to help each other under the drastic economic conditions of Ciudad Juárez. Thus, unsurprisingly, later on I found that many workers were related to each other or were old acquaintances, even from the same town or city of origin. I found brothers and sisters as well as cousins and old friends—all working in the same assembly plant.

I began to work at the electronics maquila on July 6. From June 14 to July 5, I visited the industrial parks, where I conducted some informal interviews with maquila workers; conducted informal and formal interviews with neighbors and friends of selected acquaintances; and carried out archival research, mainly in local newspapers as well as regional publications and local research reports at the Colegio de la Frontera Norte, where I was affiliated and enthusiastically supported by the director, the late Dr. Guillermina Valdés-Villalva.

I worked inside the electronics assembly plant four days a week, twelve hours a day, from 6 AM to 6 PM. Three of us (all men) joined a group of eighteen people (ten women and eight men), who were assembling a new product—the microchip (see Chapter 5). The company had just started production on the "assembling part" in April of that year. According to the supervisor, it had a high demand in the market. We were assembling microcircuits for computers.

This system of working four twelve-hour days is different from the usual system of five nine-hour days used in the assembly line globally. The former system was started in this corporation because there was a need for the constant production of the electronic fragment or part. Four groups of workers labored weekly and nonstop: two morning shifts (ours was one) from 6 AM to 6 PM and two night shifts from 6 PM to 6 AM. One of the morning shifts and one of the night shifts worked four days of the week (say, Sunday, Monday, Tuesday, and Wednesday), and the other two shifts worked the next four consecutive days (say, Thursday, Friday, Saturday, and Sunday); in fact, each shift rested one Sunday per month. Through this system of exploitation and domination, the four groups were constantly producing and reproducing the microcircuits (again, please see Chapter 5 for a cultural analysis of late industrial capitalism inside this factory).

I worked in the factory for the next six weeks. During the first three weeks of work, I was a participant observer in the assembly line: I talked, worked, sweated, ate, played, and laughed with the workers. I had informal interviews or conversations with them (whenever possible) while working and at the cafeteria while eating. The most fascinating part was listening to their conversations. The workers discussed and argued about their economic situation in the maquila and at home, rotation problems, the "best" factory, and the new workers on the shop floor. All this facilitated my research, since my questions did not seem strange to them. In reality, they openly opined and argued with me; they knew that I was a "native," although also an anthropologist. It took me about a week to two weeks, depending on how my rapport evolved with different workers, before I told them about my research. Although some of them were initially suspicious about my "research," or "*investigación*," it did not take long for them to understand that all I was trying to do was to document the working conditions in which they labored, so that one day, I hoped, policymakers, industrialists, and politicians would improve the everyday life of the maquiladora worker, which is also one of the major goals of this book.

During the last three weeks of my summer research, I arranged semiformal interviews with several of the workers as well as with other people outside the factory group, including other maquila workers, some nonmaquila workers, and friends of mine from my childhood who themselves were maquila workers.

Initial Ethnographic Findings on Late-Twentieth-Century Gender Relations in Ciudad Juárez

In the mid-1980s, Carrillo and Hernandez (1985) documented that in 1983, the maquiladora industry in Ciudad Juárez was employing mostly women: 72 percent of its labor force was female, which was typical of other sites of assembly plant production in other areas of the world, such as Southeast Asia, the Caribbean, and other parts of Latin America. Sometime in 1983, however, the maquiladora industry in Juárez began to hire men on the assembly line. By December of 1986, out of 72,369 assembly-line workers (not counting technicians), 31,087, or 43 percent, were men, and 41,282, or 57 percent, were women (Source: "Report of Thirteen Years of Work of the Maquiladora Industry," Delegación AMAC in Ciudad Juárez [1987]). The total labor force of the maquiladoras in Juárez in December of 1986 was 89,600 employees, including 11,513 technicians (who are usually men) and 5,571 administrative personnel (ibid.).

On June 15, 1987, the total labor force comprised 96,500 employees working in 224 established companies (ibid.). At that time, the labor force distribution by gender was not available. From my experience at the industrial parks and with the transportation system (which is highly utilized by the maquila workers—see Chapters 7 and 8), it seemed to me that the labor force was reaching 50 percent male and 50 percent female on the assembly line, not counting the male technicians.

During the first two weeks in which I searched for a job, I noticed that the majority of the people looking for work at the maquiladoras were men. It was common to see groups of two or three and lone males, usually young men (from sixteen to twenty-five years old) walking with their documents under their arm or holding them in their hand—just as women were seen during the first decade and a half of the maquiladora industry, and are still seen today, but not in such large numbers as before.

When asked why men were being hired, most Juarenses interviewed (both maquila and nonmaquila workers) responded that men were being hired because not too many women were looking for work at the maquila anymore and because, currently, too many factories were established in the city, implying that the labor force was insufficient for its demand.

When I interviewed Mr. Alarcón, then president of AMAC (Asociación de Maquiladoras, Asociación Civil, which is the local business association for federally registered maquiladoras), he contended that men were being hired because of the "arrival of a high number of companies in Juárez." Why was there this high influx of companies in the early to mid 1980s? The high influx of multinational assembly plants, mainly from the United States, took place because of the devaluation of the peso during the Mexican economic crisis of the early 1980s, which yielded even lower wages for the labor force, thus creating a cheaper labor force for the mostly American multinational corporations established in the border city. In 1980, there were 121 plants in Ciudad Juárez. In mid-June 1987, there were 224 factories. The number of plants in Juárez nearly doubled in less than a decade. This contributed to the turnover or rotation problem mentioned earlier, which the companies themselves created through their own competition among themselves to attract workers. The more opportunities these companies offer, the better for the workers. This is why some maquiladora workers, if unhappy with their jobs, were in a position to quit and go elsewhere, either to another plant in the same industrial park or to another factory in another area of the city.

With this high influx of companies, the maquiladora industry was not able to fulfill its need for a workforce from the previously convenient and most vulnerable labor pool—young females. In other words, throughout most of the 1980s and 1990s, the labor demand was much greater than ever before and the industry was therefore forced to hire any willing laborer, no matter what gender. Consequently, they began to hire young men (between sixteen and twenty-five years of age), and older women (that is, older than the sixteen- to twenty-five-year-old range, which was the usual range for the electric/electronics industries). Although older women were already being hired in the textile and garment industries, now they were also being hired in electronics as well. According to Alarcón, once it was realized that men could produce "more" (see Chapters 5 and 6—though he believed that this increase in production occurs because of their relative physical strength and prowess), heavy industries arrived, such as the automotive industries, which reinforced the need for specifically male workers (although most of the local automotive maquiladoras in Juárez also hire women, preferably young).

This drastic change in the labor force, mainly the incorporation of men into the assembly line, caused repercussions not only on traditional hiring practices on the part of global corporations, but also on local gender relations inside the factory, at home, and in the larger social sphere of the border metropolis. This new phenomenon also invited questions about the generally accepted notion associated with the nature of the multinational corporation, particularly the electric and electronics as well as the textile and garment industries: that they could only survive efficiently by hiring women exclusively.

It must be noted that these "new" factory men are receiving similar denigrating treatment as the women, since both are now being manipulated as a concretely gendered labor force, not just as masculine or feminine workers (see Chapter 8). For instance, each company has a different strategy for hiring men in order to discriminate against and dispose of them, if necessary, for the "reserve army of labor." Just as it was (and still is) usual to set education requirements, age limits, and tests of manual dexterity when hiring women, now men (and their bodies) are similarly being inspected and scrutinized before being given a job in the maquiladora industry.

At RCA, for example, both men and women would get hired before 7:30 AM; after 7:30, however, RCA would only hire women (men arriving to the gate after 7:30 would be rejected). At another company (Allen-Bradley), the hiring personnel would only interview men one day of the week, on Thursday, for instance. But another week, they might hire men only on Mondays. Due to these selective strategies on the part of corporations, many of the young men looking for work might spend days wandering around in the industrial parks because they were probably there on the "wrong" day and at the "wrong" time for different companies. At Camisas de Juárez, where Fernández-Kelly worked (1983, 1984), they would hire men only if they had sewing experience (if you were a woman without experience, you were considered "okay"); at Centralab, an electronics plant, they would hire men only if they were recommended by an employee or by the union. At Capcom, a sewing factory, they would not hire men, only women; while at Favesa, another sewing factory, and at Dale Electronics, they would hire both men and women any time and any day during that summer. In the case of Dale, they said that they would hire men only in some areas of production, although both men and women were assembling microchips.

This is the complexity that characterized the hiring practices of corporations in Ciudad Juárez throughout most of the late twentieth century, especially between the early 1980s and the late 1990s (see Chapters 5–8) and particularly when there was an abundant labor supply. In all these cases, it is true that women were still being hired, and exploited, in the same ways as before, though with considerable adjustments on the production line due to the presence of men on many a shop floor but also in several industrial parks—outside the plants. For instance, an interesting strategy for sorting out men before they approach the physical building of the plant is by leaving the hiring sign, *Solicitamos Operadoras* (Female Workers Needed), unchanged, even when they might be hiring men that week. Such signs kept many men who walked the industrial parks looking for work from approaching such a factory. (Indeed, it took several years for academics, who mainly drove through the parks, to realize that men *were* being hired throughout the 1980s and early 1990s, since they kept on seeing these signs.)

To be sure, these particular corporations left unchanged the signs showing the hiring of women in order to keep large numbers of potential male workers away from the plant, especially since throughout the 1980s their need for a male labor force, as a dominant force, was still not fully realized discursively, even though it had already been materialized by the mid-1980s at the local level. Interestingly, even as of this writing (2007), the maquiladora industry is still, more often than not, associated with a female labor force by many academics and policymakers, in spite of the changes that have taken place in the last two decades, especially in Ciudad Juárez.

Several multinational corporations, however, especially those that through the years have often "run out of women workers," began to put up billboards or signs advertising for both men and women, as in *Solicitamos Operadores y Operadoras* (Male and Female Workers Needed). I would like to argue that in the last two decades, multinational corporations in Ciudad Juárez have found themselves either at an early stage of this change in the gendered structure of the labor force, such as the ones just noted, or at a more advanced or mature stage, in which they were already hiring both men and women throughout the 1980s and throughout 1990s (and into the present), such as the automotive, electronics, and garment factories that I examine in the following chapters.

Even though supervisors have come to realize that working-class men might not always respond positively to orders from female figures of authority, or that they might get into fights or other altercations, causing disorder at the plant, they still hire these male workers for the following reasons: there might not be enough women applying, men supposedly talk less as they work, and they discipline each other among themselves to save face and not lose honor or their manliness. In the process, they compete against one another, which ends up increasing the production quotas for the company.

To a certain degree, the phenomenon of the incorporation of men into the assembly line verifies Diane Elson and Ruth Pearson's (1984) claim that existing traditions, such as patriarchy, can be used by companies to control women inside the factory (what they called "intensification"—see below), but I hope to show that existing local traditions, such as machismo (exalted manliness), are also being used (although less deliberately) to exploit men (see, particularly, Chapter 5). Because of this particular articulation of culture and capitalism in Ciudad Juárez, it is evident that multinational corporations manipulated not only vulnerable working-class women, but whoever was accessible and available for production when needed, be they women, men, or children, through a process that is locally and historically determined. Thus, the following argument about the gender structure of the maquiladora labor force should be reconsidered: that electronics and garment production was inherently delegated for women because of their cultural and economic vulnerability in the context of global capitalism and local patriarchy, and that, therefore, these industries could only function effectively with a female labor force on the assembly line. In this context, the following observation made by Fernández-Kelly in 1983 about the gendered structure of the maquiladora labor force under global capitalism in the second half of the twentieth century should be revisited: "Because maquiladoras must rely upon the use of cheap unskilled and semiskilled labor to maximize productivity and profits, they are led to employ the most vulnerable sectors of the working class. These sectors are increasingly being formed by women. In other words, given the constraints that guide offshore production, women constitute a close to ideal working contingent. *In this light, the incorporation of larger numbers of men into maquiladora production is unlikely*" (1983, 42; my emphasis). This quiet prediction by Fernández-Kelly about the "unlikely" increase in maquiladora men is highly influenced not only by a much-needed feminist critique loyal to gendered interests closely associated with women's plight, but also by a Marxist feminist critique that did not imagine at that time that the exploitation of men as gendered subjects could occur in the interest of capital. As Fernández-Kelly wrote: "The employment of women with acute economic needs by the maquiladora industry represents, in objective terms, the use of the most vulnerable sector of the population to achieve greater productivity and larger profits. The employment of men to perform similar operations would require higher wages, better working conditions and more flexible work schedules, all of which would increase labor costs and reduce capitalist gain" (1983, 66–67).

Regarding the use and abuse of existing traditions by corporations, I hold that there is a wide variety of existing traditions that automatically work either to the advantage of the multinationals or against them, even if temporarily. I already noted how manliness on the part of men can serve the needs of the corporation, since the male workers produce more for the company as they compete with each other. Other existing traditions, however, function to the detriment of the company. The maquiladora workers' latent belief in ghosts is an example. Let us see.

As has been documented, a substantial percentage of the maquiladora workers are either themselves migrants to the border or descendants of people who migrated from elsewhere in Mexico. Many of these workers bring their own folklore and incorporate it into the culture of the workplace. An example of this cultural adaptation is the belief in ghosts. One time, the forewoman surprised me by telling me, "Don't tell anyone, but today *una mujer* (a woman), a ghost, appeared to the guard who works in the night shift, just around 5:00 A.M." I asked, "Really? What did she look like?" She replied, "I don't know." Even though she told me not to tell anyone else, by the end of the day, she had mentioned it to everybody on our shift while we were on the bus, on our way home. The next day, while I was in the restroom, just before we started working around 5:45 AM, the lights throughout the factory went out for a few seconds. Four of the women on my shift screamed, and two of them started to cry. (I still do not know who was playing with the lights, since the lights are controlled from the main office and the main office was still locked that early in the morning).

During that day, one woman would not go to the restroom by herself; either she would go with another female worker or with the forewoman. This slowed down the production process significantly, since many a time after that day, and throughout the work week, at least two people would leave our area of production at once; nobody would dare to be left by themselves, especially on Sundays when hardly anybody else was at the plant.

This focus away from production was a loss to the company, especially when we discussed the ghost while at work. Also, due to the apparition, one female worker who was isolated in another room to carry out her work responsibility had to be moved closer to the production table where most of us were concentrated (see Chapter 5). These practices, apart from being local cultural products in themselves, can also be interpreted as subtle forms of political resistance to the tedious and monotonous work that characterizes capitalist discipline inside multinational assembly plants. Lastly, I found out that the guard who first saw the ghost had resigned a few days after his experience with the apparition, thus forcing the company to hire someone else. On the night he saw the ghost, a considerable amount of material (assembled microcircuits) had been burned and wasted, since the man would not dare reenter the room where the oven was located, which was the same place where the ghost had appeared. According to the forewoman, *la mujer fantasma* (the female ghost) was a woman who had been raped and killed in the surroundings of the factory. (Later, I return to this important topic of violence against women in Ciudad Juárez—see the epilogue).

Another example of how cultural practices can be used by the workers as a critique of multinationals is joking behavior or the telling of jokes at the production table. On some occasions, particularly when shipment delays derailed production for a few hours, I observed small groups of workers using jokes and linguistic humor to comment on exploitative working conditions and gender relations. One day, we ran out of material to assemble; they still had to bring it from El Paso. It looked like a late arrival, and did take about two hours to arrive. During this time, the workers automatically separated themselves into groups of six or four or two persons to talk about incidents at work, dances they had attended, or simply about incidents at home. During these get-togethers, when they occur, the workers have a chance to discuss their employment conditions, both in this factory as well as in other plants where they have labored.

After a while, about six of us began to tell jokes. Sometimes we would also tell jokes while working. I told them a joke that was told to me by another factory worker in the neighborhood where I used to live as a child. The joke was about a man who, no matter how much he would eat, would not gain weight; in fact, he was losing it in an exaggerated way. So, he decided to go to the doctor. The doctor told him to buy a banana and a *gansito* (a Twinkie) and to ingest them via his anus—his behind: first the banana, then the Twinkie. The man at first objected to such a prescription, but since he wanted to get healed, he followed the doctor's orders.[5] The following week nothing happened. He went back to the doctor. The doctor recommended that he be patient and try it again the following week. The man did it, but to no avail. He went back to the doctor, who now said, "Okay, this time, go to the store right now and buy yourself a banana, a *gansito,* and a stick this long (gesturing with his hands)." The man reacted: "Please, doctor, why should I do this?" The doctor then asked, "Well, do you want to get healed?" The man answered, "Yes."

The man went to the store and came back with everything the doctor had ordered. The doctor then ordered the man to bend over. "Okay," the man responded. He bent over. The doctor then inserted the banana into the man's anus and waited for a few seconds. After a while, a tapeworm came out asking, "¿Dónde está el gansito?" (Where is the Twinkie?) At that moment, the doctor smashed the tapeworm with the stick and killed it.

Everybody laughed. This gathering happened in the morning. In the afternoon, we were told how much money we were going to get as a bonus (they called it an "incentive") for the group's previous week's productivity: $900.00 pesos (at that time, the currency exchange was $1,500.00 pesos to a dollar, or 60 cents total as bonus). Right after we heard the amount, one female worker commented half-jokingly, half-mad: "Not even enough money to buy a *gansito!*" With a smile of consensus, everybody nodded.

These workers' critique of their corporate employer (which was decidedly class-based and racially specific—the general manager was a Spanish-speaking Anglo man) under late industrial capitalism on the Mexican side of the border reflects similar racially based critiques against Anglo-Americans in South Texas by the *mexicanos* interviewed by Américo Paredes in the early 1960s. The particular group of men he studied (Paredes 1968, 111–112), though mostly middle-class Mexican Americans, told jokes that revealed their resistance to the Anglos in power within their community. All of the texts that he examines in his pioneering essay about the U.S.-Mexico border tell about the struggles of poor braceros who, having being denied medical services in American hospitals, had to search for a *curandero* (a healer). This is the context in which the following joke is told to Paredes, which in turn should remind the reader that, whether in South Texas or in Ciudad Juárez, "these jests are not intended to be as funny as they appear on the surface" (Paredes 1968, 114):

They went to see Don Pedrito about a poor *bracero* who was around in Hidalgo County, and this poor man got up one night to get a drink of water and he swallowed a spider. Well, he got sicker and sicker, so they took him to the hospital in Edinburg.

And they said, "Who's going to pay?"

"Well, there's no money, I guess."

"All right. Get out!"

"So what can we do?" they said. "Nobody can pay. Let's take him over to Don Pedrito."

Well, so the little old man came and looked him over. "And what happened to him?" he said.

"Well, it's like this," he said, "This boy swallowed a spider."

"He said, "And what did they say at the hospital?"

"Oh, no! At the hospital they want money to operate on him."

"No," he said, "don't talk to me about operations. I'll take care of him right now. Let's see, turn him over for me with his ass sticking up, with his butt in the air."

They turned him over.

"Now, pull his pants down." They pulled his pants down.

He said, "But bring him out here in the yard." They laid him down in the yard.

He said, "Do you have some Karo corn syrup?"

"Well, yes. Here's some."

He gave his asshole a good smearing with it. "All right, now," he said, "everybody stand back." And he picked up a stick.

They said, "But what are you doing, Don Pedrito?"

"I'm waiting for the flies to gather," he said. "When the flies start buzzing, the spider will come out, and I'll kill it with this little stick." (Paredes 1968, 115–116)[6]

Both this joke about the spider and the one about the *gansito* speak to Mexican men's anxiety about being penetrated, either by Anglo supremacy in South Texas (see Limón 1994) or by corporate capitalism (which are not necessarily mutually exclusive, either in South Texas or in Ciudad Juárez)—an anxiety that also reproduces a machismo or masculine subjectivity that does not seem to get transcended in spite of its changing nature (see Gutmann 1996). This brings us back to the problem of working-class masculinity and capitalism—the focus of the next chapter.

These are examples of how workers incorporate traditions into the system of production, of how they use jokes to explain their working conditions, and of how they are politically aware of their plight. This cultural-political awareness is also manifested when the workers talk about previous work experiences in other factories. One worker noted that before he had come to work in this factory, he had worked at RCA for three years. Another male worker who was listening brought up the idea that at RCA they only hire newcomers from the south, or people who had no maquiladora experience — this second worker already had worked in four factories in a two-year period. I immediately asked him: "Why do you think they hire mostly newcomers?" He answered, "Porque esa gente está muy pendeja" ("Because the new ones are too inexperienced" — and, therefore, dumb about work politics). The other workers listening to him just agreed with a gesture. He continued: "These inexperienced workers still don't know what's good for them; they don't know what demands to make. Whereas with me, I will not let them treat me like a puppet. I do have a lot of experience."

As he elaborated on his position, this worker made two very important observations: (1) that corporations hire inexperienced people so that they can control them better, and (2) that after a while, the workers acquire experience and become more aware of what demands to make. Let me develop this last point.

This particular worker had already worked in four factories, in part due to the turnover problem of the industry, even though he was barely seventeen years old when we were having this conversation. In addition to this multiple-factory work experience acquired at such a young age, these workers must endure at least six continuous hours of assembling parts before lunchtime. This physically intense job, in combination with the exchange of ideas among workers, can lead to a political awareness of the existing working conditions that is itself a product of the plight they end up sharing with each other while working. If workers do not resist through widespread political mobilization, it is because of their economic needs; they do need a job, and this job, ultimately, allowed them to survive and adapt to the late-twentieth-century economic crisis in Mexico.

Revisiting Intensification, Decomposition, and Recomposition

As was previously demonstrated in the context of hiring practices, the complexity of the maquiladora labor force is also manifested here at the level of how workers are controlled or tied to the maquiladora industry. Although the roots of labor control lie in the economic conditions of the labor force within and beyond the shop floor, they become crystallized at the household level. In this context, Elson and Pearson (1984) discussed three directions that the relationship between factory work and the subordination of women may take under global capitalism, or what they called the international division of labor: (1) Intensification (already mentioned), such as when a multinational corporation deliberately tries to utilize traditional forms of patriarchal power, intensifying existing forms of gender subordination; (2) Decomposition, when factory work is used by women as a way of escaping an early arranged marriage, for instance, only to fall into a market where they become competing commodities, where it is men who exercise the choices; (3) Recomposition, as in the case when women, instead of being subordinated to their fathers, are subordinated to male factory bosses.

I found in my research that the gender aspect of these phenomena has reached far more complexity than what these analytical categories can encompass when we apply them only to women. This complexity arises from the fact that in late-twentieth-century border culture, the distribution of the labor force by gender often reached almost "half and half" on the assembly line in many assembly plants, not counting the technicians. By the mid-1980s, and throughout the 1990s, as I already noted, the distribution in Ciudad Juárez was, generally, as follows: 43 percent men and 57 percent women. Thus, gender relations in the border city now take more complex forms than the ones effectively identified by Elson and Pearson.

I believe that the notions of intensification and recomposition should not be reduced only to the case of women, because they also help explain the subordinate position of the working-class men laboring on the assembly line. While the application and transposition of patriarchal power are in actuality executed as Elson and Pearson suggested, the cultural processes by which power is ultimately sustained inside the factory constitute a multilayered matrix characterized by social, psychological, and production-related inequalities. In the case of intensification, now that the men have been drawn into the production process, this patriarchal power takes different forms. The power gets intensified in a distinct form in the case of men. Although it generally works to the benefit of the company, it does not always work that way. I already noted how men's manliness functions for the betterment of the corporation as they compete among themselves. Manuel and Teresa, two coworkers, both told me that where there are mostly men at the production table, they set a goal to be reached by everybody, and whoever does not meet it is criticized by the others—and they are criticized as males, not just as workers (see Chapter 5). This obviously yields high production quotas for the company. However, when conflict arises among the workers, fights begin, often stopping production. Nevertheless, although this shows the complexity of the phenomenon, no matter how often these conflicts occur, they are not comparable with the usual labor discipline characterizing everyday work on the assembly line.

Besides these possible conflicts, supervisors and foremen have to be more tolerant toward the men's behavior, especially when they work next to women. This was part of the reason why men were not being hired before 1983. Most men, however, would work hard to be "in good standing." Thus, I argue that the system, through time, has had to resolve this contradiction or opposition (of loyal and competitive men) by providing the means by which both kinds of men, each in their own ways, fulfill their sense of manliness, which, in the last instance, serves the system of production as well as their masculinist subjectivity.

In the case of recomposition, I found that it does not always occur in one direction, from the home to the factory. Sometimes this transposition of power is executed or exercised by women, but in reverse: from the factory to home, with some women exercising power over some men, with unfortunate violent consequences against women. Now that both men and women are working (at times in the same factory), we sometimes find conflict existing between them. Although in general most couples cooperate, often women who earn more money than their male partners become empowered over their male counterparts, while the reverse, of course, is also true. Although the latter cases have been well documented by feminist scholars, let me mention an example of the former.

I learned from male consultants, such as Lencho, that when both persons in a couple are working, and if the woman earns more income, it is possible for her to subordinate the husband, even if temporarily. Lencho says that this can happen if a woman already has a higher position (i.e., as a forewoman) and the husband is just an assembly-line operator. Since the woman earns more, she has more authority. Don Arturo, an ex-guard at a Juárez maquiladora, told me of one case in which a husband came to the factory to ask for the wife, who was supposedly working overtime. Don Arturo told him that nobody was working inside the factory that late; it was 5:00 AM. Don Manuel told the husband: "Perhaps your wife went out dancing with her friends." The husband left the place very angry. This kind of situation has led to several cases of domestic violence, including some unfortunate killings.

Juan, an ex-maquila supervisor, told me that one of his male coworkers told him that his wife, who worked at another maquiladora and who earned more than the husband, was "getting above him." According to Juan, she would not even serve lunch to his friend. When I asked Juan why his friend would not make his own lunch, especially since his wife was also working, Juan responded that his friend was so unhappy that he would not eat. Juan then told me that his friend took his wife out of the workforce. The wife then supposedly said: "I'll do it if you support me as if I was working." Juan's friend accepted the deal. Now the husband has to work a double shift. But he would not let his wife work because she was "getting above him." In the last two decades, too many working-class women have experienced violence in their intimate lives, precisely because of this cultural change. This transformation in gender relations has intensified patriarchy not only in the workplace but also at home and in the larger working-class border society.

These occurrences serve as evidence to reconsider and reanalyze Elson and Pearson's notions of intensification and recomposition, particularly when they are applied to both women and men in the assembly line and beyond. These two useful categories, although still applicable to the Juárez case, can operate in a reverse direction, back toward home (in the case of recomposition), thus reintensifying patriarchy against women, not necessarily in relation to the supervisor, but vis-à-vis other male factory workers, including some of their kin.

Finally, in spite of these gender inequalities, we must also consider moments of cooperation between men and women. Throughout my research, I found many brothers and sisters working in the maquiladora industry, though not necessarily in the same factory. In most of the cases I encountered, brothers and sisters, fathers and mothers, and daughters and sons, as well as couples, were all sharing the income responsibilities of the household. This strategy for survival has to be in operation due to the constant Mexican economic crises of the late twentieth century. Consequently, workers, both men and women, more often than not help each other by sharing transportation costs and other expenses such as buying meals at the cafeteria whenever it is necessary. In fact, this is one of the ways in which they identify themselves as workers. How and when they identify themselves as gendered subjects are ethnographic questions that I elaborate on in the following chapters.

It is important to describe the times when both genders identify themselves as workers and when the workers become gender conscious, as men and women. Until we can explain the dynamics of this process, we will not understand and appreciate the ways through which cultural and social change of gender roles occurred in late-twentieth-century Ciudad Juárez—including how existing unequal patterns of privilege were reinforced at the factory and carried out outside of it, with new forms being produced and reproduced in their trajectory back to the streets and into their homes and vice versa. Meanwhile, the changing forms of capitalist discipline, as well as the "older" cultures of the conquests, still operate as backdrop and base.

FIVE

The Political Economy of Tropes, Culture, and Masculinity Inside an Electronics Factory

[At the factory] we rest when there are blackouts. . . . Otherwise, the machine should never be stopped. Since you want the supervisors to like you, you try very hard and you manage to get as fast as the machine.

—POLO, LATE TWENTIES

As you know, when one starts working at a maquila, people try to step on your neck. If someone does not like you, that person does not help you; she leaves you on your own, even if you need help. If you do not like someone or someone does not like you, it is a matter of luck. As you know, you work in one maquila then in another one, then in another one. You then acquire experience and then you defend yourself. Then you put pressure on yourself so that no one mistreats you. When I start in a new maquila, I put pressure on me so that no one bothers me.   —LUCHA, MID-THIRTIES

They gave protective tape [for their fingers] to all the women. I never asked for it because I thought you had to buy it. I packed with my naked fingers for about a month. Maybe they thought I did not need it, that it didn't hurt me. I was staining the boxes with blood, until they noticed who it was.

—EVA, LATE THIRTIES

Introduction

The penetrating discourses of late-twentieth-century survival by male and female factory workers regarding human expectations when working under cultural, physical, and psychological pressures, especially as these are manifested on their bodies and in their vision of work, decidedly contradict the Western stereotypical notion that non-European others, such as working-class Mexicans, are lazy. Along with these personal narratives of pain and endurance, however, I have found that some sectors of maquiladora life and assembly production have reappropriated a culturally specific notion of laziness: *barra*. How this linguistic term is incorporated into assembly production can be understood by analyzing concrete material and social circumstances through which late capitalism is operating in an electronics factory established in Ciudad Juárez. Indeed, in the electronics maquila where I labored in the summer of 1987, the regionally produced concept of laziness, *barra*, became imperative (and constitutive of everyday life) for effective industrial production and for capitalist self-discipline to take place.

In this chapter, I analyze linguistic practices associated with local sociohistorical notions of laziness (reflected in the terms *barra, flojo,* and *huevón*) that have come to be in themselves particularized cultural enactments that are simultaneously turned into class performances inside an electronics factory. One of the main arguments in this chapter is that these sociocultural linguistic actions produce and reproduce a class subjectivity that enriches, especially in the eyes of the capitalist, the surplus value and the modern relations of conquest sustaining the global assembly process in Ciudad Juárez.

Through ethnographic research based on participant observation inside the electronics factory, I demonstrate how these cultural enactments and class actions surrounding "laziness" are manifested; more specifically, I examine (1) how new notions of laziness have reinforced, instead of challenging, cultural ideas of machismo (manliness and masculinity), and (2) how these beliefs and practices about laziness and masculinity are being produced and reproduced in the workplace through the production and reproduction of microcircuits for computers.[1]

Understanding Culture through Tropes

Tropes are figures of speech, and according to David Sapir, "To talk of metaphor is to talk of tropes" (1977, 3). In the last four decades, anthropologists and linguists such as Sapir, Crocker (1977), Fernandez (1986, 1991), Lakoff and Johnson (1980), and Ohnuki-Tierney (1987b, 1990) have attempted to arrive at cultural meaning by analyzing the metaphor. This theoretical framework has been called "metaphor theory." The analysis of metaphor is related to the understanding of culture. James Fernandez explains how:

> Men [sic] may analyze their experiences within any domain. They inevitably know and understand them best by referring them to other domains by elucidation. It is in that metaphoric cross-referencing of domains, perhaps, that culture is integrated, providing us with the sensation of wholeness. And perhaps the best index of cultural integration or disintegration, or of genuineness or spuriousness in culture for that matter, is the degree to which men can feel the aptness of each other's metaphors. (1986, 25)

However, Fernandez's view may be overly narrow, as Terence Turner has pointed out: "To attempt to characterize the cultural meaning of a complex process . . . in terms of a single trope (i.e., it's metaphoric) is . . . to betray as profound a misunderstanding of the nature of tropes as of cultural structures of meaning" (1987, 15). Turner argues for the relativity of tropes—metaphor and metonymy—which eventually become "refractions of the more fundamental, totalizing tropic relation synecdoche" (1987, 19). He proposes synecdoche to be the highest tropic level at which cultural meaning can most appropriately be analyzed and interpreted.

In this chapter, I make two propositions regarding these tropes in the context of the global assembly line. First, if we want to better comprehend the contribution of tropes to our understanding of culture and power on the border shop floor that concerns us here, we must follow Turner in considering synecdoche, and not metaphor, to be the highest level of tropic complexity. Second, for us to consider synecdoche as the highest level of meaning relative to culture and power, we must not treat it as a simple trope, but as a crucial ideological and ideational product and source of what I call the minor tropic relations: metonymy and metaphor.

Through these propositions, I argue that we need to reexamine metaphor theory in the context of Sahlins's structure-praxis dialectic (Sahlins 1981, 1982, 1985, 2000). I hold that the "structure of the conjuncture," as Sahlins defined it in *Islands of History,* constitutes the nest and terrain of synecdoche. Sahlins (1985, 125; 1982, 48) claims that the structure of the conjuncture articulates at the uneasy intersection between what he calls structure—"culture-as-constituted" (ideology, values)—and event—"culture-as-lived" (human behavior on the ground).[2] For example, a human being behaves in a certain way because of a certain value she or he holds. What coordinates the actual behavior and the value is the structure of the conjuncture, which, I believe, is itself a product of multiple factors: ecological, psychological, technological, social, and historical (Sahlins 1985, 125). It is a "situation qui result d'une rencontre de circonstances" (Robert, cited in Sahlins 1985, 125n). I hold that through the concept of the structure of the conjuncture, the ethnographer is better able to grasp and map out the manifestation of the particular value and behavior occurring in a specific time and place.[3] I demonstrate that it is the structure of the conjuncture, that is, the synecdoche (as a most vital trope), that should be identified and analyzed if we want to get at cultural meaning in the sociohistorical context of its respective power relations—namely, at the process through which practices and ideologies (as well as their intertwined articulation) are produced, reproduced, and transformed. To ethnographically map out the production, reproduction, and transformation of cultural dynamics and domination—occurring at the level of synecdoche, at the structure of the conjuncture—is the ultimate goal of this chapter. At the turn of the twenty-first century, I continue to believe that the definition of culture given by Franz Boas almost a century ago is still vitally relevant. He wrote:

> Culture may be defined as the totality of the mental and physical reactions and activities that characterize the behavior of the individuals composing a social group [in our case, maquiladora workers] collectively and individually in relation to their natural environment, to other groups, to members of the group itself and of each individual to himself [or herself]. It also includes the products of these activities and their role in the life of the groups. (Boas 1963, 149)

Definitions and Contradictions

It is commonly held that a metaphor synthesizes at least two distinct semantic domains through a common feature (Basso 1981, Leach 1976, Lévi-Strauss 1966, Richards 1965). It is because of this power to encompass different conceptual domains that metaphor captured the attention of symbolic anthropologists. In spite of the consensus that different domains are united through metaphor, anthropologists characterize the metaphor in a distinct way to explain different aspects of the human condition. Emiko Ohnuki-Tierney, for example, argues that although the metaphor synthesizes two different conceptual domains through a common feature, the two domains were selected precisely because they were different, rather than because they had a similar element. Consequently, because of this difference, she believes that there is tension in the actual selection of a particular metaphor (see Ohnuki-Tierney 1987b).

Other anthropologists, such as James Fernandez and Terence Turner, have made the point that a metaphor is performative. For example, Fernandez (1986, 8) defines the metaphor "as a strategic predication upon an inchoate pronoun (an 'I,' a 'you,' a 'we,' a 'they') which makes a movement and leads to performance." This notion of the metaphor as performance is a crucial aspect that helps to explain class performativity and cultural production and reproduction among maquiladora workers with whom I labored in the electronics factory.

With respect to metonymy and synecdoche, a confusion exists in the literature that I believe has led to the misunderstanding of the principles involved in tropic constitution.[4] Turner criticizes J. Christopher Crocker for reducing metonymy to a principle of part–whole. Turner makes it clear that metonymy "is not limited to the relation between parts of the same whole or order, as leaf to tree. . . . It may as easily involve contiguity or causal connection between elements of different domains, pertinent examples being the transfer of energy, power, disease" (1987, 3). In contrast, Sapir associates metonymy with a notion of "wholeness," which is different from a part-whole distinction. He defines metonymy in the following way: "Metonymies are usually identified as the substitution of one 'cause' . . .

for another: cause for effect (efficient for final cause), container for contained (formal for material), and such variants as instrument for agent, agent for act, etc." (1977, 19–20). Thus, Sapir stresses contiguity or a causal connection, as does Turner, but within the same domain. He emphasizes "wholeness" only in the sense of a "complete entity," which comprises, together, the container and the contained, the cause and the effect, and so forth. He does not explicitly discuss metonymy as a part whole relationship because he allocates those distinctions to synecdoche. Sapir writes: "Taking into account both taxonomic and anatomical classification, we get four types of synecdoche processes: taxonomic generalizing (kind for type) and particularizing (type for kind); anatomical generalizing (*whole for part*) and particularizing" (*part for whole*)" (1977, 14; my emphasis).

Sapir believes that the "whole for part" type of synecdoche is not at all ubiquitous and that, indeed, "there are a few examples . . . such as 'I am all sore' when one has a sore toe" (1977, 15). "In contrast," he writes, "the reverse . . . (part for whole) provides a huge variety of tropes." For the latter, he gives such examples as "'ten toes up, ten toes down' . . . referring to people making love; and . . . 'sail for ship'" (1977, 15).

As we can see, these part-whole relationships are treated as synecdoches by Sapir but as metonymies by Crocker and Turner (i.e., "leaf to tree"). I believe that these contradictions are due to the unsettled distinction between metonymy and synecdoche at the level of the part-whole, whole-part distinction, as well as to the insistence of treating what is called synecdoche as a regular trope (as opposed to an all-encompassing one).[5] In spite of this problem, metonymy is still characterized by the relation between a part and a whole, "contiguity or causal connection between elements of different domains" (Turner 1987, 3) or between elements of a single domain (Sapir 1977, 4). This contradiction between Turner and Sapir regarding domains is the result of the unawareness of the specific degree of conceptual knowledge that each particular domain encompasses. It is in the apparent contradiction itself that the solution is found, since part-whole and whole-part distinctions exist in both metonymy and synecdoche,[6] although the encompassing degree of each trope is different. The most complex level of encompassment (encompassing the most domains) is eventually achieved (as I try to show through ethnographic materials) in synecdoche; any level of part-whole/whole-part below this particular one is metonymic. At this highest level (not of integration, but of complexity),[7] synecdoche becomes a trope that produces metaphoric and metonymic relations, which are always relative to each other. My basic argument here is that when synecdoche is treated as the highest tropic relation, its respective contribution to cultural processes is relatively much more complex than a metaphoric or metonymic relation by itself.[8]

To bridge the gap between these theoretical propositions and practice (mine and that of the people I studied), I demonstrate this intricate symbolic process using ethnographic material collected in Ciudad Juárez. Before we step into that material, however, it is necessary to elaborate on the literary fabrication of an ideological concept that is central to my argument about the production and reproduction of culture and class on the assembly line in this border city on Mexico's northern frontier. This is the concept of "laziness." The following analysis of the discursive production of laziness in northern New Spain is critical for our understanding of the ethnographic material presented below.

The Missionary Legacy in the Colonial Production of Laziness

In Ciudad Juárez, the term *barra* is commonly used by the working-class people to call someone "lazy." *Barra* is a slang term for the Spanish word *perezoso/a,* which means "lazy." The term can be used as in "¡Cómo eres barra!" (You are so lazy), "No tires barra" (Don't be lazy), or "¿Qué pues, barra?" (What's happening, lazy?). Usually, these expressions are used among friends who might tease each other about sometimes being too lazy (the first two expressions) or simply as a form of salutation (the third form).

In Mexico, the adjective *lazy* can be used to describe someone who is not performing what he or she is supposed to perform, either at the expected time, or because the person is too slow and thus hardly moving. A "lazy" person can also be someone who has done his or her "job" poorly, for example, what was supposed to be tight was left loose. The term signifying "lazy" can be utilized by people without questioning the reasons for such performance.

All of these specific cultural practices, however, are actually measured against a Western view (founded in the history of conquest and colonization—already explored previously in Chapters 2 and 3—and here being reproduced under global industrial capitalism) of what constitutes "hard/slow work" and "who" is doing it ("Indians," "natives," "Mexicans," women, poor working-class people, and so forth). Immediately, at this ideological juncture, where "European" and non-European notions of work clash, the term *lazy,* in its many forms, becomes a political category imposed upon one or another type of dominated individuals or groups. As Edward Spicer asserted in *Cycles of Conquest* with regard to missionization in northern New Spain, "Laziness . . . was the universal complaint of Europeans about the Indians, and was symptomatic of the deep and widely-ramified differences between Western and Indian cultures at this time in regard to economic labor" (1962, 323). This ideological production of difference and social inequality was still operating in the late twentieth century with the case of *barra* as well as with another term, *flojo* (loose).

At the turn of the seventeenth century, the Jesuits used the term *flojo* to describe some of their converted "Indians" (Bannon 1974, 72–72). This categorical construction occurred when colonial evangelism became an alternative method of imperialist control. Before this mode of domination in this part of New Spain, warfare had been the only tool used by the Spaniards to conquer the "natives" (see Chapter 2).

In his drawing *Crónica de Mechoacan* (*sic;* shown in Bannon 1974, 74), Paul Beaumont depicted how the Jesuits categorized "Indians": "los inobedientes" (the disobedients), "los homicidas" (the homicides), and "los flojos" (the lazy ones—in this case, an Indian is portrayed sitting down). *Flojo,* my interest here, literally means "loose," as opposed to "tight." Thus, *flojo,* and not the formal term *perezoso,* was used in colonial times to call the indigenous people "lazy."

In his critical examination of northern Mexico's colonial history, Spicer exposed the voices of some missionaries who tell us about the economic and ideological contexts in which "laziness" became a problem for them. With the exception of the Yaquis of Sonora, for whom "there seems, in fact, to have been less complaint in regard to Yaqui habits of work . . . , indicating a high degree of Yaqui conformity to European work habits" (Spicer 1962, 295), the Opatas, the Tarahumaras, and the Seris were heavily characterized as lazy human beings by their respective missionaries.

For instance, Father Joseph Neumann, who lived among the Raramuris in the early 1700s, claimed that the "fast runners" were in fact "'simple of nature and unpolished' and 'naturally peace-loving, never quarrel among themselves,' but 'unwilling to work . . . [they had] a lazy indifference to everything good'" (Neumann, cited in Spicer 1962, 310, 311). Adam Gili, another Jesuit of German descent, but one who lived among the Seris of Sonora, wrote of "the holy sacraments which [the Seris] do not understand on account of their stupidity." He also wrote that when children grow up in that indigenous "community," they become "lazy and deceitful" (cited in Spicer 1962, 313). Lastly, in the late eighteenth century, Father Juan Nentuig systematically used the Opatas to characterize "the disposition of the Indian":

> The disposition of the Indian rests on four foundations, each one worse than the other, and they are: ignorance, ingratitude, inconstancy, and laziness. Such truth is the pivot on which the life of the Indian turns and moves. . . . Their laziness and horror of all kinds of work is so great that neither exhortation, or prayers, nor indeed much less the threat of punishment by the authorities, are sufficient to make them, by the sweat of their brows, procure the necessary sustenance of life by tilling their own lands. This love of idleness keeps them poor and needy, so that the ministering priest has to provide them during most of the year with victuals and clothing, if he wishes them to attend the instructions in their villages. (Nentuig, cited in Spicer 1962, 322–323)

Recognizing these historicities behind such politically loaded terminology as "laziness" and "Mexican," Mexican-Americans in the U.S. Southwest manifest

some measure of the legacy of colonialist control in the way some of them jokingly address each other. In fact, "¿Qué pues, barra?" (What's happening, lazy?),
as used in Ciudad Juárez by friends, resembles and parallels the linguistic expression "What's happening, Mexican?" as used by Mexican-Americans (Chicanos)
themselves. In Tucson, for example, Chicanos sometimes use the term "Mexican," which Anglos can use in a derogatory sense—meaning lazy, inferior human
being (see Jane Hill 1993)—in the same way that the Juárez border people use
barra, and which nonfriends can use to criticize someone by accusing them of
being lazy (Renato Rosaldo, personal communication, 1989). The specific meaning of both terms (*barra* and "Mexican"), however, could have derived from the
history of racial stereotypes about Mexicans (compared to European Americans
or Anglos—see Hill 1993) and indigenous peoples (compared to Spaniards) in
the Southwest and in northern Mexico: that they are lazy. Thus, this prejudicial
stereotype is not only an Anglo creation that has diffused to the Mexican border and has been incorporated into the local culture; it is also reminiscent of
the colonial Europeans working for the Spanish Empire who, as demonstrated
above, used the term *flojo* to describe the conquered indigenous peoples of the
region (for a historical analysis of these racial relations in the sixteenth century,
see Chapters 2 and 3).

   Flojo is in wide use even today. Consequently, this ideologically loaded terminology, through time and human action, gets transformed into local customs
that can take different social expressions, some of them having political repercussions on people's domination in everyday life. In the rest of this chapter, I
show how *barra* and *huevón,* the latter also meaning "lazy," are examples of such
a phenomenon.

Ethnographic Material: The Production Process—Industrial and Cultural

One aspect of the cultural alteration of the folk concept of "laziness" occurred
in the Juárez maquiladora where I carried out anthropological fieldwork in the
summer of 1987 (also see Chapter 4). Inside this factory, the workers assembled,
among other things, microcircuits. The microcircuits assembled in this global
factory provide computers with the electronic power necessary to calculate several kinds of marketable operations (mathematical, recreational, educational,
commercial, and even military). The following ethnographic description of a
moment at the workplace is a reflection of the daily events at the factory, mainly
at the production table.

   Besides the linguistic forms already mentioned in the previous section, the
term *barra* also refers to a peculiar construction tool—a five-foot-long spearlike
piece of iron that is used to dig holes where the soil is dry and harsh, which
characterizes the Ciudad Juárez hills (see Christopherson 1982, 145). On the production line where I carried out participant observation, the main instrument

for producing microcircuits was called a *barra*—a piece of iron (a beam), one foot long and one and one-half inches wide (Figure 5.1), to which an aluminum frame of a similar size, a *marco* (Figure 5.2), is attached. The *marco* is composed of sixteen rectangular one-centimeter spaces where the microchips (Figure 5.3), the major sections of the microcircuit, are inserted.

There were twelve workers at a production table: eight inserters, three machine pressers, and one inspector (see Figure 5.4). Operation 1 is performed by the inserters. They insert the *marco* into the *barra* and the chips into the *marco*. After inserting the chips, the inserter passes the *barra* and its attached frame, with its sixteen inserted chips, to Operation 2 (see Figure 5.5). In Operation 2, a prepress worker (*predoblador*) presses the frame and the chips together against the *barra* with a machine (Figure 5.6). After one press, the frame is sent through a conveyer belt to Operation 3. The last presser gives it a final press, snatches it off the frame, and gives it to the inspector. This presser then returns the *barra* through the conveyer belt back to the inserters. (I performed the work of the last presser for almost my entire stay at the factory.) Each pressed chip became a microcircuit.

Once all microcircuits are inspected, they are sent for further assembly to other areas of production: to welding, then to second inspection (this time through a microscope), and finally, they are sent to be washed in "chlorine." After "washing," the microcircuits are packed in boxes and sent to El Paso, Texas. With respect to this particular product, this is how the export processing plant operation is carried out in the international division of labor between the United States and Mexico.

During the first two weeks of my employment, the three pressers consisted of one woman and two men. The last six weeks, the three pressers consisted of a male (myself as the last presser) and two females in prepressing. Each of these two prepressers had, on the average, four inserters who would provide them with the *barras* and their inserted frames.[9]

The quota for each inserter was 453 *barras* a day. As I noted in Chapter 4, we worked a twelve-hour shift, four days a week. It usually took about four days of practice for a neophyte to meet the quota. Those more experienced received a bonus according to the number assembled above the quota. Frequently, the bonus received after a forty-eight-hour week was $2,000 pesos (US$1.25) in the mid-1980s. The hourly wage paid to the Mexican workers at that time was approximately US$.43 an hour. Thus, the need to work at optimum levels to receive a larger paycheck was indeed compelling.

Often the two prepressers and I would fall behind; we would not send enough *barras* to the other workers. When this happened, the pressure was almost unbearable. At one time, at least fifteen *barras* had accumulated in front of me, yet I could not press the microcircuits onto the barras any faster. Consequently, the inserters (those who insert chips into the aluminum frame that is attached to the

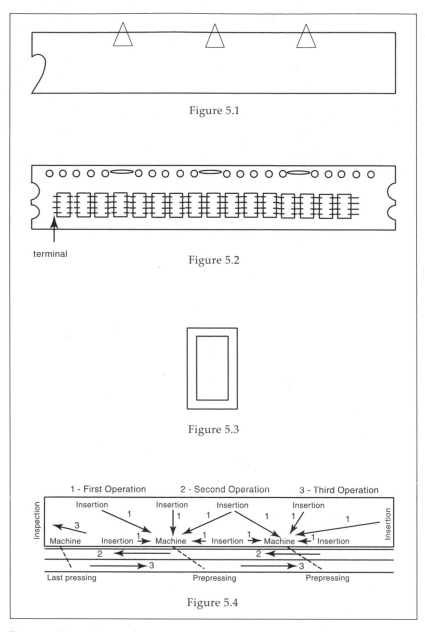

Figure 5.1

terminal

Figure 5.2

Figure 5.3

1 - First Operation   2 - Second Operation   3 - Third Operation

Figure 5.4

Figure 5.1. *Barra.* Source: Lugo 1990, 179.
Figure 5.2. *Marco.* Source: Lugo 1990, 179.
Figure 5.3. Chip. Source: Lugo 1990, 179.
Figure 5.4. Production table. Source: Lugo 1990, 179.

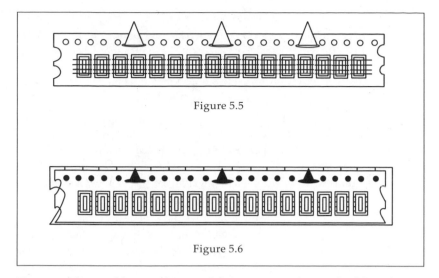

Figure 5.5

Figure 5.6

Figure 5.5. Unpressed *barra* with inserted frame, or *marco* (terminals of frame lean away from inserted chip). Source: Lugo 1990, 180.
Figure 5.6. Pressed frame on *barra* (terminals firmly pressed against the chip). Source: Lugo 1990, 180.

barra) would yell "Barras! "Barras!" out loud. While they were asking for more *barras* from us (the pressers), they were calling us "Lazy! Lazy!" since "Barras!" also means "lazy" in the Juárez working-class culture.

Likewise, if the inserters did not insert *barras* fast enough, the pressers were told by the foreman (in this case, it was a woman) to yell "Barras!" to them. Thus, all the workers, throughout most of the day, imposed pressure on each other via the expression "Barra!"—a cultural concept associated with laziness in the context of production. To understand how *barra* produces and reproduces culture (notions of manliness and masculinity and of laziness itself) through human action, an analysis of its historical and linguistic specificity must be carried out.

Historical Transformation and Cultural Reproduction

Why does *barra*, the linguistic expression, mean "lazy"? It is because *barra* is associated with two culturally specific notions: heaviness and looseness. The latter two concepts are in turn associated with laziness. Informally, an individual can call someone lazy through either *flojo* (literally "loose") or the most common slang expression, *huevón* (from the Spanish term *huevo*, "egg"; women can be called *floja* or *huevona*). Both *flojo* and *huevón* are terms used nationwide. On the other hand, *barra* belongs to the border culture of Ciudad Juárez, and more specifically to the working-class culture. However, *huevón*, the primary metaphor meaning "lazy," emerged because of the similarity in physical appearance (the ovate shape) of the two objects it connects: the egg of a chicken and the testicle of a man. It seems that *barra,* as an expression meaning "lazy," emerged from the combination of the more broadly used terms *huevón* and *flojo.*[10]

Two possibilities exist regarding the emergence of the linguistic term *barra,* meaning "lazy": one associated with the Spanish term for the (bar)room, "la barra," or "el bar," whose main feature is the drinking of liquor (these sites of recreation are places where you "kick back" or "loosen up, relax"); the other alternative is the name of the spearlike tool, *barra,* used in construction to dig holes.

The question is whether the specific meaning of the term *barra,* implying laziness, emerged from the construction industry or from the bars that have been characteristic of the Juárez nightlife since the turn of the century and that gained particular popularity during the years of the Bracero Program between 1942 and 1965. With respect to the latter, there is no evidence that the term *barra,* in the sense being described here, was used before the arrival of the maquiladora industry. Rather, this unique meaning of *barra* seems to have emerged in the late 1960s. Those males who were fortunate enough at that time to be employed in the construction industry were the ones who probably began to use the term *barra* to mean "lazy." Construction workers use a very heavy five-foot-long spearlike tool made from iron to dig holes where the ground is hard. In the barrio where I grew up in the latter part of the sixties, male teenagers would call to each other, "¿Qué pues, barra?" (What's happening, lazy?). I have observed that the expression "*barra*" is still used by the people of Juárez, even outside the factory. Let us see how and why *barra* emerged out of the construction industry in the 1960s to mean "lazy" and why it reemerged in the export processing plant where I carried out fieldwork in the mid-1980s. To understand why it could have emerged in construction, however, we first need to understand why *huevón* is associated with laziness.

Analysis of the Term *Barra*

The workers would not have associated the heavy *barra* with "laziness" if the initial metaphor for "lazy," *huevón,* did not already exist in the traditional linguistic or conceptual baggage. Thus, *barra,* when first thought of as meaning "lazy," was a metonymic transformation of the metaphor *huevón,* due to the contiguous relation (Turner 1987, 3) between *huevón* and *barra.* How did the transformation occur?

I suggest that people in Mexico began to call a lazy person *huevón* because they, consciously or unconsciously, imply that if a person is lazy, it is because his or her egg-shaped testicles/ovaries are big and heavy. (If a woman is lazy, they can call her *huevona*, adding the gender-specific ending "a," according to Spanish linguistic rules.) Thus, the two semantic domains, the poultry product, egg, and the genitals of the human male body, become synthesized in this metaphoric relationship through the similar ovate shape that each element within each domain shares: the egg of a chicken and the testicles of a man. Alonso and Koreck also document this cultural phenomenon: "In Spanish, the primary meaning of *huevos* is 'eggs.' However, in Mexico, *huevos* is also used to denote testicles and indeed, in practice, this term has become the most common meaning of the term (eggs are called *blanquillos* instead)" (1988, 121). Américo Paredes also identified this cultural practice and cautious preference in relation to folk medicine: "The doctor prescribes that an egg (*huevo*) be put on the patient's forehead, *huevo* being such a common synonym for 'testicle' that many prudish people avoid the word altogether, substituting it with *blanquillo*" (Paredes 1968, 110; italics in original).[11]

Huevo (egg), however, will not suffice to call someone lazy; it would have to be *huevón*, in the superlative sense, implying the notions of "big" and "heavy," which the speakers associate, in this case, with big and heavy testicles. Thus, in describing a lazy person through heaviness (and not through looseness, *flojo/ flojera*), *huevón* was transformed by the people into *barra* because they shared the notion that both the *barra* (the construction tool) and the *huevón* were "heavy." In consequence, I argue that the *barra* associated with laziness both in construction and in the case of the maquiladora was a linguistic product of *huevón*, and not of *flojo*, which is more closely associated with the "looseness" or "loosening up, relaxing" of the *barra* linked to drinking and to the nightlife of Ciudad Juárez. This does not mean, nonetheless, that the bar and the construction site are two mutually exclusive, separate spheres of the working-class border culture of Ciudad Juárez. Indeed, construction workers, who often visit bars, were perhaps the ones who initially *tiraron barra* (loosened up, relaxed) in the cantinas.[12]

Huevo and *huevos* (plural) are also used by Mexican males to talk about machismo (culturally specific notions of manliness) or to express attitudes regarding courage and aggressiveness with respect to other males. In this book, the concept of machismo is specifically used as a cultural practice (not an essential or biological entity; see also Gutmann 1996) closely associated with local notions of masculinity, particularly those concerned with "ordering men along a continuum of lesser or greater honour," as Salvador Reyes Nevares has described:

> The principal of honor in men is manliness. . . . Manliness implies strength of body and spirit. Further, it involves the notion of effectiveness. The man must be self-sufficient and able to solve his problem in life without hesitation or confusion. (Reyes Nevares, cited in Arnold 1977, 179–180)[13]

Consider the following example: if the wife of a man is imposing herself on him (*mandándolo*—"giving him orders"), his male friends or compadres would most likely tell him: "¡Que no tienes los huevos para mandarla tú!" (Don't you have the eggs/testicles/courage to order her?)

This association of *huevos* with testicles, and then with machismo, is also found in the American Southwest. Américo Paredes wrote the following when presenting how a man described Gregorio Cortez, a folk hero of the Lower Rio Grande border:

> A short, very dark man told me that Cortez had been just a little dark man, *chiquitito y prietito.* Ah, but what a man! All heart and testicles; that is to say, all kindness and courage. (Paredes 1958, 111)

In a footnote, Paredes explained:

> According to folk physiology, the heart is the seat of man's kinder virtues. Courage and fighting spirits reside in the testicles. (Paredes 1958, 111n)

This distinction between *huevón* (lazy) and *tener huevos* (to have testicles/courage) is important. With regard to men and machismo in particular, calling a man *huevón* in the superlative sense will insult him, especially if the target is a nonfriend. To tell him that he has *huevos* (courage, testicles) is to praise him or to suggest that he is stubborn (as in "¡Qué huevos!"); whereas to tell him that he does not have *huevos* (testicles/courage) is to offend him. Thus, semantically, *huevón* and *tener huevos* have different meanings. I discuss later how the relationship between *barra, huevón, huevos,* and machismo becomes crucial in understanding cultural and class reproduction at the factory (in the epilogue I discuss how these gendered social relations often inform violence among men and against women in Ciudad Juárez).

With respect to the tropic analysis of the *huevón*/testicles/masculinity triad, I must also note that *huevón* has a metonymic dimension, because testicles are part of a whole, the human male (metonymy, part–whole, as Turner [1987] and Crocker [1977] used it). Thus, the metaphoric dimension of *huevón* to describe a person could not exist if the metonymic relationship between testicles and a man was absent. Moreover, if a man is *huevón*, or "lazy," because perceptively his testicles are heavy, then here we have an additional metonymic relationship between heaviness and laziness, since heaviness causes laziness (according to Sapir, a cause-effect relation is metonymic).[14] However, I could also argue that heaviness is laziness—thus creating a metaphoric relationship through the common element of "being unable to move." In fact, it is because of this apparent density of meanings in the description of the principles of tropes that Sapir claims that everything is reduced to a metaphoric relation.

What is at stake in this limited characterization of tropes is that when we begin to talk about abstract ideas such as heaviness and laziness, instead of about concrete objects like "eggs" and "testicles," we are indeed talking about synecdoche—not as a regular trope, but as a discursive product and/or source of meaning for material(ized) entities. In the case of *huevón* itself, synecdoche— the wholeness constituted by both heaviness and laziness—was first an ideational/discursive product of both the metaphoric relation between *huevo* (egg) and testicle, and the metonymic relation between testicles and the human male body, achieving a conceptual level in the term *huevón*. Second, synecdoche was a crucial discursive source (the notions of heaviness and laziness) that reproduced the metaphoric relations necessary to explain a state of being (being "lazy"), and most important, gave rise to other tropes, such as *barra*.

I suggest that in the process of describing a "lazy" person, *huevón* was transformed by the people into *barra* because they shared the notion that both the *barra* (the construction tool) and *huevón* were heavy and thus, "lazy." Consequently, in this case, the notion of heaviness is the source of the relativity existing between the linguistic expressions *huevón* and *barra*. We must realize, however, that together *barra* and *huevón* constitute a different degree of encompassment or discursive terrain than *huevón* by itself, particularly in reference to synecdoche. For example, in order for *huevón* and *barra* to be similarly enacted or performed within different domains (moving someone to work faster on the assembly line or in construction), they must together constitute a new ideational or discursive "whole," different only in degree (not kind) from "wholes" that characterize one specific trope—that is, *huevón*. The new "whole" exists in the minds of the people through the sharing of the discursive notions of heaviness and laziness. This is how *huevón* and *barra* as tropes and discourse are articulated by the local people. Consequently, we come to the same conclusion found when we analyzed *huevón*: that synecdoche contains an ideological element, although with the emergence of *barra* the synecdoche relation in question acquires a higher degree of encompassment. The latter broader cultural terrain of synecdoche not only includes the already described dynamics of *huevón* in itself, but also the evident transformation that occurred between *huevón* and *barra*. This transformation occurred because the shared notions of heaviness and laziness were applied to other domains apart from the poultry product egg and the testicles of the human body: they were applied to the construction, factory, and metal domains.

The Articulation of the Past and the Present through the Performance of *Barra*

When the assembly-line workers yell "Barras! Barras!" to each other, *barra* constitutes simply a metaphoric relation, since *barra* in that particular synchronic context synthesizes the domains of (1) tools—the actual one-foot-long piece of iron—and (2) the supposedly slow and "lazy" workers (machine pressers and inserters), with "heaviness" as the shared characteristic of both elements. However, from a diachronic perspective, and from a much broader cultural context (both the border culture and the national culture), *barra* constitutes a metonymic dimension, since it has a contiguous relation to the initial and nationally used metaphor *huevón,* and to the historic fact that construction jobs represented the major source of employment for most men in Ciudad Juárez between World War II and the early eighties (also see Castellanos 1981). The latter aspect regarding political economy is not necessarily articulated by the workers at the time *barra* is enacted or performed at the workplace. The contiguous relation of *barra* to *huevón,* however, is much more conscious on the part of the workers. I have two reasons that justify this contention.

First, when *barra* is used to imply "lazy," especially inside the factory, the trope is carrying with it a "latent factor"[15] (Fernandez 1986, 54), *huevón.* The existence of both tropes operating at the same time, even though one evolved from the other, occurs because when *barra* emerged from *huevón, huevón* did not lose importance as a linguistic term to address someone as lazy; rather, it gained status—"negative status"—since calling someone "*huevón,*" especially a nonrelative and a nonfriend, can be an offensive act. This latter point regarding *huevón* as an offensive metaphor leads me to the second reason why *barra* is a conscious metonymic trope in relation to *huevón.*

From the ethnographic material that I have presented, we must realize that the factory workers have three linguistic forms for calling someone lazy. These are: (1) *flojo* (loose one); (2) *huevón* (big and heavy testicles/eggs); and (3) *barra* (the term derived from *huevón* and the actual tool). Why did the factory workers at the production table select *barra* if *flojo* and *huevón* were also part of their cultural and linguistic vocabulary? There are several reasons.

First, they did not select the first option, *flojo,* because in the context of the workplace, an actual tool called *barra* was physically immediate to them. They could conceptually and culturally relate the tool to the term *barra* that had been used to mean "lazy" outside the factory, that is, in the streets of their neighborhoods. Although sometimes the chips came loosely inserted, I never witnessed any cases where the workers associated this type of operation with *flojo* (loose one). Nevertheless, as I previously said, the term is widely used, not only inside the factory in other subcultural contexts of the maquila, but also in the larger society, particularly throughout working-class Juárez.

Second, they did not use *huevón* because, as I have already noted, in the context of competition, *huevón* can be an offensive term in situations of conflict (competition in production settings) that might lead to personal arguments (if not to physical fights), especially among men. I noted in Chapter 4 that supervisors are aware that men might not always obey the orders of the foreman, or

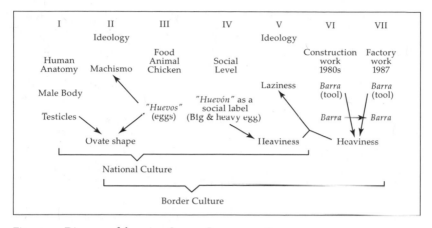

Figure 5.7. Diagram of domains. Source: Lugo 1990, 187.

forewoman, or that they might fight, causing disorder at the plant. Finally, they selected *barra* not only because they did not want to enter into physical altercations with their workmates, but also because it is a more "diplomatic" term in the culture of the factory. Having the actual tool in front of them, to an extent, detracts power from the metaphor and causes the targeted individual to move faster and not get annoyed at having been called "¡Barra!" The person would get irritated by being called "¡Barra!" only if he or she is directly targeted by all others, as in an "all against one" situation. This occurs when a new employee working his or her first week is pressured by most other workers when he or she gets behind. The first week is the rite of passage that determines whether or not the new worker will decide to keep the job.

Once we analyze this simultaneous interplay between *huevón* and *barra,* which exists in the minds of the workers and throughout time (with present and historical aspects of tropes fusing into a microcontext, as it were), the manifestation of one important phenomenon becomes evident: the concrete relation of tropes not only to culture—as Fernandez argued with regard to "metaphor"— but also to class domination on the shop floor.

Both *huevón* (a metaphor) and *barra* (metonymically related to *huevón* but also a metaphor in itself) produce a highly encompassing synecdochic relationship through the notions of heaviness and laziness. In this particular case, these form a singular synecdoche of an elevated degree as well as the specific relation between *barra* and *huevón.* It is this conceptual level of abstraction (and analysis), constituted by heaviness and laziness, that turns synecdoche into a vital discursive product and source, leaving the simple metaphoric and metonymic dimensions behind. I have reached this conclusion because no other theoretical or cultural factor could encompass all of the domains or be so pervasive, as seen in Figure 5.7.

Only synecdoche, with its discursive dimension (heaviness and laziness) spanning at least the 1960s to the late 1980s, from *huevón* itself to the coupling of *huevón* and *barra,* and from construction work to factory work (see Figure 5.7), could have managed to encompass so many domains. These domains, I believe, create a scheme or pattern (though fractured in time and space) of both class and culture. Because of the tense fusion of so many domains, I call this synecdochic dimension, following Sahlins, the structure of the conjuncture, since it is "une rencontre de circonstances," that is, "a situational set of relations, crystallized from the operative cultural categories and actor's interests" (Sahlins 1985, 125), with the concept of "interest" being related to praxis or behavior, as in the enactment or performance of the sign (in the Saussurian sense). As Sahlins wrote, "In action, the sign is determined as an interest, which is its instrumental value to the acting subject" (1985, 150). It is this structure of the conjuncture in its synecdochic aspect that produces, transforms, and reproduces culture and class on the ground, synchronically as well as historically, and therefore captures how cultural and social domination occurred, in this concrete case, throughout the late twentieth century.

Revelatory Incidents

To demonstrate the way the foregoing synecdochic process, that is, the structure of the conjuncture, reflects where the force of cultural meaning and power lies, it will suffice to present a "revelatory incident," where we (the workers and myself) were assembling microcircuits. According to James Fernandez, revelatory incidents are

> events where tropes are actually at play and where images are actually argued by . . . recognizable human agents, and where the figurative actually does something to these human agents, to their relationships with others and to their relation to their world as the figurative helps them define that relationship and that world. (1986, ix)

I argue that these revelatory incidents are products of a symbolic process, of the structure of the conjuncture, which is political in nature and is made up of ecological, psychological, social, technological, and historical factors, as I mentioned in the introduction to this chapter. One of these incidents, which manifests the unequal politics and processes of culture, is the enactment of the trope *barra* and its subsequent reproduction and transformation of masculinity at the factory, in particular, at the production table. In the attempt to produce enough microcircuits to fulfill the quota, the workers are pressured by other workers (either male or female) to labor harder and faster by being called "¡Barra!" Even though women are not associated with machismo, that is, they do not enact macho behavior *per se,* they also work faster when pressured by the term *barra.* They are being called lazy women: *huevonas.* Thus, *barra* actually becomes enacted and performed upon (Fernandez 1986). If a man gets behind, however, he might not be considered to be macho/manly; he might be thought of as not having *huevos* (testicles). Consequently, he loses status as a man, not only in the border culture but also in the Mexican national culture. The image that he might reflect is that of a nonmasculine male, especially in front of the women and other "*machista*" men. Thus, being able to keep up with the quota is, to a large extent, part of maintaining the macho image. This machismo is in turn transformed from a seemingly simple or traditional cultural practice to a system of labor control, or rather, of capitalist discipline in a new form of conquest, which includes a new hegemonic "structure."

This simultaneity of class action and cultural process is only operative because of the particular use of the trope *barra,* which reflects a synecdochic relation that is obviously ideological and political in nature—it is political because it reproduces inequalities along class and gender. In this sense, synecdoche manifests the structure of the conjuncture (see Sahlins 1981, 1982, 1985), which exists between structure (working-class machismo—culture as constituted) and praxis or action (culture as lived) or human practice (the enactment of *barra*). This "structure of the conjuncture," I hold, is responsible for the reproduction of culture—of practice and ideology, of praxis and structure (see Sahlins 1982, 43, for an explicit argument about the "dual existence of culture"; also see Chapter 9). Consequently, in making themselves work faster at the command of "¡Barras!" the men are actually reproducing themselves as machos/males, and thus are reproducing their own macho/masculine culture, and all the workers (both men and women) end up reproducing, in situ, their own working-class subjection and subjugation.

This same phenomenal reproduction of "the cultural" is documented by Terence Turner, who argues that while enacting in ritual the assertion "We become araras (macaws)," Bororo men are actually reproducing their own Bororo society. These men, however, rather than reproducing themselves as social beings to be exploited, as the maquiladora workers are doing, reproduce themselves to remain "powerful beings" in their own society. Turner writes that "Bororo men 'become araras' in order to reproduce through ritual, and thus 'become' themselves" (1987, 8). To reproduce themselves, however, especially in ritual, they become their own social Bororo beings, since "ceremonial is the mode of activity through which Bororo men reproduce, and thus pragmatically define themselves and their society as Bororo" (ibid., 6). He notes that the "realization" of this cultural reproduction, among the Bororo, can only be efficient at the level of synecdoche, "in which the metaphorically related human and arara elements become metonymically defined as the parts of a single whole of spatial and functionally effective relations" (ibid., 13).

Yet, my own trope analysis differs from Turner's in one aspect. Turner is aware of the power of synecdoche only in "cultural reproduction" terms. He suggests that metaphoric and metonymic relations are products of the "Ur-trope" synecdoche (Turner 1987, 18). I believe that metaphor and metonymy are products of synecdoche only at the level of reproduction, that is, Bororo men reproducing themselves as Bororo in ritual, or the factory men reproducing themselves as working-class macho/masculine subjects at the workplace. Reproduction in this sense, as far as I know, can only be witnessed by the analyst in a synchronic context, in which synecdoche is only seen as a source of the other tropes. It is at this level that Turner and most trope theorists, with the exceptions of Ohnuki-Tierney and Sahlins, have operated till now.

From a diachronic perspective, however, synecdoche is clearly manifested as a product of the minor tropes: metaphor and metonymy. I argue that synecdoche first emerges as a product from metaphoric and metonymic relations. Then it turns into a source only to reproduce both of the latter, which will in turn reproduce the synecdoche itself, but in an altered form. It is a circular process that is historically and contextually constituted. Indeed, this is how "the cultural" is produced and reproduced, and how culture change occurs, usually without destroying the existing cultural "base." Because of this, early in the history of our discipline, Franz Boas claimed that "all cultural forms . . . appear in a constant state of flux and subject to fundamental modifications," without, I would add, totally losing their particular distinctiveness. The more things change, the more they remain the same. Let us see how this complex dialectically diachronic process is manifested in Ciudad Juárez.

Domination's Structure of the Conjuncture in Motion

Before the foreign export processing plants, or maquiladoras, were introduced into Mexico, the synecdochic relation heaviness–laziness already existed, as evidenced by the existence of the metaphor (with its metonymic dimension) *huevón*. When *barra* emerged as a metaphor in the construction sphere, however, the synecdochic aspect of *huevón* was altered to include a reemerging trope, *barra*. At this point, *barra* and *huevón* (together) gave rise to the synecdoche (heaviness–laziness) in a new dimension, since it now encompassed the broader sphere of construction through the existence of the *barra,* the metal tool used to dig by the workers. At this broader level, synecdoche became an ideological and discursive source that could be used by the workers to call a lazy construction worker "*barra.*" From a synchronic perspective, when a construction worker is called "*barra,*" it would be apparent that *barra,* as a metaphor *in itself,* was a product of the synecdochic relation of heaviness–laziness, independent of *huevón* (just as Turner maintained that "We become macaws" emerged from the synecdochic relation of society–nature). But, as we already know, that dimension or degree of synecdoche that includes *barra* was only possible because *barra* was brought into the picture by the actors themselves when they related it to *huevón*. That particular synecdochic dimension or degree initially emerged (through human agency) out of the metaphoric and metonymic relation between *barra* and *huevón*. By adding *barra* to *huevón*, we can see cultural change operating, since it altered the synecdochic relation of heaviness–laziness. This culturally specific notion of heaviness–laziness extended itself into the mid-1980s, into the factory where I carried out participant observation.

At the workplace, a higher degree of this synecdoche appeared, further altering the sphere of what constituted heaviness–laziness. *Barra* was now enacted by factory workers, who work with automated machinery, that is, the pressing machine, something that construction workers in Mexico, for the most part, do not do. Both types of jobs constitute different subcultural atmospheres; thus, a much higher degree (or broader terrain) of encompassment emerged. This new synecdochic dimension was produced through the addition of a new tool called *barra*, used to assemble microcircuits for computers rather than to dig holes. This *barra* belonged to a new social context in which both men and women labored, together, as working-class subjects. I have concluded, then, that the heaviness–laziness dimension that operated at the maquiladora, reproducing masculine practices and values and working-class and cultural subjectivities as well as transforming them for political use, was a discursive and performative structure of the conjuncture that emerged out of the historical fact that a multinational company established its factory in Ciudad Juárez. This particular synecdochic relation was a product of a specific trope, *barra* (now the term for a microcircuit tool and a construction tool), and the relativization of "*huevón*." This synecdoche, in turn, reproduced the same tropes as they are enacted at the production table—which is the ultimate site, in this case, for the exploitation and conquest of Mexican men and women in late-twentieth-century Ciudad Juárez.

Conclusion

In summary, this tropic analysis has pointed out that, from historical and diachronic perspectives, synecdoche is produced and reproduced by the minor tropes, and that the minor tropes are, in turn, produced and reproduced by synecdoche. It is a dialectical process that is historically and contextually constituted. I have also shown not only how ideologies (machismo, notions of heaviness and laziness) and behaviors are altered, produced, reproduced, and transformed according to the social and historical contexts, but also how they persist in spite of the passing of time and the intrusion of outside agents (i.e., multinational corporations). It is this persistence, I believe, that allows for the actual integration (or disintegration), fusion (or fission), and existence (or extermination) of socially distinctive human groups and their respective cultures or subcultures—such as the border culture of factory workers of Ciudad Juárez and the "national culture" of Mexico (or the vanished Native American cultures; see Chapter 2 for more examples of the latter). The only way anthropologists, or other cultural analysts, can arrive successfully at the power matrix of cultural worlds (ours and those of "others") without dismissing internal and external factors is by identifying and scrutinizing "the structure of the conjuncture"—in this particular case, the synecdochic dimension of tropes and power at their most ethnographically grounded level, both historically and in the present.

In this instance, it was through the tropes *barra* and *huevón* that the working-class peoples of Ciudad Juárez expressed not only themselves as people with dignity but also their beliefs and practices about honor and survival. Almost three quarters of a century ago, Ruth Benedict noted that the object of the anthropologist was to understand "the different forms through which . . . [cultures] . . . express themselves" (1934, 22). In this chapter, I tried to demonstrate how maquiladora workers expressed, through working class tropes, their beliefs, themselves, and thus their "culture"—ultimately in the global context of late industrial capitalism.

In terms of the concrete realities that await the ethnographer "out there," James Fernandez has told us about the "revelatory incidents" that are the physical grounds that the sensible student of culture must identify before he or she can identify the more abstract "structure of the conjuncture," since the latter is the symbolic manifestation of the former, either synchronically or diachronically. With respect to the present and the past, I strongly agree with Sahlins that "a full anthropological practice cannot neglect that the precise synthesis of past and present is relative to the cultural order [or disorder, I would add], as manifested in a specific structure of the conjuncture" (1985, 152–153). Regarding "cultural order," or the relation between what we call "structure" and "praxis," Boas wrote:

> The activities of the individual are determined to a great extent by the social environment, but in turn his [*sic*] own activities influence the society in which he lives, and may bring about modifications in its form. Obviously, this problem is one of the most important ones to be taken in a study of cultural changes. (1940, 285)

As students of culture, society, and class (whether in cultural anthropology or in nonanthropological cultural studies), however, we must try to articulate the following theoretical metastrategy: to decipher the specific relation (either the coordination or the rupture) between structure and practice, the past and the present, the individual subject and the social group, or between culture and class, so that we can better understand human social life and its problems, not only in the late twentieth century but into the twenty-first century. I believe I have systematically demonstrated in this chapter how this complex coordination takes place at the Mexican border in an electronics factory.

Finally, I hope that full and adequate appreciation is given in the future to our understanding of the articulation of multiple *force relations*—economic, political, social, and historical (Gramsci 1971; Hall 1986), where cultural and historical meaning and practice are still waiting to be rigorously explained and interpreted—whether before, after, or during moments of conquest, in whatever forms it takes, be it in precapitalist, modern, or late capitalist societies. Regarding this complex articulation or coordination, Foucault early on took a very cautious position when he wrote:

> [The embarrassment of asking questions of causality] probably reaches its
> highest point in the case of the empirical sciences: for the role of instru-
> ments, techniques, institutions, events, ideologies, and interests is very
> much in evidence; but one does not know how an articulation so complex
> and so diverse in composition actually operates. It seemed to me that it
> would not be prudent for the moment to force a solution I felt incapable,
> I admit, of offering. . . . I chose instead to confine myself to describing the
> transformations themselves, thinking that this would be an indispensable
> step if, one day, a theory of scientific change and epistemological causality
> was to be constructed. (1970, xii–xiii)

Although I am not arguing for causality, in this chapter I have made some theoretical, ethnographic, and methodological suggestions about the ways in which "an articulation so complex and so diverse in composition actually operates." I suggest that the analysis of such an articulation allows one to better grasp how the workers' reproduction of their class exploitation vis-à-vis the performance of manliness and laziness is (as in the case of border inspections in the chapter that follows) an instance of how the unmaking of the mobilization of the maquiladora labor force was operating at the end of the late twentieth century in Ciudad Juárez.

It is to the border crossings and their inspections that I now turn.

SIX

Border Inspections

Inspecting the Working-Class Life of Maquiladora
Workers on the U.S.-Mexico Border

Introduction

This chapter tells stories of defiance and failure on the part of working-class
people at the U.S.-Mexico border as they tried to live a decent life at the end
of the twentieth century. In the process, the chapter (and the one that follows)
presents empirical evidence as to how class, culture, history, and gender articulate in the streets and factories of Ciudad Juárez. Paralleling the ethnographic
and cultural material is the theoretical underpinning of this specific chapter,
which is to revisit and reconsider the academic and conceptual phrase "border
crossings." Through an examination of ethnographic materials collected in the
Paso del Norte region and of literary (songs, poetry, and short-story narratives),
film, and historical sources, I suggest that the analytical strength of "border
crossings" as a theoretical tool can be ethnographically enriched in an empirically substantial manner by recognizing that most border crossings are more
often than not accompanied by "inspection stations" that inspect, monitor, and
surveil what goes in and out in the name of class, gender, race, and nation. After
all, as Esperanza once told Ruth Behar, not all people actually manage to cross
"to the other side" (Behar 1993). It is all really up to the inspector. Would he or
she say, "¡Pásele!" (Go ahead!), or remain inquisitively silent?

Even after having supposedly crossed the bridges between Mexico and the
United States, we must not overlook that many of these crossings are at once
densely and dispersedly populated by inspectors who are too numerous to

ignore. This is why Alejandro Morales has argued that "in general people fear and are afraid to cross borders" (1996, 23). In spite of the ubiquity of these inspectors, we, as scholars, both at the end of the late twentieth century and at the beginning of the new millennium, assumed, for the most part, too much optimism about the realities of "crossings" in the phrase "border crossings."[1]

In the same spirit with which social theorists such as Gloria Anzaldúa (1987), Juan Flores (1993), Michael Kearney (1991, 1996), Alejandro Morales (1996), Renato Rosaldo (1993), and Roger Rouse (1996) approached the complexities of everyday life in the context of "transnational circuits" in the late twentieth century, I will explore the pervasiveness of border inspections under late industrial capitalism in the Ciudad Juárez/El Paso area. I specifically focus on the everyday, regular attempts by factory workers (both men and women) to use urban spaces (city streets, buses, the shop floor, the dance floor), particularly in light of their position as legitimate citizens who are always at risk of being discriminated against. I also examine the ways they embody capitalist forms of work and leisure as they go to and from work (from home to the industrial parks and back), as they inhabit and embody factory discipline (from the shop floor to the cafeteria and to the restroom and back inside the factory), and as they attempt to enjoy their limited leisure activities (such as visiting local bars and discos). The chapter shows that Immigration and Naturalization Service (INS) inspections, quality inspections in transnational factories, door inspections at local nightclubs, and time inspections of bus drivers who labor for the maquiladora industry—all demonstrate a pervasive pattern of cultural surveillance that dehumanizes the Mexican working classes in this border city. The unmistakable existence and dispersal of power holders (border patrol officers, INS officers, Mexican health inspectors, factory supervisors, and security guards) throughout the locality continuously and systematically categorize the working-class citizenry by establishing boundaries between the workers and their many inspectors in order to place the workers on one or the other side of the socially immediate border (industrial, recreational, social, or international). These complex social inequalities have led to fatal labor practices and to concrete state/capital efforts to control local bodies, particularly the working-class population. An anthropological analysis of the dynamics of class exploitation and domination, skin-color hierarchies, and social marginalization among factory workers and others in the region enables us to tease out the cultural and historical structures of power/knowledge that shaped working-class subjectivity in Ciudad Juárez in the late twentieth century.[2]

Besides drawing on ethnographic interviews, archival materials, and the participant observation I conducted in Ciudad Juárez, I will also examine a sample of foundational theoretical texts about border crossings as well as ethnographic and testimonial accounts of border life found in other anthropological, sociological, and literary sources about the Mexican people of this particular region,

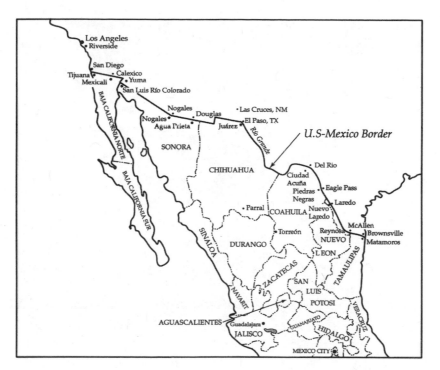

Figure 6.1. Northern Mexico and its major border cities. Map by Steve Holland in consultation with the author.

which, since 1853, includes a tristate area (see Figure 6.1): northern Chihuahua (Ciudad Juárez), western Texas (El Paso), and southern New Mexico (particularly Las Cruces). Regarding border theorizing, this particular chapter explicitly calls for a new analytical tool, border inspections, that must be added to the current metaphor of border crossings. It is *not* argued here that "border inspections" should replace "border crossings." However, it should be underscored that the former emphasizes the role of privileged power holders in enforcing boundaries and is therefore a necessary counterpart to the idea of cultural-social crossings or hybridity, which tends to emphasize an already-crossed transgression. While it is true that there are multiple borders, the chapter points out that too many of them cannot be crossed, especially if the crosser is a working-class subject. I hope to eventually show that *border inspections* are more pervasive among the *failed border crossings* of the working classes, who too often experience *border exclusions;* whereas *successful border crossings* are more characteristic of relatively privileged sectors (corporations, anthropologists, INS officers, local police, and other government inspectors), who tend to be uninspectable, and thus are able to "cross borders" much more easily, especially when compared to their unequal counterparts (factory workers, informants, migrants, and so forth).

Figure 6.2. United States Border Inspection Station, El Paso, Texas. Photograph by
Alejandro Lugo.

     With respect to anthropology, this chapter reconceptualizes "borders" as
ethnographic objects that are mainly characterized by supervision and scrutiny;
after all, too many borders in social life are products of crossroads with "inspection stations."[3] Due to its ethnographic lens, cultural anthropology, and Cultural
Studies more broadly, can productively contribute to a better understanding of
the many ways borders structure personal and collective aspirations as well as
social division. I am not arguing that the border inspections of the kind I address
here (with the exception of the problem of color) have not been documented in
the anthropological literature about the border; rather, I am proposing that it
is time to theorize them so that we no longer confuse them with border crossings. The implications of such a theoretical distinction are many, especially for
our understanding of the cultural and the material execution of power under a
transnationalized nation-state, and most importantly, for our understanding of
working-class life, not only at the end of the twentieth century but also into the
twenty-first century, particularly with the intensification of border inspections
after the September 11, 2001, attacks and after the immigration debate of 2006
surrounding HR 4437 ("Border Protection, Antiterrorism, and Illegal Immigration Control Act of 2005"), which would have criminalized undocumented immigrants and those who help them, in addition to calling for seven hundred
miles of fencing along the U.S.-Mexico border.

Heterotopias in the Context of the American Conquest of the Mexican Border: Ethnography, Songs, Poems, and Other Bordered Texts

The *corrido,* or Mexican ballad, "Los mandados," written by Jorge Lerma and sung by the Mexican mariachi singer Vicente Fernández, has been very popular among factory workers since the early 1980s. The first three stanzas of "Los mandados" go like this:

Cruzé el Río Grande nadando sin importarme "dos reales"
[I crossed the Rio Grande swimming, not giving a damn]
Me echó la migra pa' fuera y fuí a caer a Nogales
[The border patrol (La Migra) threw me out, and I landed in Nogales]
Entré por otra frontera y que me avientan pa' Juárez
[I entered through another border city, but they kicked me back to Juárez]

De ahí me fuí a Tamaulipas y me colé por Laredo
[From there I went to Tamaulipas and I sieved myself through Laredo]
Me disfracé de gabacho y me pinté el pelo güero
[I disguised myself as an Anglo and I dyed my hair blond]
Y como no hablaba inglés, que me retachan de nuevo
[And since I did not speak English, they threw me out again]

La migra a mí me agarró 300 veces digamos
[La Migra caught me about 300 times, let's say)
Pero jamás me domó: a mí me hizo los mandados
[But it never tamed me: I KICKED ITS BUTT]
Los golpes que a mí me dió se los cobré a sus paisanos
[The blows I received, I took out on their own people]

This *corrido* (or *corrida,* if you are dancing to it) is about border crossings; it is also about the persistence it takes to cross the border (on the part of the main character, a working-class Mexican man) and about the persistence (on the part of the border patrol, or "La Migra") required to stop or to tame (see "Manso" in Chapter 2) the border crosser and to block or tame the border itself. It is also, no doubt, in the same tradition as "The Ballad of Gregorio Cortez," about resistance to the blows received (see Limón 1994; Lugo 2000b; Paredes 1958; R. Rosaldo 1993). This song attempts to narrate, perhaps more than anything, the difficulty of crossing due to the border inspectors; specifically, the inescapable presence of La Migra, or the Border Patrol, throughout the international crossings between the United States and Mexico.

In spite of the concreteness of the international boundary in this border ballad, we must acknowledge that there is a critical difference between those who write metaphorically, psychologically, sexually, and intellectually about border-lands and border crossings, and those who write about the border as imposed and sanctioned by nation-state policymakers and by government officials. The concepts of "borderlands," "border crossings," and "the border" are not synony-mous. International borders are actively enforced in uniform and "with their pistol in their hand" by border patrol agents, INS/ICE representatives, and cus-toms officials (Chavez 1998; Heyman 1998; R. Rosaldo 1997). On the U.S. side of the international boundary, Border Patrol officers not only persecute undocu-mented border crossers such as the character in "Los mandados," but also, and more generally, they go after those who look (according to American Southwest cultural imaginings) like "illegal aliens," that is, Mexicans who look working class and economically and politically vulnerable. For instance, Chicano novel-ist, poet, and essayist Ben Sáenz documented and voiced the ways in which he has been harassed by Border Patrol officials, mainly because he "looks Mexican," while walking on the El Paso streets.

> The Border Patrol interrupted my daydreaming: "Where are you from?" I didn't answer. I wasn't sure who the agent, a woman, was addressing. She repeated the question in Spanish, "¿De dónde eres?" Without thinking, I almost answered her question—in Spanish. A reflex. I caught myself in midsentence and stuttered in a nonlanguage. "¿Dónde naciste?" she asked again. By then my mind had cleared, and I quietly said: "I'm a U.S. citizen." "Were you born in the United States?" *She was browner than I was* [my emphasis]. I might have asked her the same question. . . . "Yes," I answered. "Where in the United States were you born?" "In New Mexico." "Where in New Mexico?" "Las Cruces." "What do you do?" . . . "I work at the Uni-versity as a teaching assistant." She didn't respond. She looked at me as if I were a blank. Her eyes were filling in the empty spaces as she looked at my face. I looked at her for a second and decided she was finished with me. I started walking away. "Are you sure you were born in Las Cruces?" she asked again. I turned around and smiled, "Yes, I'm sure." She didn't smile back. She and her driver sat there for a while and watched me as I continued walking." (Sáenz 1992, xiii)

Sáenz's experience with state officials has its parallels with immigration offi-cials on the Mexican side. The following scene from the 1950s film *Wetbacks* (*Es-paldas mojadas*) highlights both the presence of border inspectors on the Mexi-can side of the international boundary and the problem of color encountered by Sáenz. In the following scene, a bracero (a working-class Mexican national working in the United States) named Rafael, after having experienced several in-stances of racism in the United States, returns to Ciudad Juárez and finds himself being unrecognized as a Mexican precisely because of the color of his skin:

Mexican immigration officer (MIO): So they caught you crossing the river?

RAFAEL: Yes, sir, I am Mexican. I believe I have the right to return to my country.

MIO: How would I know that you really are Mexican?

RAFAEL: What? (pointing at his own face) What about this?

MIO: That's not proof. There are many dark-skinned Americans. . . . Mexicans born over there: *pochos* [Mexicans born and raised in the U.S.], and who knows why they would want to come back to Mexico.

RAFAEL: *Pochos* do not come to Mexico.

MIO: Ah no?

RAFAEL: Well, yes, but I am Mexican. What do you want me to show you . . . do you want to see my body? [He attempts to unbutton his shirt.]

MIO: I already told you that that's no proof. There are dark-skinned French, Italians, Spanish, Lebanese, Turks, Greeks . . . all of Hispanic America. . . . Half the world is dark-skinned!

RAFAEL: But they don't speak Spanish like me, as we do. Besides, I was born in San Luis Potosí (a city and state of the same name in northeastern Mexico]. You can find that out.

MIO: That requires time and much paperwork.[4]

The point of these examples, nonetheless, is that once the person is perceived to be a working-class subject (i.e., Ben Sáenz, Rafael) and finds herself/himself at the international crossroads — in concrete border inspection stations — he or she is most likely to be inspected: literally, not just metaphorically or theoretically.

This practical distinction of our theoretical and research preferences also speaks to the seemingly synonymous notions of "the border" and "the borderlands," which tend to be lumped together by too many of us writing on the topic, including myself in an earlier study (Lugo 1997). In *Borderlands/La Frontera* (1987), for instance, the late Gloria Anzaldúa, one of the pioneers of border theorizing, attempts to distinguish between the "physical borderland" and the rest. She wrote, "The actual physical borderland that I'm dealing with in this book is the Texas-U.S. Southwest/Mexican border. The psychological borderlands, the sexual borderlands and the spiritual borderlands are not particular to the Southwest" (Anzaldúa 1987, iii).

If at times she herself conflates physical "borderland" with the U.S.-Mexico "border," Anzaldúa also differentiates between the two concepts: "Borders are set up to define the places that are safe and unsafe, to distinguish us from them. A *border* is a dividing line, a narrow strip along a steep edge. A *borderland* is a vague and undetermined place created by the emotional residue of an unnatural boundary. It is in a constant state of transition" (Anzaldúa 1987, 3; my emphasis). Thus, if the borderland is vague and undetermined and always transitional, the U.S.-Mexico border, on the other hand, has been constantly static for more than

150 years: ". . . *es una herida abierta* [it's an open wound] where the Third World grates against the first and bleeds" (ibid.).[5] Anzaldúa succinctly explains when and how the open wound within the Mexican community of the region was created: "The border fence that divides the Mexican people was born on February 2, 1848, with the signing of the Treaty of Guadalupe-Hidalgo" (ibid., 7). It has been almost 160 years since the treaty marked and enforced the place of residence for both those who belong and those who do not belong: Mexicans and Anglos, as well as *los mexicanos de un lado y los mexicanos del otro* (those Mexicans from one side and those from the other; see Oboler 1995 and Flores and Benmayor 1997 for issues of belonging and citizenship).

In *Translated Woman* (1993), Ruth Behar is both a borderlands inhabitant and a border crosser. But we should not confuse the two border subjectivities. We should not confuse Ruth, the anthropologist—the real border crosser in the power relationship—with Esperanza, the street peddler. After all, Ruth Behar can afford to buy insurance coverage to drive across the border (Behar 1995), whereas Esperanza might not even be able to secure money from the anthropologist. As Behar wrote:

> I tell Esperanza that it's fine, that she should keep the money order in case they need it later on. And then, in words I will forever regret, I follow the advice of a friend, who has told me to be firm and to say that I won't always be able to send her money whenever her son writes requesting it. I explain that I've given her half of my advance, and that so far the book *Translated Woman* has not earned any money, but that I hope it soon will, so I can give her more. . . . "*No, comadre* [Esperanza tells the anthropologist], don't be worrying about that. *No vamos a estar a pide y pide.* We're not going to be asking and asking all the time." (1995, 76)

While *borderlands* implies multiple sides, *border* implies two sides. In the case of the border between the United States and Mexico, "it divides one country with a higher standard of living from the other" (Morales 1996, 25): There is no ambiguity here. After all, Ruth can be taken to be a gringa (an Anglo), particularly in working-class Mexico, but Esperanza cannot pass [cross] as either Mexican American or as a "legal resident alien" in the United States.

Does the existence of multiple conceptions—border, borderlands, international borders, cultural borders—necessarily imply the inevitability of heterotopia? According to Alejandro Morales, Michel Foucault's heterotopia "explains border culture" (1996, 23). In *The Order of Things*, heterotopia is defined as a state of disorder in which "things are laid, placed, arranged in sites so very different from one another that it is *impossible to find a place of residence for them*" (Foucault, cited in Morales 1996, 23; my emphasis). In this particular treatment of heterotopia, the idea of a state of disorder without place or places of residence inevitably treats "the border" (*la frontera*) as an ethnographic impossibility: without a place of residence in the world. To be sure, an ethnography of multiple sites of struggle (or a multisided ethnography; see Marcus 1994) must still account for people's own sense of place in the world, no matter how chaotic or dispersed. The U.S.-Mexico border is in fact, to millions of people, more than a possibility; it is an incitement to an always unfulfilled locality and residentiality that at once reinforces nation and its privileged subjects. Consequently, it also marks as peripherals those "other peoples," similar to those "Other Victorians" in Foucault's *History of Sexuality* (1978), who are believed to belong elsewhere, in some other place of residence: on the other side, *but definitely not in a nonplace*. Indeed, it should be one of our goals to capture the immediacy of the concreteness of everyday life experiences that create the heterogeneity and heterotopia of human social life—in our case: specific encounters with Border Patrol officers, customs agents, security guards, factory supervisors, and so forth at the border between Ciudad Juárez and El Paso, between New Mexico and Chihuahua, or between Mexico and the United States.

Therefore, the concept of heterotopia can be turned into a highly productive ethnographic tool—one that would better allow us to study spatial demarcations and boundaries imposed by the state apparatus and by the privileged classes, but only if it permits, as well, an understanding of the U.S.-Mexico border as the complex place that it really is: a "place of residence" for millions of people, many of them economically marginalized.[6] Of these people, we must ask the following ethnographically grounded questions: Who crosses the border from south to north? How long do they have to wait? How many months? How many years? At what time—*de madrugada* (at dawn)? How much does it cost? Who can afford it? How many people make it alive? How many die dreaming or wishing to come across the river, across the barbed wire, or, in other contexts, across the ocean? How many are sent back or deported by force?[7]

My point about this line of questioning is to emphasize one of the major issues raised in this chapter: that not everybody manages to cross borders, especially working-class "colored" peoples. In the particular case of the border between Mexico and the United States, not everybody can afford it, in terms of money, time, or paperwork. As Leo Chavez (1998), Josiah Heyman (1998), Michael Kearney (1996), and others have documented, and as Gloria Anzaldúa noted more than a decade ago: "The Border Patrol hides behind the local McDonalds.... Cornered by flashlights.... *Los mojados* [...] are handcuffed, locked in jeeps, and then kicked back across the border" (1987, 12) to the other side. At the border inspection station, there is no "third element," no tolerance for ambiguity: you either have papers or you do not; you either convince the INS (now ICE [Immigration and Customs Enforcement]) officer that you are "American" or you do not. The ambiguity of the borderlands, cultural or otherwise, is not as common as we scholars have come to think. Therefore, undocumented peoples are not the only ones blocked or sent back. Alejandro Morales reminds us of the depth and the persistence of obstacles to "crossing" by writing about his elderly Mexican mother in Poem 29:

> My mother lost her green card. She is ninety years old and has been in the United States since nineteen hundred and twelve. If the Immigration and Naturalization Service doesn't believe she lost her green card and requires her to go to Mexico and reapply to enter the United States, a trip she probably won't survive, I will arm myself to prevent them from taking her. If they take her, it will be over my dead body. (1996, 17)

There is no doubt that there are subtle but important theoretical distinctions between border, borderlands, and border crossings, and that we need the ethnographic lens to substantiate and therefore *inspect* them. The analytical tool of "border inspections" should enrich our ethnographic accounts because it allows us to better capture the human experience in its everydayness, in this case, the conquest and domination of working-class Mexican folks.

The rest of the chapter ethnographically examines the working-class life lived by maquiladora workers as they go to work, as they labor in the transnational plants, and as they search for leisure activities at the end of the working day in Ciudad Juárez. The following sections should make manifest how pervasively "border inspections" touch, stir, and shape the lives of working-class people in this border city.

Why Maquiladora Workers Do Not Eat Chicken

I begin addressing everyday border inspections by relating them to a food-poisoning problem that affected a substantial number of maquiladora workers intermittently throughout the decade of the 1990s.[8] For reasons still not fully understood, several Juárez maquiladoras during that period sent hundreds of women and men to the emergency rooms of the local hospitals due to food poisoning occurring inside the factories. These unfortunate incidents led to inspections of factory cafeterias by federal health officials. In May of 1991, people on both sides of the El Paso–Juárez area were informed, through local television news and newspapers, about a massive intoxication of maquiladora workers at the most prestigious of the transnationals established there: RCA. Between 380 and 518 workers of both sexes had been given contaminated chicken (Pérez Espino 1995, 1B); one of the female workers died, and seven others were forced to abort late in their pregnancies. From 1991 to 1995, several additional mass-intoxication cases of factory workers were reported in the local newspapers (*Norte de Ciudad Juárez* and *Diario de Juárez*): for instance, on May 21, 1993, "30 workers became intoxicated at Corcom [a transnational electronics assem-

Figure 6.3. International Paso del Norte Bridge, a one-way bridge. It is used to drive across from Ciudad Juárez, Chihuahua, into El Paso, Texas. International pedestrians (tourists and cross-border shoppers, for instance) can walk across into either country over this bridge. All crossers pay a small fee every time they cross the bridge. Photograph by Alejandro Lugo.

Figure 6.4. El Puente de Córdoba/Bridge of the Americas, a two-way bridge. It can be used to cross (either walking or driving) from Ciudad Juárez to El Paso and from El Paso to Ciudad Juárez. This bridge is also called the "free bridge," or *puente libre,* because there is no fee for crossing it either into the United States or into Mexico. Photograph by Alejandro Lugo.

bly plant]" (Martínez 1993b, 4B); in July of 1992, the same maquiladora had been "the place of an intoxication in which 60 workers were victims" (Martínez 1993b, 4B). On May 26, 1993, less than a week after the Corcom incident, "tens of workers from 'Surgikos II' became intoxicated with meals served at the factory's cafeteria" (Martínez 1993a, 9B). On November 3, 1995, another RCA mass intoxication occurred: "Se intoxican 180 en RCA [180 Workers Get Intoxicated at RCA]." During 1995, there were two other cases in two distinct maquiladoras: "This case of intoxication (at RCA) is the second one in less than a week and the third one this year (including the case of Philips in which 105 workers became intoxicated and the case of Productos de Agua [Water Products] three months ago)" (Pérez Espino 1995, 1B).

The first RCA case of massive intoxication in 1991 was *officially* resolved through an inspection of the cooks' bodies and by blaming them for not being "clean" in the kitchen—with the utensils, with their hands, and more specifically, for not having clean fingernails. In 1993, Mexican federal officials from the Department of Health "confirmed" that the Corcom and Surgikos cases had been caused by "the poor handling of foodstuffs" on the part of cafeteria personnel. As Chief of Jurisdiction II Juan Cos Welsh told reporters: "The lack of care in the handling of foodstuffs in industrial cafeterias is the main cause behind the massive intoxications in maquiladoras" (Martínez and Cruz 1993, 3B). During the second RCA incident, Juan Lozaya, secretary of the RCA Workers' Union, made it clear that "one inspector from the Health Clinic investigated the cause of the infection by inspecting kitchen utensils, pots, and pans" (Pérez Espino 1995, 1B).

The Mexican cuisine culprits identified by the inspectors were the following: the cheese in the *chiles rellenos* (stuffed peppers) at RCA (Pérez Espino 1995, 1B), the *chilaquiles de pollo* (corn tortilla casserole) at Corcom (Martínez 1993b, 4B), and the *milanesa con papas* (tenderized, breaded steak with potatoes) at Surgikos (Martínez 1993a, 9B). At RCA in 1991, at Corcom in 1992, and since then at other assembly factories, the usual suspect has been *el pollo* (the chicken), particularly, "imported chicken contaminated with salmonella" (Cruz and Martínez 1993, 5B).[9]

Yet the Juárez citizenry was baffled and disconcerted by the ironic fact that "these foodstuffs are [also] distributed to local grocery stores, hospitals, [and] restaurants" (Cruz and Martínez 1993, 5B), yet no massive intoxications were being reported from these establishments. Furthermore, in spite of the "constant and periodic revisions to which cafeterias [were being] subjected" (Martínez and Cruz 1993, 3B), in most cases, the inspectors hardly found any serious kitchen violations or faults during the 1993 cases (Cruz and Martínez 1993, 5B). As journalist Juan Manuel Cruz noted, "The inspectors confirmed that the acquisition of foodstuffs, the quality of the products, as well as their handling and preservation, [were] adequate" (1993, 3B).

In spite of the lack of evidence regarding the mishandling of foodstuffs, local and federal health inspectors ordered cooks and other cafeteria personnel to attend "seminars and training courses [*cursos de capacitación*] on the handling and preservation of food" (Martínez and Cruz 1993, 3B). Corcom's cafeteria was closed [*clausurada*] even though "the inspectors found no fault whatsoever in the handling of foodstuffs on a second revision" (Cruz 1993, 3B).

These official inspectors, with their vigilant inspections and preventive searches inside maquiladora cafeterias, were looking for the causes of massive intoxications in the wrong place (the cafeteria) and blaming the wrong people (cooks). Instead, I suggest that we look at the structural forces (both micro and macro) of factory life, particularly at the exigencies of capitalist maquiladora production and how these multiple factors can produce incidents such as the food-poisoning cases of the 1990s. In the case of the shop floor and the cafeteria, we must examine the supervision, monitoring, inspection, and constant surveillance of maquiladora production. As I demonstrate, abusive methods of labor control are manifested at the "inspection stations" between either the shop floor and the cafeteria or between the restroom, the shop floor, and the cafeteria inside some global assembly plants. A detailed description of the rigid border inspections in the assembling production process itself will shed additional light on our understanding of the numerous cases of illness and, at times, death associated with food poisoning of the factory workers in Ciudad Juárez.

However, before examining how electric harnesses for automobiles are assembled at a maquiladora as an example of the latter system of labor control, we must follow the workers from their homes to the workplace. This should help provide the larger context, within a particular working day, in which factory inspections assault the toiling bodies.

Getting to Work: Bus Drivers, Factory Workers, and Security Guards

The capitalist forces of globalization operating on the streets of Ciudad Juárez must effectively connect the industrial parks with the working-class neighborhoods. The key material nexus in this process is the *rutera*, which is continuously used by workers to get to work. The majority of maquila workers, after thirty years of industrialization, still cannot afford to buy their own car, so they ride the *rutera*, or the *ruta*, as they sometimes call it. *Ruteras* are vans or buses that are a product of the maquiladora industry itself. They have been in existence since the mid-1960s. The articulation of neighborhoods, industrial parks, and buses, however, is not without tension. In fact, for late industrial capitalism to succeed in this endeavor, the factory workers and the bus drivers must be pitted against one other. On the one hand, the bus drivers must constantly strive to be efficient for both factory workers and (indirectly) multinational corporations.[10] On the other hand, the factory workers need a reliable labor force of *drivers* to allow them to comply with corporate expectations of arriving at the factory on time. Yet, just like the workers, only in their case on the streets, the drivers are challenged daily by the necessary balancing of time and space within a chaotic urban environment, itself largely created by the needs of late industrial capitalism.

Since the mid-1980s, most *ruteras* have been buses (which resemble American public-school buses). In the early 1980s, they were minibuses. Before that, in the late 1970s, they were vans, usually Chevy vans. Before the vans, between 1968 and 1976, most *ruteras* were four-door cars. The size of the *rutera* has grown according to the growth of the maquiladora industry. If people have a hard time getting off the buses today, imagine trying to get out of the crowded four-door cars on time. In the beginning of the maquiladora industry, cars were preferred to normal buses because the former were faster and could get to the industrial parks on time. Before the industry arrived, there were only two types of inexpensive public transportation in Ciudad Juárez: *transportes urbanos* and *transportes del valle* (buses that circulated in the urban areas and those that connected the rural valley and the downtown section, respectively). Today, the "rural" areas that previously surrounded the city have practically disappeared; the agricultural fields have become new working-class neighborhoods and maquiladora industrial parks (including the major ones, San Lorenzo, Bermúdez Park, and Río Bravo in Zaragoza, now a working-class suburb of Juárez). In this process, by the mid-1980s, the *rutera* concept (using a fast-paced vehicle to transport factory workers on time) took over, and thus most *ruteras* today are buses that circulate and penetrate all corners of the border metropolis, from Malecón Avenue (along the river in the north) to the Juárez Airport (in the south) and from Colonia Anapra in the west (now bordering Sunland Park, New Mexico) to Zaragoza in the far east (see Figures 4.1–4.3).

Consequently, as the city and the maquiladora industry grew, larger vehicles were needed. Today, the maquiladoras have helped create an urban environment in which huge buses push speed limits in the narrow streets of an unplanned and crowded city. The end results have been chaotic: automobile accidents have increased, often sending maquila workers, who are on their way to work, to the hospital.[11] Also, workers have had to adapt their bodies to the wobbling movements of the buses that (while trying to beat other buses) constantly speed up and stop, sometimes from block to block, on mostly unpaved streets in the periphery, just as they have to adapt their waist and buttocks to the wobbling moves of the chairs on which they sit at the factories (two factories where I did participant observation had this "chair problem"—see Chapter 7; also see Fernández-Kelly 1983).

Since the beginning of maquiladora industrialization in Ciudad Juárez, there have never been enough buses or vans for the thousands of factory workers who need such public transportation to get to their jobs daily. Consequently, the driver (always a male), is always expected to pick up as many people as possible and get everywhere on time. During key rush hours (between 4:30 and 6:00 AM, between 3:30 and 5:00 PM, and between 11:30 PM and 1:00 AM), it actually takes a while for someone to get out of the *rutera;* he or she has to struggle (push and shove) in the extremely crowded van or bus just to get to the door. Moreover, once in a while, a person does not want to walk the extra block. Sometimes people demand to be dropped off at exactly the place they want, not one block before, even if the *rutera* has been stopping consecutively in the previous eight or ten blocks.[12] Thus, in the actual transporting of people from their neighborhoods to the factories, the individuals who probably feel the most tension in this environment are the drivers, who must drive and produce efficiently for the maquiladora industry (which in turn provides the passengers). Drivers are the individuals responsible for taking hundreds of people to work (50–60 people easily fit on one bus at any given time). They are constantly caught in a contradiction between getting to the industrial parks on time and picking up *everybody* who is going to work, at least until the bus is full. Sometimes, workers would pressure the driver because *he* is causing them to be late.[13] But the historical and material conditions responsible for the environment they inhabit are not recognized by the actors themselves. Instead, the workers and the driver end up blaming each other. Many times on the bus, I heard workers comparing and complaining about drivers, especially on the way to work.[14]

The factory workers, however, must balance a much more immediate economic dilemma when riding the *ruteras:* In no uncertain terms, being late or being absent has serious economic consequences for the workers. In most factories, if the workers arrive late, after 6:00 AM, they lose the weekly and monthly bonuses as well as other benefits for that particular month (see Figure 6.5). At one of the transnationals where I worked, a worker can be ten minutes late without punishment. Between 6:10 and 6:30, they let you in, while keeping track of those who are tardy. After three "tardies," they "talk" to the worker, giving him or her a warning. Also, after 6:30, the guards might not let you in, sending you home for the day because the company might not want to pay you for nine hours when you have worked only eight and one-half. The guards themselves are capable of returning the workers as they see fit, as we will see below. These local inspections outside the factory are an everyday occurrence. As I recorded in my field journal (which I used to write at the end of the working day) while carrying out participant observation on the streets of Ciudad Juárez:

It rained all night. I didn't think I was going to make it. I was late today. It was already 5:25 AM. I also got wet in the rain. Four men and a woman were at the bus stop. Two *ruteras* (buses) drove by but didn't stop. Three guys began running toward Surgikos (three blocks away), where the *rutera* usually unloads some of the people. The other guy and I did not run; we walked in the same direction. The woman decided to return home instead.

Figure 6.5. In this ad, note the bonuses offered to the workers if hired: bonus for groceries (to be exchanged in local market places), $55.00 pesos ($9 pesos to a dollar at that time); bonus for being at work every day, $35.00 pesos a week; bonus for being punctual, $35.00 pesos a week. . . . If after three months there are no tardies or absences, the workers on the first shift get a bonus of $250.00 pesos, and the workers on the second shift get a bonus of $300.00 pesos. Ultimately, however, all these bonuses are conditional: the workers must be at the factory every day and on time. Source: "Aviso Clasificado," *El Diario de Ciudad Juárez*.

Another *rutera* passed by; we waved, but it didn't stop. When we arrived at
Surgikos, the three guys were still there, waiting. No one had picked them
up. By 6:05 another *rutera* arrived. It was so full. I tried to get in, but the
driver couldn't even close the door, so he asked me to get down. I did. I
waited till 6:25. It kept on raining. Finally, I caught a *rutera*. . . . It had men
and women. . . . This driver drove quite fast. This *rutera* went through San
Lorenzo, a major industrial park; then we got to Bermúdez Park, the largest
and oldest industrial park in Ciudad Juárez, where this factory is located.
I arrived at the factory at 6:45 A M. I was not the only one who was late. A
woman walked in in front of me. The factory guards did not stop us. (Field
journal, September 6, 1989)

The next day, I wrote:

I got up at 4:30, brushed my teeth, washed my face, put my clothes on, and
took off running. I arrived at the same corner around 4:45 A M, at least half
an hour earlier than the day before. A young woman around seventeen or
eighteen years of age, brunette (*morena*), with long hair down to her waist,
was already there waiting for the *rutera*. She told me that there is only one
bus between 5:00 and 5:15 A M and that it usually stops to pick up people
at this corner. This "bus stop" on September 16th Street is about a 15–20-
minute walk from where I live in the Colonia Hidalgo, one block away from
Hermanos Escobar Street. The other *ruteras,* she said, usually don't stop
because they come full from downtown, where they are stationed (there
they pick up the people who have to ride to downtown from their neighborhoods in the western and southwestern peripheries: the most populated
sectors of the city [see city population map, Figure 4.2]). Most people living
in different parts of the city—west, southwest, east, and southeast—take
one *rutera* to downtown; then another one from downtown to San Lorenzo
or to Bermúdez Park. A lot of people who live on the east and southeast of
the city work in other smaller industrial parks (i.e., Juárez Park, Oneida, or
Zaragoza) and take different routes [see city map, Figure 4.1].[15]

The first two *ruteras* that passed by were full to the maximum. They did
not stop. So around 5:40 (we should start working at 6:00 A M), the young
woman told me that we would have to walk about four more blocks east-
ward, toward Surgikos. There, she said, the *rutera* unloads some people,
confirming my experience of the day before. Actually, we had not walked
because it had been sprinkling. We walked as quickly as we could. At ten till
six, she said, "Vas a llegar tarde" (You're going to be late). Yes, indeed I was.

The *rutera* finally came, unloaded a few, and we got on and took off.
The driver, unlike the previous one the day before, drove much slower and
was picking up everybody without really worrying about many of us being

late. I had been on the bus for a block or two when the radio announced the time: 6:15. One male voice from the back of the *rutera* sarcastically told the driver: "Chofer, sube a todos los que quieran (Driver, pick up whoever wants to get on the *rutera*)." I arrived at the factory at 6:30 A M. I was thirty minutes late. The guard told us (another guy was late as well): "Run before I don't let you in." He gestured to us to run in quickly. We ran toward the gate. I guess sometimes the guards help workers in this process: or do they help the company?

Inspecting Border Inspections inside an Electric Harness Maquiladora

In August of 1991, I carried out participant observation in an electric harness maquiladora that had two work shifts. The total number of assembly-line workers was 664: 407 worked in the first shift (from 6 A M to 3 P M), and 257 labored in the second shift (from 3:30 to 12:30 P M). The morning shift, in which I labored, had 265 men and 142 women; the evening shift had 174 men and 83 women. As with the other maquiladoras where I conducted ethnographic research in 1987 (an electronics factory—see Chapters 4 and 5) and 1989 (a garment factory—see Chapter 7), most of the assembling operations were not gender specific: either men or women were assigned to them. This maquiladora was not unionized and was a direct subsidiary of a transnational corporation.[16]

The multinational corporation had a serious turnover problem. In August of 1991, 124 assembly-line workers resigned, but the company quickly hired 116 new workers in the same month. This quick turnaround in the hiring practices speaks to the abundant supply of cheap laborers, both women and men, available in the region.

The product assembled at the automobile plant under examination is the electric harness (*arnés eléctrico*). What is an *arnés*? A harness forms part of a system of energy distribution, signals and lights, which controls and conducts the electric functioning of an automobile. If Japanese plants in Juárez assemble harnesses for Toyotas, this American factory assembles harnesses for Chryslers, Dodges, Camaros, Oldsmobiles, and others. Examining the engine of my car, I could identify eight harnesses around it. There was a sticker on one of them stating, "Assembled in Mexico." I recognized the one I assembled while working there. The *arnés* has three main parts: cables, connectors, and terminals. The terminals are about one-half inch in length, and the connectors measure from one to three inches long, depending on their use. The cables, however, vary in length, from two to six feet, according to the need and use of the harness.

Each and every one of the assembling operations that I describe in what follows is heavily inspected by its respective "foremen" (*jefes* or *jefas de línea*), quality control inspectors (*inspectores de control de calidad*), and supervisors (*supervisores*).[17] All these inspectors monitor the workers' actions as well as the coordination of these actions with the assembling process.

In the first operation, the cables are inserted into connectors via the terminals. This assembling process is presented to the workers through what supervisors call "the method": "push, click, pull." The worker is supposed to "push" the terminal into the connector, then after a "click" is both heard and felt in their fingers, they can "pull," and it should not detach by pulling. This appears to be a relatively simple process as long as it is believed that you insert only one terminal at a time. In fact, each worker has to "push, click, and pull," at least six terminals, and at most fifteen, all in one bodily movement and *all* in the right places. In a particular site or zone of production called an *área*, workers have to insert the terminals as the connectors are moving slowly, but constantly, on a revolving machine called a rotary. The rotary rotates around fifty workers (twenty-five on each side), while each individual worker should remain in his or her own assigned location and insert his or her assigned terminals in the right connectors. Terminals, connectors, and cables are identified by distinct colors—green, red, yellow, and so forth—which in turn identify for the inspectors the specific worker who assembles each part. In this way, even though fifty workers labor on each production line, the supervisors, the foremen, and the quality control inspectors can easily match a particular color of an assembly part with the particular worker who assembled it.

At the end of the rotary, once the harness is inserted, assembled, and taped, it still needs one more operation (at least the one that we assembled in this particular factory): the installation of the grommet. The grommet is a round object made of dark plastic with a small hole in the middle, and powdered with a material that left my hands tasting like iron or lead. The grommet connects the inside panel of the car to the electric distribution in the engine. It comes attached directly to the body of the car. After the grommet operation, the electric harness, *el arnés,* is completely assembled and ready to be packed (twenty harnesses fit in a cardboard box. The carton is about three by four feet).

The "production process" itself is quite telling about the working life and the working conditions in the factory. The workers must still eat, they must still go to the restrooms, and they must still try to find themselves: they still joke, they still complain, and they still strategize to keep their own human agency—all of this in the context of their dehumanization. For example, signs in the restrooms of one of the maquiladoras where I worked encouraged (read: monitored) workers to wash their hands, not for the benefit of their own health, but so that they would not contaminate the material being assembled. This immediate privileging of the product being assembled, and the simultaneous inconsiderate displacement of the maquiladora worker, is also found at the automobile plant under examination. The work area is carpeted. The light green color of the carpet makes the maquiladora much more attractive to visitors (for instance, government officials and journalists) than anything else in the whole factory. Yet, when I was working there, all of us were literally warned by the supervisors that the carpet was not for the workers. The purpose of it, they emphasized, was to protect the cables and terminals whenever they were accidentally dropped. In a similar way, the protective tape provided is not always to protect the workers' fingers but often to prevent the workers from contaminating the terminals with their human flesh. This was also the case in the electronics factory where I worked in 1987: Gloves were given to us so that we would not contaminate the microcircuits. The supervisor used to tell the workers that they would not want to be responsible for such tragedies as the Challenger's explosion in 1986. (This corporation provided NASA with the electronic "parts" necessary for certain machinery, i.e., rockets and missiles). In the sewing factory where I labored in 1989 (see Chapter 7) and which assembled hospital supplies (surgery gowns), an acrylic fiber cap for the head was forced on the laborers while working so that their hair would not go into the hospital gowns being assembled: "It can kill a patient undergoing surgery," the trainers and supervisors would tell the factory garment workers.

In this context, recovering a human subjectivity at the rotary while disassembling themselves in order to assemble an electronic harness is no easy task. I interviewed Carlos, who described his experience and that of his coworkers in a similar harness maquiladora:

> Since it is very hard work, people leave constantly. They cannot take it any longer. Most electric harness factories are always hiring. Some workers only last two months, some last three months, some last longer! At the lines, our fingers get tired of grabbing the terminals. We have to press our fingers onto the terminals; often they go numb. They give you masking tape so that our fingers will not get damaged, since the terminal is pure metal. We had to work fast, very fast. It was a lot of work. For example, I used to work assembling three cables. I knew it was a lot of work: the first had eight or nine terminals to insert, the second cable had one, the third one had two or three terminals. Then, in one fraction of a minute, as the machine rotates, we only had six or seven seconds to assemble all the cables. . . . They would tell us, "You have to keep up with it. That's why you are here, because you guys are good." They would brainwash us. "Otherwise, we wouldn't have placed you here [at the rotary]," they would say. We know that it is hard work. But because it is a job, because you want them to like you, you try your best.

The former are all concrete examples of the extent to which these workers, while assembling parts, are constantly being inspected and surveilled down to their own body parts: their fingers, their own hair—and even down to the time they use to put food in their stomachs, as we will now see.

The Cafeteria: Going to Lunch

The global assembly plants located in Ciudad Juárez, in ironic conjunction with Mexican labor law, have clearly spelled out very precise rules for the workers to follow—whether it involves their assembly-line work or their breaks. These forms and strategies for controlling the working class inside the factories are found in a document accurately named *Reglamento interior del trabajo* (*Internal Rules for the Workplace*), which is given to all workers when they are hired. Specific rules relevant to our purpose at hand are Article 13 and Article 54. Article 13, for instance, declares that:

> The workers will be able to enjoy [*disfrutar*] one half-hour break during the working day. They will be able to leave the shop floor and they can use that time according to their own judgment, either to relax or to eat a meal. . . . Whenever the workers go for their meals, they should check their time card and should do the same when they come back from eating. If the WORKERS exceed the thirty-minute limit, they will receive disciplinary action according to the Reglamento [the Ruling]. (Article 13 from *Reglamento interior del trabajo* 1980, 4)

As we can appreciate, Article 13 clearly and strategically states the method of labor control regarding the workers' time and the use of their bodies. Furthermore, Article 54 identifies at least two "motives for sanction" specifically related to the uses of time (items b and c of Article 54 in the document):

> b) For not being in the area of work during working hours and without the authorization of the supervisor.
> c) For not being on time in the area of work at the beginning of each day *and at the end of each period in which workers take their lunch.* (1980, 13; my emphasis)

In this ruling, it is evident that the workers are not only being *absorbed* by the production process, but they are also being strategically *observed* by supervisors, foremen, and other figures of authority, who legitimize themselves vis-à-vis the *Reglamento.*

According to Article 13, the workers are supposed to "enjoy" (*disfrutar*) the half-hour break given to them. They are also encouraged to use their "judgment" as to whether they choose to relax or to eat during lunchtime. Is it possible to enjoy the thirty minutes, or to use them for relaxation after five straight hours of work (from 6:00 to 11:00 AM) under a rotary that keeps the workers constantly working, almost by the second? (Recall that they get up to go to work around 4:30 AM.) In spite of the fifteen-minute break given around 8:00 AM, by 11:00 or

11:30 AM, the body is more than ready to stop and to consume some food. Yet, before the workers practically run to the cafeteria, they must do two things. First, it is obligatory to check your time card before going to lunch. Article 13 makes it very clear that "whenever the workers go for their meals, they should check their time card and should do the same when they come back from eating." In order to punch the time card, one must get in line; and there are at least forty workers to an assembly line, or *línea*. It is time-consuming just to punch the time card; the punching clock immediately becomes an "inspection station" controlling the workers. The punching clock is clearly situated by management precisely as a "border inspection station" between the shop floor and the cafeteria.

And second, once you punch your time card, you have the option to either go wash your hands or go straight to the cafeteria. By this time, you realize that there are lines at both ends, in the cafeteria and in the restroom. Most people decide to go to the restrooms to wash their hands. Even if you handle contaminating material (metal terminals, powdered poliducts, and grommets), you must wash your hands as quickly as possible, sometimes because there is a line of workers behind you, pressuring you, other times because you want to get to the cafeteria as soon as possible. Most of the time, however, you do a combination of the two. By the time you get to the cafeteria, another five minutes have passed. Again, you spend between three and five minutes in the cafeteria line. By the time workers sit down to eat, they have fifteen minutes left for eating, if not less. Most workers finish their food in ten minutes (a meal may include, for instance, hot dogs, tacos, enchiladas, or fried chicken). The workers know, as the *Reglamento* says, that they "must check their time card when they come back from eating. If the WORKERS exceed the thirty-minute limit, they will receive disciplinary action."[18]

Although probably very few workers actually read the *Reglamento*, supervisors and other inspectors are in charge of the actual enforcement of these rules, especially those regarding the strategic use of time and space, that is, the use of the thirty-minute lunch break as well as the time used to monitor space and movement, both of which must *bridge* the shop floor with the cafeteria. The technical uses of the workers' bodies are hardly "acknowledged" (on the part of engineers) as being constitutive of the times and spaces (or border zones) that are being planned out and in turn inspected. This monitoring of some of the essentials of human life on the production line, with its lack of attention to the vulnerabilities of the human body, can have, and in fact is probably leading to, deadly consequences.[19]

No matter how complicated assembly production and food consumption can be inside maquiladora plants, the working-class subject (whether in the garb of a factory worker or in the garb of a cook) is always blamed for his or her condition as well as for the condition of others, such as in food-poisoning incidents. While it is true that customs should detect poorly preserved foodstuffs before they are imported into Juárez—as noted, chicken is mostly imported from the United States—the institutions themselves (hospitals, multinational corporations, and local government agencies—such as the Institute of Health) and the other privileged entities (managers, supervisors, and doctors) tend to present themselves not only as being rational and clean, but also as being innocent and therefore *noninspectable,* unlike the workers. The particular form of production in this electric harness maquiladora manifests the pervasiveness of inspection stations and other methods of control under late industrial capitalism. The highly surveilled space and the intensely controlled use of time, both of which the workers need in order to bridge the shop floor with the cafeteria, map out in concrete, material terms the coercive, nonincidental strategies of production used by transnational assembly corporations, such as RCA, Philips, and Surgikos.

Leisure Inspections, Border Moralities: Dressing Up, Going Out, and Confronting the Color Guards

The social environment, or *ambiente,* as the corporations and workers call it, at either end of the working day inside maquiladoras varies from factory to factory, often depending on the size of their respective labor force. In one of the maquilas (a garment plant) where I labored for this research (see Chapter 7), the morning-shift workers try to get out of the building as soon as possible to catch the *rutera* (to take them home), while those in the second shift simultaneously and desperately try to get into the building so that they will not be late. These timely junctures of working shifts are temporary moments of chaos: some literally push out; others literally push in. For about five or ten minutes, the two thousand workers working for this corporation met once every day in a narrow but long hallway. Needless to say, the factory is quite alive at this time of day—between 3:00 and 3:30 PM. Friends talk and sometimes yell at each other. Some of those coming in run to the cafeteria to get a Coca-Cola—*una soda*—which is very popular. Others go to the restrooms; some before they start working, others before they leave the factory. Though at least a dozen *ruteras* line up outside the building, not all workers are lucky enough to find a seat inside the *rutera.* Very often, I joined substantial numbers of workers who had to stand on the way home or on their way downtown.

Friday afternoons are a special aspect of the maquiladora *ambiente.* After 2:30 PM on Fridays, since it is payday, assembly production clearly relaxes in most factories. As in any human community dominated by industrial capitalism, receiving a paycheck lightens people's days. Maquiladora workers are no different, even if their wages are some of the lowest in the world. One of the paychecks I received was for $67,500 pesos for a nine-hour, five-day week, which included subsidized meals (which amounted to approximately $15,000 pesos). Thus, $82,500 pesos (67,500 + 15,000) was the total amount paid to the workers.

If we divide 82,500 by 2,500 per dollar that year (1989), the amount paid to the workers was $33 dollars a week. Thirty-three divided by five (days) equals $6.60 a day, and $6.60 dollars divided by nine (hours a day) equals $.73. Thus, seventy-three American cents per hour is how much the assembly-line worker was getting paid in this globalized transaction between multinationals and factory workers in Mexico.[20] These wages, which by no means constitute a living wage, must be supplemented by the wages of other relatives (parents and siblings on the part of single workers, and spouses on the part of married laborers) and by other economic strategies linked to the informal sector (Staudt 1998), such as selling cosmetics and organizing raffles, which operate in a relatively clandestine manner inside factories.

The "clandestine" selling of cosmetics (Avon, Jafra, and Mary Kay) by women is heavily inspected, and forbidden, by supervisors and other middle-management personnel, such as social workers. While the selling of raffle tickets was also inspected, it was unofficially allowed if the quota had been fulfilled. Although men do not sell cosmetics, they participate in raffles, which are sold on Fridays (when the workers get paid). Rito, a male garment worker in the factory where I labored, used to sell raffle numbers every other Friday, at $2,000 pesos per number (ticket), for which the winner would get two "botellas de pisto" (two bottles of rum or brandy). Rito was quite fast at sewing. He could roam around throughout the shop floor selling numbers as long as he was done with his quota, which was 225 gowns a day. (Rito, on his own time, was the one who taught me how NOT to bend the cloth while sewing the sleeves of the surgery gowns—see Chapter 7.) Supervisors and foremen tend to be more lenient with raffles (which are conducted by both men and women) than with cosmetics sales (exclusively done by women). Cosmetic booklets are more visible and are assumed to be more "disturbing" to the production process than individual lists of numbers and names used in raffles.

This unequal flow of a generally feminine item, cosmetics, and of a generally male item, *pisto* (liquor), whose sales attempt to complement the meager wages of the workers, is also a sign of the recent transformation of the maquiladora labor force, from almost exclusively female on the assembly line in the 1960s and 1970s to a more coed labor army in the 1980s and 1990s (see also Salzinger 2003). More importantly, the 1990s' pervasive and maquiladora-dependent deployment of couples in the *ruteras,* the workplace, bars, and discos is of major social, moral, and economic import. Indeed, several key social changes in gender relations have taken place in maquiladora working life at least since the 1980s (also see Chapter 4).

Before 1983, it was commonly believed that maquila women would dress up every Friday not just because it was the last day of the week and it was payday, but mainly because they were considered to be loose factory girls. Thus, in spite of having good reasons (getting paid) to be in a good mood (dress up), this re-

Figure 6.6. In this electronics maquiladora, the company is advertising for both male and female assembly-line workers, "*Operadoras(es),*" to work on the first and second shifts, and for only men to work on the third shift. Note the age requirement: between sixteen and forty-five years of age. The corporation is luring workers by asking them: "Do you want to earn an excellent salary? Come and sign on with us." Source: "Aviso Clasificado," *El Diario de Ciudad Juárez.*

laxed ambience has been interpreted (and inspected) as being socially immoral since the arrival of the maquiladora industry. This was and continues to be a misconception about what maquiladora life is about. In spite of this, throughout the sixties and seventies, there was a ridiculous but powerful myth in Juárez about all maquiladora women being loose, or sexually immoral. Now that men are incorporated into the assembly line (see Figure 6.6), however, and thus brothers, cousins, and husbands work alongside their sisters, wives, and other female friends, the myth is in the process of collapsing. Unfortunately, it still lives in the minds of that portion of the population that has not experienced assembly-line life and therefore is ignorant about it. This includes some journalists, local politicians, and managers (see Wright 1998), as well as the workers' mothers, fathers, and other people in the Juárez community who are hardly ever directly exposed to the working day of assembly-line workers.[21]

Just like their predecessors in the 1960s and 1970s, maquiladora workers throughout the 1980s and 1990s were nonmonolithic, but rather culturally and socially heterogeneous. While in the field in the late 1980s and early 1990s, and while visiting the city throughout the 1990s, I found very few factory women and men who could be considered sexually vulgar, even by local standards. The vast majority are struggling working-class people who want to make a well-deserved decent living and also, as Fernández-Kelly demonstrated in 1983, to have some fun.[22]

It is in this larger cultural context of work and leisure that we must appreciate the tradition, established by maquila women of the 1960s and 1970s, of dressing up every Friday just to make their lives more bearable and enjoyable. Most of the women who dress up on Fridays wear a semiformal dress. Several of them would wear jeans, high heels, and a formal or semiformal blouse, all accompanied by moderate, and often pronounced, makeup. The makeup is usually purchased in downtown Juárez, downtown El Paso (for those who have a purchasing passport), or, as I mentioned earlier, from local Avon and Jafra agents already infiltrated inside maquilas.

The cultural practice of dressing up on Fridays has influenced the men who have been hired in the factories since the 1980s. Men are not as fashionable as some of the women. This is so because working-class Mexican women, historically and culturally, are and have been expected to dress up for society, more so than working-class Mexican men. When the men change their type of outfits on Fridays, they dress in such a way that those men who do it (and it is also true that not all women dress up on Fridays) dress differently than on other days. For example, rather than wearing an old, casual pair of pants and a simple T-shirt, they wear well-ironed blue jeans and a nicely ironed dress shirt, usually cowboy style. Those men who prefer baggy pants—zoot-suit style—instead of jeans accompany them with a well-ironed white T-shirt. In northern working-class Mexican culture, a person in well-ironed clothes is usually considered to be, if it is a woman, disciplined with her persona, and, if it is a man, well taken care of by a woman (mother, wife, or sister).[23] More and more, men are ironing their own clothes, in large part due to the social transformations that concern us here. In either case, for working-class people who might not have the financial resources to consume the most recent fashions, ironing their most "decent" belongings has always been an option in contemporary modern Mexico. Social relations and expectations along gender lines inside maquiladoras are changing more and more from a female-dominated working-class culture to a factory culture life that is centered on the working-class experience of both men and women, where both members in a couple dress up, both work hard all week, both get up early, and both get paid on the same day: Friday.[24]

After work on payday, most of the workers visit the local working-class restaurants, go to the movies, go walking in the American-style malls in the city (i.e., Soriana, Futurama Río Grande, Futurama Tecnológico, or Downtown), or visit the local bars and discos. Yet, unfortunately, in Ciudad Juárez, they are not always allowed to enter some of these nightclubs. After all, the way one dresses up is not always successful at disguising one's face. Additionally, local women often inspect each other's faces, especially the faces of working-class women and girls, particularly when appearances have much to do with the type and quality of cosmetics used. Do maquiladora workers "escape the face . . . the face as fetish crossing forever crossed, the ur-border zone, the mother of all border-lands," as Michael Taussig (1998, 225, 231) would say? In analyzing one of the strategies of the Zapatista leader Subcomandante Marcos (who covers his face when negotiating with the Mexican government and the media), Taussig (1998) has recently noted that the human face is the ultimate border zone. Following my focus on scrutiny and supervision of working-class people in this chapter, I would argue, instead, that the human face is the ultimate target of bodily border inspections, and not just an ultimate "border zone," particularly in the context of the history of the conquest and of color hierarchies in Greater Mexico (see Chapters 2 and 3). For instance, one of the poems by El Paso Chicana poet Pat Mora (in Dow 1987, 32; see also Mora 1984, 36; italics in original) examines, with undeniably critical social commentary, a personal self-inspection executed by a "dark-skinned" Mexican maid:

> *"Mexican Maid"*
>
> Would the moon help?
>
> The sun did,
> Changed the *señora*'s white skin
> to red, then copper.
>   "I'm going to take a sun
>   bath, Marta, sun   bath, *sí*?"
> Marta would smile, nod,
> look at her own dark skin
>
>   and wish
>
> that she could lie
> outside at night
> bathed by moonlight,
> lie with her eyes closed
> like the *señora* wake to a new skin
> that would glisten white
> when she stepped off the dusty bus
> at the entrance to her village.

One of the main issues that emerges as a product of this kind of border inspection is the way individuals inhabiting this unequal social matrix find themselves within a discursive structure of hierarchies of color through which they discriminate against, punish, or privilege their targets.[25] For example, one common problem encountered by working-class people when trying to enter the most popular discos in Juárez is the following: Individuals who do not have "buena

Figure 6.7. This ad for the disco Amazonas announces that Fridays are for "pretty people" (*Hoy los viernes son de . . . gente bonita*), while showing images of well-dressed, light-skinned women. Source: "Gente," *El Diario de Ciudad Juárez.*

presentación" or are not considered to be "gente bonita"—meaning blond or at least white-skinned and, of course, well-dressed—sometimes are literally told at the door, "You cannot come in" (see Figure 6.7). The gatekeepers or guards, usually males, tend to use the (by now) well-known excuse that the disco club is holding a private reception. With the availability of a cultural color hierarchy (see Chapter 3), and with the cultural expectation that Mexicans should "dress up" when going out, the owners and managers of most of these nightclubs do not even [have to] bother with dress codes.[26]

In Ciudad Juárez, the discos that have been associated with this type of discrimination are Cosmos, Electric Q, and Vértigo. The politics of exclusion along color-class lines in Juárez is practiced according to the popularity, among the middle and upper classes, of the disco. The members of these relatively privileged classes include supervisors, secretaries, and other middle-management personnel (see Figure 6.8 for an ad for jobs at these levels and the "ideal" kind of person advertised for). For example, Cosmos Discotheque, during the late 1970s and early 1980s; Electric Q, during the 1980s; and Vértigo, throughout the 1990s, were accordingly avoided by most working-class maquiladora workers. Even though Fernández-Kelly identified some female maquiladora workers who went to Cosmos during the 1978–1979 period (1983, 130), she also noted, quite accurately, that most of them went out dancing to "the Malibú," a working-class club. Throughout the 1980s, working-class people attended both the Afro Bar and the Malibú (instead of Electric Q and Cosmos), sometimes called Maquilú (from the word *maquiladora*), until it burned down; and in the 1990s, maquiladora workers and other working-class people tended to go to such places as

Figure 6.8. In this ad for a "*recepcionista*" (receptionist), an image of a fashionable Euroamerican female is used. In addition to fulfilling several work-related requirements, she must have *excelente presentación* (an excellent image) and must be female as well as "preferably" single. Source: "Aviso Clasificado," *El Diario de Ciudad Juárez*.

Excalibur, Bandoleros, El Dragón, and Río Bravo (instead of going to Vértigo Discotheque).

The problem of the face-as-fetish in the Mexican community also manifests itself in color terms in the everyday life of working-class families. In her pioneering research conducted among maquiladora female workers in Ciudad Juárez during 1978–1979, Fernández-Kelly documented several instances of this color problem. One of Fernández-Kelly's female informants described her six-month-old son (her eldest child, who died of a respiratory disease) and youngest daughter, Astrid, in the following "colorful" terms:

> Of my three children, he was the best. His skin was as white as ivory (whereas Astrid is much too dark) and he was a boy too. He never gave me a day's worry until the week of his death. (Margarita, cited in Fernández-Kelly 1983, 161)

Margarita's language shows not only how children within Mexican families are distinguished by their color, but also her preference for boys (as opposed to girls) and for white skin rather than her own skin pigmentation, which is similar to that of her daughter: "dark." In a previous statement, Fernández-Kelly described mother (Margarita) and daughter (Astrid): "Astrid, a miniature replica of her beautiful mother, was four years old" (ibid., 161). At times, it is not clear whether the discourse of color in Fernández-Kelly's narrative is being used by the informants themselves. One time, when Astrid participated in a United Nations parade in Ciudad Juárez, the four-year-old girl had to wear a gown representing Albania. Fernández-Kelly depicted the mother's reaction to her festively dressed little daughter in the following manner:

> She bathed and dressed her with the care of a collector about to display her finest possession. Astrid's hair was braided, her fingernails and lips enhanced by a touch of pink. As she looked at her daughter, Margarita wondered whether Albanian women had *brown skin*. (Fernández-Kelly 1983, 168; my emphasis)

In another instance, when Astrid's father, Rubén, and one of his friends tried illegally to take the plane to Phoenix, Arizona, at the El Paso airport, Fernández-Kelly described a border inspector's—the airline clerk's—initial suspicion of them in the following terms: "At the airline counter a clerk stared at them suspiciously, observing their features, the *color of their skin* and their sparse luggage" (1983, 166; my emphasis).

That both the working-class informants and the cosmopolitan Mexican anthropologist (Fernández-Kelly) are equally captivated by the problem of color is clear evidence of the presence of this internal border (or "internal frontier," as Ann Stoler [1991] calls it), which in this particular case is a complex product of the history of conquest and colonialism. This color hierarchy, through which Mexican people regularly situate themselves, often articulates with border inspections at the crossing of the international bridge between El Paso and Ciudad Juárez.

This brings me to the border inspections experienced by two maquiladora men who tried to cross the "bridges" from Mexico into their destinations in the United States, but failed.[27] So far, the chapter has shown that border crossings associated with the workers' residential neighborhoods, the city streets, the factory shop floor, and the nightlife cannot be completely understood without their respective inspections. In the section that follows, it is argued that even in international border crossings, inspections of the working-class subject overshadow and question any theoretical reductionism associated with loose applications of "crossing borders."

International Border Crossings: Crossers Meet Inspectors

Roberto was born in Ciudad Juárez but lived and grew up in Parral, the third-largest city in the state of Chihuahua. He went back to Juárez after finishing middle school and immediately started working in the maquiladora industry on the assembly line. I met him at an electronics maquiladora where both of us assembled microcircuits for computers. At eighteen years of age, Roberto had already worked in two other maquiladoras. He told me about two of his experiences crossing the international bridge between El Paso and Ciudad Juárez; one incident related to the time he tried to get his commuter's passport (*pasaporte local*) back but failed; the other occurred when he tried, unsuccessfully, to smuggle his younger (male) cousin into El Paso. This latter failed attempt was the cause for the confiscation of his commuter's passport in the first place. In what follows, Roberto describes his encounter with an INS officer *inside* the Border Inspection Station at El Paso.[28]

> One day I went and had all the paperwork with me including the . . . letter of recommendation from the maquiladora. It was in August and I think it was the 4th or 5th of the same month. Now, this guy [the INS officer] asked me for a letter [of recommendation] from August, but I had one from the month of July. So he told me to return the next day. I went to the factory on the same day and luckily they gave me another letter [*y sí me la dieron, hasta por suerte*]. The officer had told me that that was all I needed: just the letter. So I went like all hell [*a la chingada*], and the . . . guy now asked me for a check stub from the month of August, and this was on a Thursday! So I told him: "Sir, don't be so ignorant: Tell me how you expect me to bring you a check stub from August if this is the 5th and it's barely Thursday and

I don't get paid until tomorrow, Friday" [as I already noted, all maquiladora workers get paid on Fridays]. Then he told me, angrily: "More ignorant than us are all the Mexicans." To which I responded: "Wait a minute, stop it there. . . . Fucking American trash [*Pinche gringo piojo*], what do you think you are?" "Don't insult me," he shouted back. "Then don't you do that to me, either," I yelled. Then I said: "You are also Mexican [*Usted también es mexicano*], so don't try to act like a gringo [Anglo], because I won't buy it." Then he said: "If you don't bring me an August check stub, forget about me giving back your passport." Then I told him: "Go fuck yourself: I don't want it anymore [*Pues váyase a chingar a su madre: ya no lo quiero*]." . . . So I grabbed all my forms and papers. I finally told him: "What the hell do I need the passport for?" . . . [Then Roberto continued:] I don't know why the fuck I went: I don't like it when others treat me like that. That's my rage [*Es el pinche coraje que me da*]. I don't know why we go there begging. What does that fucking country have that Mexico does not have? I will never go there again. There is no real need to go to the other side [*No hay necesidad real de irse al otro lado*]. . . . My mother had been waiting for me [in the waiting area], and she asked me about what happened. I just said out loud: "Let's get the fuck out of here [*Vámonos a la chingada. Vamos a mandarlo por un tubo al pinche viejo*]." [The latter expression is another way of saying "*Me hace los mandados*," which, like the corrido "Los mandados," means that Roberto will continue to challenge and resist the officer's orders.] My mom then told me: "With your kind of temperament [*carácter*], you will never get any papers back." "I don't care," I told her.

This same critique of the U.S. government's practice of exclusion (represented in the INS officer), especially when dealing with working-class Mexican nationals, either at the border or once inside U.S. territory, was also voiced by Don Ernesto, who is now in his sixties. He was a bracero in the 1960s and became a maquiladora technician in the 1970s and 1980s in Ciudad Juárez. Based on his experience as a bracero, Don Ernesto shared with me his assessment of this kind of encounter with the American government—via state officials:

In reality, the United States is very self-interested. . . . When a Mexican man works, he is appreciated: Americans really want him, they help him, right? But if they find an anomaly with a Mexican worker, then they kick him out. And none of the man's good deeds are taken into consideration when he's deported. I say this because I saw it myself while living in the United States.

Edgar, an ex-maquiladora worker in his thirties who is now a construction worker, tried to move to California in his search for a better job, but he was detained at an unexpected "inspection station" very near Los Angeles. Edgar, who was born and still lives in Juárez, told me about his attempts to cross into the United States: once in 1977, once in 1983, and once in 1988. The latter two attempts only make sense vis-à-vis "Los mandados," as a persistent struggle to challenge La Migra—especially after Edgar's encounter with inspections and inspectors in the United States in 1977, which is recounted in the following:

EDGAR: A friend of my father's drove us all the way [to California] in his car. And we almost made it, but in Riverside, this dude [*bato;* see Limón 1994] took out his bottle of liquor [*botella de pisto*]. He pulled the bottle out and drank the whole thing—took the last swallow—but the police saw us. It was the police, not La Migra. They asked if we had identification. "We don't have any," we said. We were underage. I was sixteen years old.

ALEJANDRO: Then the police called La Migra?

EDGAR: No. They themselves took us to the Immigration office. They'd asked if we had papers, and we said, "No." [Edgar laments:] We were already there, we were so close [*Ya estábamos allá, ya nos faltaba cualquier cosa*]. But they kicked us out to Mexicali. We would ask for food in houses, and people would give us beans, fruit. . . . We went through Chihuahua . . . no . . . they didn't let us go through Chihuahua. We passed through Mexicali, Sonora, Nayarit, Guadalajara! We were down there; it took us fifteen days to get to Juárez. When we arrived at Juárez, I was very skinny. If I'm skinny now, I was worse. We looked all black [*todos negros*], all dirty.

ALEJANDRO: How did you finally arrive in Juárez?

EDGAR: We arrived in Torreón and stayed at my [paternal] cousin's house. From there, they gave us money for the trip to Juárez.

ALEJANDRO: So when they caught you guys, your dad was with you?

EDGAR: The four of us were in the car: my father, the driver, César (my uncle), and me. We were pretending to be asleep, but the policemen woke us up and asked for our identification.

ALEJANDRO: Your father did not admit that you were his son?

EDGAR: No. That's what my uncle from California told my dad: "You should have said that they were your kids, and they would have done nothing to them." But my dad responded: "If I had said that, they would have taken me, too. One never knows what the police are going to do."

ALEJANDRO: So all three times you tried to cross, it was *de mojado*—as a wetback? [In northern Mexican Spanish, the phrase "*de mojado*" is a qualifying adverb, not a noun.]

EDGAR: No. The third time I had a permit.

For Edgar, passing, or crossing, with a permit over the official bridge is not considered an illegal transgression. If people cross legally with a permit, they might not necessarily feel that they have transgressed, even if their intention·is to remain illegally in the United States. In fact, Roberto also tried to reclaim his passport to be able to cross legally. One of the important distinctions in the way the two young men dealt with the inspectors is in their response to real, pistol-in-hand authoritarian state figures. Roberto challenged the immigration officer, but neither Edgar nor his father was able to talk back to either the police or La Migra. The potential for resisting a real Border Patrol agent, a real police "officer," and a real immigration "officer" is influenced and often determined by the structural (mainly economic) positions of those being inspected: Roberto had a job, though poorly paid, at the maquiladoras; whereas Edgar and his father, as unemployed construction workers, were jobless and therefore much more vulnerable in relation to the inspectors.[29] Today, although they occasionally visit the United States (they all have commuter's passports), Roberto, Edgar, and Don Ernesto (mentioned above) continue to live in Ciudad Juárez, with no plans of ever leaving Mexico.[30]

Conclusion

The life of working-class people at the U.S.-Mexico border is so fragmented, and yet so systematically inspected, that a culture of rebellion, or of class mobilization, was not found—not even in "the blurred zones in between" the borderlands (R. Rosaldo 1993). In fact, these border inspections allow us to see how class was being unmade in late-twentieth-century Juárez. One reason for this is that some of these zones are not so blurred; in fact, they are heavily inspected, supervised, surveilled, and monitored. Regarding cultural borders, inspections take place not only across such social hierarchies as gender, age, and class relations, but also within them (between workers and supervisors, between men and women, among men, among women, and so forth). In other words, as Sherry Ortner noted, we must consider the sites of internal politics "not just between chiefs and commoners or landlords and peasants but *within* all the local categories of friction and tension: men and women, parents and children, seniors and juniors; inheritance conflicts among brothers; struggles of succession and wars of conquest between chiefs . . . and on and on" (1995, 177; italics in original).

Consequently, the main difference between the analytical phrases "border crossings" and "border inspections" is that the latter leads to the analysis of the depth and breadth of the many "inspection stations" deployed throughout the social, political, economic, and cultural borders and borderlands characterizing human social life at the turn of the twenty-first century. Ultimately, "border inspections" should allow us to better inspect, in our social analyses of border crossings, who in fact crosses and who doesn't—both metaphorically and literally. The present chapter demonstrates that there are many kinds of inspectors in human social life, and they are all relatively privileged: health inspectors vs. cooks, men vs. women, whites vs. nonwhites, capitalists vs. factory workers, supervisors vs. assembly-line operators, gatekeepers vs. bar visitors, heterosexuals vs. gays and lesbians, parents vs. their children, husbands vs. wives, tenured faculty vs. assistant professors, professors vs. students, anthropologists vs. informants, police state officials vs. the citizenry, doctors vs. patients, and bosses vs. subordinates (so the supervisors, gatekeepers, and health inspectors in this chapter will, at the end of the day or at the end of the week, be inspected by their own respective bosses). These inspectors, or oppressors, do indeed reside on *both sides* of the racial and international border, and throughout the borderlands.

Only detailed border ethnographies (about the nation-state and its socially diverse citizens in their transnational contexts) that are theoretically informed by cultural analyses of borderlands, border crossings, and border inspections will lead us to better anthropological and sociological accounts of human social life in the twenty-first century, including the making and unmaking of the working classes. Any attempts to understand or explain one (cultural borders and their inspections) without the other (government-planned, militarily secured international fencing) will be incomplete—at best.

Although incidents do happen when crossing borders, border inspections themselves are more than incidental. There is no doubt that so far we have assumed too much about the "crossings" in the phrase "border crossings." Perhaps we should not cross or "drive" so fast over the "bridges" that we can't give proper consideration to the analysis of the difficulties presented to most underprivileged subjects when they try to cross a border—be it international, cultural, racial, or industrial. Privileged entities such as anthropologists and transnational corporations can cross the border much more easily than our informants and/or the factory workers can. As we saw, some workers might have difficulties even getting to the cafeteria. Most of these late-twentieth-century underprivileged individuals, as Behar aptly notes about the undocumented who try to cross into the United States, "put their life on the line simply to find [or keep] a little back-breaking work" (1993; 241). Thus, Behar (like most anthropologists, including myself), more often than not, is the border crosser, but not necessarily Esperanza. And even when Esperanza crosses, she (like Edgar and Roberto) gets sanctioned: she becomes, in the critical words of Behar, a "literary wetback" (1993, 234).

By examining border inspections metaphorically, literally, and ethnographically, I tried to enrich the concept of "border crossings" so that we can challenge more effectively not only "totalizing discourses in the name of culture . . . and . . . nation" (Ong 1995, 368), but also the evasiveness of late capitalism as well as its concreteness (which presents itself in the name of jobs to the underprivileged at the U.S.-Mexico border). There is no doubt that social life in the late twentieth century was (and continues to be in the new millennium), in large part, about border crossings. Here I argued that border crossings, and the class and cultural experiences they produce, cannot be properly understood without an analysis of the border inspections that constitute them.

I would like to end this chapter with a return to the *corrido* "Los mandados," mentioned earlier, and with Gloria Anzaldúa, the pioneering border theorist who defined the *corrido* in the following apt way: "Corridos—songs of love and death—are usually about Mexican heroes who do valiant deeds against the Anglo oppressors. . . . The ever-present corridos narrate one hundred years of border history, bringing news of events as well as entertaining. These folk musicians and folk songs are our chief cultural mythmakers, and they make our lives seem bearable" (1987, 61). Thus, in the spirit of making the lives of working-class border crossers more bearable, particularly in their plight against their varied inspectors or oppressors—who actually reside on both sides of the racial and international border and throughout the borderlands—I offer the last two stanzas and chorus of "Los mandados," which go like this:

Por Mexicali yo entré y San Luis Río Colorado
[Through Mexicali I entered and also through San Luis Río Colorado]
Todas las líneas cruzé de contrabando y mojado
[All the lines I crossed as a wetback and smuggled]
Pero jamás me rajé. Iba y venía al otro lado
[But I never gave up. I came and went back and forth to the other side]

Conozco todas las líneas, caminos, ríos y canales
[I know all the border crossings: roads, rivers, and canals]
Desde Tijuana a Reynosa, de Matamoros a Juárez, de Piedras
[From Tijuana to Reynosa, from Matamoros to Juárez, from]
Negras a El Paso y de Agua Prieta a Nogales.
[Piedras Negras to El Paso, and from Agua Prieta to Nogales.]

La migra a mí me agarró 300 veces, digamos
[La Migra caught me about 300 times, let's say]
Pero jamás me domó: a mí me hizo los mandados
[But it never tamed me: I KICKED ITS BUTT]
Los golpes que a mí me dió se los cobré a sus paisanos.
[The blows I received, I took out on their own people.]

SEVEN

Culture, Class, and Union Politics

The Daily Struggle for Chairs inside a Sewing Factory
in the Larger Context of the Working Day

At 12:30 during the thirty-minute lunch break, I had a chance to better see the factory. Its improvised aura was underscored by the metal folding chairs behind the sewing machines. I had been sitting in one of them during the whole morning, but not until then did I notice that most of them had the well-known emblem of Coca-Cola painted on their backs. I had seen this kind of chair many times in casual parties both in Mexico and in the United States. . . . In any event they were not designed in accordance to the strenuous requirements of a factory job, especially one needing the complex bodily movements of sewing. It was therefore necessary for women to bring their own colorful pillows to ameliorate the stress on their buttocks and spines. Later on I was to discover that chronic lumbago was, and is, a frequent condition among factory seamstresses.

— MARÍA PATRICIA FERNÁNDEZ-KELLY, *FOR WE ARE SOLD*

In the kitchen with the mint green walls and the dark pink cracked cement floor tiles, two women sit across from one another talking, a tape recorder between them. Our chairs creak and are not very comfortable; they are cheap wicker chairs that have become worm-eaten over the years.

— RUTH BEHAR, *TRANSLATED WOMAN*

Introduction

Both María Patricia Fernández-Kelly in 1983 and Ruth Behar in 1993 spoke briefly about chairs. They spoke about them, however, in quite different contexts. In Behar's case, chairs were used to produce a specific critical knowledge (a series of interviews focused on the gender, class, and ethnic struggles of Esperanza), materialized in a book to be sold mainly in the academic world. *Translated Woman* is not only a product of several friendly and intimate conversations between two *comadres* (friends), but more important for our purposes in this chapter, a commodity that resulted from the unequal relation between the anthropologist and her informant. In the case of Fernández-Kelly, chairs were used to produce an assembled item to be sold to the masses in the world market: jeans. The jeans, in this case, were a concrete product not only of factory workers and the sewing machines, but also of the colorful pillows. In spite of these differences, the chairs in both situations were inadequate for the purposes used, yet were ultimately (and ironically) central to both the production of critical knowledge against social injustices (through the enactment of feminist/Marxist anthropological interviews and participant observation) and the production of commodities (books and jeans) to be sold in the world market.

What follows is a study of the roles chairs (and seats) played in cultural transformation in Ciudad Juárez, in class making and unmaking, and in the politics of everyday life inside a unionized sewing factory. If, for most American cultural anthropologists from the last two decades, the term *politics* generally tends to go uncontested (usually implying for us "power relations" or pervasive inequalities), the term *cultural,* I believe, is less articulated. In the particular sewing factory where I did fieldwork in the summer of 1989, what was so "cultural" and political about chairs became very evident. The class subjectivities of factory workers were profoundly affected by specific political and material practices that aggressively confronted them once they became part of the global assembly line in the maquiladoras of the border city under study. This situational process articulating class and culture was manifested in the ways the workers changed the manners they were taught about respect and caution when they found themselves in newly encountered situations.

More specifically, my argument here is that under ruthless working conditions of late capitalist production (i.e., a shocking unavailability of chairs for all sewing workers in a particular maquiladora), commonly expected courtesies and notions of respect were transformed into cutthroat competitive performances enacted in altercations between workers over the use of chairs and other critical furniture (i.e., the best secondhand sewing machine). Furthermore, just as workers' cultural senses got displaced into struggles over decadent tools of production, I found myself studying "things" more than "people" and the base more than the larger structure of power in the workplace. Yet the complex sociopolitical articulation of the shop floor itself, the workers' many strategies, and the lack of any positive role played by the local union must be deciphered to elucidate both the cultural politics of the daily struggle for chairs as well as the unstable and fragmented interconnection between the global economy and the workers' strategies for survival.

The ruthless working conditions, the cutthroat competitive performances among workers, and the struggle over decadent tools of production often led to the unmaking of class, that is, to the impossibility of class mobilization against capital, in this specific case, the American multinational corporation, and against a labor aristocracy that defended its own and the company's own interests.

The notion of respect in the cultural setting of maquiladora production must be understood in the context of a fast-paced society in which there is much competition and aggressiveness tied to a way of life associated with production (on the part of the workers), with profit (on the part of the multinationals), and with being on time (especially on the part of workers, managers, and bus and truck drivers). One of the main purposes of this chapter is to show how the working-class subjectivities of men and women were rudely displaced and sometimes shattered once they entered the factory under study. It is precisely in this (not always symbolic) violent encounter with late modernity that I present the culturally specific ways of life the workers lead *just before and as they were being subjected* to a new border Juárez culture and to a new and unexpected culture of a poorly managed multinational sewing factory.

What follows are selected field notes from the period in which I conducted participant observation in the summer of 1989. The criteria used in the selection of the excerpts consisted mainly of my own personal sense of which moments could most vividly represent not only how I experienced the time, the place, and the people I encountered, but more importantly, the extent to which they clearly manifest what it meant to work in this particular maquiladora. I also considered the effectiveness with which the ethnographic excerpts represent the complex manner in which workers' subjectivities were involuntarily transformed in a politicized context of resistance—resistance not only to production but to a way of life they themselves must reproduce.

I tried to give coherence and remain loyal to the field notes by maintaining the chronology that produced them. I wrote my field notes either at the end of each workday or during the subsequent weekend. The observations I made and some of the stories the people told me inside the factory were selected in such a way that they would elucidate my theoretical arguments in this chapter—particularly the transformation of culture and the reproduction of the working-class experience as well as the complexity, at the everyday level, of making class mobilization impossible.

Ethnographic Material: Notes from the (Battle)Field

FRIDAY, JULY 28, 1989

Went looking for a job. I went to Bermúdez Park. I began at the north side of the industrial complex and walked south. I visited several factories. Actually, eleven of them, until I found one that was hiring today. I remembered that two years ago I had discovered the complexity of multinationals' hiring practices by going from plant to plant looking for work. I did the same

thing this time. This was the only way in which I could find out the extent
to which they were hiring men. I visited the following maquilas: Cummins,
Ark-less Componentes, Baxter-Promédicos, General Instruments, ACSA
(Appliances and Components), Componentes e Interruptores, Productos
Edmond, Delmex, Marsh Instrument, CCE, and lastly Hospital Supplies
(a pseudonym).

Each company had different strategies for hiring: some of them were
hiring only women, most of them were hiring both men and women, one
of them was hiring only men (Cummins). Some of them wanted letters of
recommendation (a new requirement that was nonexistent in 1987; this
requirement replaced the notarized letter, proving no criminal offenses in
the past, which was required of the men).

After having gone to all of the foregoing factories, sometime between
10:00 and 11:30 AM, I went to Hospital Supplies. A female guard was
standing in front of the building. When I asked her for an application, she
told me to go around the southern side of the building—to the gate. As I
walked in the direction she suggested, a young man in his early twenties
asked me if I was looking for a job. I told him, "Let's go get an application." Both of us walked to the gate. When we got there, the guard (another
woman) asked if we had our birth certificates with us. I had mine with me.
The young man who had followed me did not. There was some reluctance
on his part. He thought that in that maquila blood was extracted during the
medical test and that it did not pay well. I did not want to risk not finding
a job that day. So far, that was the only factory that was hiring. (It was a
Friday. Four of the maquilas I visited told me that they would be hiring on
Monday.) He left; I stayed.

The guard then told me to wait. At that moment, two guys approached
us and asked for an application. Only one of them was looking for a job.
He looked about seventeen years of age. Then another young male arrived
and asked for an application. Then the female guard opened the gate and
told us to go inside and to go around the building and to look for an office.
We found it, and once we were there, a secretary sent us to a room where
about thirteen young persons were filling out applications. The three of us
waited for about three minutes. Then a young woman in her early twenties
wearing a white gown gave each of us an application to fill out. While most
of the people in the room were done with their applications as soon as we
arrived, I noticed that five of us were still working on them: the other two
(besides the three of us who had arrived late) were two brothers, obviously
and visibly handicapped. Since they could not coordinate their fingers properly, they were still working on their applications.

The sixteen of us included four women and twelve men. After we filled
out the application, about thirty minutes later, they took all of us to the

nurse. She checked our blood pressure and gave us an eyesight test. Since I had left my glasses at home, I could not see well. The women were given a pregnancy test.

We went back to the previous room. At about 1:30 PM, they took us to the cafeteria for lunch. It was given to us free. The cafeteria was crowded. There were men and women, young and middle-aged, all dressed in blue, especially their gowns and head covers. We had a choice of meals. I had hot dogs; the other option looked like some kind of stew. They also gave us soft drinks (Coca-Cola, Sprite, Wink, or Fanta, all products distributed by the Coca-Cola company). After we ate, we went back to the waiting room. They told us to wait for a woman who was to interview all of us. She was supposed to have arrived at 2:00 PM. She arrived at 2:40. In the meantime, we just sat there, sort of smiling, sort of serious, sort of tired, sort of sleepy. Someone desperately mentioned that those who had arrived before the last three of us had been there since 9:30 AM.

All of a sudden, four men stood up and walked out. Two of them mentioned that the cafeteria was too dirty. Twelve of us remained. All except three were between sixteen and twenty years of age. At around 2:30, the woman in the white coat (perhaps a social worker) walked in and asked every single one of us the following questions: (1) Where are you from? (2) How did you learn about the job? and (3) What is your name?

This is how I learned that out of the twelve, only three were from Juárez (the two handicapped brothers and myself). The others were three from Mexico City, two from Torreón, one from Durango, one from Monterrey, and two from southern Chihuahua. Finally, the lady who was going to interview us arrived. She called us into another room one by one. Those returning from the interview would call the next interviewee. The interviewer, however, first called the two handicapped brothers. When they returned, they did not sit down. They began to walk out. Then I asked them: "Are you leaving already?" Both kept walking, with one of them answering: "They said (well at least to us) that they were going to let us know through a telegram [an old practice of the early maquiladora industry] . . . that's what they said."

He did not believe his own words. Yet he was not sure whether they meant what they had said. None of us had an explicit reaction. Some of us just sort of looked at each other. There was only silence.

When my turn came up, I went to see the lady. Her office was at the end of the hallway. I passed through two offices. All she said was that we were going to sign the contract later on today. She did not ask any questions. She did not mention any telegram. However, she told me that the medical doctor would check us over. I went back to the room to wait for the doctor, with all the others.

We waited for about an hour. Finally, the doctor arrived. We went to see him. I was always one of the last ones. He saw every single one of us individually, very briefly. When I went in, he asked questions regarding family illnesses or diseases such as diabetes and heart attacks. He asked if I smoked cigarettes or marihuana. I told him I did not smoke anything. Then he said, "There is one thing wrong with you, right?" (He had seen the results of the eye test.) "Yes," I said, "my sight is not too good." He then said, "Estás bien ceguetas, 'mano. Necesitas a un perro que te cuide" (You are very blind, brother. You need a dog to guide you). I told him that I wear glasses but that I had forgotten to bring them with me (actually, I did not want to look too "different" from the other workers). He did not say my eyesight was a problem for the job. By this time no one had mentioned the product to be assembled. This is what he said next: "Roll down your pants and show me your penis." I sort of hesitated but did what he had ordered. He looked at it and said, "OK." He then said, "Gracias, Alejandro." I walked out. The doctor was in his late thirties, early forties—a light-skinned Mexican male. I realized that most of us looking for work were dark-skinned or on the darker side. [Note: This observation on skin color was added after I left the field.]

I went back to the waiting room. We were supposed to wait for the contract. At 4:30 PM, the lady who had interviewed us walked in with a set of papers for each of us to sign: a job contract, Social Security documents, a union contract, and a checking-in card, among other things. They were seven documents in total. I was the only one who had a pen, being an anthropologist. She lent pens to everybody else. She said that after we signed all the sheets (hojas) to take them to her, but to show up Monday morning at 6:00 AM for training. One of the young men asked about the salary. She told him that we would be told about it later.

We signed all the sheets with each other's help. All of us went to her office. I turned in everything except my pen. Just before I walked out of her office, she yelled at me, "Alejandro!" I went back to her. She said, "Where is my pen?" I answered, "Look, see it. I was the only one who had one with me." "OK, thank you," she said.

She was a twenty-six- to thirty-year-old [light-skinned] woman. Four of us walked out of the building together. Then I asked, "What are we going to assemble here?" (¿Qué vamos a hacer aquí?). Arturo (the person who had asked about the salary) and Raúl answered, "Gowns—those used in hospitals [Batas—para hospital]." "It is a sewing factory," Arturo said. "See you Monday," I told them. All of us dispersed toward the street to catch a rutera. It was 5:00 PM.

MONDAY, JULY 31, 1989

I arrived at Hospital Supplies at 6:03 AM, more or less. I went into the waiting room. All of us were there by 6:10, except Arturo, who was from Mexico City (DF: Distrito Federal). A lady in white and in her late twenties walked in and took us to the second floor of the building to the "training room." She began by telling us the history of this maquiladora, our privileges, and, of course, our responsibilities, which they called GMP's (GMP stands for Good Manufacturing Practices). She used the English abbreviation but pronounced it in Spanish. We had four presenters in six hours, all of them women, including the union representative. This factory, unlike most others, does have a union. The union representative was a woman in her early forties. She said she had been working for ten years at Hospital Supplies. The factory started in 1970 with forty workers. In 1989, it had two thousand workers. The union is affiliated with the CTM (Confederación de Trabajadores Mexicanos/Confederation of Mexican Workers), the largest national union of workers in Mexico, but which is also a major political arm of the PRI (Partido Revolucionario Institucional/Institutional Revolutionary Party). The general secretary of the union within the factory is, at this time, the city's deputy for the PRI in Ciudad Juárez.

We had breakfast at 7:30 and, later, lunch at 1:00 PM. The trainer explained that they have three departments in Production: Gowns (Batas), Fabrication (Fabricación), and Packing (Empaque). In Fabrication, they make the sheets for hospital beds. It is not clear why they call it Fabrication. The gowns are those used in surgery by doctors and those given to patients.

All presenters, except the union representative, emphasized that we have to be very careful because these products are used in hospitals during surgeries. They told us that the patient undergoing surgery could die if a hair of ours is left on the assembled product and then sneaks into the body of the patient [see Chapter 6 as well]. They even claimed that being careless with our factory ID card could cause problems at the American hospitals — if they accidentally found one!

The respect and status accorded to these medical supplies reflect the respect unconditionally given to the medical community internationally. This strategic form of authority was also used to control the workers' behavior when assembling the hospital supplies.

At around 2:30 PM we went in to the shop floor for the first time. They gave us a tour of the place so that we could see the whole manufacturing process. There were people of all ages, between sixteen and fifty years of age, and of both genders. There was no gender specificity in the operations being performed. Interestingly, "in order to protect the products," anyone inside the shop floor must wear a cap and gown — all in blue.

Then we went into the actual training room, where several sewing machines were located. There, we were assigned to different machines to do different operations. Four of us were sent to a machine to thread a needle (actually the older ones: myself, Arturo, and two women who probably were in their early twenties. I seem to have been the oldest of the group, twenty-seven years old). The different operations were: Rivet (Remache), Cuff (Puño), Collar (Cuello), and Sleeve (Manga). One man went to Rivet, one woman went to Collar, one woman to Cuff, and four of us went to Sleeve (one begins the latter operation by learning to thread needles). The other five workers were sent right away to the shop floor. They were sent to Folding (Doblado; folding the finished gown or the sheets) in prepacking or Applying Glue (Poniendo Goma) to a plastic that supposedly protects the sheets from germs. The trainer (*instructora*) told us that Collar, Rivet, and Cuff took one full day of training, while those in Sleeve would take three to five working days. From that time on until the end of the day (3:30 PM), we were told to thread the needle(s) (*ensartar abujas*), which is the first stage of training. [The correct term in Spanish for "needle" is *aguja,* but most working-class people say *abuja.* Thus, following working-class etiquette, *abuja* will be used in these ethnographic excerpts.]

The four of us had a very hard time inserting the thread into three different places on the machine. The sewing machines are Singer 261. I do not know what year, but they look very old; for sure, secondhand. You need to have very good eyes, especially for one needle, which is practically hidden and has a very small hole. Arturo became anxious and desperate very quickly. He started saying that he was not going to come the next day; that it was too hard to thread and that the pay was too low ($63,000 pesos a week—$20 American dollars). Pretty soon, the two female workers in "261" (as this operation came to be called) began complaining, though less decisively. One woman is from Durango (a quiet, humble woman); the other woman, who is a bit more talkative—though not as vocal as Arturo—is from Mexico City. I did not say anything, perhaps because, as an anthropologist, I had to stay there to study the situation. I complained, however, whenever I couldn't thread the needle (*ensartar*). By the end of the day, the two men (Arturo and myself) had threaded the three needles only once during the whole day; the woman from Durango had succeeded twice; and the woman from Mexico City, three times.

TUESDAY, AUGUST 1, 1989

Today I arrived at Hospital Supplies at 6:30 AM. I was thirty minutes late, due to the slow *rutera* that picked me up this morning.

Because I am going through training, they did not say anything to me for being late. I told the trainer the reason I was late. She did not make a comment. She just said, using the formal *usted* form but giving me an order, "Begin to thread needles" (Comience a ensartar abujas). Two people were missing: Arturo from Mexico City and Cristina, the woman from Durango who had been sewing the collar.

We worked threading needles until noontime. It is very difficult. If you don't have good eyes, forget it. Yet they hire as many workers as possible, even if they don't see well. The company figures that if the workers want or need the job, they'll stay with it and still produce for the company (after all, assembly-line labor is very cheap to them).

As with almost anything in manufacturing, it is a frustrating process. The woman from Mexico City said, "I think I am going to quit; I'll be walking out of here blind and with a hunch on my back." As she implies, threading puts strain on your eyes and your back. The other two women in Rivet and in Cuff were working quite fast. For almost the whole morning, we stayed by ourselves, since our instructor was training more newcomers in the other training room (later I learned that there were sixty additional applicants).

At around 12:30, the trainer asked those of us in 261 to start practicing with the foot pedal, in order to control the machine. She gave us some sleeves to sew over the stitching, just for practice. This was the second step in the training for the 261 operation. At around 2:00 PM, twelve of the newcomers came into our room. They were ten women and two men. Everybody looked like a teenager between seventeen and nineteen years of age, except for a woman who seemed to be in her middle twenties.

The trainer assigned them to their positions. Most of them, including one male, were placed in 261. They began threading needles. We were already practicing with the machine. Since the trainer was very busy, threading needles was all they did all day long.

At around 2:30, she told us to begin sewing long sleeves (*mangas largas*), joining two sides of the same rectangular cloth to form a sleeve. This was the third stage of training. The rules for sewing a sleeve were to sew in a straight line, without wrinkling the cloth, and also to unsew (i.e., rip out the stitches) if a mistake was made. Thus, for training purposes, we have to sew and unsew and resew. I tried doing that until the end of the day, 3:30 PM.

I got home, had dinner, watched the TV news, and fell asleep around 7:30 PM. I got up at 4:30 AM the next morning.

WEDNESDAY, AUGUST 2, 1989

Because we are in training, we don't have to check in with a card. Everybody was there, the newcomers and those in my group. The woman from Durango showed up. Arturo, again, did not show up. I don't think he is coming back, since he thought the work was too difficult and poorly paid. He was right of course.

The woman from Durango said that she did not come yesterday because she was too tired from Monday. She and her husband, along with another friend, came to Juárez to look for work.

During the whole day we worked on making sleeves. For some reason, I kept folding and wrinkling one side of the sleeves. I took a few sleeves to the trainer so that she could see what I was doing. She said that she wanted to see "how" I was sewing them. I kept on "folding" them. Everybody was watching. The trainer is very direct and somewhat strict. I didn't get nervous. I think that my experience at the electronics factory was more frustrating because it was the first time I had been confronted with producing something under an authoritative gaze. In 1989, I am also much older than in 1987, and more experienced in doing both "field" and assembly work. This is important because I am not young (sixteen or seventeen) and I am not a young female barely starting to make a living. I am also not a new migrant at the border. In fact, I knew at that moment that I was the anthropologist learning, not the working-class apprentice.

These last three days, I had breakfast and lunch not only with those of my group but with those who happen to do the same operation (261). These are the woman from Durango and the woman from Mexico City. Today, another woman joined us. The woman from Durango is married and has been in Juárez since February. Her husband works in another maquila. The woman from Mexico City came on vacation but decided to stay and work to see if she can get a commuter passport to go to El Paso. She has the U.S. in mind, however. At one time, she said she wanted to learn English. She is single and hates the *moyotes*, "mosquitoes," a word she says she learned in Juárez. The woman from Monterrey is married and came along with her husband and a friend or cousin. They are staying in a boardinghouse.

Today at lunch, these three women and myself sat together and all of a sudden began to talk about where we were from. All three of them told me that I did not look like a guy from Juárez. The woman from Monterrey said that I did not have the accent of a Juarense. I said, "Maybe I don't use the same slang. But do you think the people of Juárez have an accent?" She said, "Yes, they have a certain rhythm."

For the first time someone is telling me that I do not speak like a Juarense. Maybe after all this time in the United States (New Mexico, Wisconsin, California), my border accent has changed, even though my wife grew up in Juárez and we speak to each other in Spanish. Maybe there is an element of change since 1987 and, thus, I am not the same "native" anymore. On the other hand, I remembered that I was talking to new migrants, who,

more than anything, have heard the slang of Juárez, which also changes
throughout time. I also realized that I have not used any slang there. It has
not been necessary. What comes together here are the different identities
that Renato Rosaldo discusses in his new book [*Culture and Truth,* 1989].
In this case, they have to do with gender, class, region, and accents or
rhythms.

In the conversation, the woman from Mexico City mentioned that there
are some very mean people in Juárez. She told us that she and her friend
were in the *rutera,* and that they saw a vacant seat available. She said that
when she was going to sit down, another woman in the *rutera* immediately
took the seat. She thought that that was a very aggressive attitude on the
part of the other woman.

On top of that, the unfriendly woman and two of her friends began
insulting them by calling them *"pinches chilangas pendejas"* (the closest I
can come to this expression in English is "miserable fucking people from
Mexico City"). Ever since the arrival of migrants from Mexico City, after the
1985 earthquake, a war has been waged against this specific population.
They are victims of a stereotype: that people from Mexico City are trick-
sters, aggressive, and deceitful. In fact, there are car bumper stickers sold
in the whole state of Chihuahua stating "Si amas tu patria, mata a un chilango" (If you love your country, kill a person from Mexico City). In Ciudad
Juárez, these migrants from Mexico City are recognized right away through
their accents.[1]

The woman from Mexico City was telling us that she was furious. She
said that the *rutera* was crowded and that they kept making fun of them
until the *rutera* arrived downtown, about a half-hour ride. She told us that if
tomorrow she does not come back, it is because she got involved in a fight
and would probably be in jail.

When we went back to the training room, the woman from Durango
could not find her purse. She had left it there and she shouldn't have done
that. Later, she learned that two of the newcomers had hidden it. At the
end of the day, she informed the trainer about the incident, but then the
newcomers accused her of being a *rajona*—a "tattletale."

We spent the rest of the day sewing/assembling sleeves. Those in one-
day training were sent to the lines downstairs. The trainer told us that
tomorrow we would be given the two sleeves and would assemble the
whole gown.

THURSDAY, AUGUST 3, 1989

Took the *rutera* on time and arrived at the maquila at 6:00. I was a bit nervous because I was barely getting the sleeves straight. On my way to the

training room, I saw two of my friends (the woman from Durango and the woman from Mexico City). I told the DF woman, "I guess you did not get into a fight." She said, "No, they took the other *rutera;* they better stop it; they don't know what awaits them" [the unlikelihood for a reencounter in Ciudad Juárez relates to the fact that it hardly ever happens that the same people from the previous day take the same *rutera* on the following day].

When we went into the training room, a few newcomers were already there. Two men and three women. I noticed right away that my chair had been changed. I looked around and saw that one of the newcomers had it. I told him: "You have my chair, *que pues.*" He said, "No, *bato,* I've always had this one." "Oh really? . . . OK, I hope I find mine." I looked around and, of course, I didn't find it. But I found another one that also had a cloth cover, as my earlier one had. It only had it on the sitting section, not on the backrest area, of the chair. All of the other chairs were pure wood, much harder to sit on [though highly improvised, these chairs are not the metal folding chairs that Fernández-Kelly documented].

Here, as in the other factory where I assembled microcircuits, the chairs, the machines, and most other equipment are obviously secondhand. Is this the new high-tech maquiladora? This condition of the workplace very quickly turns into a battlefield, where the workers, at least the most aggressive ones, try to get the best chairs, the best machines, and so forth. This aspect of work turns into a way of life in which the ideology of "survival of the fittest" dominates.

The new migrants, who are sometimes very quiet and "well-mannered" to begin with, either become victims of the situation or true defenders of their "own." With time, the workers, who may have initially been non-self-interested, become incorporated, in mind and soul, into a capitalist form of life and discipline, where if they do not become flexible, they do not fit in and survive the system. But since they have to eat, they opt for changing to the new ways; in order to remain, they must immediately transform their own cultural subjectivities.

I was surprised, when returning from lunch, that my chair had been taken again, this time by a woman. She just took it. She just kept on working, as if the chair had always been hers. What was I supposed to do? Or what is someone, either from southern Mexico or Juárez itself, supposed to do when he or she has been taught to respect what belongs to others? I went back to work, now with a third chair.

While all of us were working, it was obvious to everybody that the gowns that belonged to the guy who first took away my chair had disappeared. He was desperately looking for them. Two of the young women had hidden them. He finally found them. The situation had turned into a quiet game. Resistance? Is the company providing the poor working conditions for the workers to control them? (We will see.) While watching what was happening, I remembered that at the electronics factory where I had worked two years earlier the workers hid and stole one another's colorful pillows.

This type of behavior in the factory is for the most part quiet and silent. If something that "belonged" to you gets lost, usually you remain silent yourself, lest they think that you are a big mouth, unmale, a tattletale—you name it.

The fourth and last stage of my operation was to sew both sleeves and attach them to the rest of the gown. The trainer explained very well how to sew them. However, she did not really explain what the piece of cloth to which the sleeves are attached looked like; so I spent about thirty minutes to an hour just trying to figure out the shape of the cloth she had placed in front of my machine. We worked all day trying to make the gowns. It was so frustrating. In trying to sew the whole gown, I was screwing up what I had learned before (how to sew the sleeves themselves).

By this time, the newcomers had already learned how to thread the needle and how to control the sewing machine. They were already learning how to sew the sleeves. One of the new young men was very fast and good and was already at our stage—sewing the whole gown. He is around nineteen and from Parral (a colonial mining town in southern Chihuahua), but was raised in Mexico City. He was faster than everybody, including women.

MUSIC: The last two days they have tuned the radio to "Radio Mexicana." About 45 to 50 percent of all songs are by Vicente Fernández; 30 percent by Juan Gabriel and his interpreters (Rocío Dúrcal and Lucha Villa); and 20 percent by Gerardo Reyes, Antonio Aguilar, and José Alfredo Jiménez—all very popular mariachi singers.

While in the *rutera,* after 3:30, I talked to a woman who had worked six years at Hospital Supplies, but quit because there was no opportunity to be promoted. She said it was too political to get the new openings. She applied and applied and was never called. She is working third shift in another factory. Her new job allows her to take care of two children who go to school. She told me that there are some assembly-line workers at Hospital Supplies who have been working there for eighteen years, since the factory opened.

FRIDAY, AUGUST 4, 1989

The *rutera* driver had the radio on a station where a song by Juan Gabriel was playing: "Ciudad Juárez Is No. 1." The station then played "La hierba se movía" (The Weed Was Moving), after "Juana la cubana"—all *cumbia* songs. I arrived at Hospital Supplies on time. Today I worked all day doing gowns. Practiced, practiced, and practiced. I did about fourteen gowns, none of them perfect. Everybody in 261 did several of them. The guy who is good at it did about twenty that qualified! He was told he might be taken to the main floor on Monday. The rest of us were told nothing.

Today I "talked" to the trainer. She has been working there for ten years, four as an instructor, four as forewoman, and two as an assembly-line worker. She told me she was studying high school through the maquiladora's educational program, a product itself of the late 1980s and of the general problem of turnover in the maquila industry.

In the cafeteria, the food tastes good to me and is practically given as a bonus, another product of turnover and the result of the competition among multinationals in Ciudad Juárez [see Chapters 4–6]. Rotation allows the corporations to compete for the workers. This situation benefits the workers through the creation of such programs as subsidized meals.

Hospital Supplies has a training program; neither the electronics factory where I worked in 1987 [see Chapter 5] nor the automobile maquiladora where I labored in 1991 [see Chapter 6] had a training program for new workers.

MONDAY, AUGUST 7, 1989

In the *ruteras*, we now see couples. These people are from Mexico City, Veracruz, Chiapas, and Puebla, not just from Torreón, Zacatecas, and Durango, as used to be the case before the mid-1980s.

TUESDAY, AUGUST 8, 1989

Worked all day but made mistakes again. She did not take me down. Got home, but fell asleep till the next morning.

WEDNESDAY, AUGUST 9, 1989

A very important day. Cristina, the woman from Durango, was told by her newly arrived husband that "any of the *ruteras* will take you downtown." So she took a *rutera* whose route is through the "Rivereño"—a highway along the Río Bravo, literally adjacent to the U.S.-Mexico border [see city maps in Chapter 4]. When she saw the American flag from the distance, she thought she was in El Paso, Texas. She became very scared. She thought her relatives would miss her. I asked her, "But didn't you think you had to have a passport to go there?" She said, "I did not think of anything. I saw the flags and I thought, 'We're in El Paso.'" She said she did not ask anyone because she was embarrassed. She got off the *rutera*. She then realized she was still in Juárez. She took the next *rutera* downtown.

Cristina also mentioned that a woman and a man got into a physical fight inside the *rutera*. She told me that no one defended the woman and that in the "south" (*en el sur*) a woman would not get into any fight with a man, and that any man would have defended her.

Incident about the Woman Who Cried

The trainer yelled at a woman; the trainer is very strict. She spent too much time asking the trainee "Do you understand me or not? . . . Yes or no? . . . Yes or no?" (¿Me entiende o no? . . . ¿Me entiende o no?). The trainer can be very authoritative even by using the *usted* [formal "you"] form, here not implying respect but distancing. The trainer is directly responsible for twelve of us in that room, plus forty additional ones. Yet the trainer abused her authority by yelling at the female trainee. In the end, the trainer said she was really sorry.

Everybody was listening. Some of the workers thought the woman was stupid to cry . . . to let someone humiliate her. Some of them said, "There is so much work in other maquilas." At lunch, I talked to her. She told me the following: (1) "I became confused by her orders"; (2) "The operation is actually easy"; (3) "I could handle the previous operation and the trainer changed me to this place"; and (4) "I am in need. I have three children. This is August, and in September two of my children will go to school (last year only one was going to school). I need to buy them things. If I change maquilas, I cannot be caught in 'between' weeks not having any money [when someone starts working in a maquiladora, they don't get paid until the second week of work]. Besides, what if they don't like my work over there? This is why I am staying here."

At 2:37, the trainer decided to take me down to the line. She actually took three of us down. All of us were nervous. First they gave us meal tickets for the rest of the week. The woman from Mexico City did not feel ready to go onto the shop floor. She was just nervous, as I was. The trainer took me to the "temporary supervisor." She took me to Line X to a *jefe de línea*, or "foreman." There was no machine for me. It was 3:00 PM. He asked me to help count the gowns. I did that for twenty minutes. In Line X, everybody uses the 261 machine. There are more men than women. On the shop floor, the music is loud.

THURSDAY, AUGUST 10, 1989

Today they assigned me a sewing machine. Most machines are older than those used in training! The foreman was patient with me. One *chilango* assembly worker yelled at me and said, "Don't be stupid. Do it like this" (No seas güey. Hazlo así). The quality control people checked on me. Most of my gowns did not make it. It is a lot of work to repair them.

My girlfriends from training looked for me to ask how my job was.

Most workers stop at 3:00 PM. They clean their area in about ten or fifteen minutes. They wait for the foreman to give them their time cards (checkout cards). They will pay me tomorrow for the first time. Tomorrow is Friday and the end of the second week.

There were more men on the shop floor than what I expected (from my readings about the garment/textile industries). Many of them look very young, many of them look much older, thirties and forties. It is a real mixture of ages and genders.

FRIDAY, AUGUST 11, 1989

In the *rutera*, unlike last Friday, there was no radio on. I arrived at 5:45. For the first time, I had time to have coffee and sweet bread (*pan dulce*) at the cafeteria—something I had been waiting for. It was very delicious and awakening. I went into the working room at exactly 6:00 AM.

The foreman assigned me to another sewing machine, the place where I was to stay. I had to begin all over. Not all the machines function in the same way. All of them need to be tamed to your own abilities. It took me about forty-five minutes to get sort of used to it.

Amalio, from Celaya, Guanajuato, was assistant to the foreman and did not like Juárez.

A female worker was very helpful in teaching certain tactics or strategies for sewing fast. She was actually helping another man while I was watching. The woman in quality control seems to be very understanding. The foreman is actually indifferent toward me. This morning when I entered, the problem of the chairs reemerged. This time on the shop floor. I picked one up. The "owner" went to ask for it in a nice way. I was new. I did not know it was his. Later, the foreman and Amalio found me a chair. I left for a few seconds to go get something when I saw a young woman taking my chair with her. I said, "Hey, you're taking my chair. They just brought it to me." She just smiled. The foreman happened to be passing by, a thirtyish male. She didn't say anything. She just dropped it. Maybe she saw two males. Maybe she only saw the foreman with his yellow gown (this color marked the difference in power between foreman and worker). Mine and hers were blue. We were both at the same level. I could have been more aggressive if she had resisted. But I am not aggressive. More than likely, she could have taken it if the foreman had not been there. It was not my intention to intimidate her. That chair had been given to me in my production line. The young woman was from another production line. I wonder what happens when a young woman, newly arrived to the city, takes chairs from sewing workers who are gang members in their neighborhoods? How is the chair negotiated in these sites of gender, region, and age struggles?

In this production "line," using the 261 machines, there are four women and about six or seven men. It is still not clear where "Line X" ends. After 2:30, and since it is payday and Friday, it is almost party time. Production pressure clearly relaxes [see Chapter 6].

This afternoon I interviewed a social worker who works in personnel for an automotive factory in Juárez. Basically, she made the following important points regarding how personnel departments view the maquila worker in 1989. She stated quite clearly that (1) the assembly-line operator (*operador*) has the power in the maquiladora [this is, of course, incorrect]; (2) some of them work only the week of training (once they are trained, they might start with increases in salary or bonuses in other factories); (3) *pirateaje*, or "pirating"—when maquilas steal potential candidates from other maquilas—occurs when jobseekers just don't get to certain maquilas before they are hired, as I was hired at Hospital Supplies. The social worker argued that at one time, she and her coworkers were sent out to the streets by the manager to convince workers to come to their plants—this is pirating (*pirateaje*) among maquila managers. She also told me that everybody gets hired (except the handicapped, as we saw). She told me that they cannot just "select" who they want to hire. If twenty persons arrived looking for work, all of them get hired, especially on those strategic days when they have vacancies. This is the situation in the late 1980s in some maquilas. This explains why it was relatively easy for me to get a job, either in 1987 or in 1989.

MONDAY, AUGUST 14, 1989

It was a Monday—terrible! I didn't really feel like going to work. . . . The *rutera*, as usual, was crowded. The driver drove fast. Two young female workers were talking about the difference between this driver and others. I arrived at the factory at 5:25—unbelievable! Several people were already there. I went for my head/hair cover, but didn't punch in because the foreman had my card. I went to get coffee and bread; I like the biscuits, *bisquete* in Spanish, and the *quekis* (cupcakes). Other pieces of bread are *pan blanco* (white bread similar to French bread), *cortadillo, esponjas,* and *campechanas*—the last three are all decorated with sweets.

Time went by quite fast. Pretty soon, five minutes till 6:00 came, and I had to go in there. Boom! Surprise, my previous chair was missing. Shit! I had to look for one, probably someone else's. I found one that seemed not to be labeled. While I was getting the sewing machine ready, the "owner" of the chair approached me. I said, "Look, take it! I'm new here. I don't really have a chair." One of the workers was absent, so I grabbed his for today. We'll see what happens tomorrow.

After breakfast, I . . . worked till lunchtime, from 9:25 to 12:50. The foreman checked my gowns. He took them to another table, almost next to mine. He counted them. He said there were seventeen. *How could there be only seventeen?* I thought. I couldn't have done only nine gowns in almost four hours [since I had done eight gowns from 6:00 to 9:00 AM]! I felt very frustrated because I thought I had done more and I did not get to count them myself. I began to wonder whether someone had stolen the gowns. Could they do that? Could someone's work be miscounted or stolen? Of course it could. Tomorrow *I'll* count it.

I couldn't work anymore. I only did seven or eight more. It's a good thing that they don't bother you too much, especially in these times when the worker is more able to choose a factory than the other way around. I learned that even though the worker has to work as fast as possible, he or she has to keep track of how many he or she makes. This situation can create problems between workers, between the one who counts and the assembler. They'd better agree. If they don't, arguments are likely to emerge. Two elements pit workers against each other: the chairs and protecting their own produce. As I have noted before, in this way newcomers learn to be self-interested, since they ironically have to protect what is temporarily "theirs." It seems to be difficult to do any type of sharing in these two circumstances.

Lupe was unhappy because she wanted the air conditioner by us. Other groups had it. Why couldn't we? She was pissed. For this reason, she did not finish the standard—the quota. She said, "How can I finish when I'm so hot?" Even though the company hires two thousand workers, it does not have air-conditioning, at least not on the shop floor. Lupe told the foreman, "You come and sit down here to work in the heat."

TUESDAY, AUGUST 15, 1989

Got there at 6:00 AM. Checked in. Went into the huge working place. This factory is the size of three or four basketball gyms. My chair wasn't there; someone had also taken my little table where sleeves are placed to be assembled. A woman told me who did it. My sewing machine was all messed up (*desordenada*). Somehow, all of this was expected. Why doesn't management give a good chair and tables to everybody? I began sewing very late. It was a very frustrating day. For some reason, I spent about one and a half hours on one gown.

I was pissed at what had happened with the chair, machine, etc. Thus,

I could not work well. I cannot explain my frustration and fury. I even thought of quitting. I wanted to tell everybody about the chairs. Everybody has to get there early in order to protect their place; yet you have to produce. Is this possible in the late twentieth century?

Today we were told to stop at 3:15 instead of 3:00. The pressure from management was being felt. Lupe was saying that in another line, even those who went over the standard quota could not stop sewing.

The Gum Incident

We are not supposed to chew gum. Supposedly, Lupe had some. She insisted she didn't have anything in her mouth. The quality control guy said her voice sounded like it did! Lupe said that that's how she speaks—that is how her voice sounds. They insisted. She said she didn't have any. The man stopped. Then Lupe told Pedro, the foreman, that she actually swallowed it. Then one of the men sewing heard that and said, "Se te van a pegar las tripas"(invoking Mexican parents who tell their children not to swallow gum because their intestines—tripes—will stick together forever). She said jokingly: "I don't care."

WEDNESDAY, AUGUST 16, 1989

Today I made thirty-eight gowns, but Amalio wrote down forty. This is how the workers help each other, by writing down more than what they actually do.

Again, I couldn't find a chair. I finally found one, but it was pretty ugly. I was in pain all day. The chair wobbled too much. By noon I was already pissed. I thought of quitting again. I couldn't stand my back. This is how all seamstresses (men and women) hurt their kidneys. I was particularly furious because I had hurt my back very badly typing a paper for one of my professors in Wisconsin (he would not accept late papers). Physically, I could not take the job anymore. But I have to be patient because I have to get more information.

I had forgotten that the electronics factory also had a problem with chairs. This factory went to the extreme, though. Is this a general problem of the maquiladora? In fact, in this maquila, aggressiveness emerges as the first thing in the morning: trying to find your chair.

THURSDAY, AUGUST 17, 1989

The chair again! Finally, one was sort of assigned to me. The best I've had, but still old. Today I made fifty gowns, or two "bags."

Today the social worker talked to me. She came to my machine. She came to remind me that after a month of working there, I can use the other services (i.e., savings within the company). She asked me how I was doing. I told her that I was happy with the food and with the people. But I told her I did not like the chairs. She blamed it on the workers. That after five years the chairs get old and that people don't take care of them. I asked myself, "But how can the workers not take care of the chairs? They just sit on them. I never witnessed any "chair throwing." When under production, how can you harm a chair? Her response was a traditional cop-out among non-assembly-line workers within the maquilas (as we will see). [It is not that easy to question authority directly, especially when you are reminded that your opinion does not really matter; they always find a way out].

Today, I missed my line while coming back from breakfast. Two women laughed at me when they noticed that I was looking for my machine in the wrong place. Actually, they all look the same, the gowns, the machines. The hair covers and the gowns, by the way, conceal the gender of the workers. In the latter way, through the unisex uniform, everybody becomes just a worker. [This homogeneity is a reminder that they are a class, but one that, nonetheless, does not guarantee political mobilization.]

FRIDAY, AUGUST 18, 1989

Started working. Surprisingly, by ten till nine (just before breakfast) I had assembled twenty-five gowns. Surprise. By the end of the day, I had finished sixty-three gowns. Amalio wrote down sixty-five. I am really making progress. I already know how to sew right. All I need is speed (with efficiency): I need to coordinate every movement into one single flow, as the experienced workers do. In order to increase our productivity (but not necessarily our paycheck), body coordination is critical. This takes practice; repetition makes production work. A week ago I was making thirteen or fourteen a day. Today, I made sixty-three. Truly, I do not know how this is happening. As in the martial arts, practice of some movements, no matter how complex they are, makes them more perfect every time. This repetition in the factory, which is certainly class-based, erases traditional gender conceptions about who is or is not able to perform sewing. In the late 1980s, the instructors, supervisors, foremen, and managers know this political aspect of work performance.

By this time, I have been on the shop floor one week and one day (after close to two weeks of training). I made sixty-three. Arnulfo, who has been on the shop floor three weeks today, made seventy-five. I am catching up with him, unintentionally. Other workers are comparing me to him. Even Arnulfo asks me about my pace. I don't want to tell him that I've done "X" amount. I don't want any of my actions to cause pressure on him, especially from Amalio, Lupe, or from the woman working next to him. They are all watching me and him (I am the newest; he is second to the newest).

I have decided that since I was given four weeks to do the standard (253 per day), I can afford to slow down. I have to remember that I am the anthropologist. Sometimes I forget. The machine and the responsibility to produce take you over, no matter who you are. I don't want to cause any trouble for the workers, even though, in the normal order of things, someone other than me could have been slower or faster than Arnulfo. This type of pressure applied by the workers themselves is characteristic of industrial capitalism; thus, at times, the presence of a supervisor is mainly symbolic of the power structure, which pits workers against one another.

Yet, individual abilities may appear conflicting in working contexts where formalized standards are set from the outside or from the top. In fact, setting standards constitutes a goal that everybody should attain. Those who do not meet them get into trouble. This is, of course, part of pressuring the workers to work faster. In sewing, this is how surplus value is extracted and secured. Once the engineers set the standard (and the local universities trained them to do so), the workers will reproduce both the conditions that reproduce capital (profit) and the conditions that keep them there [see also Chapter 5]. Here, this occurs through the process of internalizing the idea that he or she must not get behind any other worker who has the same (or less) time as the target. There is no real sense of competition with someone who has been there longer than you have.

MONDAY, AUGUST 21, 1989

I talked to Juan, another worker, about the chairs. He agreed that I should talk to the union delegate about the problem with the chairs.

TUESDAY, AUGUST 22, 1989

The quality control person, a male, reports to the quality control supervisor, a female. He checks on us—Lupe, Berta, Juan, Víctor, Arnulfo, myself, Marta, etc. Gender relations can be very complex in the maquiladoras of the late 1980s, especially once we scrutinize the hierarchy. Also, there are two male foremen and at least eight forewomen.

WEDNESDAY, AUGUST 23, 1989

THURSDAY, AUGUST 24, 1989

I was too tired all day and yesterday. I can't write anything. Hardly anything new happened.

FRIDAY, AUGUST 25, 1989

It's been a tiring week. By 2:30 PM I didn't want to work anymore. The fore-man gave me two more gowns to repair. I repaired them by 3:00.

Two of those who entered with me resigned. Luis resigned because he was paid only $20,000 pesos from the last week worked. Even though he was incapacitated due to illness, the company should have paid him 60 percent of his salary. This is considering that he was supposed to stay at home. But he went to work two of those days. In spite of that, he was only paid $20,000 pesos (about $8 dollars), actually for only the two days he worked. He went to talk to the social worker, the foreman, and other people in the office, but everybody said that it was not their area, their jurisdiction. He went to the union's delegate, but he said he could not do anything. Because of all this, he opted to resign.

The other person was the woman from Mexico City. First, she said she was bored. Then she said they wouldn't pay her the "incentive" (extra money earned for extra material produced). She was told to make forty-five boxes, and she would make fifty-five or sixty. She also said that the fore-woman yelled at her in front of everybody. The woman also said that the pay was very low.

MONDAY, AUGUST 28, 1989; TUESDAY, AUGUST 29, 1989;
WEDNESDAY, AUGUST 30, 1989

In the restrooms, there is a sign that reads "The washing of your hands is important for the quality of our product" instead of saying "The washing of your hands is important to your health and for the quality of our product." [This privileging of the product over the worker is the most common and serious problem that characterizes the three maquilas in which I worked — see also Chapters 5 and 6.]

I've been very tired all these days. I was very sick Monday night and Tuesday morning. I did not go to work on Tuesday. Today, they gave me the following form to sign:

Control of Absenteeism

We remind you that to play a good part at work, your disposition is important in order to carry out your daily activity in the workplace and in order to get along with the co-workers (*compañeros*). Your exact, punctual attendance is favorable to the company of which you are a part. Thus, we ask you to explain the motives or reasons that made you absent on August 29, 1989. If you have a document justifying your ab-sence, please give it to us.

[I wrote the following:] I was sick to my stomach. (Me enfermé del estó-
mago.)

Good relations are possible only through communication.

Signature of male or female worker   Supervisor
Firma del (a) trabajador(a)

THURSDAY, AUGUST 31, 1989

[Important finding]
Thirty-seven people work on Line X: two men assembling the whole gown; a
man and a woman doing the sleeves; two women and two men doing rivets;
two women and five men sewing the sleeves; four women in glueing; two men in
cuffs; two women on the collar; five men and three women at two folding tables;
a man and a woman checking the sleeves; two men counting the sleeves; and
one man counting the gowns. There is one additional quality control male.

FRIDAY, SEPTEMBER 1, 1989

The demand for perfection from others is tied to the discipline a worker is
expected to have vis-à-vis other workers. Here [as shown in the previous
chapter] notions of manliness are manifested quite explicitly and without
mercy. If a woman is careless, she is just being "stupid," but if a man is
careless, he is not only stupid but also useless and unworthy as a male, at
that specific moment. This is also part of the masculinization going on not
only in sewing factories but in the assembly line of the maquiladora industry as a whole, at least in Ciudad Juárez. That women are being displaced in
the process is evidenced in this sewing factory, where I know of two male
supervisors and several male quality control people who have been promoted from the assembly line.

MONDAY, SEPTEMBER 4, 1989

Chairs are still the problem. I should talk to the union people.
     A new guy began to work today. He is seventeen and from Delicias, a
small city in southern Chihuahua. He went to elementary school and had

one year of middle school, or *secundaria,* as it is called in Mexico. The instructor from training brought him and said to me: "Ahí se lo encargo" (Please watch him in case he has questions or problems). He is very smiley. He has been in Juárez only two weeks.

I talked to a woman who was in training with me. She told me that they fired Alicia and that Antonia quit. She went back to school. The woman who had mistaken Juárez for El Paso when she took the *rutera* that circulates along the river also quit.

TUESDAY, SEPTEMBER 5, 1989

Today I made 110 gowns. I don't know how I did it.

The factory has a special program for workers who recommend friends (not relatives) as future new workers; whoever brings in the most, that person gets to go to Carlsbad Caverns or White Sands, both in southern New Mexico.

After work, the *rutera* was full to its maximum. It was sort of funny that after we passed San Lorenzo, someone released some gas and, believe me, it smelled so bad. It was very funny and embarrassing for some.

WEDNESDAY, SEPTEMBER 6, 1989

For some reason, I did not work as hard. That is, I only made seventy-five gowns. I've been eating with Juan. He is a very hardworking young man. He has worked in Río Bravo [an automobile maquiladora in another industrial park], an automotive factory where he assembled electronic harnesses. He left because of the low pay over there. Río Bravo would not let him resign. He had to resign after he began working in this factory.

When I went home in the *rutera,* it was very humid and hot.

THURSDAY, SEPTEMBER 7, 1989

I have not been able to talk to the union people. They say that they are busy. They are always with someone when I go into their office. Yesterday, the woman did not pay attention to me. Today, I didn't even walk in. The delegate was busy when I went to talk to him. He was telling other workers about how Christmas holidays consisted of eleven days (not fourteen, as some workers thought), if they work three Saturdays consecutively (maquila workers would rather work on weekends so as not to work on December 26 and on January 2; they work these days in advance). Tomorrow I have to talk to the union people about the chairs.

This is a very politicized plant. The general secretary of the union is deputy to the PRI. I do not want to get the workers in trouble. It is not easy to talk to them about problems. It takes time to make friends. Sewing is a very individual/lonely job; there is little time to create networks. It takes years on the job.

Pedro, the foreman, told me today to try to do more gowns. This is the first time he has put pressure on me. I worked harder, but only made 107 gowns.

The new worker talks about how his "ass" (*cola*) hurts from the chair. He is so clear and straightforward. His cousin also works there and eats with him. He now makes twenty-two to twenty-five gowns.

In the *rutera*, around 4:30 PM, there were some workers with books: English/Spanish. I asked one of them where he was studying. He said, "Capcom." He said they have classes after work, two hours a day of English and computer classes. He said that there were seven people in his class. Most people are too tired to stay after work.

Teaching English to the workers is a great idea. This is a product of the creation of bonuses or services to attract more workers. If workers had more time, they would definitely take advantage of this program.

FRIDAY, SEPTEMBER 8, 1989

I took the *rutera* for the last time, it seemed. It was crowded as usual.

The new worker was there. He grabbed a weird chair. He fixed the back of the chair, which was quite loose. Then he told me that the small table where we place the gowns was wobbling like a donkey—it would not stand still. This is why he said it was a moving donkey. His spontaneity in the use of *cola* (ass) instead of the more vulgar *culo* and his associating the table with a donkey reflect his newness to the border city and his background in the country. So far he has not demanded a better chair, and all the ones he has used are obviously bad, so no one has requested them. Sooner or later, he might ask for a better chair, which he will have to defend.

He was telling me that Juárez is ugly, that he does not like it. "I don't even like Chihuahua [City], where I was born," he said. I asked why. He just said, "Juárez is too ugly." As I noted earlier, he has a cousin who visits him, "checks on him." His cousin is from the same area, but he has been in Juárez for a few years now. He also said that he used to come to Juárez every so often, since he was five years old. They eat together.

Juan's machine was working very poorly. He had to be moved. Today his paycheck was $127,000 pesos—minus $20,000 for savings with the union; $6,000 for saving in the maquila, which the company will double; and $1,000 for food. He received approximately US$40, or $100,000 pesos. He's been working there for three months.

At breakfast, Arnulfo told me that he liked one of the new women who was eating near our table. He walked behind her until she went upstairs to the training room. A female guard was coming down the stairs.

Many couples meet each other in the maquilas. It is obvious that both men and women enjoy seeing other attractive women and men in the workplace. It is a social place where you can meet people. When Fernández-Kelly was in Juárez in the late 1970s, women had to go to the discos to meet men [see Fernández-Kelly 1983].

Verónica resigned today. Her one-year-old son in Torreón [city located in the state of Durango] is sick. She has to leave.

Just before lunch, I talked to the union's delegate. I asked him who I should talk to. It was not a personal problem, but a problem I saw with the chairs in general. I explained to him that most of the new people and some of the older ones have to look for a chair in the mornings mainly because someone else takes it away or because the people of the second shift leave it somewhere else. I told him that there were enough chairs but that not all chairs were of the same quality. He asked me, "How is your chair?" I said, "Mine is now fine, because I told Pedro about it, but at the beginning I had problems." I also told him that these conditions could cause problems between the workers. He said, "I have not received any complaints." I emphasized that problems have not developed because usually someone sacrifices his or her chair in order to avoid problems, but that the problem was still there. Then I directly asked, "Wouldn't it be possible for the union to suggest new chairs to the company?" He answered, "The problem really belongs to each individual. If he has a problem with a chair, he should tell me, and we'll bring one for him. It is like the machine. If you have problems with it, you tell Pedro or the mechanic. The same with chairs. I have not seen anyone come to me for this. Until enough people, or a considerable number of people, tell me, then I present the problem to the union. The individual has to complain. If they don't tell me, I cannot do anything."

Then I said, "But don't you think the chairs are old? The workers do not have to tell you. Some chairs do not even have backrests." He said, "But unless they come to me, I cannot take it to the union as a problem."

It is ideological rhetoric to blame the workers for the poor working conditions under which they work, especially when their own jobs are, by the same token, temporary. Under these circumstances and in times of frequent turnover, how can the worker speak up and truly organize? By particularizing a generalized experience, the company and the union avoid having to make a financial investment that they do not want to carry out simply to save on expenses. As long as the factory keeps producing profits without any investment in "technology," the workers will keep fighting for the chairs and will keep on thinking that that is the order of things.

When you are told as a new employee to look for a chair and to defend it, and you see that everybody is doing the same thing, you tend to see that environment as axiomatic in the workplace—"It is part of the job." To ask or resist or demand a new chair, or a better chair, not only for you but for your coworkers, is to destruct or to attempt to change the conditions that received you. At the beginning, you feel you don't have the authority or seniority to speak up. With time, you find your own niche. You defend it, and you let other people adapt as they go along. They will finally adapt to the circumstances, or leave. In other words, those who stay learn to live with the problem instead of solving it.

This situation reproduces itself mainly because the company gets new people every week or every other week. The workers' first priority is to make a living. These conditions may persist for years, as indeed they have.

I talked to Juanita after lunch and told her about the problem. She believed people should get together and talk to the delegate. She said that at one time several people demanded a new or better chair, but that they talked to Pedro, the foreman, and not to the union delegate. She said that the other day, a week ago or so, they were counting the machines. Maybe it has to do with the chairs. She also told me that Lines B and C have office-type chairs, really nice ones. (These two lines produce the most, out of the thirty lines in existence.)

I went to talk to Pedro and told him about how I noticed that everybody tells him about the problem with their chair. "Why don't you suggest to the union to tell the company to get new chairs?" He answered, "I cannot talk to the union. The union is supposed to protect you guys from us. We are not unionized. Only the assembly-line workers and the cafeteria people are part of the union. I am an "employee of trust" (*empleado de confianza*), working for the company. Therefore, I cannot get into the union business. This is why I cannot do what you're asking me."

What a deliberate contradiction, I thought: The union delegate has not received complaints in a group (individual complaints are not enough), and the foreman receives them but cannot do anything (after all, he protects the interests of the company) because he is not unionized. This comfortable situation for the multinational obviously marginalizes the workers, even if they complain.

I went straight to the union office. Because in previous attempts the female union representative had been talking to someone else, this time I knocked at the door to ask if I could talk to her. She said, "Seguro, pásele y siéntese" (Sure, come in and sit down).

I told her about the problem as I had told the union's delegate and the foreman, except that I added that there were rumors that they were already looking into the chair problem. She said, "Yes, that's what I wanted to tell you. In Lines B and C, we placed new chairs because it had been reported that there were some chairs missing, that there were not enough, not that they were in poor condition." Then I said, "It is pretty obvious that the chairs are quite old." She added, "They are reconstructing some to compensate for those that are missing. But what I wanted to tell you is that in one of the lines, C, they [the workers] made a big deal (*hicieron todo un circo*) about the new chairs. They didn't like them; they claimed that it was going to hurt their kidneys, and so forth [*y todo eso*]."

Then I asked, "What about the other line?" "In the other one, they have not said anything. You can go investigate if you want. Go ahead and ask."

"When did this happen? When did they introduce the new chairs?" Then she said, "You are new, right? . . . about two months ago. They were gonna wait for the people's reaction. . . . They're still waiting for the others." My last comment was: "Well, OK. Thank you very much. I just wanted to tell you about the problem. Thank you." I walked out.

What is strange about the whole thing is that the foreman and the union delegate acted ignorant about the new chairs in other lines. When I talked to the workers in my line, they quickly noted that Lines B and C had better chairs than theirs. They did not mention that the other chairs were new, however. Next Monday I will go in the morning and ask some workers from those two lines about their chairs, when they got them, and what they think about them, and in the case of Line 102, what, exactly, they don't like about them.

There already exists a contradiction between the union's delegate of my line and the woman in the union's office. It is obvious that the union operates differently with regard to its delegates, the workers, and the company's personnel. The foregoing shows three different truths about the union's practices: (1) The union delegate should have known about the new chairs in other lines; (2) that workers in different lines have different or better chairs is a problem; and (3) the workers tend to see each other as invaders, making one another more aggressive and less attentive to the fact that it is the company's problem, and not that of the individual worker who has to protect and defend his or her chair in order to assemble the desired product and quota.

MONDAY, SEPTEMBER 11, 1989

I was supposed to go today only to check what kind of new chairs had been introduced and why the people in Line C rejected them. I walked into the place at five minutes before 6:00 AM. I went straight to the area where the affected lines (B and C) were, without checking in (I wasn't sure if there was a blacklist). I didn't see anyone I knew. I walked to Line C. There were three people working, two women and a man. I didn't know who to go to. I picked a woman and approached her. I said, "Excuse me, since when do you have these chairs?" She answered, "A bit before the heat started" (*Poquito antes de que empezara el calor*). *El calor* (the heat) in Juárez usually begins in June. This means that the chairs were probably introduced in May. It is close to what the woman from the union had said (about two or three months ago). Then I asked her, "Do you like them?" She answered, "I never liked them. I liked the fixed ones better." "You mean you didn't have those that spin around?" She answered, "Yes, but we had the fixed ones first. These plastic ones are very hot and slippery. We sweat a lot. This is why I don't like them." Then I asked, "Did you complain about this?" She answered, "Yes, but they reported me" (*Sí, pero me reportaron*). "Who did?" "The forewoman" (*La jefa [de línea]*). "Why?" I asked. She answered, "Because I didn't accept the chair. Two other women also rejected them. So they reported all of us. The *jefa* told Yolanda (from personnel), who came to talk to me [these are the kinds of group leaders that Peña (1997) highlighted in his ethnography]. She stood there and told me, 'Come here, I need to talk to you.' I said, 'You come.' She did. She asked me why I didn't like the chair. I told her that she should have asked us, the workers, about what kinds of chairs we needed. The one who told the office and union people about which chairs we wanted were those in white [supervisors and other members of personnel wore a white gown; line leaders wore a yellow gown; and assembly-line workers wore a blue gown]. But what do they know about chairs? They don't sit all day like us. Then Yolanda said, 'We can't buy more expensive chairs. Besides, only three have rejected them. Line 101 has not said anything.' Then I said, 'I don't know why they haven't. You don't have to buy more expensive ones. I'm just telling you that my back hurts with this chair and that the plastic makes me sweat too much, which is very uncomfortable.'"

Then I interrupted her and asked, "How long have you been working here?" "Thirteen years" (Trece años), she said . . . "Before these chairs, how long did you stay with the older ones?" She said, "I don't remember. Anyway, I told Yolanda (the woman from personnel) to erase me from the report: 'You cannot report me just because I don't like the chairs.' She said she would, but she never erased me."

Then I asked, "What about the union?" She answered, "The union listens to those in white (company's personnel) and to those inside [those inside the main offices: middle management]. They are working together. They should listen to us, because we are the ones sitting down all day. We should have a meeting. But we haven't had a union meeting in a year."

While I was listening to her, I felt a touch on my shoulder. It was someone I knew close to my line. He reminded me that it was about time to start working. While the lady was talking to me, she was sewing on a 261, doing the same task as my position. I also felt nervous because I wondered what her forewoman would say to her. Then I asked, "Why do they make such a big deal reporting (blacklisting) you, just because you wanted another chair?" At this time, three workers approached us and told me briefly about the problem. They said that they were not changing theirs because Line B and others in their line were not saying anything. They were also afraid of getting reported or blacklisted.

I told the woman that the chairs in our line were too old and that I wanted to see how things were working there. She asked, "What line are you working in?" "Line X," I answered. "Thanks," I said, and walked out of the factory. As far as I knew, my research about the chairs was done.

I went to resign around 5:00 PM. Workers resign in order to get paid for the week they did not get paid for in the beginning (we must remember that when they enter a factory, the workers don't get paid until the second week). I was uneasy the whole day.

Within the factory and in the midst of an apparent peace characterized by music, whistling, and good food, there was a kind of repression.

When I resigned, the secretary very courteously asked why I was leaving. I said that I was moving to Chihuahua City. "How was training?" I answered, "Good. The trainer is patient." "How was your foreman (*jefe*)?" "He is a good foreman." "What did you like the most?" "The food." "What didn't you like?" "The attendance bonus and the chairs." The secretary said, "Thank you," with the usual administrative indifference toward assembly-line workers. I still had to go to the factory the following week just to pick up my last check.

Conclusion

Very quickly, the men and women who arrived at the particular sewing maquila where I conducted fieldwork had to survive by appropriating an outspoken and aggressive attitude. This cultural appropriation and transformation is an example of how a multinational corporation, through mismanagement, enhances and, to a large extent, produces a certain aggressiveness on the part of the workers (male and female), along with their own subjugation. This aggressiveness is later used outside the factory, especially in the public vehicles the maquila workers must use to go home and to work. This unfortunate social process demonstrates how a specific cultural transformation produced in a specific factory reproduces the way of life that has characterized Ciudad Juárez at least since the advent of late capitalism in the area: a fast-paced everyday life controlled by strict uses of time and space in which individuals do not have the means to adapt to the new situations without transforming their cultural subjectivities—that is, out of choice. Even though this transformation meant that both men and women could share work experiences as a class, it did not necessarily lead them to transform the working conditions inside the maquiladora where they labored. The repressive regime was everywhere: in the air, the chairs, the quota, their sweat. It is here where chairs become political. They are "political" in different senses at the crossroads of class, gender, age, education, and regionalisms, particularly in relation to the factory union (which worked more for the company than for the workers), and in relation to the working conditions. Needless to say, none of these categories is mutually exclusive. All these elements led to the unmaking of class as a mobilization tool, especially when the company and the union repressed even the minor complaints. In this context, the chairs acquired a different culturally and politically hegemonic meaning according to the survival needs and the forms of domination of the workers.

In this chapter, "politics" also took on another meaning, one relevant to the politics of academics and how we produce knowledge, especially the historical and personal contexts under which we produce it. This question is also related to the different ways Behar and Fernández-Kelly generated ethnographic information in the specific examples cited in the introduction to this chapter. The ethnographic depictions in this chapter were in fact a combination of Fernández-Kelly's encounters with "things" (the chairs, the sewing machines, and the pillows) and Behar's exclusive encounter with a human being—Esperanza. The specific form of representation selected above was highly influenced and informed by (1) historical developments in late-twentieth-century American anthropology, especially after incorporating the critical messages of *Writing Culture* (1986), edited by James Clifford and George Marcus, and of *Women Writing Culture* (1995), edited by Deborah A. Gordon and Ruth Behar; and by (2) concretized circumstances of what it meant to do "participant observation" in the maquiladora industry of Mexico during the last two decades.

Even though *Writing Culture* was published in 1986, and I went to Juárez to do fieldwork for the first time in the summer of 1987, the impact of this publication on doing ethnography had not been felt yet (at least not in Wisconsin). At that time, as is perhaps evident in the previous chapter, I was more worried about how to get a job in the maquiladora industry (not necessarily an easy endeavor) than about the politics of representation (something that was to scrutinize fieldwork itself and the process of extracting knowledge from strategic subjects). By 1989, once I was at Stanford, and having discussed Foucault with my cohort group and some professors, the problematic relation between the doctor and his patient, the teacher and the student, the juror and the accused, the priest and his devotee, the craftsman and his apprentice, had been smoothly transferred to the uneasy and inescapable power relation between the anthropologist and the informant.

In other words, by the summer of 1989, I was afraid to do fieldwork. More specifically, I was not sure if it was ethical to extract information from "informants" even with their "consent" and even if "their" voice was democratically incorporated into the narrative. I quickly realized that "finding" someone who would provide me with information was so imposing in itself that giving people a "voice" when we write tends to conceal the pervasive inequalities that characterize the process of searching for "informants." It still conceals the "spy" in all anthropologists. The question that I pose with regard to this matter is the following: Is it possible, convincing, and ethical to produce ethnographic knowledge without interrogating "informants"? Is it possible to destabilize the gaze upon the informant per se and center our academic and political preoccupations on specific situations by positioning ourselves without, once again, taking over? After all, the academic arena, and not that of the masses, in spite of our attempts, remains a privileged site where decisions take place as to what, when, and how knowledge is to be published.

Despite these serious questions and fears, I still felt I had to discover and uncover the cultural and political processes through which maquiladoras or multinational corporations extract profit from men and women in the garment industry. I felt I still needed to analyze the ways in which cultural practices were incorporated into the industrial process and how these practices differed from one place to another; in this case, did the role of the cultural in a garment factory differ from the role it played in the electronics factory where I had done participant observation in 1987? This question inevitably leads us to the concrete—to those differences in size, number of workers, type of capital investment—and to questions of institutionalized politics, more specifically, to such critical interrogations as to whether the workers were unionized or not.

In 1983, Fernández-Kelly distinguished between the two types of capital investment that had characterized the maquiladora industry up until then. Among factories of the electric/electronics type, she identified higher investments of capital—capital that comes from economically powerful direct subsidiaries such as General Electric, Honeywell, and Texas Instruments. These multinationals tended to hire younger women, those between sixteen and twenty-three years of age. She also noted that most factories of the garment/textile type tended to be subcontractors for companies that dominated (and still dominate) the retail clothing industries. She properly noted that these latter types of factories were technologically unsophisticated, if not backward, and offered low economic security (due to unexpected cycles and ruptures in clothing styles and market trends).

These (garment) types also offered extremely poor working conditions to the workers they hired. An example of such an aberration would be the already-cited Coca-Cola chairs used for garment production. Because of this difference in capital investment, Fernández-Kelly accurately argued that in 1979–1980, when she conducted her pioneering fieldwork, the garment/textile types of maquiladoras focused on hiring the most vulnerable sector of the labor market: older women with children who could not compete with the young labor force utilized in the more prestigious electronics/electric factories. The latter maquiladoras could afford, at that time, to apply strict measures of control regarding the labor market they privileged (from its beginning in 1965 to 1980): younger women.

As I noted earlier, in 1983, due to the devaluation of the peso and due to the concurrent arrival of the automobile industry, the maquiladoras began to hire not only men but anyone who was willing to work (except, as we saw, the handi-capped). Throughout the 1980s, the labor demand increased and the previously desired supply (women: young ones in electronics and older ones in garments) substantially "contracted." Thus, in the late 1980s, I found that most (but not all) multinationals could not afford to privilege a specific sector of the labor force, either through age or sex discrimination. As we have seen, it is now evident that both men and women, young and old, are more and more sharing the same ex-ploitative production process.

This historical incongruity was, of course, also manifested in the sewing fac-tory where I worked in 1989. It could not be characterized in the same way as the garment plants of the late 1970s, which were mostly staffed by a female labor force. As we saw, the sewing plant where I did fieldwork resists facile categoriza-tion, either with regard to gender or to the age of the workers. In fact, Fernández-Kelly's warning to me in 1986 about how we must avoid representing the maqui-ladora as monolithic applied to my work during the late 1980s and early 1990s, as it has also applied to the late 1990s and into the present (see the work of Wright [1998] and Salzinger [2003], for instance). Interestingly, with regard to capital investment, Hospital Supplies did not follow the characterization that Fernández-Kelly gave to this kind of industry in 1983. It was a direct subsidiary instead of a subcontractor; yet, as a direct subsidiary, it did not offer the sophis-tication in technology or working conditions usually associated with electric/electronics subsidiaries of powerful corporations. Nonetheless, it claims to be a "prestigious" corporation representing the major provider of hospital supplies in the world.[2]

As was evident in my field journal, my major goal turned into clarifying whether the "chairs" were and had been the crux of the problem, not only for ethnographic production, manufacturing production, and union politics, but also for the health of the workers and for the possibility for them to organize around issues of class. Through an analysis of chairs, I hoped to show that poli-tics and power inequalities are articulated by the common people in the realm of the mundane and not exclusively in their relation (though unequal) with the larger structures of power that pervade their institutionalized lives (i.e., as part of the nation-state, the global economy, and even "management," which to them might seem to be as distant as the president of AMAC or the president of their corporation, for that matter).

Besides this politicized atmosphere, the turnover problem, which the maquiladoras themselves created (due to their own search for cheap labor in one strategic locality—Ciudad Juárez) and which they were confronting since the early 1980s, made it unfeasible to develop long-lasting relationships with the workers, since they themselves, for economic reasons already identified, unexpectedly moved from factory to factory, looking for the better maquila. In fact, of the sixteen individuals who started working with me, by the end of my stay in the factory (five weeks later), only one person remained.

In this chapter and the previous two, I addressed not only the theoretical problems of cultural reproduction (how workers reproduce themselves as masculine or disciplined class subjects) and cultural transformation (how workers transformed themselves into more aggressive agents of production), but also the political and social ramifications of the fact that the continuing conquest of the Mexican working classes is taking place in late-industrial-capitalist settings. Yet there is still hope for effective class mobilization, accompanied by cultural dignity. Interestingly, in other not-too-distant historical and geographical contexts, not having access to a seat or a chair led to broad social revolutions, such as the civil rights movement in the United States. A booklet celebrating Black History Month states the following: "1955. Rosa Parks, a Montgomery, Ala., seamstress, refuses to give her seat on a bus to a white man. Her arrest sparks a 381-day bus boycott and begins the modern Civil Rights Movement" (*Famous Dates in African-American History*, 2000)

In the following chapter, I bring together, theoretically and empirically, two major aspects of cultural life in late-twentieth-century northern Mexico: class and gender experiences and their respective implications for our understanding of the life and death of working-class women and men at the border from an explicit feminist perspective.

EIGHT

Women, Men, and "Gender" in Feminist Anthropology
Lessons from Northern Mexico's Maquiladoras

Societies . . . that place positive value on . . . the involvement of both men
and women in the home seem to be most egalitarian in terms of sex roles.
When a man is involved in domestic labor, in child care and cooking, he
cannot establish an aura of authority and distance.

— MICHELLE Z. ROSALDO, "WOMAN, CULTURE, AND SOCIETY"

I started working. I wasn't going as fast, but I was sewing kind of constantly. When I went to breakfast (three hours later), I had assembled eight
gowns (last Friday, by this time, I had three or four). At breakfast, Arturo,
a guy I briefly met while in training, sat with me. He is nineteen. He told
me that a guy last Friday did sew his finger accidentally—five strikes. . . .
Arturo was telling me that even after the accident occurred, he kept on
working. According to Arturo, the guy claimed it did not hurt; so he kept
on working for about two hours. He went to the nurse and she gave him
a Band-Aid. Apparently, the nurse did not send him home because he had
agreed to stay. . . . After two hours the guy's lower arm went numb. The
guy could not work anymore, so he had to leave. According to Arturo, he
did not show up today.

— ALEJANDRO LUGO, "FRAGMENTED LIVES, ASSEMBLED GOODS"

THE FIRST EXCERPT—taken from Michelle Rosaldo's 1974 "theoretical overview"—manifests two areas of social analysis not fully appreciated by the feminist anthropological literature: (1) Michelle Rosaldo's concrete recommendation
for social change in the West—to bring men into household obligations; and (2)
her theoretical and practical strategy for the systematic study of men as gendered
subjects in feminist anthropology as early as 1974.[1]

Together, the two quotations above bring to light, first, Michelle Rosaldo's
insightful observation regarding the aura of authority and how it might be challenged; and second, a brief ethnographic attempt on my part to explore her
intriguing suggestion: whether or not men who work in a "domestic" site (a

garment factory) can establish an aura of authority in relation to women.[2] Transnational assembly plants, and especially garment factories, have been historically perceived as what I call "domesticated" public spaces, both metaphorically and literally, mainly because they have been associated with women. Diane Elson and Ruth Pearson, for instance, describe what they call "the changing forms of the subordination of women" (1984, xiii) in the development of capitalist social production as follows: "Though one form of gender subordination, the subordination of daughters to their fathers, may visibly crumble [once they find work in global factories], another form of gender subordination, that of women employees to male factory bosses, just as visibly is built up. . . . In study after study the same pattern is revealed: the young female employees are almost exclusively at the bottom of this hierarchy; the upper levels of the hierarchy are almost invariably male" (ibid., 33).

Before men were hired in the early 1980s in transnational factories at the U.S-Mexico border, the following characterization of what I will call the "domestication" of women, either at home or in the factory, would have applied as well to female factory workers in Ciudad Juárez: "But the problem is not simply that young women may, through factory work, escape the domination of fathers and brothers only to become subordinate to male managers and supervisors, or escape the domination of managers and supervisors only to become subordinate to husbands or lovers. There is also the problem that the domination of managers and supervisors may be withdrawn—the woman may be sacked from her job—while the woman is without the "protection" of subordination to father, brother, husband" (Elson and Pearson 1984, 33).

In what follows, I return to Elson and Pearson's discourse of domination/subordination, analyzing it in the current context of narratives about the domestic and the public, both as they appear in Michelle Rosaldo's work and as they might relate to the Foucauldian notion of "the subject" as "always already subjected" (Grossberg 1996), "suggesting forms of power which subject and make subject to" (Foucault, cited in Alonso and Koreck 1988, 119). In this chapter, I will extend Michelle Rosaldo's use of "the domestic" into the "already domesticated" as an element of particular "forms of power which subject [domesticate] and make subject to."

Throughout this project, my main theoretical, methodological, and practical proposition is that feminist studies of women (usually done by women) and feminist studies of men or masculinity (usually done by men) do not necessarily add up, either together or separately, to studies of gender—that is, to studies of both men and women. In fact, when a sole feminist analyst comprehensively examines both men and women, new and productive categories of theoretical analysis and politics can emerge. To accomplish these objectives, I reflect on two broadly conceived interrelated projects for feminist anthropology, both of which constitute the main body of this chapter. "Part I: Rereading Michelle Z. Rosaldo's Domestic and Public" reexamines how the late M. Rosaldo's recommendations for social change were incorporated into her theoretical conceptualization of "domestic" and "public" and how her critics (including herself in 1980), while ignoring her practical suggestions for social transformation, disapproved of her early theorizing. "Part II: Refocusing 'Gender': Destabilizing the Aura of Authority" explores several theoretical issues regarding the production of gender identity in specific social sites (i.e., late-capitalist shop floors addressed in the last three chapters) where both men and women are involved in the same activity (either assembling microcircuits for computers, electric harnesses for automobiles, or hospital supplies).

More concretely, Part II attempts to show that when both men and women are taken into consideration by the social analyst, the following theoretical and empirical problems seem to develop: (1) gender differentiation based on either biology or social tradition often loses significance for the actors involved, particularly if we examine "moments" of negotiation (Collier and M. Rosaldo 1981; Yanagisako and Collier 1987, 1994) that do not necessarily privilege either men or women (in M. Rosaldo's hypothetical cases of egalitarianism, when both men and women are involved in domestic chores; in my ethnographic cases, when both men and women are on the assembly line); (2) the narrow (though often useful) vision of studies of men becomes evident in either a prefeminist, masculinist text (in this case, I revisit Napoleon Chagnon's ethnography of the Yanomamo) or in more recent feminist attempts (in this particular instance, I present my own ethnography of maquiladora workers); and finally, (3) our understanding of gendered subjectivities gets broadened by opening other avenues for feminist practice: for instance, domestic/public is transcended along with *simplistic* masculine/feminine distinctions.

Ultimately, I argue here that when both men and women are treated as gendered subjects in feminist projects, our usual analytical conceptions about gender, identity, and power are redefined, and, consequently, new political repercussions come to the fore, particularly a class identity among the workers that does not necessarily collapse when issues of both genders are examined.[3] To carry out this analysis, I bring together selective ethnographic materials from the previous chapters to suggest that by comprehensively considering both men and women in capitalist societies, feminist studies of gender should inevitably contribute to studies of class, and in the process, better grasp the plight of working-class women and men at the border in late-twentieth-century northern Mexico.

Attaining these goals, however, requires a specific ethnographic sensibility: skills that perhaps can only be acquired through a feminist consciousness and feminist anthropological training, as the one provided by the social lens of the late Michelle Zimbalist Rosaldo.

Part I: Rereading Michelle Z. Rosaldo's Domestic and Public

1 *domestic*/adj 1: of or relating to the household or the family . . .
TAME, DOMESTICATED 5: devoted to home duties and pleasures
2 *domestic* n 1: a household servant.
Domesticate vt *-cated, -cating* 1: to bring into domestic use; ADOPT 2: to
fit for domestic life 3: to adapt (an animal or plant) to life in intimate association with and to the advantage of man
domesticity n 1: the quality or state of being domestic or domesticated
2: domestic activities or life   —*WEBSTER'S NEW COLLEGIATE DICTIONARY*

Sexual asymmetries and visions convey what is "really" going on elsewhere, at another political epicenter.
   —ANN LAURA STOLER, "CARNAL KNOWLEDGE AND IMPERIAL POWER"

In 1974, M. Rosaldo had a clear and definite political agenda: "to understand the
nature of female subordination and the ways it may be overcome" (1974, 24). To
this extent and in conjunction with most contributors to the M. Rosaldo and
Lamphere volume (*Woman, Culture, and Society*), her interest was, as Sherry
Ortner stated, "of course more than academic" (1974, 67).

   Following the major anthropological tenet of the time—the search for universals, for what was "broadly human"—M. Rosaldo believed that the subordination of women was a cross-cultural phenomenon (1974, 19; Lamphere 1987, 16).
What constituted women's subordination for Rosaldo was in essence a "sexual
asymmetry" embodied in "the fact that male, as opposed to female, activities
are always recognized as predominantly important, and cultural systems give
authority and value to the roles and activities of men" (M. Rosaldo 1974, 19).
Though she was quite cautious in differentiating the theoretical implications of
valued and devalued activities from the philosophical and political question of
the subordinate status of women, M. Rosaldo tried to justify her stance regarding universal subordination by presenting specific ethnographic material (see
1974, 12–21, 28–41). More generally, she perhaps followed Ortner's position: "I
think the onus is no longer upon us to demonstrate that female subordination is
a cultural universal; it is up to those who would argue against the point to bring
forth counter examples" (Ortner 1974, 71).

   To what extent have M. Rosaldo's critics of the 1974 position brought
"counter examples"? Since then, for instance, Karen Sacks (1979) argued for
the complementarity of gender relations, Eleanor Leacock (1981) analyzed so-
called "egalitarian societies," and Peggy Sanday and Ruth Goodenough (1990)
have invited feminist anthropologists to go beyond the "second sex" syndrome.
However, alternatives such as these, which emphasize a move away from as-

suming too much about gender inequalities, were heavily questioned by Sylvia Yanagisako and Jane F. Collier (1987) and by Louise Lamphere (1987). As Lamphere stated:

> Women . . . are rarely the "articulators" of decisions that involve the entire band or community. . . . Usually this role falls to a male, though older women are not entirely excluded. The lack of recognition of this "male bias" in the way decisions are made . . . is, in my opinion, one of the critical deficiencies in the egalitarian hypothesis. (1987, 24)

Paradoxically, however, and perhaps optimistically, M. Rosaldo still hoped that we could achieve a certain form of egalitarianism, as we will see.

Power and Gender, Biology and Practice

Although M. Rosaldo's *preoccupation was more with finding ways to overcome* the apparent universal oppression than with explaining the universalism itself, she tried to understand why the activities of women were devalued cross-culturally, especially in comparison to men's practices. Her aim in this attempt was the search for the identification (in ethnography and in society) of the "sources of power" that kept women subordinated, *as well as those that would help them escape the subordination* (1974, 18) — or the devalued status. Thus, she proposed a "structural model" constituted by two dichotomous categories (public and domestic) that "underlay" the local "evaluations of the sexes" (1974, 23), that is, the culturally specific values attached to male and female activities. The cultural values given to the sexual asymmetry were in themselves "sources of power." They could work either *against* women as sources of domination and oppression or, as M. Rosaldo would prefer, *for* women as sources of empowerment and transformation.[4]

In 1987, Yanagisako and Collier, though critical of M. Rosaldo's use of domestic and public as "merely elaborations and extensions of the same natural fact: the biological difference between men and women" (1987, 15), still depend quite significantly on the notion of values applied to cultural practices carried out by men and women. They wrote regarding their concept of "systemic inequality":

> We begin with the premise that social systems are, by definition, systems of inequality. This premise . . . conforms to common usage. By most definitions, *a society is a system of social relationships and values. Values entail evaluation. Consequently, a society is a system of social relationships in which all things and actions are not equal.* (Yanagisako and Collier 1987, 39; my emphasis)

This focus on values, as we have seen, was one of M. Rosaldo's main theoretical and practical preoccupations, as early as 1974. Yanagisako and Collier were extending "evaluation" to general studies of society, culture, and history—a direction, I believe, M. Rosaldo would have taken.

The explanatory element that Yanagisako and Collier gave to M. Rosaldo's uses of domestic and public, however, is interpreted differently by Lamphere. She noted, "Rosaldo did not attempt to *explain* women's subordination through the dichotomy, but saw it as an underlying structural framework in any society that supported subordination and that would have to be reorganized to change women's position" (1993, 75; italics in original). M. Rosaldo herself stated it quite explicitly:

> The opposition does not determine cultural stereotypes or asymmetries in the evaluation of the sexes, but rather underlies them, to support a very general (and, for women, often demeaning) identification of women with domestic life and of men with public life. These identifications, themselves neither necessary nor desirable, can all be tied to the role of women in child rearing. (1974, 23–24)

More than three decades later, it should be evident that in 1974, M. Rosaldo was trying to come to grips with the ways men and women were given a social "identification," or in more recent terminology, how they (or their identities) were produced socially, or, more concretely, how the asymmetry supported "a very general (and *for women, often demeaning*) identification of women with domestic life and of men with public life." Because of their socially produced inequality, according to Rosaldo, these particular characterizations of men and women are "neither necessary nor desirable." Nonetheless, they provided a "framework for conceptualizing the activities of the sexes" (1974, 33). By "activities," Rosaldo means human action, behavior happening on the ground—actual experience. With regard to the question of biology, she wrote, "I would suggest that anything so general as the universal asymmetry of sex roles is likely to be the result of a constellation of different factors. . . . Biology may be one of these, but biology becomes significant only as it is interpreted by human actors and associated with characteristic modes of action" (ibid., 23).

Plan of Action

The major arguments made so far must be well understood: (1) that M. Rosaldo formulated her theoretical model in order to identify the "sources" of power that subordinate women (here I stress, as I think she did, the sources of power and not the "subordination"); (2) that she was theoretically and politically concerned with how women and men were given social identities (my phrase; her term: "identifications"); and (3) that she saw the problem of women as emerging mainly from their culturally enacted role as child rearers, and not so much as life givers. As she held, "These identifications [of public and domestic] . . . can all be tied to the role of women in child rearing" (ibid., 24). To subvert or transform the latter state of affairs, Rosaldo delineated two possible sources of empowerment:

> By using the structural model as a framework, we can identify the implications for female power, value, and status in various cross-cultural articulations of domestic and public roles. . . . The model . . . permits us to identify two sorts of structural arrangements that elevate women's status: women may enter the public world, or *men may enter the home.* (ibid., 35–36; my emphasis)

Having handy Sacks's (1974) critique of Engels, it would not have been terribly illuminating to accentuate that women must enter the "public sphere." Instead, without denying such a strategy, it was the possibility that men could be brought into the "home" that stimulated Rosaldo to suggest that equality of the sexes could be obtained. That is, only through such an alternative could cultural evaluations of the activities of men and women be given equitable value. After all, she had found in the ethnographic literature of the time that

> societies . . . that place positive value on . . . the involvement of both men and women in the home seem to be most egalitarian in terms of sex roles. When a man is involved in domestic labor [i.e., as among the Ilongot, the Arapesh, and the Mbuti; see M. Rosaldo 1974, 40–41], in child care and cooking, he cannot establish an aura of authority and distance. (ibid., 39)

As I noted earlier, the latter statement about men involved in "home" activities and not establishing "an aura of authority" has not, as yet, been questioned (or even addressed) in the feminist anthropological literature. I will try to address it in Part II of this chapter. For the most part, the main focus in feminist anthropology has been on women. As Judith Shapiro noted about the gender literature in anthropology: "The focus is on women. . . . Moreover, much of the recent cross-cultural research is not only about women, but by women, and in some sense, for women" (1979, 269). In this selective process of trying to "permit a grasp of women's lives," many feminist scholars forgot, as M. Rosaldo noted in 1980, that "men and women ultimately live together in the world." Yet, she argued, "We will never understand the lives that women lead without relating them to men" (M. Rosaldo 1980, 396; also see Behar 1995; Brandes 1980; Carrillo 2002; Ebron and Tsing 1995; Gilmore 1990; Gutmann 1996; Herzfeld 1985; Lancaster 1992; Limón 1994; Ong 1995; Salzinger 2003; Shapiro 1987).[5]

Not surprisingly, then, as early as 1974, M. Rosaldo concluded her widely misunderstood feminist piece with the following suggestion for our society:

> We must, like the Ilongots, bring men into the sphere of domestic concerns and responsibilities. . . . The Ilongot example . . . suggests that men who in the past have committed their lives to public achievement will recognize women as true equals only when men themselves help raise new genera-tions by taking on the responsibilities of the home. (1974, 42)

Some Repercussions, No Feminist Reaction

In the case of the United States, specifically in middle-class circles, bringing men into the "home" or into such activities as cooking their own meals, driving their kids to daycare centers, and helping to redefine their wives' reproductive lives has perhaps been more influential in whatever autonomy women have achieved today than is commonly thought. Yet this does not mean that these new men and new women escape the hegemony of domestic/public discourses. For in-stance, in her study of new reproductive technologies (particularly amniocen-tesis—prenatal diagnoses), Rayna Rapp argues that while recent medical tech-nology allows women, "like their male partners, to imagine voluntary limits to their commitments to children," it "does not transform the world of work, social services, media, and the like on which a different sense of maternity and the 'private' sphere would depend" (1997, 138). Interestingly, Rapp does not reflect on M. Rosaldo's early work but makes the following apt claim: "Moreover, that 'private' sphere and its commitment to child bearing is now being enlarged to include men. Fathers, too, can now be socially created during the pregnancy, through birth-coaching and early bonding. These new fathers may also claim the right to comment on women's motives for pregnancy and abortion in powerful ways" (ibid., 138).

Thus, M. Rosaldo's framework of the domestic and public can still explain the gendered politics of everyday practices (although "private" is not synony-mous with "domestic," Rapp's specific usage is part of the hegemonic dichotomy Rosaldo was challenging). We, as scholars writing at the turn of the twenty-first century, must recognize that the identification of cultural and spatial male and female schematic worlds, or their inversions, is not necessarily futile; on the contrary, we must continue the disclosure of what Pierre Bourdieu calls "the schemes of the sexual division of labor and the division of sexual labor," since they manifest symptoms of broader hegemonic relations. As he convincingly argued with regard to Kabylian society in Algeria,

> The opposition between . . . man, invested with protective, fecundating virtues, and woman, at once sacred and charged with maleficent forces . . .

is reproduced in the spatial division between male space, with the place of assembly, the market, or the fields, and female space, the house and its garden, the retreats of *haram*. (Bourdieu 1977, 89).

Unfortunately, Bourdieu provided no critical commentary on the cultural positions of women. Nonetheless, he elaborated on how the correlation of space and gendered activities permeates other realms of everyday life by noting that "this spatial organization (matched by a temporal organization obeying the same logic) governs practices and representations—far beyond the frequently described rough divisions between the male world and female world, the assembly and the fountain, public life and intimacy—and thereby contributes to the durable imposition of the schemes of perception, thought, and action" (1977, 89–90).

Perhaps much more intriguing is Ann Stoler's critical observation regarding "sexual asymmetries" in colonial cultures: "Sexual asymmetries and visions convey what is 'really' going on elsewhere, at another political epicenter. They are tropes to depict other centers of power" (1991, 54). I argue that these tropes and their respective logical schemes of perception, thought, and action are deployed throughout the city and throughout the different industrial parks of Ciudad Juárez, particularly in the context of the recent changes in the gender structure of the labor force.

Interestingly, however, both the feminist movement and the gender literature have generally responded to M. Rosaldo's agenda very much as the kibbutz social movement in Israel responded to gender issues. Judith Shapiro wrote about the kibbutz that

> the attempt to achieve [sexual] equality is generally a matter of trying to turn women into social equivalents of men. . . . Women had to be given the opportunity to work in agricultural production, in developing industries, and in the army. There was, however, no comparable effort to get men into the kitchens and laundries. (1991, 276–277n40)

Indeed, Rayna Rapp discusses how "white middle-class women," in their individualist fight for choice, "may be 'becoming more like men,' freer than ever before to enter hegemonic realms of the culture from which they were formerly barred, but at the price of questioning and altering their traditional gender identity" (1997, 138). In Rapp's otherwise lucid analysis of amniocentesis, there is no comment on the possibility, essentialist notwithstanding, of the "new fathers" becoming social equivalents of women: unlike their female counterparts who get transformed into social males, they remain men, but shift from biological into socially created fathers (through birth coaching, for instance).

Lest there be misunderstanding, the point of this discussion is twofold: that

domestic/public narratives affecting both men and women continue to reproduce themselves, and that their identification in particular spaces, like the factory shop floors, for instance, might help demonstrate some of the social victo-
ries, and the lost battles as well, of the feminist movement itself, especially in the
context of late capitalism at the turn of the twenty-first century.[6]

We the Victorians: Historical Realizations, Static Applications

In her 1980 article, "The Use and Abuse of Anthropology," M. Rosaldo reconsiders
her 1974 position by reanalyzing her use of human universals, her use of dichotomies, and her abuse of Western concepts. Undoubtedly, after Reiter's 1975 historical contextualization of our folk concepts of the domestic and the public, and
their respective association with women and men, Rosaldo suggested and clarified that her model was dichotomous because such dualities had constituted in
our culture a heritage from Victorian England. This ideological legacy, she agreed,
we have not escaped (M. Rosaldo 1980; interestingly, Anzaldúa [1987] explored
these dichotomies in Spanish, Mexican, and Aztec discourses about gender).

This valid recognition on her part, which mainly traces her theoretical position historically and culturally, does not, however, necessarily make invalid the
ethnographic cases she used in 1974. In the examination of the secondary texts
presented, the reader is not so naive as to not distinguish between M. Rosaldo's
imposition of the dichotomy and the data that those ethnographies provided.
In fact, the latter were simply illuminated by M. Rosaldo's interpretation. After
all, we must remember that ideology in different contexts can be put to different
uses. As we have seen, her specific political purpose of the application of the
dichotomy was opposed to that of Victorian thinking—bringing men into the
household.

Moreover, M. Rosaldo was interested in power relations and, being a cultural
relativist, in cultural variation. When she thought of "sexual asymmetry" in 1974,
she was not thinking of how "gender works" (1980, 399), as she believed in 1980.
Instead, her preoccupation concerned the ideological "sources of power" that
tend to produce or give rise to the asymmetry. Indeed, it was the purpose of
her essay to present an agenda about how to subvert the nature of the Western
asymmetry. Perhaps without fully knowing it, she was already making a critique of Victorian ideology. Thus, her belief in 1980 that she was "assuming too
much" with her use of the two spheres is, more than anything, the result of the
influence of her critics. Realizing that her theoretical framework was based on a
hegemonic Victorian tenet does not necessarily make the ethnographic material
Victorian. As she noted in 1980 about the empirical element in the dichotomy
debates:

> My earlier account of sexual asymmetry in terms of the inevitable ranking
> of opposed domestic and public spheres is *not . . . one that I am willing to*

reject for being wrong. Rather, I have suggested that the reasons that account made sense are to be found not in empirical detail, but in the categories, biases, and limitations of a traditionally individualistic and male-oriented sociology. (M. Rosaldo 1980, 415; my emphasis).

M. Rosaldo was a product and an example of a social transformation (the feminist movement): by bringing men into the "home," she was turning the Victorian dichotomy (and capitalist ideology) on its head.[7] As she argued about the public in the domestic: "When *public decisions are made in the household,* women may have a legitimate public role" (M. Rosaldo 1974, 39; my emphasis). And so, I argue, there must be domesticity—"the quality or state of being domestic or domesticated"—both in terms of gender and in terms of class, in (so-called) public terrains of struggle, such as the Juárez maquiladoras.

Michelle Rosaldo's Articulation of Theory and Practice

Michelle Rosaldo's practical political agenda and her theoretical formulations went hand in hand. They could not be, and should not have been, separated. The alternative itself was not taken into consideration by her peers in the 1974 book. She wrote, "None of the other papers in this volume consider this alternative," that of bringing men into the household. Her critics have ignored her most specific political strategy. Yet, by separating the dichotomous framework (domestic and public) from the concrete recommendation for change in our society, they managed to conveniently discard her theoretical proposition (see, for example, Comaroff 1987; Leacock 1981; MacCormack and Strathern 1980; Sacks 1979; Strathern 1988; Yanagisako and Collier 1987). Perhaps having considered "the Michelle Rosaldo case" closed, the following did not challenge her critics: Behar and Gordon (1995); di Leonardo (1991); Ginsburg and Tsing (1990). (In fact, in two collections from the late 1990s addressing gender issues—*Situated Lives: Gender and Culture in Everyday Life* [1997], edited by Louise Lamphere, Helena Ragoné, and Patricia Zavella, and *Gender's Place* [2002], edited by Rosario Montoya, Lessie Jo Frazier, and Janise Hurtig—Michelle Rosaldo is completely absent from the discussion about what constituted feminist anthropology in the late 1990s; since my coauthored collection on M. Rosaldo [2000], Ellen Lewin's [2006] *Feminist Anthropology: A Reader* has incorporated Rosaldo's 1980 essay into the history of feminism in anthropology.)

We must realize that gender relations can only be better understood by analyzing the complex sociopolitical processes affecting both women and men in their culturally and historically ordered worlds (Lugo and Maurer 2000; M. Rosaldo 1980; Yanagisako and Collier 1987). One of the initial attempts to deal with men as gendered (i.e., domesticated) subjects was already theoretically and politically inherent in M. Rosaldo's pioneering formulation. By 1980, she invited feminist scholars "to ask just how it comes about—in a world where people of both sexes make choices that count—that men come to be seen as the creators of collective good and the preeminent force in local politics" (M. Rosaldo 1980, 414–415). Thus, without leaving behind the feminist project for social justice, we must systematically study men as culturo-historical products themselves, and with the same care and rigor undertaken when studying women.

With regard to gender, in the preceding four chapters I attempted to show, through ethnography, how maquiladora women and men are socially produced in class, historical, and cultural terms—with a specific purpose in mind, as we will now see: to identify the conditions that (will allow us to) destabilize men's aura of authority over women and hopefully create the conditions that will limit the process of class unmaking while identifying those that may foster class mobilization in the future.

Part II: Refocusing "Gender": Destabilizing the Aura of Authority

1 *private* / adj 1 a: intended for or restricted to the use of a particular person, group, or class b: belonging to or concerning an individual person, company, or interest c: (1) restricted to the individual 2: carried on by the individual independently of the institutions 2 a (1): not holding public office or employment (2): not related to one's official position: PERSONAL 3 a: withdrawn from company or observation b: not known or intended to be known publicly: SECRET c: unsuitable for public use or display
1 *tame* adj 1: reduced from a state of native wildness especially so as to be tractable and useful to man: DOMESTICATED 2: made docile and submissive: SUBDUED 3: lacking spirit, zest, or interest
    syn TAME, SUBDUED, SUBMISSIVE shared meaning element: docilely treatable
    ant fierce
2 *tame* vb, *tamed; taming* vt 1 a: to reduce from a wild to a domestic state b: to subject to cultivation 2: to deprive of spirit: HUMBLE, SUBDUE 3: tone down: SOFTEN vt: to become tame-tamable
tameless /adj not tamed or not capable of being tamed
                    —WEBSTER'S NEW COLLEGIATE DICTIONARY

A few of the younger men retired after a single blow, privately admitting to me later that they pretended to be injured to avoid being forced to fight more.
                    —NAPOLEON CHAGNON, YANOMAMO

The whistling of the people is important. When someone drops something noisy, or forgets to wear his or her hair cover, everybody whistles. In Juárez, you are expected to be perfect in your behavior. You cannot be

weak, forgetful, or careless. To present yourself as such would only show
that you are not capable of doing what you are expected to do. Thus, if you
drop something, or forget to cover your head after the break or after lunch,
they will whistle, mainly the men. One time, the whistling was so constant
(apparently, the target had not noticed it was he who had been whistled at;
most of the time you think it is someone else) until one guy finally yelled,
"¡Tu gorro, pendejo!" (Your cap, stupid!).

—ALEJANDRO LUGO, "FRAGMENTED LIVES, ASSEMBLED GOODS"

As has been noted throughout this book, men began to be employed in maquiladoras (global assembly plants) in the early 1980s: in electronics, garment, and
automobile assembly lines.

Strongly believing in "participant observation," I worked as an assembly-
line operator in three maquiladoras, one electronics (Chapter 5), one garment
(Chapter 7), and one of the automobile type (Chapter 6). I was interested in
studying both men and women, especially the interactions between them inside and outside the factory. It never occurred to me to study either exclusively
men or the issue of masculinity *per se*. While I asked both men and women
about their conceptions of machismo, I never asked about their own local conceptions of "masculinity" or how they defined "the masculine," "manliness," or
"manly" virtues (see Gutmann 1996, 2000). After all (I now ask myself), did
feminist scholars approach the "woman question" in terms of the "feminine"?
How far would they have gone if they had continued along those lines? In trying
to understand men, how truly critical is the issue of the "masculine"? Regarding these kinds of questions, though related to women, Michelle Rosaldo knew
better. As early as 1974, she examined or asked questions about the *activities of
women,* not about their femininity; even more important for our purposes here,
in 1980 she argued that women's place in society was a product of "the meaning
[their] activities acquire through concrete social interactions" (1980, 400).

Most ethnographic studies about men by male anthropologists (e.g., Herdt
1981; Herzfeld 1985; Lancaster 1988, 1992, 1997; Limón 1989, 1994; Lugo 1990)
have focused on the cultural construction of "masculinity" or "manliness"
(machismo) with reference to men, and not necessarily in relation to "gender."
Thus most of these works do not engage directly with feminist theorists or with
feminist theorizing about gender (for an unfortunate attempt by a male anthropologist who caricatures feminist anthropology, see Gilmore 1990, 23–24). And
in the cases where more serious and sophisticated theorizing occurs (for instance, Comaroff 1987; Lancaster 1992, 1997; Scheffler 1991; Valeri 1990), it has
not been applied to concrete innovative ethnographic projects that would enrich
our representations of *both* men and women—gender relations—in feminist
anthropology. Two major contributions, however, are Matthew Gutmann's ex-

traordinary (1996) work among working-class Mexican men in Mexico City and
Lancaster's exceptional (1997) essay on Guto's working-class life and sexuality in
a Managua barrio.[8]

Yet, perhaps ironically, we cannot claim that before the feminist movement
men were not being studied. After all, was it not this privileging of men in earlier
prefeminist ethnographies that triggered feminist anthropology in the 1970s?
To what analytical degree is it possible to claim that those studies were "in fact"
studies of masculinity?

With these questions in mind, I examine below certain social occurrences
that Yanagisako and Collier call "moments when practice and meaning are negotiated together" (1994, 198). My analysis of such moments of negotiation consists of a juxtaposition of my own ethnographic narratives of maquiladora men
and women conducting their workday with Napoleon Chagnon's ethnographic
descriptions of Yanomamo men as aggressive/violent masculine subjects. This
juxtaposition serves several purposes: (1) it shows one treatment of "masculinities" in what Renato Rosaldo calls "a classic ethnography"; (2) it shows the critical difference between Chagnon's masculinist, prefeminist vision and my own
feminist consciousness—a product of my specific graduate training in the 1980s;
(3) it shows the limitations in exclusively examining men's lives in "masculine"
terms; (4) it tries to show how maquila men's lives as well as Yanomamo men's
experiences cannot be described by excluding from our analyses men's vulnerabilities as part of their gendered subjectivities (i.e., feeling frightened, intimidated, and ineffective); and, finally, (5) by focusing on these feelings of vulnerability, it also sheds light on M. Rosaldo's analytical insight, though inverted, that
"when public decisions are made in the household, women may have a legitimate
public role" (M. Rosaldo 1974, 39; my emphasis). In other words, when this same
insight is applied to men in public settings, that is, when "domestic" decisions
are made by men in public settings, the "domestic" is inevitably turned into the
"private/personal/intimate," allowing or leading men to play a legitimate and
necessary, though not always desired, "domestic" (if not tamed/domesticated)
role (see Chapter 2 for other discourses on taming, or Mansos, during the colonial period).

Yanomamo Men: The Fierce, the Frightened, and Chagnon's Masculine Heroics

We would raise the question, nonetheless, of whether a postmodern feminism can afford, any more than modernist feminism, to be a project for
women only.   —JUDITH NEWTON AND JUDITH STACEY,
                                "REFLECTIONS ON STUDYING ACADEMIC MEN"

Whereas feminist anthropological projects of gender, after 1970, were consciously,
decidedly, politically, and explicitly about, by, and for women, during the clas-

sic period of anthropology (more or less between 1920 and 1970), most studies of culture and society were, for the most part, unconsciously and "apolitically" about men, by men, and probably for the men who dominated the academy. This confusion of masculinity with culture and society is quite evident in *Yanomamo* by Napoleon Chagnon (there have been several editions: 1968, 1977, 1983, and 1992; all citations herein are from the 1992 edition). Chagnon's ethnography can be read in many different ways: as a study of marriage, kinship, and descent; as a study of warfare; as a study of cultural ecology and social structure; or, perhaps more simply but more exactly, as a study of sedentary gardeners and hunters who live in dispersed villages in the Venezuela-Brazil Amazonian border and who speak the Yanomamo language. Perhaps for historical reasons related to the birth and development of the classic ethnography (see R. Rosaldo 1993), the text is believed to be, and is presented by Chagnon as, a study of a whole people and their culture. After all, the first three editions of Chagnon's case study were subtitled "The Fierce People." After he consulted with some Apache friends of his, Chagnon dropped the subtitle because they (not he) felt that "some white people might read the wrong thing into a word that attempted to represent valor, honor, and independence" (Chagnon 1992, xvi).[9] In spite of this change in the title of his book, Chagnon not only confuses the notion of "fierce" with violence (he explains to the readers the different "levels of violence"—chest pounding, side slapping, club fighting, and raiding), but he also confuses what he thinks is a study of the "Yanomamo culture" with, at best, a study of masculinities, and at worst, a study of a few men who acted "violently." Allow me to present three moments in which feeling fear and feeling intimidated by others were probably more common in his ethnography than the acts of fierceness Chagnon believes he is describing.

Chagnon identifies two men (Rerebawa and Kaobawa) as his key informants: Rerebawa is in his early twenties, and Kaobawa, the head of the village, is in his early forties. According to Chagnon, "Of all the Yanomamo I know, [Rerebawa] is the most genuine and the most devoted to his culture's ways and values" (1992, 31). Whereas "Kaobawa is older and wiser, a polished diplomat," Rerebawa "is fierce and capable of considerable nastiness" (ibid., 31). Chagnon presents at least two examples of Rerebawa's "ferocity," one being when he challenged Bakotawa, who had an affair with one of Rerebawa's potential wives:

> Rerebawa challenged Bakotawa to a club fight. . . . He hurled insult after
> insult at both Bakotawa and his father, trying to goad them into a fight. His
> insults were bitter and nasty. They tolerated them for a few moments, but
> Rerebawa's biting insults provoked them to rage. Finally, they stormed an-
> grily out of their hammocks and ripped out roof-poles, now returning the
> insults verbally, and rushed to the village clearing. Rerebawa continued to in-
> sult them, goading them into striking him on the head with their equally long

clubs. Had either of them struck his head . . . he would then have the right to take his turn on their heads with his club. His opponents were intimidated by his fury, and simply backed down, refusing to strike him, and the argument ended. He had intimidated them into submission. . . . Rerebawa had won the showdown and thereafter swaggered around the village, insulting the two men behind their backs at every opportunity. (1992, 22)

While I would like to emphasize the rage, the process of intimidating, and the submission (taming/domestication) of two men (father and son), Chagnon wants to emphasize the fury and anger of Rerebawa, but with a strategic purpose in mind: to get at people's genealogies: "He was genuinely angry with them, to the point of calling the older man by the name of his long-deceased father. I quickly seized the opportunity to collect an accurate genealogy and confidentially asked Rerebawa about his adversary's ancestors" (1992, 22). Evidently, Chagnon's seizing of violent occasions to trace genealogical relationships constitutes an extreme methodological strategy of classic anthropology's privileging of social structure over structures of feeling. This theoretical preference omitted what M. Rosaldo would have emphasized: that when individuals make private/ personal decisions (tolerating insults, experiencing rage, and feeling intimidated into submission) in public places, they tend to play a culturally legitimate "domestic" (if not domesticated) role. Thus, while masculinist decisions or feelings of fury do not escape Chagnon's ethnographic sensibility (particularly in figuring out social networks), other public forms of intimate "identifications" become blurred if not erased before his analytical gaze. In leaving out of his analysis what he would probably consider *nonmasculine* vulnerabilities of men (feeling fear and being intimidated), Chagnon reduces, or rather elevates, "the Yanomamo," particularly Yanomamo men, to masculine—in this case, fierce—proportions.

In a second example of what it means to be "fierce," Chagnon tells us that

Rerebawa has displaced his ferocity in many ways, one incident in particular illustrates what his character can be like. Before he left his own village to take his new wife . . . , he had an affair with the wife of an older brother. When it was discovered, his brother attacked him with a club. Rerebawa responded furiously: He grabbed an ax and drove his brother out of the village after soundly beating him with the blunt side of the single-bit ax. His brother was so intimidated by the thrashing and promise of more to come that he did not return to the village for several days. I visited the village . . . shortly after this event had taken place; Rerebawa was my guide. He made it a point to introduce me to this man. He approached his hammock, grabbed him by the wrist, and dragged him out on the ground: "This is the brother whose wife I screwed when he wasn't around!" A deadly insult, one that would usually provoke a bloody club fight among more valiant Yanomamo.

The man did nothing. He slunk sheepishly back into his hammock, shamed, but relieved to have Rerebawa release his grip. (1992, 30)

While I would like to call attention, once again, to the shame, the fear, and the intimidation felt by Rerebawa's brother (we do not get his name), Chagnon repeatedly ignores these public demonstrations of domestic/ated feelings among the Yanomamo and instead makes the observation that Rerebawa "has a charming, witty side as well." Yet just as he provided Chagnon with genealogies, Rerebawa also seems to have given the most charming treatment to the anthropologist (unlike the blows given to his cultural peers). For instance, Chagnon wrote, "He is one of few Yanomamo that I feel I can trust. I recall indelibly my return to [the village] after being away a year. . . . He greeted me with an immense bear hug and exclaimed, with tears welling up in his eyes, 'Shaki! Why did you stay away so long? . . . I could not at times eat for want of seeing you again!' I, too [Chagnon continues], felt the same way about him—then and now. . . . Of all the Yanomamo I know, he is the most genuine and most devoted to his culture's ways and values" (1992, 30–31).[10]

Thus, even though Rerebawa intimidated everyone else in the village, Chagnon considered him a typical Yanomamo, with all kinds of evidence to the contrary.

One last example of the terror felt by the young men (and the avoidance practiced by older men) should suffice to demonstrate that Chagnon's ideal spectacle about "fierceness" was mostly in his own *masculinist* imagination. He wrote:

Some of the younger men in Kaobawa's group were reluctant to participate in the fighting because *they were afraid of being injured, remaining on the periphery so as to not be easily seen.* This put more strain on the others, who were forced to take extra turns in order to preserve the group's reputation. At one point Kaobawa's men, sore from the punishment they had taken and worried that they would ultimately lose the fight, wanted to escalate the contest to an ax duel. . . . Kaobawa was adamantly opposed to this, as he knew it would bring bloodshed. He therefore recruited the younger men into the fighting, as well as a few of the older ones who had [*sic*] nothing but demand the *others* step into the arena. . . . *A few of the younger men retired after a single blow, privately admitting to me later that they pretended to be injured to avoid being forced to fight more.* The fighting continued in this fashion for nearly three hours. . . . Kaobawa and the headman from the other group stood by with their weapons, attempting to keep the fighting under control but not participating in it. (1992, 180; my emphasis)

This chest-pounding duel, which eventually led to "women and children from both groups . . . fleeing from the village, screaming and crying" (ibid., 183), was a product of a feast. Even though the relationship between the two groups remained "somewhat strained and potentially hostile," Chagnon ends his analysis on a sort of happy, structural-functional note: "In general, feasts are exciting for both the hosts and the guests and contribute to their solidarity. . . . Of the six feasts I witnessed during the first 18 months I spent with the Yanomamo, two of them ended in fighting" (ibid.).

In spite of the complex life lived by the people Chagnon studied and in spite of his (almost exclusive) interaction with men—and not all of them "violent"— Chagnon not only reached explicit conclusions about culture, society, social structure, and the nature of violence in human beings, he also reached implicit conclusions about Yanomamo men as if they all were exclusively "masculine" and, thus, fierce beings.[11]

From Masculinity Studies to Gender Studies

In Chagnon's ethnography, and most visibly in the ethnographic films he made, women (as gendered subjects) are present but hardly ever discussed. For that to occur in anthropology, it took a feminist turn in the discipline, a shift driven quite effectively by the female generation of Michelle Rosaldo. This feminist turn included not only a feminist critique of gender roles; it also implied (though informally) some kind of anthropological training in the development of a feminist sensibility and consciousness on the part of the ethnographer—something that Chagnon and most anthropologists of his generation either rejected or simply did not get. By the mid- and late 1980s, the period in which I was a graduate student at UW-Madison and Stanford, several of my feminist professors (who were themselves trained in a critical feminist and/or Marxist anthropology in the late sixties and seventies) were reshaping a theoretically pervasive and ethnographically convincing kind of feminist anthropological tradition that their students, female or male, could easily incorporate into their general training of the discipline (if they so desired) and into their general vision of the social and academic worlds they inhabited. Yet in the 1990s, perhaps ironically, the move from Women's Studies and Masculinist Studies to Gender Studies was mostly characterized by gaps and contradictions, particularly concerning the production of a scholarly field that would genuinely and rigorously take the feminist study of gender—of *both* men and women—to task.

With the intention of exploring possibilities, below I displace or change the focus on masculinity to refocus on "gender" in order to (1) challenge more effectively the aura of authority (as M. Rosaldo suggested) and (2) argue that neither men nor women can be properly understood separately, especially in the class-based, cultural contexts of maquiladora production in the late 1980s and throughout the 1990s. Following M. Rosaldo's inquisitive logic, I would like to address in this section two interrelated questions: (1) Are gender subjectivities extended into class identities when both men and women are incorporated into public social spaces, such as maquiladoras?; and (2) Is the aura of a gendered authority effectively challenged in this process and can this lead to class mobilization?

In 1990 and in Chapter 5 of this book, based on my 1987 fieldwork experience in a maquiladora (where the workers and I assembled microcircuits), I made several arguments about gender, culture, and late capitalist production (Lugo 1990). I examined how sociohistorical notions of laziness constitute in themselves cultural enactments or performances that enrich, in the eyes of the capitalist, the global assembling process. More specifically, I tried to show how new notions of machismo (manliness and masculinity) were produced and reproduced through the production and reproduction of microcircuits on the assembly line. This production and reproduction of culture and gender identity occurred (1) through the public enactment of *huevón(ona)* and *barra*—two different linguistic terms that mean the same thing: "lazy"—and (2) through the cultural expectation, on the part of Mexican men, to have *huevos,* or "courage/strength," in everyday life (here the metaphor *huevos,* translated as "eggs," implies "testicles" or "balls"). The most important tool necessary to assemble the microcircuits was a *barra,* a piece of iron (a bar). The multiple uses and multiple meanings of the term *barra* led me to give an ethnographic description of how gender and class exploitation took place simultaneously.

From a particular Latin Americanist perspective, it is evident that analysis of that factory was implicitly dominated by the machismo/*marianismo* (which assumes that all women must be, to different degrees, moral extensions of the Virgin Mary) distinction, commonly associated with gender differences in Latin America (see Twinam 1989, 120). Yet it is more true that part of the psychological pressure the men felt when they got behind was a product of the negotiation taking place not only with other men, but also with the women who were assembling at the same production table. In other words, the reproduction of masculinity was not only a male thing (see also Gutmann 1996); it acquired deeper meaning precisely because of the power behind the women's gazes. Interestingly, however, in spite of this masculinist cultural process, and just as M. Rosaldo argued, men cannot easily establish an aura of authority precisely because of the involvement of both men and women in the same kind of activity.

This transfiguration in the dynamic of the workings of authority has unintended and unexpected consequences for the transformation of gender identity and subjectivity. If, in this particular global factory, being masculine meant keeping up with the quota in an efficient manner, then the women at the production table also engaged in a "masculine" praxis of their own. Thus, biological notions of femininity and masculinity collapse when, for example, social and productive effectiveness is the dominant discourse domesticating and taming all workers (both men and women) as gendered, and, more importantly, as class subjects, that is, as exploited workers.

Without this specific analysis of "gender" and class subjectivity, it is possible, though a serious theoretical problem, to reduce complex social processes to either men or women. Without this analysis, "class" would be fractured into simplistic gendered categories. Under these specific circumstances of global production (with both men and women producing), where it is uncertain whether the worker will be effective or not, gender identities are improvised and negotiated, specifically at the production table. In this negotiation, gender acquires class tones. For instance, one day, we ran out of material to assemble in the electronics maquiladora discussed in Chapter 5. While we were waiting, a young man (teenager) seriously commented that he had a headache. In the border city of Ciudad Juárez, working-class men often joke with the linguistic expression, *dolor de cabeza,* or having a "headache." Metonymically, *cabeza* or "head" can be jokingly taken to mean the head of the penis (just as "head" is used in the American expression "giving head"). Consequently, when the young man seriously said, "Me duele la cabeza," a young woman immediately responded by yelling, *¡Sumo!* an expression meaning "Fuck You! [with the head of my penis]," which is commonly used by males to express real and ideal sexual domination over others, but here it is appropriated by a woman. Feeling challenged in their own subculture, the men nodded with a smile, whereas other women simultaneously showed, with a different kind of smile, both a sign of approval of the cultural inversion or cultural shift taking place and a sign of momentary disassociation from "that type of women" (*ese tipo de mujeres*). Thus, as we can see, the appropriation of male discourse on the part of women often dissolves facile masculine/feminine distinctions; yet it does not necessarily transcend or transform the class-based male ideology that often marks as *locas,* or "loose," the women who cross conventional gendered boundaries.

Nonetheless, we must still ask the following question about the workers: What strategies do they (men or women) have for coping with group pressure (which, when applied while they are actively assembling a product, is not dissimilar to the group pressure felt by the young Yanomamo men in chest-pounding duels)? Just as Yanomamo men "remain on the periphery so as to not be easily seen" and "pretended to be injured," maquiladora workers sometimes opt for simply leaving the job, especially if the pressure gets too high. This is part of the turnover or rotation problem that characterized maquiladora production in the last two decades of the twentieth century. The following description by Carlos about what it means to work under pressure in an automobile maquila, where he assembled electric harnesses (also see Chapter 6), vividly explains what experiences might lead a worker (*male or female*) to simply quit:

There was a quota. The line where I was working had to produce between 150 and 200 harnesses . . . it was a lot. If we ran out of material, then you rested. If a person got behind, as one of my [male] friends used to do . . . [pause] . . . he would always get behind, always. He was five persons behind me. I was the last one. He had very long cables . . . do you understand? . . . Very long cables. Where they were hung, the cables would make three big circles. When my friend would pull the cables, he would get desperate because he would not pull them right. With the preoccupation that the machine was rotating, he would get behind. Then everybody would fall behind . . . everybody: the five persons behind him and five guys between us. So the machine would have to be stopped. Since no one wanted to get behind, all the workers [women and men] would get piled up on each other, trying to assemble their own cables. See, the machine could not be stopped. The most it would stop was two or three minutes, and that was a lot. (Lugo 1995, 142–143)

After a long workday, Carlos and his friend (they lived in the same neighborhood) would go home and dream about work. He told me that they used to joke with the supervisor by asking him who would pay the extra hours labored. The supervisor would ask, "What extra hours?" Carlos would answer: "The evening hours. We go home and dream that we are inserting terminals. Who is gonna pay for those hours?" When I worked in the electronics maquila assembling microcircuits and distributing *barras* through the conveyor belt, I used to dream that I was passing *barras* to the other workers. My wife used to tell me that I kept on giving my pillow to her while I sat (asleep) on our bed. Carlos then told me that he and his friend resigned, both on the same day.

In the garment maquiladora where I conducted fieldwork in 1989, notions of aggressiveness, which tend to be associated with the masculine *in men,* were more characteristic of *the workplace* than of either men or women; this is the case even if it is through gendered subjects that these cultural practices and class actions are manifested. As we saw in the previous chapter, in this particular garment factory, there were not enough decent chairs on which to sit to sew the hospital gowns we were supposed to assemble. Cultural notions of respect for *lo ajeno* (what does not belong to you) or in favor of Latin American *caballerismo* (expected gentleness toward women) on the part of men (as when giving the chair or the seat to a woman) had to be discarded if the workers wanted to carry out their jobs. It is impossible to sew without a chair in garment factories. Yet, every morning at 6:00 AM, workers had to confront others in their daily struggles for chairs. The chair had to be negotiated every morning, along with their working-class dignity and, of course, their gender subjectivity.

The following journal entries from my field notes depict the gendered working conditions under which the workers and I negotiated chairs in the garment *maquiladora:*

Monday, August 21, 1989—Víctor was looking for his chair. Finally, he came to me; he said mine was his. Juan, another worker said, "Don't believe him" (*No te creas*). Víctor insisted. I said, "Go tell Pedro (the foreman). He assigned it to me." Víctor did not say anything. He just wanted a chair. I don't know why no one is assigned one. It's even good for productivity. I liked that chair. At the end of the day, I marked it with "Lugo" on it. I went to tell Pedro that because so many people were absent, if the owner shows up tomorrow, I would give it back to him or her. Then Pedro, the foreman, said, "No, defend it! Defend that one!"

On the next day, August 22, 1989, I wrote the following:

Remember, I was to defend my chair, the chair I had labeled "Lugo." I was hoping that a *cholo* (a gang member) would not have it. But then, to my surprise, a young, quiet (sixteen- or seventeen-year-old) woman had it. I went to her and said, "Excuse me, this is my chair" [*Oiga, esta es mi silla*]. She said, "I always use this one." Then I asked, "Were you here yesterday? Why didn't you have it?" She answered, "Yesterday, everything was very confusing, so I ended up with another one." I said to her, "Pedro told me to label this one. Tell Pedro to assign you one" (by this time, I do not know why I insisted on assigning chairs). While talking to her, I couldn't help but realize that she was so young [I was twenty-seven years old at that time]. Yet, I was told to "defend" that chair. I remembered my feminist instructors from graduate school [Ann Stoler, Florencia Mallon, Maria Lepowsky, Jane Collier]. I thought about Fernández-Kelly (through her book). I could see their faces inside my mind. Believe me, you gals, I didn't mistreat her. I've learned from your teachings. We didn't have a discussion or argument about the chair; we had a dialogue. I was aware of gender relations (power) there, at that moment. I was gentle to her. I even felt bad when she was giving the chair back to me. She said, "I'll talk to Pedro. I'll tell him to find me one." . . . When I went to my place, I saw her grabbing another chair [from another machine]. I went to her and said, "Make sure you label that one." . . . She said, "I always use this one or the one you have. So I'll stay with this one." "Label it," I said again. She answered, "I'll recognize the chair." Of course, I felt ridiculously patronizing and stupid. Both of us had different ways of approaching the chairs. . . . When I came back, María thought the young woman was taking away my chair. She said to me, "If that chair is yours, make sure you claim it . . . (*Que a usted le valga*)." María had described the attitude that one has to have under these working conditions. Whether the person is a woman, a man, a young woman, an older woman, an older man, or a younger man: you must defend your chair. It was survival of the fittest in the late twentieth century inside a multinational assem-

bly plant. Yet, the young women are and can still be at a disadvantage. This
is why the feminist arguments of Fernández-Kelly, Stoler, Mallon, Lepowsky, and Collier came to my mind at that particular moment. I saw and experienced the situations they claim injure particular women, especially the
young ones. However, I saw Lupe, an older woman [with seniority], defend-
ing her positions regarding chairs, fans, gum, etc., not only from older men
with experience, but also from inexperienced male newcomers.

It is evident that many times, and depending on their circumstances, gender identities and notions of "aggressiveness" cannot simply be defined either
as masculine or as feminine: these meanings can be uncertain and tend to get
negotiated, in this case, as M. Rosaldo would have suggested, precisely because
both men and women are involved in work activities that are given the same
value—either by the capitalist or by the coworker. In this regard, notions of Latin
American *caballerismo* on the part of men, as in "giving your chair to a woman,"
had to be discarded (in fact, it is common nowadays, when the workers get on
the *rutera* hoping to find a seat where they can rest, to see men *not* giving their
seat to women who might be standing on their way home at the end of a long
working day). Consequently, the question of "the masculine" or "the feminine" is
not always the right question to ask, even if it seems that the question of gender
is the issue. It is thus clear that the social context and the circumstances themselves (late capitalism) had a dominant role in producing aggressive practices
and subjectivities that are, in the end, class based.

Social reality, however, either in its negotiated or inverted version, does not
necessarily transcend the power inequalities that still place subordinate/domes-
ticated subjects at a disadvantage in the process of negotiation. Men and women
in Ciudad Juárez, for example, are still victims of patriarchal ideologies: some
physically stronger men still injure the weaker males in violent fights, which take
place inside and outside the factories (in the buses, in the streets of their neighborhoods); some of these men batter their wives and girlfriends. Physical violence against women, children, and gay men is one of the most common problems the Juárez community still associates with the use and abuse of authority
and physical strength, whether on the part of male police or on the part of other
victimizers of violence, who tend to be males (I have noticed, however, that most
male victimizers of violence are nonmaquiladora men: they tend to be street
vendors, construction workers, drug dealers, and bus drivers). In the epilogue, I
briefly examine a few of the deadly cases of violence against women and girls. In
this chapter, however, it will suffice to argue that the cultural meanings given to
these occurrences relate more to discourses of power—which disembody gender from the body itself—manifested in particular contexts of class, than to es-
sentializing notions of a masculinity and a femininity exclusively inscribed on
already-naturalized male or female bodies (see Ginsburg 1997).

Conclusion

The particular displacements of gender identity examined in this chapter—the unpredictability, uncertainty, and unexpected inversions and subversions of gender relations and gendered subjectivities—are products of the destabilization (at strategic moments) of the aura of male authority in gender relations. These social products and social transformations, however, were not imagined by Michelle Rosaldo when she proposed her hypothetical recommendation for social change in Western capitalist society: bringing men into household obligations. Thus, it seems that a more extensive and multilayered concept of gender is our best option for understanding and examining relations among men, among women (not explored here), and between men and women in the multiple "fields" of feminist anthropology.

In this chapter, I have made several arguments. In "Part I," I suggested that Michelle Rosaldo's articulation of theory and practice was reflected through complex (instead of simplistic) understandings of "domestic" and "public" spheres and through the political spaces her theorizing tried to create for the social transformation of gender relations, at least in capitalist societies. Bringing men into household obligations and responsibilities, she thought, would not allow men to establish an aura of authority and distance vis-à-vis women. I argued in "Part I" that her critics misunderstood her political project and, in consequence, her theoretical project as well. "Part II" examined the social repercussions and theoretical implications associated with "bringing men into the home," or with destabilizing the aura of authority in an ideologically and materially unfixed space where both men and women participate. Through ethnographic detail, I tried to address the following question: are gender subjectivities inevitably extended into class identities when men *and* women are incorporated into the global assembly line (an economic sector historically associated with female labor in Ciudad Juárez, Mexico)?

Before attempting to answer this question, I analyzed certain limitations with studies of men in relation to men (as opposed to "gender") by using as an example Napoleon Chagnon's masculinized representations of "the Yanomamo." In critically examining Chagnon's ethnographic representations of Yanomamo men, I made the following arguments: first, that if we are going to focus on men in ethnography and consider in turn only their "strengths" in our analysis (just as Chagnon focused exclusively on masculinist fury and on being fierce), we end up not only with poorly understood, reductionistic notions of the "masculine" in men, but also with masculinist representations of what are otherwise complex human beings; second, a more accurate description of this human complexity in men and women requires particular ethnographic sensibility and training— skills that perhaps can only be acquired through class and feminist consciousness and feminist anthropological training, similar to the one provided by the sophisticated lens of the late Michelle Zimbalist Rosaldo (and of several female anthropologists of her generation). Finally, I argued in this section, though implicitly, that the new generations of feminist anthropologists, especially those trained in the first decade of the twenty-first century, should have the capacity to carry out (if the analyst so desires) a gender analysis of class that transcends either the *masculinist* studies of the classic tradition (which should not be reproduced in any form or content in the future), or the kind of studies of women that, according to Michelle Rosaldo, "by stressing female action," fail "to ask just how it comes about— *in a world where people of both sexes make choices that count—* that men come to be seen as the creators of collective good and the preeminent force in local politics" (M. Rosaldo 1980, 414–415; my emphasis).

In "Part II," I also juxtaposed Chagnon's analysis of Yanomamo men with my own analysis of factory men and women at the U.S.-Mexico border. Through such juxtaposition, I raised certain theoretical issues that, I believe, redefine our conception of "gender" in feminist anthropology. For example, I have demonstrated that in destabilizing the aura of authority, there are no empirical grounds for reducing either masculinity to men or femininity to women. In this process, I have also claimed that men, if they are to be studied, should be understood through both their strengths and their vulnerabilities as human beings. Here, I emphasized vulnerabilities: feeling fear, being intimidated, getting hurt, being careless, feeling pressure (at work or in dreams), and finally, feeling physically ineffective, whether among maquiladora men or among Yanomamo men. This discussion of "the domestic" and of private and personal feelings of men in so-called public places constituted as well my reflections on the theoretical insights M. Rosaldo had for inversions in gender relations: just as she claimed that "when public decisions are made in the household, women may have a legitimate public role" (1974, 39), I also argued that when undesired personal decisions are made in public settings, men often do play a legitimate and necessary "domestic" (if not domesticated/tamed) role.

In the maquiladora cases examined here, an aura of static, pervasive, or persistent authority on the part of men could not be established precisely because both genders are actively involved in the same activities, and on more or less equal terms. This was M. Rosaldo's suggestive hypothesis, which I tried to put to the test.

Despite the undeniable self-presentation of men and women according to what they believe to be a culturally acceptable image along masculine and feminine lines, the complexity of everyday life should remind us, at least those of us who study human beings in their sociohistorical contexts, that questions of "the masculine" and "the feminine" should be addressed not through our powerful (but probably false) assumptions of what biology and society should dictate, but rather through our analyses of power, class, color, and gender—of how human beings (both men and women) interact and negotiate their cultural and class subjectivities in particular social contexts, in this case, under late capitalism in the postcolonial context of the U.S.-Mexico border.

To conclude, just as Michelle Rosaldo tried to invert the domestic/public dichotomy, I tried to show that the "masculine" and "feminine" subjectivities of men and women, respectively, are also inverted on the shop floor, often transcending what it means to be a man and what it means to be a woman, yet articulating a class identity that could bring them together for political (class) mobilization. As Catherine MacKinnon noted in the early 1980s about the political potential of feminist analyses of class: "Feminism turns theory itself—the pursuit of a true analysis of social life—into the pursuit of consciousness and turns an analysis of inequality into a critical embrace of its own determinants. . . . The pursuit of consciousness becomes a form of political practice. Consciousness raising has revealed gender relations to be a collective fact, no more simply personal than class relations. This implies that class relations may also be personal, no less so for being at the same time collective" (1982, 30). Then, in spite of the Cold War discourse, she is still able to suggest from the past, to those of us who are still documenting the conflict between labor and capital at the beginning of the twenty-first century, that "the failure of Marxism to realize this may connect the failure of workers in advanced capitalist nations to organize in the socialist sense with the failure of left revolutions to liberate women in the feminist sense" (ibid.).

The reidentification of these problems of identity and politics is just the beginning of our understanding of the unintended consequences of the destabilization of the aura of authority in gender and class relations. These are the particular social contexts that constrain, transform, and, finally, give shape to what Michelle Rosaldo called our "identifications." By the same token, I hope that these observations make evident that our traditional conception of what constitutes gender studies or studies of gender must also be transformed into an analytical notion (that is sensitive to class and race issues but) that encompasses specific studies of both men and women, and not only studies of women or studies of men.

Unless we search for alternative and alternating imaginings, we, as critical scholars and as citizens, will not be able to challenge effectively the "unmaking" of the working classes in Mexico and around the world—an unmaking that continues to reproduce itself in the twenty-first century.

III

Alternating Imaginings

Reimagining Culture and Power against Late Industrial Capitalism and Other Forms of Conquest through Border Theory and Analysis

border n. 1: an outer part or edge 2: BOUNDARY, FRONTIER . . .
4: an ornamental design at the edge of a fabric or rug
syn BORDER, MARGIN, VERGE, EDGE, RIM, BRIM, BRINK
borderland n. 1 a: territory at or near a border: FRONTIER
b: an outlying region
borderline n.: line of demarcation
bordure n.: border surrounding a heraldic shield
— WEBSTER'S NEW COLLEGIATE DICTIONARY

Ania Loomba: Now some people have offered a critique of Subaltern Studies saying that if you try and combine Foucault and Gramsci, it's like trying to ride two horses at the same time. And Gyan Prakash answers by saying then we all need to become stunt riders! . . . I wanted to ask you to comment in a little more detail on what you think is the potential of such combinations. Is this a productive tension at all between Foucault and Gramsci?
Edward Said: Extremely productive . . . the attempt to bring the two together involves in a certain sense breaking up the Foucauldian narrative into a series of smaller situations where Gramsci's terminology can become useful and illuminating for analytical purposes.
— EDWARD SAID, "IN CONVERSATION WITH NEELADRI
BHATTACHARYA, SUVIR KAUL, AND ANIA LOOMBA"

Introduction: The Borders of Border Theory

If we wanted to carry out an archaeology of border theory, how would we identify its sources and its targets?[1] Where would we locate its multiple sites of production and consumption, formation and transformation? What are the multiple discourses producing images of borders almost everywhere, at least in the minds of academics? In trying to answer these questions, though more with an exploratory spirit than with a definitive one, let us say that the sites, the sources, the targets, and the discourses can be variably characterized by the following: previously marginalized intellectuals within the academy (i.e., women and other minorities); the outer limits of the nation-state (i.e., the U.S.-Mexico border region); the frontiers of culture theory (i.e., cultural borderlands compared with cultural patterns); the multiple fronts of struggle in Cultural Studies (i.e., the war of position); the cutting edge of theories of difference (i.e., race, class, gender, and sexual orientation); and, finally, the crossroads of history, literature, anthropology, and sociology (i.e., Cultural Studies).

In this final chapter, I argue that to understand its political and practical importance, we must reimagine border theorizing (one that articulates to culture, capitalism, and conquest) in the realm of the inescapable, mountainous terrains of Power (Derrida 1978; Foucault 1978) as the latter has operated through the expansion of Western empires since 1492 (see Chapters 2, 3, and 5), and as it has overlapped in the academy, in culture theory, in the global contexts of late industrial capitalism (Chapters 4–8), and, in the last analysis (and perhaps most important), in the realms of the changing "nation" (Anderson 1991) and "state" (Hall 1986)[2]—under which current transnational academic practices continue to be enacted.

This privileging of the "nation-state" on my part relates to a current theoretical and political concern that has practical implications for the opening of more inclusive spaces under globalization, especially for the twenty-first century; for *the deterritorialization (and reterritorialization)* of the nation, politics, culture and border theory; and, finally, for human agency (Martín-Rodríguez 1996; Morales 1996; Ong 1995). For Alejandro Morales (as noted in Chapter 6), "Michel Foucault's concept of heterotopia explains border culture," and "life in the chaos of heterotopia is a perpetual act of self-definition gradually deterritorializing the individual" (1996, 23, 24). Regarding feminist practice in the global setting, Aihwa Ong argues that "diasporic feminists (and we should all be somewhat mobile to be vigilant) should develop a denationalized and deterritorialized set of cultural practices. These would have to deal with the tough questions of gender oppression not only in that 'other place' . . . but also in one's own family, community, culture, religion, race, and nation" (1995, 367). Finally, just as Manuel Martín-Rodríguez, following Deleuze and Guattari, argues that a "minor language" can erode a "major language from within," I argue that the border region, as well as border theory and analysis, can erode the hegemony of the privileged center by denationalizing and deterritorializing the nation-state and culture theory, respectively: "In other words, minor languages erode, as it were, a major language from within, deterritorializing it, breaking up its system's supposed homogeneity" (Martín-Rodríguez 1996, 86)—without uncritically reterritorializing it.[3]

Much more specifically, my analytical framework in this chapter is the following: I draw the contours of two theoretical parallelisms, both constituted by seemingly disconnected conceptual preoccupations. On the one hand, there is the critical articulation between Gramsci's notion of the *state and its dispersal* and Foucault's notion of *Power and its deployment;*[4] on the other, we have Anderson's critique of the nation and R. Rosaldo's critique of culture in anthropology. I am particularly interested in Gramsci's uses of the terms "state," "force relations," and "war of position" and how they might relate to Foucault's "relations of force" and his faith in "the strategical model rather than the model based on law," as well as his strategic belief that "politics is *war* pursued by other means" (Foucault 1978, 93; emphasis added). I argue here that these connections of resistance against folk notions of the "head of the king [and] the spell of monarchy" (Foucault 1978, 88–89), that is, "the state/the law,"[5] are quite telling in themselves about the ways in which we have come to think about social life and culture inside and outside anthropology, which is my interest here. These critiques call for multiple discourses, wars of position, situated knowledges, positioned subjects, and different arenas of contestation in everyday life. Thus, the analysis presented here should help explain not only the recent production of theories of borders in resistance to our Westernized imagination but also how the latter system of domination is traced back to the sixteenth and seventeenth centuries (see Chapter 2). I strategically examine this complex sociohistorical articulation between border theory and the West, within anthropology, by juxtaposing Anderson's critique of the nation as an imagined community with Rosaldo's critique of culture as shared patterns of behavior (also see Chapter 5 for my juxtaposition of Foucault, Sahlins and Boas).

By reflecting on these parallelisms—that between Gramsci's notion of the state and Foucault's notion of power (both being *dispersed* entities) and between Anderson's notion of the imagined community and R. Rosaldo's cultural patterns (both being *homogeneous* entities)—I hope to show how border theory at the turn of the twenty-first century in anthropology (i.e., R. Rosaldo's "cultural borderlands") cannot be properly understood without situating it in relation to changing discourses about the state (both colonial and modern), the nation, and culture in the nineteenth and twentieth centuries, at least as these imagined categories and periodizations are examined in the works of R. Rosaldo (*Culture and Truth*, 1993), Anderson (*Imagined Communities*, 1991), Foucault (*The History of Sexuality*, Vol. 1, 1978), and Hall ("Gramsci's Relevance for the Study of Race and Ethnicity," 1986), as well as throughout this book.[6]

By locating border theory at the crossroads of culture theory in anthropology, and at the crossroads of ideologies of the state and the nation, which in turn produced "anthropologies" that represented national hegemonic traditions (American, British, and French), I hope to show the political and epistemological limits under which we teach, write, do research, and theorize. One of my main arguments here is that border theory itself can contribute effectively to the exploration of these limits, as long as it is recognized to be (as theories of social life tend to be) a product of the codification of a "multiplicity of force relations . . . which by virtue of their inequalities, constantly engender states of power" (Foucault 1978, 93).[7]

The Current State of Culture: Cultural Borderlands vis-à-vis Cultural Patterns

Cultural borderlands should be understood, first of all, in relation to the previous dominant discourse about culture: cultural patterns. Renato Rosaldo has been very precise about the limitations of what he calls the "classic vision of unique cultural patterns":

> It emphasizes shared patterns at the expense of processes of change and internal inconsistencies, conflicts, and contradictions. By defining culture as a set of shared meanings, classic norms of analysis make it difficult to study zones of difference within and between cultures. From the classic perspective, cultural borderlands appear to be annoying exceptions rather than central areas of inquiry. (1993, 28)

Although I agree with R. Rosaldo's critical assessment of the social and political implications of the ideology of "cultural patterns," my vision of the way those cultural patterns have been created in the theoretical imagination of classic anthropologists is a bit different. In fact, the historical process through which we have come to theorize and think about culture, society, cultural patterns, and borderlands should be reconsidered if we want, as Foucault argued, "to cut off the head of the king" (1978, 88).

I propose here that the attempt to decipher the complex relation between structure and practice was and has been a dominant thinking channel or tool through which the concept of culture has been imagined, though more implicitly than explicitly. Let us see how the latter contention is manifested in the writings of some of anthropology's major and recent practitioners. By considering the sociopolitical and historical context in which anthropologists wrote, I hope to shed some light on why, after all, a discourse on culture and society emerged, especially in the context of capitalism and imperialism. The following discussion will eventually bring us back to an analysis of the role of the state, the law, and the nation in shaping our formulations of the concept of culture and of social life in general.

As previously noted in Chapter 5, Marshall Sahlins has explicitly associated the concept of culture with a double existence: "In the dialectic of culture-as-constituted and culture-as-lived we . . . discover some possibility of reconciling the most profound antimony of social science theory, that between structure and practice: reconciling them, that is, in the only way presently justifiable—as a symbolic process" (1982, 48). Regarding "society," however, Sherry Ortner has also identified a dialectical polarity in what she calls "practice theory," which constitutes the attempt to understand "how society and culture themselves are produced and reproduced through *human intention and action*" (1984, 158; emphasis added). In 1984, Ortner argued that "the modern versions of practice theory . . . appear unique in . . . that society is a system, that the system is powerfully constraining, and yet that the system can be made and unmade through human action and interaction" (ibid., 159). Ortner's similar treatment of both "society" and "culture" is less conspicuous, for our purpose here, than the way she imagines these theoretical constructs through pervasive critical dualisms: system and action, human intention and action. Sahlins's imaginings about culture, as lived and as constituted, also reproduce the pattern I am exposing here: the double existence of culture (see Chapters 5–8 for how these concepts relate to "class" and to specific ethnographic examples for the U.S.-Mexico border).[8]

Sahlins subjects this dialectic in culture to his "structure and history" approach (1981, 1982, 1985; see also R. Rosaldo 1980), whereas Ortner associates the dialectic in society with a general theory of "practice" (1984). Ortner in fact argues that this focus on "practice" emerged in the early 1970s as a result of such historical conjunctures as the New Left movement; she also suggests that "practice theory" became articulated in American anthropology when Bourdieu's *Outline of a Theory of Practice* was translated into English in 1977 (Ortner 1984).[9]

In what follows, I suggest that the dominant anthropological notion of culture is one that is constituted by the articulation of beliefs and action, structure and practice, culture as constituted and culture as lived, and/or system and action, and that it is the historical product of a specific "academic" response to the political relation between the state/the nation and its citizens—a relationship that can be traced to the nineteenth century. In fact, these larger sociohistorical forces became crystallized in Western academia through Durkheim's ([1893] 1933, [1912] 1965) own peculiar invention of "society" and through the German/ American production of "culture" in Boasian anthropology.

Culture and the State

Before the late 1960s, certain socioeconomic and political events of the Victorian era contributed to the continued suppression of the explicit treatment of the structure/practice relation embedded in the concepts of "culture" and "society": to talk about human practice or praxis was to talk about history, conflict, change, and social transformation—theoretical concepts that could easily expose the colonial and capitalist encounters/enterprises of the nineteenth century and the first half of the twentieth century. Thus, until the early 1970s, the discourse on culture and society in the social sciences, and especially in anthropology, was dominated by the systematic analysis of the coordination of such dualisms as the individual and society, the individual and culture—ignoring the realities of "practice" (for examples of this pattern, see Barth 1966; Benedict 1934; Durkheim [1893] 1933, [1912] 1965; Malinowski 1944; Radcliffe-Brown 1952).

Consequently, due to the political suppression of conceptual binaries that included "practice" (praxis), the notions of "society" and "culture" were to be discussed in terms of "order," "harmony," "rules" (Durkheim [1893] 1933, [1912] 1965), "shared patterns of beliefs" (Benedict 1934; Boas 1963), and an antichaotic condition (Weber 1977). Political scientist Perry Anderson has appropriately noted that the work of Emile Durkheim, like that of Max Weber and Vilfredo Pareto, was haunted by "a profound fear of the masses and premonition of social disintegration" (1968, 4). He claims quite explicitly that sociology at the turn of the twentieth century "emerged as a bourgeois counter-reaction to Marxism," which, of course, was arguing at the time that class conflict was inevitable. It must be noted, however, that Durkheim was as much against the greedy capitalist on the loose at the time as against the "immorality" of the masses. Both of these threats confirmed for him, as an employee of the French state, the need for rules to monitor and control both the working classes and the utilitarian entrepreneur.

The intensification of class conflict had emerged as a product of industrial capitalism within the "West"; additionally, broader sociopolitical tensions were generated as a result of the retraction of some European colonialisms due to the nineteenth-century nationalist movements in Spanish America and Central Europe. The expansion of U.S. colonialism at the turn of the twentieth century into the Philippines and Puerto Rico, for instance, also contributed to a generalized problem of the body politic within and outside the West (see B. Anderson 1991; Flores 1993, Foucault 1978; Hall 1986). Foucault[10] and Stuart Hall treat 1870 as a key historical moment regarding, respectively, the production of new sexualities and the expansion of the new imperialist colonialisms. According to Gramsci and Hall, this period in the latter part of the nineteenth century constitutes a historical transition in the nature of the "State" from a monarchical, dynastic body politic and its subjects to a "State" (read: nation/nation-state) in which the subjects become citizens, and thus, become loosely tied to the direct control of a centralized, lawlike apparatus; in this new political regime, individuals are indirectly monitored through the state's *dispersal of power* (Foucault 1978; Hall 1986). This process must be properly explained in the historical and geographic contexts of each newly emerging nation around the world.[11]

Stuart Hall describes Gramsci's vision of this critical transformation in Western history in this way:

> Gramsci bases this "transition from one form of politics to another" historically. It takes place in "the West" after 1870, and is identified with "the colonial expansion of Europe," the emergence of modern mass democracy,

a complexification in the role and organization of the state and an unprece-
dented elaboration in the structures and processes of "civil hegemony."
What Gramsci is pointing to, here, is partly the diversification of social an-
tagonisms, the "dispersal" of power, which occurs in societies where hegemony is sustained, not exclusively through the enforced instrumentality of
the state, but rather, it is grounded in the relations and institutions of civil
society [schooling, the family, the factory, churches and religious life, and so
on]. (1986, 18)

In addition to these institutions of civil society, Foucault adds "a multiplicity
of discourses produced by a whole series of mechanisms operating in different
institutions . . . demography, biology, medicine, psychiatry, psychology, ethics,
pedagogy, and political criticism" (1978, 33). Regarding their dispersal, Foucault
explicitly and forcefully noted, "So it is not simply in terms of a continual extension that we must speak of this discursive growth; it should be seen rather
as a dispersion of centers from which discourses emanated, a diversification
of their forms, and the complex deployment of the network connecting them"
(ibid., 34).

Weber (1958) documented the bureaucratization of modern institutions
around the same time, after 1870 and into World War I. The "war of position" necessary for effective political resistance against the dispersal of power, and characterizing the new state of the "state" is powerfully stated in military terms:

> The "war of position" . . . has to be conducted in a protracted way, across
> many different and varying fronts of struggle. . . . What really counts in a
> war of position is not the enemy's "forward trenches" (to continue the mili-
> tary metaphor) but "the whole organizational and industrial system of the
> territory which lies to the rear of the army in the field" — that is, the whole
> structure of society, including the structures and institutions of civil society.
> (Hall 1986, 17, paraphrasing Gramsci)

Today's realization of the transformation of the nature of the cultural (from
homogeneity to heterogeneity) as manifested by both "Cultural Studies" and
the postmodern preoccupation with "dispersal," has clearly influenced Renato
Rosaldo's redefinition of "culture" in terms of "borderlands," fragmentation, and
contestation (as opposed to the exclusivity of shareability, coherence, and uni-
formity). It is necessary to quote Rosaldo at length from his book *Culture and
Truth* (1993):

> The fiction of the uniformly shared culture increasingly seems more tenu-
> ous than useful. Although most metropolitan typifications continue to
> suppress border zones, human cultures are neither necessarily coherent

nor always homogeneous. More often than we usually care to think, our everyday lives are crisscrossed by border zones, pockets and eruptions of all kinds. Social borders frequently become salient around such lines as sexual orientation, gender, class, race, ethnicity, nationality, age, politics, dress, food, or taste. Along with "our" supposedly transparent cultural selves, such borderlands should be regarded not as analytically empty transitional zones but as sites of creative cultural production that require investigation. (207–208)

In the past, from the moment Marxism became a threat to the late-nineteenth-century European order, Marx and his followers were not only negatively sanctioned (suppressed) in major sociological and anthropological circles, but "metropolitan typifications" of culture and society (i.e., Durkheimian and Weberian traditions) quite willingly continued "to suppress" any alternative means of studying and analyzing social life in its entirety, that is, in a manner that such phenomena as disorder, chaos, fragmentation, contestation, resistance, and "the border zones" could be rigorously scrutinized (in Chapter 7, which focused on cultural transformation, I dealt with disorder, chaos, fragmentation, and contestation as these are manifested in the daily struggle for chairs in a sewing factory). The notion of "cultural borderlands" is also closely associated with social identities or cultural diversity—that is, age, gender, class, ethnicity. However, for purposes of explaining what Ortner calls "human intention and action" or what Sahlins denotes as "structure and practice," Renato Rosaldo still depends on the dual aspect of social life (structure and agency) that, I have argued, has characterized our imaginings about both culture and society.

For example, in his examination of recent ethnographic experiments and in the new social analysis that he proposed, Rosaldo noted:

> Modes of composition have changed because the discipline's research agenda has shifted from the search for structures to theories of practice that explore the interplay of both structure *and* agency. In such endeavors, knowledge and power are intertwined because the observer's point of view always influences the observation she makes. Rather than stressing timeless universals and the sameness of human nature, this perspective emphasizes human diversity, historical change, and political struggle. (1993, xvii–xviii; italics in original)[12]

Thus, if the initial understanding of the "state" was complicit with rules, laws, and order, which must be followed or obeyed by its citizens or subjects, Victorian anthropologists (British, American, and French) quite willingly, with the same juridical attitude and "morality," traveled to other "non-Western" societies uncritically searching for the rules, traditions, orders, and coherent social systems to which human subjects (or informants, in the anthropologists' case) must accommodate and adhere. By "uncritical," I mean that these early-twentieth-century scholars did not necessarily articulate in their writings the politics of the state over the production of social science itself. It is also true, however, that the dominant discourse on "law and society" had a key humanitarian angle that was used against an earlier vision of "natives" as lacking law and therefore having no rights to life and property.

Nonetheless, the Victorian focus on morality, order, and the state, with its many angles, dominated the anthropology practiced until the early 1970s, when the civil rights, New Left, and feminist movements and the decolonization of previously colonized "nations" disinterred Marxism (or Gramscian Marxism in England) from the academic cemetery deliberately constructed by "metropolitan scholars" (see R. Rosaldo 1993, chap. 1). Now that we recognize that "modern societies" constitute "arenas" of different social contestations, are we looking for similar contestations, fragmentations, dispersals, disorders, and chaos in "other"[13] societies, just as our ancestors looked for order, shared patterns, and coherent systems here and elsewhere?

Perhaps what is of major importance here is that our metaphors of social life have also been transformed along with our notions of culture, society, and the state. There has been a very persuasive replacement, not only displacement, of a metaphoric trope: the biological organism, which was supposed to maintain itself in equilibrium through systemic (political) order and (social) harmony, has been decidedly supplanted by the "war" metaphor, which sheds light on how "society" and "culture" constitute hegemonic battlefields where contestation itself (instead of reciprocity) is inescapably pervasive (see Chapter 6 on "border inspections" and the section "Notes from the (Battle) Field" in Chapter 7). As Foucault suggestively questions, "Should . . . we say politics is *war* pursued by other means?" (1978, 93; my emphasis).[14]

Although Gramsci's work on the state and culture was "rediscovered" in England as late as the 1950s and 1960s as a result of the sociopolitical movements of Birmingham, England (see Raymond Williams's *Politics and Letters,* 1979), through Gramscian "Cultural Studies" in American academia, the state has come to be imagined vis-à-vis its dispersal of power within "civil society" by being deployed on a battlefield of multiple social relations. Since the mid-1980s, through the critiques of such scholars as Renato Rosaldo, Donna Haraway (1986), and James Clifford (1986), American anthropologists began rigorous (re)search on the deployment, dispersal, and, ergo, fragmentation of society and culture, where identities and experiences are constantly being contested in specific sites or localized centers of power, such as the factory, the cafeteria, the city streets, and the buses (see Chapters 4–8).[15]

Nonetheless, despite the influence of cultural Marxism, the notion of culture being used in Cultural Studies has a strong connection to the culture concept constituted by "structure and practice," and that has characterized the academic imagination about the social and the cultural. Paul Willis, in his classic *Learning to Labor*, stated the following with regard to his use of the "cultural": "I view the cultural, not simply as a set of transferred internal *structures* (as in the notion of socialisation) nor as the passive result of the action of dominant ideology downwards (as in certain kinds of marxism) but at least in part as the product of collective human *praxis*" (1977, 3; my emphasis; note the inevitable duality structure/praxis). Following Gramsci, Hall presents the following definition of culture:

> [One might note the centrality which Gramsci's analysis always gives to the cultural factor in social development.] *By culture, here, I mean the actual, grounded terrain of practices, representations, languages and customs of any specific historical society. . . . I would also include that whole distinctive range of questions which Gramsci lumped together under the title,* the "national popular.". . . They are a key stake as objects of political and *ideological* struggle and *practice*. (1986, 26; my emphasis, but original italics on "national popular")

The dual aspect (ideology/practices, structure/praxis) associated with a general definition of culture, although not central, is self-evident. Along with this implicit double existence, in the last two decades, we have simultaneously treated, much more explicitly, culture as an arena of different social contestations. James Clifford notes, "Culture, and our views of it, are [*sic*] produced historically, and are actively contested" (1986, 18). He adds, "Culture is contested, temporal and emergent" (ibid., 19). Its temporality, its instability, its contingency, and thus its fragmentation all give form to the theory of borderlands that R. Rosaldo (1993) and Anzaldúa (1987) call for in and outside social analysis.

Yet to limit the concept of culture to "contestations" while not recognizing its double life (as we tend to do regarding new theories of borders, culture, and social life) is to confuse culture with Gramsci's notion of the "State" in "modern societies." As Stuart Hall correctly argues about Gramsci:

> Gramsci elaborates his new conception of the state . . . it becomes, not a thing to be seized, overthrown or *smashed* with a single blow, but a complex formation in modern societies *which must become the focus of a number of different strategies and struggles because it is an arena of different social contestations*. (1986, 19; my emphasis, but original italics on "smashed")

In fact, I must emphasize that Gramsci associated culture not only with practices and representations but also with the "national popular." Why are culture and the idea of nation or nationalism so closely interrelated by Gramsci?

Culture and the Nation: Imagined Communities

At the turn of the twenty-first century, both culture and the state are perceived to be dispersed as well as consolidated or centralized. Yet some of us have privileged, in the last two decades of the twentieth century and even today, the dispersed and the fragmented. How were nationalism, the state, the nation, and culture perceived in the nineteenth century? In its classic mode (as Renato Rosaldo so eloquently reminded us and Chagnon's *Yanomamo* confirmed), culture was imagined, almost exclusively, to be shared, patterned, and homogenous. So, in a similar way, throughout the nineteenth century and the first half of the twentieth century, the nation, according to Benedict Anderson, came to be imagined in homogenous time, and as an imagined community: "The nation is always conceived as a deep, horizontal comradeship. Ultimately it is this fraternity that makes it possible, over the past two centuries, for so many millions of people, not so much to kill, as willingly to die for such limited imaginings" (1991, 7).[16]

These imaginings—whether from the first decade of the 1800s (Creole nationalism, i.e., Mexico); or from the 1820s or the 1850s of Central Europe (so-called vernacular/linguistic nationalisms, which were opposed to the hegemony of Latin); or from the "official nationalism" prior to the end of World War I (a nation/dynasty combination)—all culminated in the now-threatened "nation-state" that became the international norm after 1922 and at least until the 1970s. By the 1970s, the nation-state was politically and economically transcended, or at least challenged, by the strategic fragmentation of the manufacturing production process around the globe under late capitalism. In the specific case that has concerned this book, the Mexican state has been challenged by the deployment of mostly American maquiladoras not only throughout Mexico (thereby intensifying Mexico's dependency on foreign capital) but throughout the border metropolis of Ciudad Juárez; they are located in more than seventeen industrial parks strategically established in different sections of the city (see maps in Chapter 4).[17]

Thus, the imagined community Anderson identifies in the idea of the nation is the imagined (shared) community R. Rosaldo identifies in the classic anthropological concept of culture, which was conceptualized in the period of "official nationalism" and discursively deployed throughout the consolidation of the "nation-state" (between 1922 and 1970).[18]

Two major historical forces (or, in Gramsci's terms, *"force relations"*) that led to the nation as an imagined community were the emergence of print capitalism (the novel and the newspaper) and the gradual collapse of the hegemony of Latin (a collapse that gave rise to vernacular nationalisms within Europe).[19] Before these major historical and complicated political processes led to the initial versions of the nation (before the nineteenth century, more specifically, before 1776), the political imagination regarding such taken-for-granted conceptualizations as "society" or "social groups" was characterized by fragmentation, inter-marriage, and cultural and social heterogeneity—all predating a homogeneous imagined community.

For instance, Benedict Anderson has written in relation to this prenation, premodern stage, "The fundamental conceptions about 'social groups' were centripetal and hierarchical, rather than boundary-oriented and horizontal" (1991, 15). With regard to the dynastic, monarchic realm, Anderson notes that "in the older imagining, where [kingship] states were defined by centres, borders were porous and indistinct, and sovereignties faded imperceptibly into one another. Hence, paradoxically enough, the ease with which pre-modern empires and kingdoms were able to sustain their rule over immensely heterogeneous, and often not even contiguous, populations for long periods of time" (ibid., 19). Regarding sexual politics, Anderson states that "in fact, royal lineages often derived their prestige, aside from any aura of divinity, from, shall we say, miscegenation? For such mixtures were signs of superordinate status [thus] . . . what 'nationality' are we to assign to the Bourbons?" (ibid., 20–21). Consequently, assigning an essentialized identity about nationalism or culturalism to any subjectivity, before the nation, was not only difficult, but probably impossible (see my analysis of prenation, dynastic, monarchic, and heterogeneous New Spain and New Mexico in Chapter 2, where I argue that "the Mansos" and "the Aztec Empire," for instance, were ethnic labels invented by the Europeans).[20]

It is evident that heterogeneity preceded the "imagined community"—the nation, the nation-state, nationalism—all of which, I argue, influenced our academic notions of culture and society during the late nineteenth and most of the twentieth century. Thus, the heterogeneity discovered in the late twentieth century in theories of borderlands and fragmentation should not be limited exclusively to the collapse of classic norms from the mid-1960s to the mid-1980s; rather, our theories of culture, society, and identity should be analyzed in the contexts of much longer historical processes, such as (1) the monarchic kin relations in sixteenth-century New Spain and Spain; (2) the first attempts "to cut off the head of the king" in the early nineteenth century; and (3) the political transformation and/or reproduction of the nation-state throughout the twentieth century. This book has attempted to provide a comparative analysis of the heterogeneity of the late twentieth century and the heterogeneity associated with prenation contexts and politics in the sixteenth and seventeenth centuries; it is not that heterogeneity cannot coexist with homogeneity, but this strategy might serve as a point of departure from a possible prison of border thought.[21] At the same time, however, we must recognize that such identities as class, gender, sexuality, and ethnicity, as they were (and still are) articulated in the late twentieth century, are, in large part, products of the 1900s; in particular, they are products of a long history of resistance—the working-class, feminist, gay and lesbian, and civil rights movements of the 1960s (including the Chicano movement's "reimagined" Aztlán—see Chapter 2) as well the decolonization movements of Africa and Asia since the late 1950s (R. Rosaldo 1993).

We can now claim, then, that at the turn of the twenty-first century, the "State" has been strategically dispersed, both by current Gramscian thinking and by multinational corporations in this historic moment characterized by the dispersal of manufacturing production processes (as well as commodity consumption) throughout the world (i.e., the three maquiladoras examined in Chapters 5–8). Unfortunately, Benedict Anderson not only ignored the role of late capitalism in the redefinition of the nation-state after 1965 (when the maquiladora industry arrived in Mexico); he also did not perceive that the Fascism of Mussolini had been produced through and by the ideology of the nation, which Anderson himself limits to an amorous feeling of patriotism. Anderson also ignores the major threat to the formation of the nation-state in the first decades of the twentieth century: the attempt to internationalize (read: denationalize, deterritorialize) the working classes.

It is perhaps at this analytic juncture that we must systematically articulate R. Rosaldo's theory of multiple subjectivities (so much needed for our understanding of the politics of difference under state citizenry) with pervasive late capitalism—which can be characterized not only by the fragmentation of the production process but also by the fragmentation of the working classes as a labor force (women, men, younger, older, educated, migrants, married, single, and so forth; see Chapters 4–8). Is it possible to reconcile the following seemingly irreconcilable statements about the politics and economics of difference? First, Rosaldo argues, "Social borders frequently become salient around such lines as sexual orientation, gender, class, race, ethnicity, nationality, age, politics, dress, food, or taste. . . . [S]uch borderlands should be regarded not as analytically empty transitional zones but as sites of creative cultural production that require investigation" (1993, 207–208). And second, Marxist feminist June Nash notes regarding the current global accumulation of capital that "sectors of the labor force based on gender, ethnicity, age, and education within both industrial core and peripheral nations are differentially rewarded and these differences, along with wage differences, between nations, determine the long-run movement of capital" (1983, 3).

Adding the wage differential to the "borderlands" equation does not allow us to separate "border zones" as "sites of creative cultural production" from "border zones" as "sites of lucrative manufacturing production" in the globalization of capital (for example, the electronics maquiladora, the automobile plant, and the sewing factory examined in Chapters 5, 6, and 7, respectively). Thus, is the theory of borderlands a critique or handmaid of capitalist discipline in this historical moment? Historically and theoretically, it can be both. Just as we must extend cultural borderlands into a critique of late-capitalist production, so we must transform the political economy of June Nash into a critical, global theory of multiple cultural subjectivities, which in fact R. Rosaldo offers. After all, one alternative lies in situating our theoretical concepts about social life not only in the larger contexts of history, colonialism, nationalism, and power (see Chapters 2 and 3), but also in micro-contexts of cultural specificity (see Chapters 4–8) as well as in the Foucauldian recognition that academic research

> is a question of orienting ourselves to a conception of power which replaces ... the privilege of sovereignty with the analysis of a multiple and mobile *field of force relations,* wherein far-reaching, but never completely stable, effects of domination are produced. . . . And this, not out of a speculative choice or theoretical preference, but because in fact *it is one of the essential traits for Western societies that the force relationships which for a long time had found expression in war, in every form of warfare, gradually became invested in the order of political power.* (Foucault 1978, 102, my emphasis)

In a post-9/11 world, and with the American invasion of Iraq as well as today's assault on Mexican immigrants, we are, at least in part, returning once again, at the beginning of the twenty-first century, to a situation in which "it is one of the essential traits for Western societies that the force relationships find expression in war, in every form of warfare."

In this broader context, it is worthwhile to note that through the ethnographic descriptions of class and cultural struggles throughout this book, we have turned R. Rosaldo's ideas of cultural borderlands into a simultaneous theory of class borderlands. Besides the need to identify in the world concrete situations concerning specific political mobilizations where people do in fact get together in street protests or in strikes at the workplace, for example, the fiction of a "shared class" seems, as Rosaldo argues about a "shared culture," "increasingly more tenuous than useful." I argue here that "social classes" are also characterized by border zones and that they are "neither necessarily coherent nor always homogeneous." Consequently, the working-class lives of the factory workers under study are always "crisscrossed by border zones, pockets and eruptions of all kinds," including, I will add, cultural ruptures. This book has demonstrated, then, that "class borderlands" should also be regarded as creative sites of culture and class making and unmaking, both of which demand additional investigation within and beyond officially recognized borderlands.

From the Nature of the State to the State of Nature

The emphasis in this book on war, contestation, and power relations in society and culture along class, gender, and color lines, more than on a faithful commitment to Communist utopias, constitutes a strategy of resistance and opposition to the extreme conservatism permeating Durkheimian thinking, which dominated academic social thought throughout most of the twentieth century. The latter influential paradigm, however, was tied more to Thomas Hobbes, who wrote for an earlier British monarchy, than to Durkheim himself, who was reacting against late-nineteenth-century labor unrest (Anderson 1968). In assigning the generalized transformations of societies to specific historical periods—for example, to 1870s historical events or, for that matter, to 1970s political occurrences and outcomes—one runs the danger of reducing the complexity of human relations to socially situated experiences (practice), which are in turn transformed into generalized visions of the world (structure). The problematic trick presents itself when the latter (structure) are confused with the former (practice), not in the recognition that one can lead to the other. The impermanence of either "structure" or "practice" allows for the analysis of the *unintended* consequences of "culture" and its politics, past and present.

"Situated knowledges" (Haraway 1986) in themselves are not necessarily, and have not always been, part of the "war of position" that Gramsci promoted. Durkheim's position about the state, morality, and society was situated as well, but relative to the state's need of the times, to restore so-called social order—both from capitalist rapacity (the greedy capitalist) and from worker unrest. Under late capitalism, Durkheim's vision of the sovereign state is in fact being politically challenged by multinational corporations, particularly in Mexico, but more specifically at the U.S.-Mexico border, and by a much-needed border theory that is produced by border subjects who claim citizenships that transcend boundaries (see Anzaldúa 1987; Lugo 1997, 2000b; Morales 1996; R. Rosaldo 1993).

Throughout most of the history of social science thinking, and even as early as 1642, Hobbes argued in his *Leviathan* ([1642] 1958), and in Latin (that is, before "the nation"), that the state of nature is inherently about chaos, disorder, and war, and that the only remedy is to impose a sovereign—the king—so that order and harmony will exist. Thus, we must realize that actual social life does not tend to obey "official mandates" or the most recent "theoretical paradigms." Human relations did not necessarily transform themselves from "chaos" to "order" under Hobbes, nor from "order" to "chaos" under Marx, nor (back again) from "chaos" to "order" under Durkheim, nor will they change from pure "order" to pure "disorder" under Gramscian, postmodernist, and borderland thinking.[22] Thus, just as culture changes, so does the state; needless to say, our concepts about them are also transformed according to distinct historical specificities.

Social life changes and reproduces itself both through cultural-historical contingencies and through the arbitrary, though still symbolically constituted, imposition of a politically legitimated force. It is our business to study the former and a matter of human integrity not only to scrutinize the latter but, more importantly, to prevent it. It is necessary that we continue our analytic flow from "Culture" to "culture," from the "State" to the "state," from "Order" to "order," from "Patterns" to "patterns," from "Chaos" to "chaos," and from "Border Crossings" to their "border inspections," as well as from "gender studies of women and gender studies of men" to "studies of gender" that comprehensively include both women and men. As Geertz persuasively noted in 1973, the anthropologist still "confronts the same grand realities that others . . . confront in more fateful settings: Power, Change, Faith, Oppression . . . but he [*sic*] confronts them in obscure enough [I'd say clear enough] places . . . to take the capital letters off them" (1973a, 21). It seems, after all, that one of postmodernism's major contributions to sociocultural analysis is, as Benítez-Rojo argues in *The Repeating Island: The Caribbean and the Postmodern Perspective,* its "lens," which "has the virtue of being the only one to direct itself toward the play of paradoxes and eccentricities, of fluxes and displacements" (1992, 271), that is, toward the simultaneous play of order and disorder, coherence and incoherence, chaos and antichaos, contestation and shareability, practice and structure, culture and history, culture and capitalism, and finally, patterns and borderlands (R. Rosaldo 1993). We should not privilege a priori one or the other; instead, we must continuously suspend each category in order to analyze the eccentricities of each. It seems to me that only by following these suggestions was I able to juxtapose the analysis of "assembled parts" in maquiladoras with the analysis of the fragmented lives of the maquila workers who assembled them, and I was able as well to examine the everydayness of late industrial capitalism as compared with the encounters of conquest and colonialism in the sixteenth century—all in the larger contexts of history and the present, the global economy and the local strategies of survival, and, finally, in the more intricate, micro-contexts of culture and power, as we saw in the preceding chapters. Ultimately, and without leaving the question of *meaning* behind, I suggest that we, as social analysts, must face the challenge to truly balance the interpretation of human culture and its borderlands with their respective inspections.

Conclusion

By examining Gramsci's notion of the state and its dispersal, Foucault's notion of power and its deployment, Anderson's critique of the nation, and R. Rosaldo's critique of culture, I have tried to spell out my critique of cultural analysis, Cultural Studies, and culture and border theory as these overlap one another in nationalist, capitalist, late-capitalist, colonialist, and related projects of politically legitimated force. My specific argument throughout this final chapter, however, has been fourfold. First, I have argued that our own folk conceptions of culture and society have been historically constituted by such dialectic dualities as beliefs and practices (Boas 1940), "symbolic structures and collective behavior" (Geertz 1973a, 251), structure and agency (Bourdieu 1977; R. Rosaldo 1980, 1993), human action and intention (Ortner 1984), and culture as constituted and culture as lived (Sahlins 1981, 1982, 1985).[23] Second, I have asserted that our received academic conceptions of culture and border, and of social life for that matter, have been heavily (but, for the most part, unconsciously) influenced by our capacity and incapacity to acknowledge the distinct transformations that the nature of the Westernized "state" has gone through in the past two hundred years (the academic recognition of everyday experiences along the U.S-Mexico border region is a manifestation of this transformation, especially with the creation of Free Trade [Border] Zones around the world). Third, I have contended that these academic conceptions of culture and border have been the historical products of either political suppressions or political persuasions and other types of resistance (i.e., the emergence of minority scholars who have experienced life at the borderlands) to the center's domination. Finally, I have argued in this chapter that culture, constituted by both beliefs and practices, is not necessarily always shared or always contested, and that the crossroads and the limits or frontiers of these beliefs and practices (border theory) create, in turn, the erosion *from within* of the monopoly of culture theory as "cultural patterns" (to follow Martín-Rodríguez 1996, 86).

Regarding anthropology as a discipline, we must ask: What is the role of anthropologists in the production of a cultural theory of borderlands in the interdisciplinary arena? Anthropologists today can certainly redefine themselves vis-à-vis the emergent and newly formed academic communities that now confront us. At the turn of the twenty-first century, as Renato Rosaldo has argued, anthropologists must strategically (re)locate/(re)position themselves in the current scholarly battlefield of power relations.

To be effective in this conceptual/political relocation, however, both anthropologists and nonanthropologists who think seriously about the cultural must ask themselves the following question (which Roland Barthes would pose to anybody regarding the nature of interdisciplinarity): Is the concept of culture an object of study that belongs to no particular discipline? Only an antidisciplinary mood would allow us to answer in the affirmative. A cultural theory of borderlands challenges and invites academics to recognize the crossroads of interdisciplinarity, where "ambassadors" are no longer needed. Once the challenge and the invitation are accepted, border theorizing in itself can simultaneously transcend and effectively situate culture, capitalism, conquest, and colonialism, as well as the academy, at the *crossroads* (including the inspections), but only if it is imagined historically and in the larger and dispersed contexts of the nation, the state, the nation-state, and Power (Foucault 1978).

Finally, at certain times we must question the tropes we tend to privilege the most—"culture," "nature," "humanity," "class," "race," "*mestizaje*," "border," "gender," "power." In this case, I prefer the "nonimagined community" as opposed to the "imagined one," for as Anderson told us, imagined communities kill people and people die for them. More importantly, we need to understand and explain the symbolic process—the structure of the conjuncture, that is, the complex articulation of culture, capitalism, and conquest both in the sixteenth and seventeenth centuries as well as in the late twentieth century and into the present—that has made it possible, over the past five hundred years, for so many millions of people, in this case in the Americas, not so much to die as to die slowly (and at times abruptly) *so that others may live well-off.*

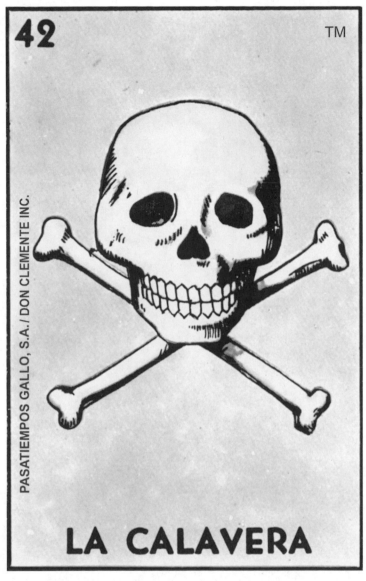

LA CALAVERA

The skull/*La calavera*. "Remember, I told myself: You are already part of the dead men and dead women [of Ciudad Juárez]" (Sergio González Rodríguez 2002, 286).

TEN

Epilogue

> *These borderlands are spaces where,* as a result of expansionary wars, colo-
> nization, juridico-immigratory policing, coyote exploitation of émigrés and
> group vigilantes, *formations of violence are continuously in the making.* As
> racialized confrontations, these have been taking place since the Spanish
> began to settle Mexico's (New Spain's) "northern" frontier, what is now the
> Anglo Americanized Southwest.
> —NORMA ALARCÓN, "ANZALDÚA'S *FRONTERA*" (MY EMPHASIS)

> As in other parts of Mexico, in this northern region, certain bodies (white)
> are held in higher esteem than others are. Although the women were in-
> deed targeted for their gender, perhaps even more significant are racial
> and class hierarchies that constitute their identities as women.
> —ROSA LINDA FREGOSO, *MEXICANA ENCOUNTERS*

HISTORICALLY, THE IMPRISONMENT of the marginalized classes, especially Mexican men—both peasants and proletariats—has been part of the cultural life lived in Mexico at least since the first two decades of the Porfiriato in the late nineteenth century—with the institutionalization of the rural police—and at least since the consolidation of the urban police state in postrevolutionary Mexico. Due to these unequal relations between the modern Mexican state and its citizens/subjects, it is very common for many, if not most, working-class men to fall into the hands of the police, at least once in their lifetime, and too often for quite unpredictable reasons. Consider the following situations in which Héctor, a young garment maquiladora worker, found himself, just on one weekend in Juárez. He told me of the following incidents on a Friday afternoon; he had been absent the previous Monday. He explained: "Remember you told me to go out once in a while? Well I went out, but the cops stopped me and I spent a night in jail." "But why?" I asked, with a feeling of guilt. "What happened?" His answer was quite elaborate:

> See, last Saturday, we worked some extra hours. Alberto and another guy invited me to go to a party in the evening. We had some *birrias* [beers].

233

Not many, just a few. The party was supposed to be over there by the Municipal Gym [in old downtown area], so we were walking by "La Mariscal" [a notorious bar street, parallel to Juárez Ave., where most of the discos are found]; in order to go to the party you have to go through that street. The three of us were walking along that street when all of a sudden two policemen in a car stopped us. One of them asked us where we were going. I said that we were going to a party. At that moment, the cop said, "Your breath smells like beer . . . we're gonna have to take you with us." "Are you talking to me?" [Héctor asked.] Then one of my friends asked what was wrong with smelling like beer, since we were not drunk. The cop interrupted him by saying, "Do you want to go with him, too?" Then I said very quickly, "OK, ok, let's go." They took me to the municipal jail. Once I was inside, they made me pay $35,000 pesos [about thirteen dollars, half of his paycheck]. Then, when I walked outside, two other cops stopped me again and said, "Where are you going?" I said, "Wait a minute, I already paid inside." They said, "Shut up! Let's go inside!" They took me to another office. [The old municipal jail had one office on each side of the building]. The cops took me to the other office where they didn't know anything about me. They took me to another room and hosed me with cold water, with all my clothes on. I didn't say anything. I was all calmed. I didn't want to get mad. They left me there all Saturday night and Sunday morning and afternoon. I got out at 6:30 PM.

I then asked Héctor, "How did the other guys in the cell treat you?" He answered:

They would stare at me, but I would stare back at them. There were *chavos* [guys] my age and *señores* older than me—*no cholos* [not gang members]. I was in cell "1." They said that there are a lot of *cholos* in cell "8." On the next day, they told me that it was time for me to leave, that I had already paid. I had given the second cops 35,000 more pesos. [He earned around $80–90,000 pesos a week; thus, the cops took most of the money.] When I walked out, my cousin was outside. [Héctor was staying in Juárez with his cousin, as most newly arrived migrants do]. She paid another $35,000 pesos so I could get out of jail. I did not know that until my cousin told me. We ended up paying about $100,000 pesos.

Then I told Héctor, "You probably were cursing me in there, since I encouraged you to go out." He did not reply to my statement immediately. He hesitated, then he said, "It can happen to anybody. This time it happened to me." "Be careful, don't walk in strange places," I uselessly said. Then Héctor made the following observation: "Si no son los polis, son los cholos [If the cops don't get you, the gang members will]." He continued, "My cousin told me, 'Que se me durmió' [You should have known better], since the cops probably just wanted money. I should have offered them some cash out there in the street." I underscored what he said, "That's usually what they want."

Héctor did not go to work the next day [Monday] because he had to sleep. He told me that for the weekend starting on that Friday, he was taking a break; that he was not going to work any extra hours.

Policemen in Juárez are known for intimidating the citizenry rather than protecting it. Although Héctor did not know about "la mordida" (bribing) in Juárez, he was trying to adapt to the border "way of life"—the life of thousands of working-class men and women.

The criminalization of the working classes, in its political, economic, and transnational guises, has produced its criminals, but it has also criminalized innocent working-class subjects like Héctor. In fact, in the last decade, young working-class Mexican women in Ciudad Juárez have also been targeted, but with a brutal sexual twist. Because of the pervasiveness of the repressive state in underprivileged Mexico, the ubiquitous presence of the prison in the life of thousands of Juarenses is not surprising. In this context, the sexualized embodiment of the police state in journalistic descriptions of border violence is not just a simple stubborn tendency toward sensationalist journalism on the part of the local newspapers, particularly during the last two decades.

In fact, the presence of the police state in cultural and social, as well as legal, texts is historically and politically grounded not only in the modern and contemporary history of northern Mexico (and beyond) but also in the transnational economic presence of late industrial capitalism in the border region. The Mexican state continues to support the presence of multinational corporations in the region precisely because the country depends on them as the "benevolent" employers of a willing and needy labor force. The Mexican government apparatus and its respective kin network of elite entrepreneurial families also support the transnational companies and their subsidiaries by repressing labor unrest when it occurs and by acting, more often than not, openly indifferent, to say the least, toward violence against factory workers, particularly vulnerable young women.

Yet this assault by capital and the state on working-class women is closely associated with another layer that must not be ignored: a patriarchal system constituted by unequal gender rights in which men of any class are privileged as men, while women, especially working-class women, are treated as second-class human beings by either their male counterparts or by elite men, as we shall see. Consequently, what can be empirically substantiated in Juárez since the wave of violence against women was identified in 1993–1994 is a product of a combination of sociohistorical forces, including (though not exclusively) the transnational articulations and ruptures associated with late-industrial-capitalist production (especially the exploitation of women); the increase and intensification of local drug consumption and trafficking (particularly of heroin and cocaine); state impunity at the local, state, and federal levels; and last, and just as serious, a male-centered patriarchal system in which men continue to believe that they own not only women and women's lives, but also women's right to live or die—including how they die, especially dark-skinned working-class girls and women.

At this juncture, working-class women in Juárez are being triply oppressed culturally (through gender ideologies) and legally (through legal impunity and indifference): by a violent patriarchal system of gender domination, by a capitalist system of class exploitation, and by a Mexican state apparatus that values economic and political interests over the human rights of its most-vulnerable female citizens.

On March 13, 2002, dozens of women, representing several human rights groups, including a substantial number of NGOs concerned with violence against women in the northern state of Chihuahua, arrived in Ciudad Juárez after a 235-mile-long march from Chihuahua City, the capital of the state. They walked for five days through the Chihuahua desert before reaching their destination: the Paso del Norte Bridge in downtown Juárez. The name they gave to their march gives definition to their main purpose: "Éxodo Por La Vida: Ni Una Más" (Exodus for Life: Not One More Victim"—*El Paso Times,* March 14, 2002, 1B). The women, most of them of middle-class background, identified themselves as "Mujeres de Negro" (Women in Black/Mourning) and represented such NGOs as "Nuestras Hijas de Regreso a Casa" (Bring Our Daughters Home) and "Mujeres de El Barzón" (*Norte de Ciudad Juárez,* March 14, 2002, 7A).

Since 1993, hundreds of women and girls have been brutally murdered in Ciudad Juárez. The figures given by NGOs, local and state governments, and the media (local, national, and international) vary from 300 to 400, and even 600, depending on the sources and the discourses: legal, journalistic, or popular. On March 14, 2002, the day after the march, the state government, which was at that time under a PRI (Institutional Revolutionary Party) governor (Patricio Martínez), released the following "official" figures of the sexual crimes: 177 women killed from 1992 to 1998 (when the state governor, Francisco Barrio, was a PAN-ista (a member of the opposition party, PAN—National Action Party) and 91 women assassinated between 1998 and 2002 during Patricio Martínez's governorship. In total, the two kinds of figures given in the report totaled 268 cases (*Diario de Juárez,* March 14, 2002, 1 and 4A).

The state government further claimed that out of 268 cases, only 76 cases could be classified as "multiple homicides" or "serial killings," while the rest (192) were interpreted as "situational," meaning "passional," "imprudent," or drug-trafficking related (ibid., 4A).

According to this report, which was treated as "the truth about the cases of homicides against women," the 76 cases considered "serial killings" could be further divided in the following manner: 56 occurring while Francisco Barrio was governor, with only 8 of the cases "solved"; and 20 carried out during Patricio Martínez's term (or at least up until the day when the report was released), with 15 already "resolved"—or "*resueltos.*" This self-congratulatory kind of official report also noted that those "responsible" for the latter 15 cases were already at the tribunals—in jail—all of them waiting for the verdict (*Norte de Ciudad Juárez,* March 14, 2002, 7A).

Politically, the main objective behind the report was, ultimately, to attempt to delegitimate quite valid counterdiscourses, which, for the most part, had lumped together hundreds of femicide cases under one rubric: serial killings/multiple homicides, whether these were perpetuated by the so-called Los Rebeldes ("Rebels"), Los Ruteros (from *rutera*—"The Bus Drivers"), or El Egipcio ("The Egyptian"; please see below, as well as the documentary *Señorita extraviada* (2001), by Lourdes Portillo, who managed to convincingly connect some of the cases to the Juárez police). Interestingly, since March of 2002, the Juárez bishop and the Bar and College of Juárez Lawyers (all men) openly accused NGOs (mostly constituted by women) of exaggerating and politicizing the murders for their own purposes. For instance, the Juárez bishop claimed that "for now [since October 2001] serial killings against women have stopped, in spite of the fact that NGOs search to aggrandize the list of killed women by including even those women who are assassinated by their husbands" (*Diario de Juárez,* July 9, 2002, 3A). Additionally, Filiberto Terrazas, a representative of the locally and highly influential association of lawyers, accused NGOs "of putting pressure on the authorities only for capricious politics" (*Diario de Juárez,* July 29, 2002, 9B). According to the journalist Luz del Carmen Sosa, Mr. Terrazas also observed that "there exists such a huge number of NGOs that nobody knows who they are or where they come from. . . . Imagine if a group of delinquents form an NGO and then demand to have important information about the progress of our investigations. . . . Each crime, each investigation requires special treatment; no one can talk about 'the homicide cases of Ciudad Juárez' as a whole" (ibid., 9B).

The next day, representatives of NGOs, such as Adrián Delgado of "Casa Mi Esperanza" and Lucha Castro of "El Barzón," made it clear that Mr. Terrazas should not have generalized about all NGOs either and that most of these organizations worked to help "underprivileged persons from all sectors of the community" (*Diario de Juárez,* July 30, 2002, 2B).

In spite of the debates in the locality, since 1993 the criminal courts have barely managed to associate a total of 23 cases with a handful of men, all of them put in prison almost immediately, most of them with tenuous and questionable connections to the specific crimes: 3 cases have been associated with Abdel Latif Sharif (1995), 6 cases with "Los Rebeldes" (1996), and 14 (6 cases in 1999 and 8 cases 2001) with "Los Ruteros," who have never constituted an "organization." The only case that has been partially resolved is the case of "El Tolteca," a bus driver who raped and tried to kill a fourteen-year-old girl, who in turn managed to survive and told her story. Yet the state and local governments associate him with having also killed at least one more woman, in 1999, a specific case presented below.

At least since 1996, when the members of "the gang" Los Rebeldes were captured, there have been very convincing reports that a majority of these working-class men, if not all those captured, were or have been tortured. A lawyer working on the 2001 case of the bus drivers was assassinated because he had evidence that two of his clients had been tortured. As a consequence of the human rights abuses of both women and men, families on both sides — that is, relatives of the women who were raped and killed (and often disappeared) and relatives of the accused men — have been demanding justice from the "authorities."

This is the context in which I would like to make a case for going beyond the discourse of serial killings, though without denying them. I would like to suggest that many of the brutal murders of working-class women in Ciudad Juárez are indeed "unorganized," yet of equal legal value in relation to the cases that are, in actuality, a product of "organized crime." We must not legally devalue the unorganized cases of deadly domestic violence, for instance, precisely because they might be used (if they are not already being used) by the powers that be in Ciudad Juárez to hide or cover up the sexual crimes committed in an "organized" manner. Ultimately, both kinds of gender crimes, unorganized and organized, must be addressed and solved by the Mexican citizenry and state.

Consequently, I would like to displace the binary categories of homicide cases identified by the Mexican state, such as "multiple homicides" and "situational" ones, in order to turn their cultural and legal importance on its head. In this process, I would argue that the "situatedness" of everyday death in Juárez is culturally, historically, and economically constituted, and therefore at the heart of the matter of what it means to be a female citizen or a male citizen in a postcolonial and transnational setting in this Mexican border city. Whether as cultural citizens-subjects or as legal citizens-subjects, these working-class men and women are already subjected to, or subjugated under, the law and a culture of power, and for these reasons, find themselves in unequal, violent situations in their everyday life in this border city.

As the bulk of the ethnographic chapters showed, I did anthropological research (participant observation and ethnographic interviews) in Ciudad Juárez in 1987, 1989, and 1991. Between 1992 and 1995, I lived in El Paso, Texas (across the border from Juárez). For almost ten years, I collected stories of violence in Ciudad Juárez from the local newspapers. During the three fieldwork periods in which I did participant observation inside the three maquiladora plants, I lived in three different working-class *colonias* (neighborhoods) located in the west, north, and southwest of the city. To get to work, like the majority of the workers, I took one bus from the *colonias* to the downtown area and then a second bus from downtown to the industrial parks, which are located in the east and southeast of the city. I recorded in specific detail the time I got up in the morning (4:30 AM), the time it took me to wait for the bus, and the time the bus took to get to the industrial parks. I also recorded the street corners and avenues where the buses picked up the workers and the length of time it would take to get home in the afternoon, after the working day. All along, I kept in mind, and also interviewed, some of the workers who labor on the second shift, from 3:00 PM to 11:30 PM. In addition to documenting the working day, I also attended many of the recreational centers the workers attend, usually on the weekends: discos, bars, restaurants, and parks.

After 1993, when the systematic killings of girls and young women began to be identified by organized women's groups, audiences where I delivered papers would ask my opinion about the killings. My answer tended to be that while I studied culture and capitalism, I was not studying the killings *per se*. Since April of 1999, I decided to devote time and energy to the problem. Since 1993, the Universidad Autónoma de Ciudad Juárez (Autonomous University of Ciudad Juárez) has been collecting newspaper articles on violence against women (not only killings but also sexual assaults and domestic violence). I have reviewed their archives and have read the documentation of the years from 1993 to May of 1999. Because the violence against girls and women has not stopped, I have been accumulating additional newspaper articles on violence in Ciudad Juárez.

The material is overwhelming and rich in detail, especially with regard to the violence in Juárez since the early 1990s, among the working classes as well as between the lower and upper classes; yet it is materializing more concretely in a truly complex "violence of conquest" by working-class men and upper-class men against working-class women—and girls. It is, in fact, extremely painful to read the many graphic descriptions. Some of the women and girls were brutally killed, but not raped: most of these women and girls (from what I have been able to read) really defended themselves . . . to their death.

Violence against women and girls is so pervasive that in 1998 alone, without counting the killings themselves, according to the *Diario de Juárez*, 160 cases of sexual abuse and 228 cases of rape were reported. As of April 21, in the first three and a half months of 1999, there were 32 cases of sexual abuse and 76 of rape (*Diario de Juárez*, Wednesday, April 21, 1999, 7C). Regarding deaths and violence in general, in the month of February 2000, 93 people died, 65 from violent deaths and 28 from natural causes. The former included assassinations, traffic accidents, suicides, drug overdoses, and burns, among other causes: 77 were men and 16 were women. In the previous month (January 2000), 137 people died: 106 were men and 31 were women (*Diario de Juárez*, March 4, 2000). In the first six months of 2002, there were 30 suicide cases in Ciudad Juárez (*Diario de Juárez*,

June 16, 2002, 15B). From January 1 to August 2, 2002, there were 786 cases of robbery at gunpoint (*Diario de Juárez,* August 6, 2002, 6B). In that same year, 82 individuals died from drug overdose in Ciudad Juárez (*Diario de Juárez,* August 6, 2002, 6B). The following "extra-official" statistics of homicide cases, not broken down by gender, for the year 2000 and for the first seven months of the years 2001 and 2002 were quite discouraging (*Diario de Juárez,* August 2, 2002, 12B):

2000: 130 cases
2001: 127 cases (Jan.: 22, Feb.: 14, Mar.: 7, April: 21, May: 26, June: 20, July: 17)
2002: 182 cases (Jan.: 22; Feb.: 31, Mar.: 32, April: 32, May: 27, June: 15, July: 23)

Consider the following questions and reflections that inform and guide this epilogue. Why has it become, it seems, so easy to think of raping and killing girls and women in Juárez? Is killing women a part of the cultural "logic" of gender and sexual relations between men and women in Mexico? Is there a specific sexual discourse that is dominant in and closely associated with the border city itself? Why is it being expressed in such a way that hundreds of women are getting killed in specific ways, at specific times, and kidnapped from specific places?

To be sure, from most of the cases I have read, there are usually two or more men involved in these kidnappings and rapes. In fact, most of the women who have escaped their rapists and potential killers have actually escaped in large part because they lived to tell that it was "a" man, one man, who tried to "hurt" them. It is, indeed, physically difficult if not impossible for anyone, male or female, young or old, to escape two or more violent men who simultaneously attack a person, especially a girl or a young woman. As Chicana feminist theorist Gloria Anzaldúa warned in the mid-1980s under the rubric "Intimate Terrorism": "The world is not a safe place to live in. . . . Woman does not feel safe when her own culture, and white culture, are critical of her; when the males of all races hunt her as prey" (1987, 42).

Journalistic Discourses and the Law: Imprisoned Narratives

1993: The Case of a Woman Who Escaped

On November 11, 1993, a young woman who escaped her killers told the police the story about what happened. The journalists then publicized the incident in one of the Juárez newspapers (*Diario de Juárez*):

The victim who survived, a 19-year-old woman, declared that one of the three women (a 15-year-old) had been stabbed with a knife, but she is not sure if the stabbed woman died, since she (the 19-year-old) took advantage of an altercation or argument among the rapists and escaped [ran away] in the company of another woman (a 20-year-old). When kidnapped, the three young women's hands and mouths had been tied (*amordazadas*) and their eyes had been covered with a handkerchief. The woman said that on Saturday evening, she was walking by one of the streets in Gema industrial park, where she was intercepted by a vehicle (she does not remember the characteristics) and immediately a man of high stature, light skin, and black hair got out and forced her into the car. She told the police that inside the vehicle there was another man and two other women whose eyes were covered with a cloth and their hands were tied. All three of the women were taken to a place where, once their eyes were uncovered, they could see that it was the Cerro Bola [the local Juárez mountains]. The 19-year-old said that one of the men attacked all three women sexually. The other man just held them tight so that the other could rape them, but when his accomplice stabbed the 15-year-old girl with a knife in the abdomen, the two men got into an argument [one of the men did not want to "hurt"—*lastimar*—women] and the other two women escaped. The victim of rape does not know if the other adolescent died, since all she could do under so much shock was run and escape. The mother of the supposedly deceased girl has not filed a complaint—*a demanda*—in the Juárez Police Department.

To contextualize this particular escape I should note that until September of that year, there had been seven reported killings: on February 17, a woman was found at the corner of Violeta and Cobre Streets (to the north of the city); on May 3, the body of a pregnant woman was found on Ortiz Rubio Avenue (to the east of the city); on May 12, a strangled and raped woman was found in the surroundings of the Cerro Bola (Bola Mountains of Juárez); on June 4, a woman was stabbed and (completely) incinerated—her body was found at the Anapra dump (to the west of the city); on June 10, the dead body of a woman who was raped was also found with a material object inside her anus. The body was found on the Altavista High School playgrounds (to the northwest of the city); on August 29, a strangled woman was found at the Senecú government-subsidized housing (to the southeast of the city); and on September 1, another woman was raped and strangled to death (*Diario de Juárez*, September 1, 1999).

1999: The Case of a Woman Who Could Not Escape

In the spring of 1999, according to a detailed article published in *El Diario de Juárez*, five bus drivers were captured, but they subsequently declared that they had been tortured and forced to make and sign a number of legalized declarations or dispositions. According to the police, José Gaspar Ceballos Chávez, "El Gaspy," accepted his participation in six of the killings against women who died on: June 26, 1998; October 4, 1998; December 9, 1998; January 31, 1999; February 16, 1999; and March 3, 1999. The main local newspaper published a declaration describing one of the killings (the one that supposedly happened on October 4, 1998). "El Gaspy" declared the following:

> It was at the beginning of October, I don't recall the exact day, and it was about noon or one o'clock when a group of friends came to my house— they were "El Tolteca," "El Kiani," and "El Samber." [Note: These are local nicknames. "The Tolteca" is the bus driver who was captured after one of his rape victims, a fourteen-year-old factory worker, escaped alive and told the story. "The Tolteca"—perhaps under torture—turned in the other bus drivers to the police. "El Gaspy" continues :] They arrived in a '69 Nova, a two-door car. I remember the car had clear windows. . . . They told me to get in the car to go cruising and just to have fun. I got in the car and we went by the Avenida de los Aztecas and went to the house of "El Tolteca." [These are not fictitious names.] I don't know his address, but it is an adobe house. Then, from there, we went to buy more beer. We cruised all throughout Juárez, partying until dawn. When it was almost dawn (*ya había amanecido*) at about six in the morning [Note: an hour at which many maquiladora workers go to work], we headed toward the crossroad of Avenida de los Aztecas and Ponciano Arriaga, where the Tolteca stopped the vehicle and, without turning off the engine, put it in "park." He said that there was a woman standing near the corner and that he liked her and that he was going to ask her if she wanted a ride (since the Tolteca was the one who was driving). I remember the woman standing near the corner—she was tall, with long black hair down to the shoulders, slim, and about 21 years of age. She was wearing a big black blouse and had a big bosom. Since I did not like her, I did not do anything (*no se la hice de pedo*). When the Tolteca got out of the car, "El Samber" became the driver, and the Tolteca talked to the girl and asked her if she wanted a "ride," but she responded that "No" [and] to "Go away." But the Tolteca insisted with the idea of "the ride," and the *muchacha* (girl) told him to go away and yelled: "Vete, baboso (Go away, you slime)." In reaction to that, the Tolteca embraced the girl by force and forced her into the car and sat her between him and "El Samber," the driver. I and El Kiani stayed in the backseat. The Tolteca told el Samber to drive toward the dump, close to the mountains. When we arrived, the Tolteca told us: "Stay away—I go first," so the rest of us got out of the car.

This woman was raped by all three men but was, supposedly, killed by "El Tolteca," according to the declaration.

2001: The Case of the Young Woman Who Disappeared for Being Late to Work

According to one of the local newspapers, Claudia Ivette's mother used to go meet her at the bus stop, just a block from their house in a working-class neighborhood. One night, the daughter did not get off the bus. One family member told the journalist: "She never arrived. We looked for her in all the hospitals, in the local jail; we went on Friday to the bank to see if she had gone there to withdraw money." Claudia Ivette disappeared on Wednesday, October 10, 2001. Her family told the reporter that "on that day she went to the maquiladora where she worked on the second shift. She was supposed to be at work by 3:30 in the afternoon. Since she arrived two minutes late, the guard sent her home. She never arrived. She did not have any money with her, since the company offers free transportation for the workers at night; she thought that all she needed that day was money for the two buses that usually took her to the factory" (*Diario de Juárez*, November 8, 2001).

Claudia Ivette's funeral took place in November 2001, after the government claimed it had "identified" her body in a "cotton field," which is located across from the AMAC (Association of Maquiladoras) building, and where the bodies of seven other women were found. In spite of the funeral, Claudia Ivette's mother is still not completely sure that the "bag of bones" she was given were those of her daughter.

2002: Cases of Women Who Died at the Hands of People Who Knew Them

(1) June 2002: "Woman, Raped and Killed" (*Diario de Juárez*, June 3, 2002, 1B); "Woman's Assassin Turns Himself In" (*Diario de Juárez*, July 31, 2002, 12B). Her name, age, and occupation: Lucila Silva Salinas/Dávalos, age 30, sex worker. His name, age, and occupation: Juan Antonio Ramírez Varela, age 24, parking attendant (ibid.). "I Killed Her Because She Did Not Want to Go Out with Me" (*Porque no me hizo caso*) (*Diario de Juárez*, August 1, 2002, 10B). "She Ended Relationship, He Killed Her" (*El Mexicano*, July 31, 2002, 1). "Woman's Killer Captured" (*Norte de Ciudad Juárez*, July 31, 2002, 8A). This latter article contained the following information: (A) "A fine was imposed on two police agents [a woman and a man] who stole the purse of the raped/killed woman [Lucila] when they found her body. The two agents were laid off due to loss of trust" (ibid.). (B) "Lucila's relatives noted that she was originally from Chihuahua City, and that she lived in concubinage and that she was the mother of three children, whose *patria potestad,* or 'custody,' she had lost" (*Norte de Ciudad Juárez*, July 31, 2002, 8A).

(2) August 2002: Julieta Enríquez Rosales, age 39, mother of four children, was violently beaten by her common-law "husband," who beat her with bricks; he

had been jealous and on drugs (alcohol, cocaine). He had gone to pick her up from the maquiladora where she worked. She died a week later. The man fled the city (*Diario de Ciudad Juárez*, August 2, 2002, 13B).

2003: The Case of the Music Store, the Computer School, the Restaurant, and the Nightclub

Like several other social justice activists involved in the struggle to stop the violence against women and girls of Ciudad Juárez, two persistent journalists, Sergio González Rodríguez (2002, 2003) and Diana Washington-Valdez (2005), have risked their lives to provide the public with detailed information about the complexity of the matter surrounding the organized crime behind many of the killings of young women and girls in the border city. It was in 2003 when González Rodríguez published an article in *Norte de Ciudad Juárez* (Monday, August 25, 2003, 5B), that contained the following narrative, which itself is part of an FBI intelligence report produced on February 24, 2003, by the FBI office of El Paso, Texas. It is based on the declaration of a particular individual who confessed to FBI agents that s/he knew another person, simply described as "witness," who had been witness to aspects of the organized killings. The information presented in the FBI report, or the report itself, according to the article (and also noted by Diana Washington-Valdez in her 2005 book) is already in the hands of Mexico's federal officials (for sure, as of August 2003).[1] The section of the report that I have selected here reads as follows:

> In Ciudad Juárez exists a place [a nightclub] called . . . , which is located on Juárez Avenue. . . . According [to the witness], he knows who is responsible for the homicides of the girls abandoned in the Ciudad Juárez areas. [The witness] told me that Licenciado . . . , along with his assistant (a guy with a mustache, skinny and arrogant), work together as "lookouts" to recruit new girls. Those two get in touch with girls who visit the music store called . . . which is located on [name of street], across the street from the [city church]. The girls go inside the music store, and as they exit, they find themselves followed. While they are being followed, without them noticing, other *jóvenes* [young men] approach them and ask them personal information for a computer school . . . which is located on the same street. In one way or another, these girls are contacted to go to the restaurant owned by the Licenciado . . . whose name is. . . . The restaurant is, in turn, located close to the nightclub [mentioned above]. Once inside the restaurant, the girls are tied up, and with their mouths taped, they are taken to an alley where prostitutes proliferate. The one in charge of transporting these girls is named [Alias], who owns . . . [another club that is close to the nightclub

mentioned above]. [Alias] is part of the Juárez Cartel, which operates in other nightclubs [as well], such as . . . [Alias], together with his assistant nicknamed . . . or ["real" name] (if this is his real name), are in charge of paying the police to dispose of the dead bodies. Warning: The new Juárez police chief, the engineer . . . is first cousin of the assistant [to Alias].

According to the article in *Norte de Ciudad Juárez*, the FBI report adds that the Licenciado, owner of the restaurant, "'collects proof of the victims' hair, kept at the nightclub . . . , in order to show to the customers as trophies' and that 'there is also an attic [area] in the ceiling of the nightclub where [more] evidence of the killed women can be found.'" "The report," the *Norte* article notes, "continues in the following way: 'The truth, señores, seems to be too incredible.' But 'all the disappeared [women] have something to do with having been seen for the last time in the surrounding areas close to the places mentioned in downtown Juárez.' The informant, according to González Rodríguez, concludes the report [in the following manner]: 'There are plans to kill four more within the next two weeks. The truth: I was so inconsolable after I took the witness [*al testigo*] home, but that night, I could not sleep. I beg you, señores, please do something to put an end to this.'"

Because the Mexican government, at any level—federal, state, or local—did not take action when the report was made public (and hasn't taken any legal action as of this writing), a group of journalists, including Diana Washington-Valdez (2005), took matters into their own hands at that time and visited the places mentioned in the report. According to González Rodríguez, [Alias] denied any accusations to Diana Washington-Valdez during a phone interview. And the person in charge of the restaurant rejected all information by reiterating "not knowing anything" of such matters, although he accepted that the place was frequently visited by prominent families, such as . . . Interestingly, according to González Rodríguez, the ex-police chief, "who resigned on March 18, 2003, noted [*precisó*] that rich and powerful important persons [*personajes*] are involved in the assassinations of women" (*Norte de Ciudad Juárez*, August 25, 2003, 5B).

I join all those who have worked tirelessly to try to stop the violence against girls and women in calling for any individual, including Mexican government officials, to "speak up" about anything substantial they might know regarding who is (still, as of 2008) committing these crimes, so that the legal process in search of organized crime against working-class women can begin. If working-class men, like Héctor, can be put in jail simply for drinking a few beers, why is it that powerful and wealthy Mexican men, some of whom could be descendants of the white Spaniards who controlled the area during the colonial period, cannot be brought to court, like the darker, working-class men, for allegations that

Maquiladora men and women during May Day parade, marching and calling for a
"Stop" to violence against women: *Alto a la violencia contra las mujeres.* Photograph
by Alejandro Lugo.

they, too, might be responsible for the actual killing of economically vulnerable
working-class women and girls? After all, as Diana Washington-Valdez makes
clear in her examination of the killings:

> Neither one man alone nor one specific group in particular is responsible
> for all the Juárez [sexual] killings. Suspects include serial killers, copycats,
> gang members, drug dealers, and an influential group. None of the true
> criminals of this long decade of serial sexual killings has been placed in
> jail. As long as the true criminals remain free, no woman will be safe in
> the streets of this border city. It is clear that corrupt government officials
> have covered up the crimes and have protected the assassins. Due to official
> complicity, these deaths amount to crimes of state, and are, according to
> what was expressed by an FBI agent, crimes against humanity. (Washington-
> Valdez 2005, 237; my translation)[2]

All these "journalistic" narratives offer, among many other things, something
in common ethnographically: we find, in all of them, the specific times of day
and the specific places in the border city where these crimes of state and crimes
against humanity were perpetrated. I propose that we should not ignore the importance of specific cultural spaces and temporalities associated with the deadly

late-capitalist way of life and with state terror in Juárez, both of which are leading to the nonstop multiple killings of women and girls. These kinds of places and times, I argue, need to be surveilled by all members of the Juárez community surrounding vulnerable working-class women. So far, the state, the maquiladora industry, and the media have ignored, for all intents and purposes, the families' call for justice and prevention, which consists of countersurveying the surrounding spaces and times traveled by daughters, sisters, wives, and/or young mothers as they go to work or to school.

I suggest that the menace and reality of death that many women and girls have experienced might be challenged and probably stopped by a strategy of countersurveillance (in addition to legal international recourse)—that is, a temporary but highly strategical countersurveillance of the everyday time and space inhabited and embodied by the women who are the target of these killings. This countersurveillance of "opportunist men," whether poor or wealthy, should start at the grassroots level and should be supported and enhanced by the international community concerned with social justice and with women's and human rights.

Historically and theoretically, we must recognize that these deployments of sexuality in the border region throughout the late twentieth century and into the new millennium are contrary to Foucault's eighteenth- and early-to-mid-nineteenth centuries' deployment of sexuality in the sense that the latter discourses escaped the working classes, according to Foucault, "for a long time" (1978, 121). Where this analysis overlaps with Foucault's discussion is that both deployments of sexuality (in either the early nineteenth century or in the late twentieth century) give way to a particular kind of subjectivity where "at the juncture of the [female] 'body' and the [factory] 'population,' sex [has become] a crucial target of . . . Power." But in the Juárez case, power has been lately organized around the menace of death and not the management of life.

Thus, it seems that, unfortunately, we have come full circle at the U.S.-Mexico border at the end of the millennium, since what Foucault identified about the two centuries that concerned him was "a power organized around the management of life rather than the menace of death" (1978, 147).[3]

A final word: During his tenure, President Vicente Fox could have begun the investigation of some members of the elite families who might be involved in the sexual killings. If the general conditions of the current everyday life continue to reproduce themselves or get worse, or simply do not substantially improve for working-class women and men, as well as for indigenous and poor dark-skinned Mexican people, either by 2010 (during the centenary of the 1910 Mexican Revolution and the bicentenary of the 1810 Wars for Independence) or by 2019 (during the five-hundredth anniversary of the beginning of the conquest of Mexico in 1519), Mexico's own quest for a more dignified life might turn, if not more deadly, certainly more challenging than anything we have seen thus far, not only in the northern and southern borderlands but throughout continental Mexico, for whoever governs the country as well as for the "governed."

It must be noted that most of the young women and girls killed since 1993 would still have been young, in their early to midtwenties or early to midthirties by either 2010 or 2019, respectively.

Chapter Two

1. What I would like to underscore, though it is beyond the limits of this chapter, is the fact—downplayed in both Cline 1972 and Encinias, Rodríguez, and Sánchez 1992—that in conquering Mexico and in moving "north" and "west" and conquering and occupying the Southwest, the Spaniards and the Americans, respectively, dominated (and often exterminated) thousands of indigenous peoples they encountered. For one of the best analyses and, perhaps, the most rigorous presentation of the genocide during the colonial period in the Southwest and Northern Mexico, see the volume *New Views of Borderlands History* (1998), edited by Robert H. Jackson. Unfortunately, this much-needed scholarly text does not include either a discussion or substantial historical materials on Paso del Norte.

2. In this section, I demonstrate what has not yet been substantiated empirically—either by rigorous official historians or by historically misinformed nationalists—that "'Mexico' was the term the Spanish used to refer to the former Aztec empire" (Julyan 1998, 241).

3. Another result of the Battle of Cintla with historically relevant dimensions is the appearance of Malinal (or Malinalli) or, as she is more commonly known, "La Malinche," "a Spanish corruption of the reverential form of this name (Malinaltzin)." She was later baptized with the name Marina (Cortés 1986, 464). With regard to the postbellic encounter in Cintla, Pagden noted: "She was given to Cortés with some Indian women after the battle of Cintla, and given by him to [Alonso] Puertocarrero. She returned to Cortés when Puertocarrero was sent to Spain [as Cortés's messen-

ger to the king], and acted as his mistress and translator during the conquest" (ibid., 464). We will see how Malinche's role as translator and mistress to Cortés during the conquest tends to be exaggerated and discussed outside any historical process. In the Fifth Letter, written in 1525, Cortés himself clarifies that "Marina . . . had been given me as a present with twenty other women" (Cortés 1986, 376).

4. It has not been "proven" by historians whether Cortés actually wrote this "First Letter." The document treated here was found by the Scottish historian William Robertson in 1777 and has been considered "a notarial copy of a letter from the municipal council of Vera Cruz" and is part of the Vienna Codex (Pagden 1986, liii–liv). Pagden believes this letter, "which customarily replaces Cortes's 'missing' First Letter, bears all the stamp of his personality, and was no doubt written largely to his dictation" (ibid., xx). Having read all five letters written between 1519 and 1525, I have no doubt that Cortés is the author of this "First Letter." I do not believe, as Pagden does, that he dictated it to someone else. Considering the effective strategies of manipulation Cortés used throughout the conquest, it seems that he himself wrote it, using the third person ("the captain," "Fernando Cortés," etc.).

5. His interpreter at this time was Gerónimo de Aguilar, who had learned Chontal Maya while in captivity among the Maya from 1511 to 1519. Gonzalo Guerrero and Gerónimo de Aguilar were the sole survivors of a shipwreck in 1511 on Las Víboras Islands. Guerrero "became an Indian to all intents and purposes," and it is believed that he urged "the Indians to resist the Spaniards" (Cortés 1986, 453n22). According to Diego de Landa, Guerrero was eventually killed by a harquebus (ibid., n25). Aguilar, however, joined Cortés's army as interpreter and served as linguistic mediator between Cortés and Marina, who spoke Nahuatl from birth and Chontal Maya from her captivity among the Maya in Tabasco (she is believed to have been originally from either Oluta or Jaltipan in Veracruz). Thus, Pagden noted the following regarding the translations taking place at that time: "She translated into Maya for Aguilar, who then translated into Spanish, though later she seems to have acquired enough knowledge of Spanish to translate directly" (Cortés 1986, 464n26; see also Martínez 1990, 67–68).

6. It is well known that Cortés always exaggerated the number of fighters on the opposing side as well as the type of information supporting his numbers. After all, as J. H. Elliot has warned us, "[The First Letter] should . . . be read, as it was written, not as an accurate historical narrative but as a brilliant piece of specific pleading [and heroism to Charles V]," for Cortés had rebelled, without the king's knowledge, against the governor of Cuba, Diego Velázquez (1986, xx). Elliot adds to our reading of this representation of the initial situations of conquest by also claiming that "the first letter from México [sic], then, was essentially a political document, speaking for Cortés in the name of his army, and designed to appeal directly to the Crown over the heads of Velázquez and his friends in the Council of the Indies" (1986, xxi–xxii).

7. I disagree with Donald Robertson, who traces the use of "the abbreviated form Mexico" to 1545, though I strongly agree that the phrase "Mexico City" should not be taken for granted. He wrote: "The name Mexico City is another source of confusion [in addition to "Aztec Empire"]. The native name was Tenochtitlán; in the Early Colonial Period it was called Mexico-Tenochtitlán, and by about 1545 the abbreviated

form Mexico was preferred. For simplicity and consistency we shall call it Mexico City or Mexico, especially when the Colonial capital is meant" (1959, 6).

8. We must keep in mind Alexander Humboldt's 1822 observation that "New Spain" "was a name given at the beginning, in 1518, to the province of Yucatan. . . . Cortés expands the denomination of New Spain to all of Moctezuma's empire . . . whose actual territory was not as extensive" ([1822] 1998, 200; my translation from Spanish to English from text in Guzmán Betancourt [1998], whose volume *Los nombres de México* is the best on the topic since the 1993 controversy mentioned at the beginning of this chapter).

9. In the next chapter, I discuss *The Broken Spears*, a text considered to be the indigenous (Aztec) version of the conquest of Mexico. As we will see through the current chapter and the next one, I explicitly juxtapose Spanish and indigenous voices for purposes of historical and critical analysis and, I hope, appreciation of "what actually happened."

10. Doña Marina ("Malinche") mostly lived in an involuntarily subordinate position to Cortés. That Marina was closer (not necessarily romantically, but in their roles as interpreters) to Gerónimo de Aguilar than to Cortés during the conquest is suggested by the following observation by Pagden about the confusion of who Marina's "partner" was: "Marina's relations with Cortés have been the subject of a good deal of romaticization . . . , but it seems that far from being an obviously devoted couple[,] some of Cortes's soldiers took Marina to be Aguilar's wife (she must certainly have spent much of her time with him), a mistake repeated by Muñoz Camargo" (Cortés 1986, 464–465n26). The problem with such a statement is that it tends to reproduce the misogyny directed at Marina by blaming her for the effectiveness of the Spanish through the uncritical supposition that she slept with Cortés during the conquest. Diego Muñoz Camargo, a mestizo author of the *History of Tlaxcala*, wrote in the last half of the sixteenth century, as did other authoritative Spanish chroniclers such as Bernal Díaz del Castillo and Bernardino de Sahagún. Thus, it is not necessarily a "mistake" to confuse the role of Marina/Malinche during the conquest. That Cortés gave Marina in marriage to Juan Xaramillo in 1524 (Cortés 1986, 464n26; see also Conway 1940, 70–71) speaks to the involuntary nature of Marina's role as mistress to Cortés (also see note 1). After all, we must remember that some women arrived with the Spaniards: with Cortés came Beatriz Hernández, María de Vera, Elvira Hernández and her daughter Beatriz, Isabel Rodrigo, Catarina Márquez, and Beatriz and Francisca Ordaz; with Pánfilo de Narváez came María de Estrada, Beatriz Bermúdez de Velazco, Beatriz Palacios, and Juana Martín (see González Obregón 1959, 445). Pagden presents a family tree for Cortés that includes his two legitimate wives and their children: Doña Catalina Xuárez Marcaida and Doña Juana Ramírez de Arellano y Zúñiga; the latter had six children—Luis, Catalina, Martín, María, Catalina, and Juana; the former had no children, and it is believed that Cortés killed her (see Martínez 1990, 53–53). Cortés's illegitimate wives and their respective illegitimate children are the following: Doña Marina/Martín, Doña Antonia Hermosillo/Luis, Doña Leonor Pizarro/Catalina Pizarro, Doña Isabel Moctezuma/Leonor, and an illegitimate daughter, María, whose mother's name is not known (Cortés 1986, 531). Pagden incorrectly believes that "[Marina] bore Cortés a son, Martín, who seems to have

been a favorite child. He was legitimatized by Clement VII in 1529 and left one thousand gold ducats a year for life in his father's will" (Cortés 1986, 464n26). Although Marina's son was legitimated, he was not a favorite; the Martín who was made Marqués del Valle was the legitimate son of Juana Ramírez, and *not* Marina's child (see González Obregón 1959, 69, 70; and Conway 1940, 72).

11. Cortés left some inheritance for the two illegitimate/mestiza daughters (Doña Leonor and Doña María). In his will, he called them "natural daughters": "En tal caso les sean dado [a Doña Leonor y Doña María, mis hijas naturales] para sus gastos y alimentos a cada una dellas en cada un año sesenta mil marquedis y lo Restante vuelva y la aya al dicho Don Martín, mi hijo [legitimate, not Marina's Martín; see previous note], subcesa de mi estado o los que en el subcedieron" (Cortés, cited in Conway 1940, 34-35).

12. The editors to this edition of the epic poem also noted that "Nueva México, as it was called in the sixteenth century, stems from the Spaniard's hopeful association . . . between the unknown lands to the north and the fabulous Aztec Empire found by Cortez" (Encinias, Rodríguez, and Sánchez 1992, 3n1).

13. I disagree with Robert Julyan's explanation about the emergence of "Nuevo México" (in the masculine form) during Ibarra's travels. Mistranslating from Spanish into English, Julyan writes: "The first documented use of the name New Mexico came in 1563 when Don Francisco de Ibarra, after his appointment as governor of the Mexican province of Nueva Vizcaya, referred to the region to the N as *un otro* or *Nuevo Mejico*, 'another' or a 'New Mexico'" (1998, 241; italics in original).

14. Philip Burden (1996, 77-78) has identified a map from 1587 by Richard Hakluyt. Hakluyt lived in Paris from 1583 to 1588 while he was chaplain to the English ambassador to France, Sir Edward Stafford. According to Burden, "Here we find the first mention of *Nuevo Mexico* on a printed map, and the first appearance of an inland lake in the west. This knowledge probably derives from Antonio de Espejo, who was sent out as a rescue party in 1582 to find three missing Franciscan friars. . . . The account of this voyage was published in Madrid, 1586. Later in the same year Hakluyt published it privately in Paris and was instrumental in its translation and publication in French" (Burden 1996, 79). It is well known that Antonio de Espejo did get to cross the Río del Norte in 1582 (see Encinias, Rodríguez, and Sánchez 1992).

15. With regard to the invocation to "Aztlán," the editors properly note: "The reference is to the Aztecs, whose historical-legendary origin in the north, in the general area of the new lands being explored and settled, intrigued the Spaniards, always hopeful of encountering similar societies in that area" (Encinias, Rodríguez, and Sánchez 1992, 3n2 of English column).

16. I would like to thank Elea Aguirre for gracefully and in a timely manner pointing out this "Anglo" use and abuse of "Rio Grande." Interestingly, if the Spaniards' cultural logic was dominated by binary oppositions of reality, Anglo Americans since the nineteenth century have not been shy about imposing their legalistic frame of mind onto the region. Their attempt to tame the unpredictable river and label it "illegal"(!) was documented by Timmons (1990, 325n54) in the following account of a 1920s shift of the river during Prohibition, which dislocated the then Texas–New

Mexico boundary north of Ciudad Juárez—in between El Paso, Texas, and Las
Cruces, New Mexico:

> J. J. Bowden has called attention to an unusual situation that developed in the
> 3600 block of Doniphan Drive [which still traces the borders between New
> Mexico and Texas along the river] when the Rio Grande shifted its bed, leaving
> a small tract of New Mexico land lying east of the highway. In 1927 the Supreme
> Court of the United States ruled that the boundary was a fixed line, that the river
> had moved physically but not legally [!]. The tract then became the site of several
> cocktail lounges, mixed drinks being at the time legal in New Mexico but not in
> Texas." (Timmons 1990, 325n54)

In the mid-nineteenth century, the American federal government officialized the
distinction between the Río Bravo (for Mexicans) and the Rio Grande (for Americans) in the Treaty of Guadalupe Hidalgo of 1848 (see Article 5, in Griswold del Castillo 1990, 187). In this regard, I disagree with Julyan about the Americans' preferred
name for the river during the nineteenth century. Julyan wrote: "The name Rio del
Norte persisted even after the American occupation in 1846 and routinely appeared
on American-made maps. But by the end of the nineteenth century, the present
name had begun to supplant the older name and now is firmly established, at least in
the U.S." (1998, 295).

17. Since 1659, Paso del Norte/Ciudad Juárez has maintained a religious site in
honor of the Virgen de Guadalupe. The cathedral and a chapel are located in the same
general area where the mission was founded, which is today's old downtown Juárez.

18. Anthropologist Morris Opler (1983, 388; italics in original) writes that "they
were called *mansos*, 'tame, peaceful ones,' by the Spaniards because it was one of the
first words these Indians used to greet them." I do not endorse Opler's suggestion
that the indigenous peoples could have used a term denoting "tame" to describe
themselves—for an exceptional historical situation, see note 19 below.

19. The idea that *manso* is somehow connected with the haircuts of the local
peoples is also mentioned by Opler: "Zarate Salmeron [1629] and Benavides [1630]
give Gorretas, 'caps,' as an equivalent of Mansos, because their haircut gave the im-
pression that they were wearing caps" (1983, 388). It should be noted that the difficulty northern agents of conquest had with names of peoples and places stems from
the inadequate availability of translators. In their conquest of what became northern
New Spain, the Spaniards would kidnap specifically targeted indigenous men and
women and teach them Spanish so that, in turn, these captives would translate from
local indigenous languages. But, as before, there was strong resistance to translate.
In one important case, Doña Inés refused to be a "second Malinche." As Encinias,
Rodríguez, and Sánchez (1992, xxxi) note, "Doña Inés, born at San Cristóbal, as a
child had been taken by Castaño de Sosa to be trained as an interpreter. 'Her parents
and almost all of her relatives were already dead, and there was hardly anyone who
remembered how Castaño had taken her away,' wrote a colonist. She, however, had
resisted her role as interpreter for the Spaniards and refused to become a 'second

Malinche, but she does not know the language or any spoken in New Mexico, nor is she learning them,' lamented the Spaniard. Doña Inés had craftily won her freedom from the Spanish." As far as I know, there is no systematic study of "Doña Inés" and the important role she did or did not play in the conquest of New Mexico.

20. This same cultural logic of conquest informs Chagnon's (1992) description of the Yanomamo as "fierce"; see Chapter 8 in Part II of this book.

21. Anthropologist Morris Opler, perhaps the main specialist on the indigenous/colonial history of the El Paso/Juárez/Las Cruces region, considered the term "Manso" to be one of the "Obsolete Group Names" (1983, 387) for "Apache," which in turn is an "English word . . . from Spanish *Apache,* which was first used by Juan de Oñate, on September 9, 1598, at San Juan Pueblo" (ibid., 385; italics in original). Opler elaborates on "Manso" in the following:

> Manso. Mansos was a term employed for Apaches who were friendly to the Span-
> iards and Mexicans and used especially for a small group of Apache continually
> friendly with Mexicans and Papagos [sic] who lived in the area south of Tucson.
> Manso also was used, first by Oñate in 1598, to refer to a group around El Paso.
> . . . The first descriptions of the Mansos never give any evidence that they were
> Apacheans, and the denomination Apaches Mansos may well be due to the fact
> that they became close allies of the Apaches. (1983, 388)

22. For one indigenous voice about what happened during the massacre in Acoma Pueblo in northern New Mexico during December 1598–January 1599, I strongly recommend the historical essay "Acoma Pueblo" by Velma García-Mason (1979).

23. The strategic use of dogs during conquest and occupation came to the surface once again in Iraq in 2003, particularly the abuse and torture of Iraqi prisoners by American military personnel at Abu Ghraib prison.

24. The state of New Mexico requires only one car plate, unlike Texas, Arizona, and California, which require two plates, one on the back of the car and another on the front.

Chapter Three

1. All informants' names have been changed to preserve their privacy.

2. For "cultural invisibility," see R. Rosaldo (1993), who examined it in the context of citizenship both in the Philippines and in Mexico.

3. For the importance of whiteness within the state of Chihuahua, especially during the late-nineteenth-century wars against the Apache, see Alonso 1995; also see Orozco 1992.

4. For a specific cultural analysis of whiteness in Namiquipa, Chihuahua, which does not necessarily extend to the border region and therefore does not include a border analysis, see Alonso 1995.

5. For indigenous/black disarticulations, see Laura Lewis's important work — mainly 2000 and 2004 — on the Costa Chica area.

6. For decades, scholars have acknowledged that the term "Aztecs" in this par-

ticular context is a misnomer (see also previous chapter for other relevant analysis). In his *Mexican Manuscript Painting of the Early Colonial Period: The Metropolitan Schools,* Donald Robertson noted: "The Náhuatl-speaking peoples of the Valley of Mexico have been called Aztec in reference to the 'Aztec Empire.' However, the term 'Aztec Empire' is itself a misnomer; the political organization of Central Mexico in the beginning of the sixteenth century was neither an empire nor a nation-state. The Empire was in fact a Triple Alliance of the city-states of Tlacopan (modern Tacuba), Texcoco, and Tenochtitlán (modern Mexico City); the last was the dominant city at the time of the Conquest" (1959, 5). See also Guzmán (1989) for perhaps, in my opinion, the best analysis of the Spanish Conquest.

7. Interestingly, with regard to the preference of some Cuban Americans, Puerto Ricans, and Mexican Americans in the United States to call themselves "Hispanics," Ana María Alonso and María Teresa Koreck have argued that the latter term "'whitens' by giving voice to a hypostasized Spanish essence while simultaneously erasing from the field of discourse the African and Indian heritage of peoples of Latin America"; furthermore, Alonso and Koreck accurately contend that "the 'whitening' and assimilationist connotations of 'Hispanic,' on the one hand, and the continuing construction of Spanish-speaking peoples as inferior (but useful) *'brown'* bodies, on the other, are among the contradictory practices which mark out the terrain of contemporary cultural and political struggle" (1988, 102, 103; my emphasis). For an elaboration of my analysis of the relationship between Border Studies and Latina/o Studies in anthropology and beyond, please see Chapter 6.

8. García Sáiz (1989, 24–28) provides a very useful "taxonomic chart" mapping out the twenty-five *castas,* which were colorfully depicted in several seventeenth-century paintings. The racialized definitions of seven of these *castas* will suffice to demonstrate the mixed heterogeneity of these social relations: *Criollo* refers to a "person of Spanish or European heritage born in Spanish America"; *mestizo* refers to the "offspring of one (white) Spanish parent and one Indian parent"; *mulatto* refers to the "offspring of one (white) Spanish parent and one Black parent"; *zambo* refers to the "offspring of one Black or Mulatto parent and one Indian parent"; *castizo* refers to the "offspring of one Spanish parent and one Mestizo parent"; *morisco* refers to the "offspring of one Spanish parent and one Mulatto parent"; *albino* refers to the "offspring of one Spanish parent and one Morisco parent"; *coyote* refers to the "offspring of [a] Mestizo [man] and [an] Indian woman"; and *"Ahí te estás"* ["Stay where you are"] refers to the "offspring of one Mulatto parent and one Mestizo Coyote parent."

How much of this *casta* categorization refers to color differences produced by interracial marriages, and how much refers to interracial marriages produced by color differences (both of which ultimately lead to the impossibility of reducing current populations in Mexico to simple black/white, Spanish/Indian, or mestizo/indigenous dichotomies) is a research project in itself beyond the scope of this chapter. Yet the social meaning attached to unequal color hierarchies, in spite of their multiplicity, speaks to class, gender, and ethnic/racial differences. For instance, while the white *criollo/a* or Spaniard (male or female) was almost always represented as civilized and well mannered, the dark-skinned mulatta was almost always represented in *casta* portraits as violent, especially beating up her husband, who in turn could come from diverse *castas*/representations (see several examples in García Sáiz 1989).

Chapter Four

1. According to figures from the 2000 Census, the whole state of Chihuahua had 3 million residents, and the whole country of Mexico, approximately 97.4 million: 50 million women and 47.4 million men (*Diario de Juárez,* Special Report, June 22, 2000, 9A).

2. *Diario de Juárez* documents that as of January 2000, there were 229,478 employees in the maquiladora industry in the border city (April 30, 2000, 1F). As of 1999, nationally, there were 3,297 assembly plants that hired 1,947,000 workers (*Diario de Juárez,* June 11, 2000, 3F). In April 2000, a report on the state of maquiladoras at the border noted that "Ciudad Juárez is considered to be the main border zone where the most important foreign transnationals have opened their doors to create more than 10,000 jobs annually" (*Diario de Juárez,* April 30, 2000, 1F).

3. See previous note. It is very difficult to find precise figures on the number of workers according to gender. For instance, in the *Bulletin of the Association of Maquiladoras* for the month of July 2000, they list 106,377 workers for thirteen industrial parks: 44,413 women and 49,716 men! Since it is impossible to find exact numbers, what I would like to underscore is that tens of thousands of men have been working on the assembly line, at least since the mid-1980s.

4. During elections, Ciudad Juárez gets divided into three main electoral districts: District 02, District 03, and District 04. The New Juárez is principally constituted by District 03. As of January 15, 2000, District 03 had 266,066 registered voters (Mexican citizens eighteen years of age or older), whereas District 02 had 231,358 and District 04 had 255,764 (*Diario de Juárez,* "Special Report: The Power of the New Juárez," June 26, 2000, 10A–11A). Specific studies of the voting participation of maquiladora workers need to be carried out. In this chapter, I use these figures mainly as one additional way of mapping out the growth and the reality of the working-class population due to the growth of the maquiladora industry in Ciudad Juárez in the last two decades.

5. In his fascinating study "Folk Medicine and the Intercultural Jest" (1968), Américo Paredes convincingly argues that these kinds of specific cultural jests (that represent Mexican doctors and/or *curanderos* avoiding surgical operations even in difficult cases of illness) do in fact reflect a generalized form of critique of modern science (hospitals, medical doctors) on the part of many working-class Mexicans: it is often believed that hospitals, besides being too expensive, are places where doctors may move too quickly toward operating/invading their bodies.

6. These particular jokes contain universal motifs found around the world, particularly what folklorist Stith Thompson identified as "Foolish imitation of healing" and "Means of ridding person of animal in stomach" (cited in Paredes 1968, 108, 109). Américo Paredes explains: "There are several methods by which animals that have introduced themselves into people's stomachs are disposed of. For example, in [Thompson's] B784.2.1., reported from Ireland, Italy, and the United States, 'The

patient is fed salt or heavily salted food and allowed no water for several days. He [*sic*] then stands with mouth open before a supply of fresh water, often a running brook. The thirsty animal emerges to get fresh water.' Thompson does not tell us if the animal is then beaten to death. Then there is motif B7842.1.2, reported from India, about which Thompson tells us, 'A husband ties a cock near his wife's feet so that a snake-parasite in her stomach will come out to catch the cock. The snake is then killed by the husband. Thompson does not tell us how the snake comes out of the woman's body, an important omission, especially for the psychoanalytically ori ented investigator" (Paredes 1968, 108). Without providing a gender analysis of these texts (something that escaped Paredes and other male anthropologists of his gen eration—see Chapter 8), he does identify the specificity of the Mexican *curandero*/ doctor: "But our curandero is not reticent about explaining his methods, in fact, has a logic all its own, based on a folkish kind of empiricism one might say. The hit-or-miss character of many folk remedies, their far-fetched sense of causality . . . all come in for ridicule [in these jests]" (Paredes 1968, 108–109).

Chapter Five

1. This chapter is a more elaborate version of the article "Cultural Production and Reproduction in Ciudad Juárez, Mexico: Tropes at Play among Maquiladora Workers," published in the journal *Cultural Anthropology* (see Lugo 1990).

2. An "event" constitutes human behavior (action, activity) to the extent that "the event (any event) unfolds simultaneously on two levels: as individual action and as collective representation" (Sahlins 1985, 108). Similarly, with regard to "structure and event," Renato Rosaldo (1980, 23) wrote in his introduction to *Ilongot Headhunting 1883–1974*, "In this book . . . I shall develop an analysis of society and history conceived as the interplay of received structures and human activity." Later in his piece, Rosaldo stated that "given the present state of the art, the problem is to show the articulation of structure and event in human cultures" (1980, 109; also see Rosaldo 1993). For a profound analysis of the disarticulation or "rupture" of this dichotomy and its politi-cal repercussions, see Taussig (1987). Also see Chapters 7 and 9 in this book.

3. Sahlins sees the concretization of the "structure of the conjuncture" as a "situa-tional synthesis" (1985, xiv) or as a "situational set of [historical] relations" (1985, 125n). His focus is on a "situation." My focus is on presenting the multiple forces that lead to, or produce, a particular "situation," which in turn coordinates particular values and behaviors (structures and events), synchronically as well as diachronically.

4. I am aware that "the literature on the tropes is varied and beset by congenial disagreement" (White 1973, 33n13; see his two-page footnote for a concise review of this literature, from Petrus Ramus to Giovanni Giambattista Vico to Claude Lévi-Strauss to Emile Benveniste). Allowing for so many (perhaps too many) different views may be overly lenient, and it may not be a good excuse for the conflating of distinctive cultural and linguistic processes that can get confused due to the semantic disagreements among theorists. I agree with James Fernandez when he says, "In our analysis of objects behaving . . . there seems always to remain something ineradicably subjective. . . . Scientific inquiry of this kind is not only hypothetical about objects;

it is predicative upon subjects. . . . Nevertheless, I suggest that more clarity can be achieved in the practice of such 'subjective objectivity'" (1986, 60).

5. Hayden White (1973, 34) mentions that some thinkers treat synecdoche as a sort of "species" (1973, 31n) of metonymy. Fernandez (1986, 50, 69n20) and Lévi-Strauss (1966) are two of them.

6. See White (1973, 34–36) for a similar argument and discussion about this particular relation between metonymy and synecdoche.

7. I differ from philosopher Hayden White in two respects: (1) White treats synecdoche explicitly as an "integrative" concept (1973, 34, 35); I see it as complexly encompassing (in my view, White should have reconsidered his use of the term "integrative," since it implies or resembles a functionalist argument, which I do not think he postulates); and (2) White characterizes the three tropes (metaphor, metonymy, and synecdoche) "as 'naïve' (since they can be deployed only in the belief in language's capacity to grasp the nature of things in figurative terms)" (1973, 36–37). His argument is mainly that they are "naïve" because the actors, in playing with these tropes, are not as self-critical or self-conscious of their world (1973, 37) as they are in their use of "irony." On the contrary, I find all tropes to be politically loaded. In claiming this, I am not implying that language, in itself, has "the capacity to grasp the nature of things in figurative terms." I propose here that the actors (through their own histories and particular experiences) are sometimes forced to try self-consciously or unconsciously to "grasp the nature of things in figurative terms" in order to adapt to their stable or changing conditions of life, in this case, to global assembly production through their own bodies.

8. I, like White and Turner, see the complex coupling of metaphor and metonymy (the return to the whole) as synecdochic. More than three decades ago, Hayden White proposed the "fourfold analysis of figurative language (metaphor, metonymy, synecdoche, and irony), since it had "the added advantage of resisting to fall into an essentially dualistic conception of styles which the bipolar conception of style-cum-language promotes" (1973, 33n13). For my own purposes with regard to the analysis of cultural process and trope occurring on the assembly line, I try to decipher a trichotomy—the relation between metaphor, metonymy, and synecdoche (also see note 15 for another important triadic relationship to be considered in this ethnographic analysis).

9. As you can see, these operations are not gender specific per se; either a man or a woman could perform them. This generic aspect at this particular factory contradicts the gender specificity that most feminist scholars have claimed would be perpetuated on the assembly line. The fact that men have been hired in substantial numbers since the early 1980s for assembly-line work, and are being paid the same wages as women, questions their thesis. I have discussed this issue in more detail in Chapter 4.

10. A search for the origin of any social practice, in particular the origin of linguistic terms, is inherently limited. More ethnographic research among construction workers of Ciudad Juárez is needed. Nonetheless, it is still our responsibility to try to decipher the complexity of the interconnections between cultural beliefs, linguistic terms, and actual human practice—to the best of our knowledge.

11. *Blanquillo* (singular) or *blanquillos* can be directly translated as "little white one/s." *Blanquillo* is diminutive for *blanco* (white).

12. As far as I know, no ethnographic work has been carried out among construction workers in Ciudad Juárez. Alicia Castellanos's (1981) solid sociological analysis on Juárez does incorporate important general detail data on the working-class labor force until the late 1970s. A thorough ethnography on masculinity and construction work in Ciudad Juárez as a border city is highly needed. I found that some of the men who worked temporarily in construction in the late 1970s and early 1980s ended up working in the maquiladoras throughout the 1980s, and some even into the 1990s. In fact, a few of the maquiladora men I interviewed did work on occasional construction jobs whenever they could, especially on the weekends.

13. Machismo has also been explained through class analysis by arguing that it serves as a "safety valve" for letting off steam produced by the inability of working-class men to have control over their own lives. Women, children, and "ineffectual" men thus become targets for their frustration (see Ehrenreich 1983 for interesting treatments of machismo in the context of class per se; for machismo, race, and class in the context of what I consider the conquest of Mexican peoples and how it affects economically marginalized men, see Anzaldúa 1987 and Limón 1994). For a decade-old ethnography on machismo in Mexico that is already a classic in cultural anthropology, see Gutmann 1996; for a study of the sexual politics among Mexican men and its impact on vulnerable men and their masculinities in Guadalajara, Mexico, see Carrillo 2002.

14. I am grateful to Emiko Ohnuki-Tierney for having pointed out to me this "cause-effect" aspect of heaviness/laziness.

15. Using Edward Evan Evans-Pritchard's work among the Nuer, Fernandez wrote the following to give an example of a "latent factor":

> Statements such as "twins are birds" are made in relation to a third term: "They are statements as far as the Nuer are concerned, not that A is B but that A and B have something in common in relation to C" [Evans-Pritchard, cited in Fernandez]. The latent generic characteristic which they have in common and which associates them is spirit [as in my case, what associates *barra* and *huevón* is laziness–heaviness]. They are both manifestations of spirit [of laziness]. There is a triadic relationship involved. (Fernandez 1986, 54)

Thus, the latent factor could be argued to be one ethnographic manifestation of the structure of the conjuncture (please also see note 8 above, where another relevant triad [metaphor, metonymy, and synecdoche] is underscored as well).

Chapter Six

1. The scholarly literature on "border crossings" is vast. Among many others, the following are key texts—in anthropology: Alvarez 1995; Behar 1993, 1995; Berdahl 1999; de Genova 2005; de Genova and Ramos-Zayas 2003; Gordon 1995; Heyman 1991, 1998; Hill 2003; Kearney 1991, 1996; Kelleher 2003; Lavie and Swedenburg 1996;

Limón 1994; Lugo 1997, 2000a, 2000b; Olwig and Hastrup 1997; Ortiz 2003; Paredes 1958; R. Rosaldo 1993; Spyer 1998; Taussig 1998; Vélez-Ibáñez 1996, 2004; Wilson and Donnan 1998; in Latina/o Studies: Anzaldúa 1987; Bonilla et al. 1998; Castillo and Tabuenca Córdoba 2002; Flores 1993; Fusco 1995; Jackson 1998; Maciel and Herrera-Sobek 1998; Michaelsen and Johnson 1997; Morales 1996; Pérez-Firmat 1994; Saldívar 1997; Torres-Saillant 2002; Valdivia 2005; Vila 2000, 2003. The field of Social Justice Studies, which often articulates with Legal Critical Race Theory, has produced some of the most compelling applications of border analysis and border social critique, such as Bejarano 2005; Romero 2003, 2005; and Staudt and Coronado 2002, among others.

2. A much shorter version of this chapter was published in the journal *Cultural Dynamics* 12, no. 3 (2000):353–373, with the title "Theorizing Border Inspections." I am deeply grateful to Angharad Valdivia, Matt García, and Josiah Heyman for their concrete suggestions, which I tried to follow in the rewriting and elaboration of this particular piece. Needless to say, I am solely responsible for any errors.

3. My idea about "inspection stations" is not a product of the academic literature. During the first decade after my parents brought me to the United States in 1973, I crossed the international bridges at El Paso, Texas (see figures 6.3 and 6.4), so many times that I noticed early on as a child (and especially after waiting for hours inside my parents' car to cross) that the building complex (where inspectors monitored the crossers) was officially named "Border Inspection Station" (see Figure 6.2). We also lived intermittently in Gadsden, Arizona, five miles away from the San Luis, Arizona–San Luis Río Colorado, Sonora, boundary.

4. For an excellent analysis of this film and many others on braceros, see Maciel and García-Acevedo's "The Celluloid Immigrant" (1998). Although these authors examine this particular scene, they do not comment on "the problem of color" as I consider it here. Interestingly, Central American migrants who hope to cross illegally into the United States via Mexico encounter a similar kind of border inspection once they are in Mexican territory. Research on Central American immigrants in Mexico needs to be conducted. For instance, in the state of Chihuahua alone, where Juárez is located, in the year 2000, 1,250 "migrants" from Honduras, Guatemala, and El Salvador had been detained in the first four months of the year (see *Diario de Juárez,* May 2, 2000, 1A: "Caen 227 migrantes centroamericanos"). In addition, in June, 63 "undocumented" people were captured (see *Diario de Juárez,* June 25, 2000, 1A). In September of the same year, 20 Guatemalans who were "roaming the streets" were detained in Ciudad Juárez (*Diario de Juárez,* September 17, 2000, 3B).

5. In 1853, the Gadsden Purchase created today's international boundary from the Rio Grande/Río Bravo at the El Paso/Juárez/southern New Mexico crossings to the current California/Arizona borders with northwest Mexico. What has changed and remains consistently contested is the way the "border" is interpreted by scholars, artists, and policymakers. For instance, "the border" can be the end or the beginning of a country (a territorialized nation-state); the margin or the center of cultural production; or the way of life for millions of people in economic, political, or sexual transitions.

6. In addition to Alejandro Morales, Josh Kuhn (1997) provides another produc-

tive analysis of the notion of heterotopia in border studies, specifically in relation to diasporic and transnational musical productions.

7. In 1999, 350 individuals (men, women, and children) died by drowning or dehydration or were gunned down (by American ranchers, Border Patrol officials, criminals roaming unofficial border crossings) or run over while attempting to cross into the United States (*Diario de Juárez,* June 11, 2000, 1A and 3A). As of June 11, 2000, 100 persons had already died while trying to cross illegally that year (ibid.). According to Ricardo Martínez, an official working for the National Institute of Migration in Mexico, the INS deports 192 Mexicans a day. As of February 2000, 10,000 Mexicans had been deported since the beginning of the year. Mr. Martínez declared that in 1996, 49,000 undocumented Mexicans were returned to Mexico; in 1997, 67,000; in 1998, 70,000; and in 1999, 76,000 Mexicans were deported (see *Diario de Juárez,* February 23, 2000, 1B: "Deporta EU cada día a 192 indocumentados [mexicanos]"). These figures include Mexicans who were caught while trying to cross and undocumented Mexicans who were already in the interior continental United States (ibid.).

8. The heading for this section is influenced by the subtitle to Bridget O'Laughlin's classic feminist-Marxist essay "Mediation of Contradiction: Why Mbum Women Do Not Eat Chicken," in which she argued that among the Mbum Kpau (a society in the Republic of Chad), "women eat neither chicken nor goat for fear of pain and death in childbirth, the bearing of abnormal or unhealthy children, or even sterility" (1974, 302). While this cultural practice of not eating chicken is associated by O'Laughlin with bride wealth as a system of male dominance (senior males vis-à-vis junior men and women), in this section I am interested in highlighting that the fear of eating chicken among maquiladora workers (both men and women) in the 1990s, precisely when food poisoning occurred, is based on multiple emergency cases (documented below) and therefore connected to the real possibility of getting ill, dying, or losing babies as a result of the food eaten in maquiladora cafeterias. As we will see, this caution about eating chicken is associated with late capitalist production and not with any local cultural knowledge about a connection between chickens and maquiladora workers.

9. One of the ways in which maquiladora workers make these kinds of incidents bearable is through joking (also see Chapter 4). It is still common to make a joke in Juárez about eating "pollo a la R" in connection with the RCA chicken poisoning events. If someone has chicken to offer for dinner, for instance, the cook might say: "Vénganse a comer pollo a la R" ("Come eat RCA chicken"). With NAFTA and the consequent arrival of Church's Fried Chicken and Kentucky Fried Chicken, the workers articulate in their own ways their critique of late capitalism. Interestingly, though not surprisingly, even though most of the chicken is imported from the United States, customs officials on either side of the border were not inspected by anyone during these incidents.

According to an article in *Diario de Juárez,* "90 percent of chicken meat that is consumed in this border city comes from the United States, and the rest comes from the interior of our Republic, mainly from Torreón and Monterrey" (June 8, 2000, 1A). And the same article claims that "purchasing the whole chicken, legs, or thighs is cheaper in the United States than in Mexico." This is why the importation of chicken is attractive. In the same article, it was noted that chicken breasts and chicken wings are cheaper in Mexico.

10. These *ruteras* are independently owned by concessionaires who emerged precisely to provide transportation service to maquiladora workers in the late 1960s. According to Desarrollo Económico de Ciudad Juárez, a local government agency, in 1991 there were 1962 *ruteras* in circulation, all owned by eighteen different concessionaires, who in turn hired the drivers (1991; see tables 2.2.2–2.2.4 in booklet). These *ruteras* served the percentage (so far undocumented) of workers (out of approximately 130,000 maquiladora laborers in 1991) who did not own cars at that time (see *Diario de Juárez*, April 20, 2000, 1F, for figures of maquiladora workers in Ciudad Juárez for 1985: 76,284; 1990: 121,143; 1995: 152,937; and 2000: 229,478).

11. The local *Autoridades de Vialidad*, the Authorities of Motor Vehicles, noting a positive change from January to April 2000, stated that "we used to have 60 to 70 automobile accidents per week [in the city]. Now we regularly get 40 to 50" (*Diario de Juárez*, April 26, 2000, 1B). Unfortunately, adding the accidents from January to June of the same year gave a total of 8,000, or 44 accidents a day! "According to statistics from the Motor Vehicle office, 39 persons died from being run over, 26 died in car crashes, and 4 died in car turnovers . . . this high incidence of automobile accidents . . . is very similar to what happened in 1999, when there were 16,455 accidents that caused the deaths of 142 persons" (*Diario de Juárez*, June 29, 2000, 1B).

12. Interestingly, as the violence against women increased throughout the 1990s (see epilogue), this strategy (demanding to be dropped off as close to home as possible) became not just a personal whim but a matter of life or death.

13. Tragically, with the increase in the number of women killed in the context of impunity and corruption regarding the enforcement of the law in Ciudad Juárez, there have already been some cases in which bus drivers were accused of raping and killing maquiladora women and girls.

14. Local authorities, as well, do not recognize the role of the maquiladora industry as one of the "factors" leading to automobile accidents in the city. Inspectors in charge of ticketing drivers keep track of "infractions." Between January and August 2000, the following were ticketed in the city (the figures were *not* broken down by type of driver: *rutera*, taxicab, average citizen, and so forth): 49,166 for speeding, 34,501 for going through a red light, 29,028 for missing stop signs, 25,773 for driving without a license, and 12,970 for not using a seat belt (*Diario de Juárez*, September 9, 2000, 1B). The average number of infractions per day was 620. According to the Motor Vehicle office, factors in an automobile accident include: vehicle, driver, street or highway, degree of traffic, artificial lighting (as opposed to driving in the dark), and the weather. Due to all of these factors (which do not include the industrial way of life!), the Office of Transit inspectors made the following call to the Juárez citizenry: "We ask people to please adjust their time due to possible delays, and we recommend that they obey the law, since there are various types of 'stops.' But there is only one genuine 'stop' in front of a stop sign: to stop completely" (*Diario de Juárez*, September 9, 2000, 1B).

15. Due to competition among multinationals, many maquiladoras offer "Trans-

porte Especial" (Special Transportation, which is a new form of *rutera* that works for specific companies) so that workers can be transported, free of charge, from the industrial parks to the neighborhoods, especially for those who work on the night-shift, or to the downtown area.

16. This was the third maquiladora in which I carried out participant observation (summer 1991). After my experience in two other assembly plants (one in 1987 and one in 1989), my purpose there was to observe and compare the technical aspects of the assembling process itself. Having collected data on the technicalities of the assembling of microcircuits (an electronics plant) and on the assembling of hospital gowns (a garment plant), I simply wanted to collect information (i.e., how an electric harness is assembled) on an automobile type of maquiladora for comparative purposes. In both 1989 and 1991, I entered the factory as any other applicant, following Fernández-Kelly's strategy (1983): as anthropologists with a Mexican birth certificate, both of us were able to walk from factory to factory and ask for an application, which would hopefully get us an interview, like any other worker (see Chapter 4). This strategy is, of course, awkward but very productive. Although in all three cases I applied for jobs through the latter process, in 1987 I was recommended through a contact in that factory. Getting recommended is not an uncommon practice (also see Fernández-Kelly 1983). For obvious ethical reasons, the identity of the corporations where I found myself doing participant observation, and the identities of the workers who volunteered inside and outside the factories, must be completely protected.

17. For the best discussion of middle-management personnel inside maquila-doras, particularly the role of managers and supervisors, see the monumental work by Devon Peña (1997). For one of the best feminist analyses of gender dynamics on the management ("American") side of these transnationals, see Wright 1998. Some American personnel consider the shop-floor section of these assembly plants "the Mexican side" (Wright 1998).

18. Between 1:00 and 2:30 PM, the restrooms are very popular, not only in this maquiladora but in most places around the world where the mode of capitalist production has allocated 12:00 noon as the critical time for the consumption of food so that the consumers can continue working, at most, until 5 PM. In this factory, however, the visitors to the restroom are several of those who have been working at the rotary and who end up having a ten- to fifteen-minute lunch. Their body tends to be in continuous movement. Thus, the visits to the restrooms tend to be, if not crowded, far from private.

Something peculiar that I have observed and experienced among male Mexican factory workers (I have no experience with, nor did I interview anyone about, the women's room) is that when they try to defecate knowing that others are around them, they do not necessarily release the gases with the same easiness one finds in men's restrooms, say, at the American universities I have attended or, for that matter, at men's restrooms in major hotels where the American Anthropological Association meetings are held. This particular practice is complicated when one considers another aspect of the culture of late capitalism: graffiti and its discontents. Even though graffiti has become characteristic of restrooms in most public buildings in both Mexico and the United States, in places where bodily discipline is expected if not enforced, writing on walls and doors might lead to a specific loss of privacy, not only for those who were the authors. Such is the case with the automobile maquila under discussion. If the female factory workers Aihwa Ong studied in Malaysia found spirits in the toilets, the male factory workers I worked with found no privacy in them.

In the men's restrooms of this factory, none of the toilets had a door for privacy. The lateral dividers in between the toilets allowed the restrooms of the maquiladora to be only slightly different from toilets at prisons, where they tend to be placed in the open—in the middle of empty cells. Otherwise, and apart from the fact that these restrooms are usually clean, I could make the case that the male workers defecate without any privacy. That these workers care about their privacy is demonstrated by their attempt to cover themselves with their own working gowns. Both the specific circumstances of defecating almost in an open or unprotected space and the peculiar humbleness among these working-class men about releasing loud airs in such "public" space produce a digestive uncomfortableness quite unimaginable. Some of the workers conditioned their bodies and stomachs to carry out such biological needs only in the privacy of their own home.

When I asked one of the supervisors why the men's toilets did not have their own individual doors, she responded: "The company is tired of painting and painting over the writing on the walls and doors at the restrooms. As punishment, the company decided to take down the doors." Would parents of university students tolerate such measures being taken by administrators of their children's schools? It is obvious that this abuse of authority is more a sign of power than an example of administrative or managerial illogic.

19. While no one should be shocked that factory workers punch time clocks and that supervisors supervise, we all should be concerned not only about their health rights but their political rights as well: These workers are putting pressure on each other while some of these corporations put additional pressure on them, precisely by, among other things, forcing them to punch the time clock four times a day, twice during lunchtimes (in the garment plant where I labored in 1989, the workers did not have to punch the time clock at lunchtime; the line leader was responsible for his/her assembly line). Devon Peña's general assessment of the *jefe* or *jefa de línea* or *grupo* (line leader) in his description of maquiladora relations of production inside factories can be summarized as follows:

> There are two different types of workers directly involved in productivity super-
> vision in the maquilas: group chiefs and first-line supervisors. The group chief
> is a regular assembly-line operator selected by management as a group leader
> on the basis of performance and behavioral standards. Group chiefs are selected
> from among the assembly operators who consistently produce at higher levels
> compared to other workers. Among industrial sociologists, these workers are
> known as rate-busters because they surpass the productivity standards informally
> set by the primary work groups. In the maquilas, these rate-busters are derisively
> called *santanitas,* presumably in reference to the Mexican dictator General Santa
> Anna [Santa Anna is known to have betrayed Mexico by selling almost half of its

territory to the United States during the Mexican-American War of 1846–1848].
Others refer to them as *rompecolas,* literally "ass busters," and yet others call them
simply *traicioneras* (female traitors). . . . Group chiefs receive economic and non-
economic incentives for their co-optation: for example, bonuses, gifts, tolerated
absenteeism or tardiness, and after-hour entertainment hosted by male supervisors. (Peña 1997, 116–117; italics in original)

My experience with group chiefs in the three maquiladoras where I carried out
participant observation (in 1987, 1989, and 1991) was not politically uniform and was
certainly more diverse along gender lines: I found both male and female line leaders
in all three factories (see also Chapters 5 and 7). Although some of them clearly
aspired to be part of lower management, and therefore did not always listen to assembly workers' complaints at the everyday level (see especially Chapter 7), they were
not necessarily always already "co-opted." Even though I did encounter line leaders
who were nonunionized, for instance, and therefore *empleados de confianza* (trusted
company employees), for the most part, they were socially (and often politically) vulnerable, especially in relation to other workers (as the label *traitors* demonstrates), in
spite of the additional privileges that Peña identified. The emergence of line leaders
in my ethnographic description in the rest of the book coordinates much more
(though not always exclusively, as will be seen in Chapter 7) with Fernández-Kelly's
assessment of their structural position:

As with factory guards, supervisors and group leaders are frequently seen by
workers as solely responsible for their plight at the workplace. Perceived abuses,
unfair treatment and excessive demands are thought to be the result of supervisors' whims rather than the creature of a particular system of production. That
explains, in part, why workers' grievances are often coached in complaints about
the performance of supervisors. . . . They [group leaders and supervisors] are
also the receivers of middle and upper management's dissatisfaction, but they
have considerably less power and their sphere of action is very limited. Many line
supervisors agree that the complications they face in their jobs are hardly worth
differences in pay. (Fernández-Kelly 1983, 126–127)

20. A 1999 document advertising Juárez to multinational corporations proudly
compares this border city with other areas around the world where similar assembly
plants are located: for 1989, the Desarrollo Económico de Ciudad Juárez calculated
the cost of labor per hour in Juárez to be $1.22 (without showing how they arrived
at this figure). For Hong Kong, they show $2.79 per hour; South Korea, $3.34; Sin-
gapore, $3.15; Taiwan, $3.53; Puerto Rico, $4.39; Japan, 12.49; U.S., $14.32. For 1996,
the last year accounted for in this document, the cost of labor per hour was $1.24
("Ciudad Juárez, Chihuahua, 1999," 1999). In December 2000, the minimum wage
in maquiladoras in Juárez was $37.90 pesos a day (at 9 pesos to a dollar), which is
complemented by bonuses, including free meals, and, at times, free transportation.
Even assuming that the most "productive" workers took home $400.00 pesos in their
paycheck every week in November 2000, they were still earning only ninety-eight

American cents an hour: 400 divided by 9 (9 pesos to a dollar) equals 44 dollars a week. 44 divided by 5 (5 days a week) equals $8.80 a day. 8.80 divided by 9 (hours per day) equals $.98 cents an hour.

21. In her fascinating study of "maquiladora mestizas" working on the "American side" (the management section) inside assembly plants, Melissa Wright documented the following: "Reference to prostitution when discussing women employees came up on more than one occasion in my research. . . . For example, when I asked one of the production managers, Roger, to describe the labor force, he said, 'Some of these girls have second jobs. You know, I've even heard that some work the bars.' The message that you cannot tell the difference between a prostitute and a female maquiladora worker was common in my interviews" (Wright 1998, 119–120).

22. One of Fernández-Kelly's main informants, Sandra, reminded critics of maquiladora workers (then and now) that "factory work is harder than most people know. As long as you don't harm anybody, what's wrong with having a little fun?" (Fernández-Kelly 1983, 132).

23. Gloria Anzaldúa has also noted the importance of gender inequalities in relation to ironing: "At a very early age I had a strong sense of who I was and what I was about and what was fair. I had a stubborn will . . . *Terca*. Even as a child I would not obey. I was 'lazy.' Instead of ironing my younger brothers' shirts or cleaning the cupboards, I would pass many hours studying, reading, painting, writing" (1987, 38; italics in original).

24. In Chapter 8, I deal with the theoretical implications for feminist literature of studying both men and women (also see Lugo 2000a and Lugo and Maurer 2000). I have basically argued that studies of women (women's studies) are one thing, studies of men are another (men's studies), and studies of both women and men are yet another: a completely different theoretical and ethnographic project enriched by the class experience of both women and men as "workers."

25. Latin Americanist historians have documented the pervasiveness of what Alejandro Lipschutz (1944) called a "pigmentocracy." Following the arguments and the documentation provided by Magnus Morner (1967) for Latin America and by Ramón Gutiérrez (1991) for colonial New Mexico, Suzanne Oboler describes this complex racialized process:

[Pigmentocracy] was a racial system whereby whiter skin was directly related to higher social status and honor, while darker skin was associated with "the physical labor of slaves and tributary Indians" and, visually, with "the infamy of the conquered." . . . [T]his extreme color consciousness was often accompanied [in the colonial period] by equally complex legal and social restrictions concerning marriage, taxes, residential settlement, and inheritance. Intermarriage among whites, "pure mestizos," and Indians, for example, was permitted—increasingly so, toward the end of the colonial period—but marriage of "pure bloods" to blacks and mulattoes required authorities' permission. And insofar as miscegenation, particularly among the lower sectors of the hierarchy, was also perceived as a real or potential threat to the established order, Afro-Indian marriages were strictly forbidden. The Spanish notion of *pureza de sangre,* or purity of blood, was thus embedded in the New World aristocracy's understanding of the interrelated concepts of race, social status, and honor. (Oboler 1995, 21)

The material that follows manifests, I argue, the undeniable existence, in today's postcolonial present, of the social effects of this colonial past (see also Chapter 3 in Part I).

26. Also, a dress code would force them to reject American tourists. Most American tourists—both white and black—are usually allowed to go in, since they are assumed to have dollars to spend, even if they are wearing shorts and tennis shoes. In this context, many Mexican American tourists do additional negotiation; they pass/cross into these discos by dressing up, of course (shorts and tennis shoes would not necessarily do for these Americans), and by speaking English as they wait in line and particularly when they are in front of the gatekeepers. In this way, the Mexican sector of the American border population distinguishes itself from the pesos-earning darker-skinned maquiladora workers and from the lighter-skinned Mexican population that does not speak English; but they can overlap with their dollars-earning, racially diverse American visitors. As a customer (and for a time a regular) in several Juárez discos while I lived in the Paso del Norte region until 1995 (when I left for Illinois), I was exposed to these strategies while waiting in line to go in.

27. Maquiladora women, of course, have also tried to cross the border. Given the fact that since the late 1970s, researchers have documented the plight of Juárez maquiladora women (see Fernández-Kelly 1983; Peña 1980, 1997; Ruiz and Tiano 1987; Staudt 1986; Tiano 1994; Wright 1998; Young 1986), my privileging of two economically vulnerable male maquiladora workers in this chapter is done with the intent of complementing both the feminist literature on maquiladora women (including my own previous writings that have focused on the feminist perspective) and the other ethnographic chapters in this book (Chapters 4, 5, 7, and 8), which also deal with both men and women.

28. The presentation that follows in the form of a dialogue between "informant" and "anthropologist" is influenced by R. Rosaldo and Flores's call for academics to treat the individuals we interview as "analyzing subjects, as people with valuable perceptions about their . . . situations" (R. Rosaldo and Flores 1997, 85; also see R. Rosaldo 1993 about the subaltern as analyzing subject).

29. Research needs to be done on how more senior or elderly working-class Mexican folk (whether Roberto's mother, Edgar's father, or Alejandro Morales's mother) respond or relate to much younger Border Patrol officers, police deputies, and customs and INS or Homeland Security officials. At this point, I can only offer personal impressions about what I have seen in the Juárez–El Paso area: After a long life of struggle, they seem to quietly observe how they themselves and their own younger loved ones cope with what has been old news (to most of our elderly), at least since the 1930s depression—that is, the ever-present possibility of being inspected and interrogated, at best, and of being sent back, at worst. In the case of Edgar and his father, it must be noted that border inspections often produce rigid borders or boundaries where least expected: the father denied the son in front of the inspectors.

30. More and more since the mid-1980s, migrants from southern states in Mexico

(Veracruz, Chiapas, Oaxaca, and the state of Mexico), in addition to those who migrated to Juárez in the 1960s and 1970s from such northern states as Zacatecas, Coahuila, and Durango, are deciding to reside in Juárez once they are sent back to Mexico by INS and U.S. Border Patrol officials. As Jorge Morales narrated: "Ciudad Juárez used to be just a place to cross into the United States. I tried two times, but both times they sent me back. Alone, without money, and without family, I decided to find a job here [in Juárez] so that I would save money to return [to Coahuila], since I did not want to return penniless. Besides, there were no jobs down there, so it did not make sense to return right away. That happened fifteen years ago: Here I found a job, I found a house, I found a wife, so I stayed here" (*Diario de Juárez,* June 10, 2000, 3B). Since 2000, with the emergence of China as one of the most attractive sites for low-cost labor under global assembly production, Ciudad Juárez lost some of its competitiveness in the world market, losing between 20,000 and 30,000 maquiladora jobs in 2001–2004.

Chapter Seven

1. Sociologist Pablo Vila's excellent ethnographic work (especially 2000) documents this general problem in Ciudad Juárez, particularly the regional divisions intensifying border life even further.

2. For the best elaboration of the complexities of the turn-of-the-century constitution of the maquiladora industry in Ciudad Juárez, especially as it relates to shop-floor conditions since Fernández-Kelly and Peña published their work and since I did fieldwork on various shop floors, please see Salzinger 2003.

Chapter Eight

1. A different version of this chapter appeared in my *Gender Matters: Rereading Michelle Z. Rosaldo* (2000), coedited with Bill Maurer. Small but important adjustments have been incorporated into this chapter in the spirit of reconceptualizing a productive "U-turn" toward a Marxist-feminist analysis of class for the early twenty-first century.

2. For a different, though not totally unrelated, use of "domestication"—as a form of empowerment on the part of particular groups of women who have "domesticated" public places in England and in Argentina—see Schirmer 1994, 203–216.

3. Catherine A. MacKinnon best articulated the classic Marxist feminist concerns associated with what seemed inevitable tensions between class analysis and gender analysis. She wrote, "Marxists have criticized feminism as bourgeois in theory and practice, meaning that it works in the interest of the ruling class. They argue that to analyze society in terms of sex ignores class divisions among women, dividing the proletariat. . . . Feminists charge that Marxism is male defined in theory and in practice, meaning that it moves within the worldview and in the interest of men. Feminists argue that analyzing society exclusively in class terms ignores the distinctive social experiences of the sexes, obscuring women's unity. . . . Marxists and feminists thus accuse each other of seeking (what in each one's terms is) reform—changes that

appease and assuage without addressing the grounds of discontent—where (again in each one's terms) a fundamental overthrow is required. The mutual perception, at its most extreme, is not only that the other's analysis is incorrect, but that its success would be a defeat. Neither set of allegations is groundless. In the feminist view, sex, in analysis and in reality, does divide classes, a fact Marxists have been more inclined to deny or ignore than to explain or change. Marxists, similarly, have seen parts of the women's movement function as a special interest group to advance the class-privileged: educated and professional women" (1982, 3–4). That MacKinnon wrote her essay in dedication "to the spirit of Shelly Rosaldo in us all" is a clear reminder of what kind of gender analysis M. Rosaldo aspired to carry out before her untimely death. I will return to MacKinnon's key proposition regarding gender and class at the end of this chapter.

4. Jennifer Schirmer has provided explicit examples of these sources of power as forms of empowerment. For example, she has shown how the Plaza de Mayo Madres of Argentina have used photographs of children and of the disappeared to subvert or domesticate the public plazas: "The Madres have used the conservative image of women without husbands to care for them, together with photographs of children, to appeal to a 'natural order' that the state does not respect. . . . Photographs also serve to reassert the presence of the disappeared in the mind of the public and to negate the 'chronicle of announced death.' Photographs exhibited publicly break the state's monopoly over memory and, together with the domestication of politi-cal space, serve, in turn, to substantiate these women's political shape and purpose" (Schirmer 1994, 204). Schirmer also gave a captivating example of domestication of public space from England. The Greenham Common women who have protested nuclear weapons since the early 1980s "domesticated" with a sofa the "roadway on which camouflaged missile convoys exercised maneuvers": "In March 1987 a Cruise missile truck convoy, returning from driving missiles around on the Salisbury Plain to 'distract the enemy,' found the turning to the main gate at Greenham blocked by a dilapidated sofa upon which three women sat chatting. When the convoy arrived, one of the women said in a very matter-of-fact tone through a megaphone . . . , 'As you will notice, this road is now occupied by women. The road is now closed. The road is now closed. Please turn back and go away'" (ibid., 207). Schirmer's work in Latin America and in England is a reincarnation of Temma Kaplan's classic work on Barce-lona (see preface in Lugo 2000a): Both show, it seems to me, how M. Rosaldo's ideas about the mobilizing potential of the domestic were in the air, so to speak. In the case of marches protesting the Mexican government's impunity and injustice associated with more than four hundred murder cases of young women and girls in Ciudad Juárez (see epilogue), it is mainly the mothers who created a vital social movement based on the mobilization of their domestic rights as child rearers who lost their beloved daughters (also see Bejarano 2002).

5. For a much-needed examination of the gender and sexuality of academic anthropology, see Dubois 1995; Lewin 1995; Lutz 1995; Newton and Stacey 1995; and Tedlock 1995—all in Behar and Gordon's *Women Writing Culture* (1995). Also see the relationship of my "feminist" subjectivity with Chicana feminisms, white feminism, and Chicano Studies (Lugo 2003).

6. In this regard, *New York Times* journalist Patricia Cohen recently reported
on changes in gender relations in the United States ("Signs of Détente in the Battle
between Venus and Mars," May 31, 2007, A13). More specifically, Cohen comments
on research that concludes the following: "Women and men are becoming more
alike in their attitudes toward balancing life at home and at work. The gender revolution is not over, [researchers say,] it has just developed into a 'gender convergence.'"
Cohen quotes a conference paper by Molly Monahan Land and Barbara J. Risman,
who define "gender convergence" as "an ever-increasing similarity in how men and
women live and what they want from their lives." Cohen also notes that according to
research carried out by Kathleen Gerson, "Convergence shows up more in younger
parents." After conducting 120 in-depth interviews with men and women ages eighteen to thirty-two, Dr. Gerson found that Generation X fathers spent more time with
their children than did baby boomer fathers, and that both sexes aspired to the same
ideal: "a balance between work and family." These findings, I believe, challenge us
to produce a feminist theory of gender that better accounts for women-men interactions such as these occurring at home and beyond, especially in capitalist societies
of the twenty-first century. To be sure, a full analysis of these changes cannot be
carried out without recognizing class distinctions; in other words, the experience of
working-class men and women will most likely differ from the experiences of their
middle-class counterparts.

7. In a not very different context, MacKinnon made a similar analytical argument
with regard to feminism (orthodox gender analysis) and Marxism (orthodox class
analysis): "Feminism stands in relation to Marxism as Marxism does to classical political economy: its final conclusion and ultimate critique. Compared with Marxism,
the place of thought and things in method and reality are reversed in a seizure of
power that penetrates subject with object and theory with practice. In a dual motion,
feminism turns Marxism inside out and on its head" (1982, 30).

8. Lancaster's highly original piece is in "a league of its own" in both anthropology and feminism; its analysis of Judith Butler's theory of performance in the
context of Guto's own personal feelings and social practices at home and beyond
is a major contribution (unsurpassed so far) to feminist theory in anthropology,
even though Lancaster is not examining, ethnographically, both men's *and* women's
sexualities per se (for a related theoretical discussion of performativity, see Lugo and
Maurer 2000).

9. See Chapter 2 for my analysis of European visions of savage (Apache)/civilized
(Spaniard) and fierce(Apache)/tamed (Pueblo/Manso) peoples during the imperialist
encounter at the U.S.-Mexico border in the sixteenth and seventeenth centuries. This
section on Chagnon and the assessment in Chapter 2 should produce the following:
Yanomamo is to Chagnon in the Amazonian borderlands what Apache is to the
Spanish colonizer in the northern Mexican borderlands.

10. I would like to draw attention to an interesting parallel between Chagnon's
own representation of his main informant, Rerebawa, and Devon Peña's own representation of his key informant, Juana Ortega. In his attempt to document struggles
of resistance among maquiladora workers, Peña situates Ortega throughout his
ethnography in very strategic ways, ultimately to make a much-needed critique of

co-optation inside maquilas. The sociological ethnographer first introduces Juana Ortega in a multidimensional manner: "She has a bit of the terrorized victim that is Ford's automaton and a lot of the rebel that is more akin to Ludd, the original machine-smasher" (1997, 8). Then, Peña moves his description of Ortega toward an antivictim narrative sustained by its fictive opposite (a stereotype of maquiladora workers)—a narrative that erases the majority of the working-class laborers in Ciudad Juárez: "I do not see a quiescent victim in Juana Ortega. She is both an oppressed worker and a tireless agitator for workers' rights. Her oppression does not reduce her to the status of a helpless victim. She is too dignified for that. . . . She does not fit the stereotype of the happy Juárez factory worker impatiently yearning for the next paycheck to hurry on across the border in search of a Big Mac and fries at the gleaming, golden-arched temple of North American capitalism. While she readily accepts the wages she needs to help a family survive, she remains critical of the excessive gringo appetites that fuel the growth of the maquila industry" (1997, 9). Eventually, Peña is explicit about how "Ortega is one of the most politicized maquila workers that I have ever spoken to over the course of ten years of field research in Juárez" (1997, 200). This realization on Peña's part does not, however, allow him to see that among workers themselves, the line between resistance and aggressiveness is not always clearly delineated. For instance, Peña interprets the following anecdote as an example of "the importance of friendship networks in the subaltern life of the factory," and as evidence for how "Juana Ortega was perhaps exceptionally effective at preventing co-optation" (1997, 18):

> It has to do with how the group works together, whether or not the group has a sense of solidarity, a feeling that, hey, we are all in the same position here. . . . Every so often someone would almost violate this trust and solidarity. . . . One was when the managers came and performed a new series of time and motion studies in order to increase the standards and improve efficiency. . . . We had to be careful to make certain none of us did the best we could. . . . One of us, Sara, almost blew it. . . . But we created a diversion, a fake accident, that got the engineers off her. While they saw to the "accident," I went over and reminded her that she was obligated to the group, to keep a lower pace, and then she did. (1997, 118)

In very different contexts, but similar in their analytical tone and use of key informants, both Chagnon and Peña are unable to see the politics of intimidation at work, one for focusing too much on "fierceness," the other for focusing too much on "resistance."

11. I would like to make it clear that Chagnon and Peña do not share political ideologies (especially regarding the subaltern), and that my respect and appreciation for Peña's (as well as Fernández-Kelly's) pioneering work on maquiladoras led me to do ethnographic work at the U.S.-Mexico border. Yet I find it necessary to make the following methodological comparison between Chagnon's ethnography of the Yanomamo and Peña's ethnography of maquiladora workers: Chagnon's key informant, Rerebawa, was fierce; Peña's key informant, Juana Ortega, was a resister; Chagnon's focus was on the nature of violence; Peña's focus was on issues of resistance; Cha-

gnon used Rerebawa to get at genealogies in villages; Peña used Juana Ortega to get at networks of resistance in maquiladoras.

In spite of the problem of focus regarding the overuse of his key informant and an overprivileging of struggles of resistance in trying to understand maquiladora life in Ciudad Juárez, Peña's body of ethnographic and political work is an admirable one that will be difficult to duplicate. In these notes, I just wanted to identify for future scholars (who should not commit the same mistakes that I and my generation have committed) a few but important limitations tied to methodology more than to moral or ethical commitment in Peña's (1997) *Terror of the Machine.*

Chapter Nine

1. A different version of this chapter appeared as "Reflections on Border Theory, Culture, and the Nation" in *Border Theory* (1997), edited by Scott Michaelsen and David E. Johnson. Both my article in *Border Theory* and this particular version of it are dedicated with *mucho cariño,* admiration, and gratitude to one of my most important teachers, Renato Rosaldo.

2. In this chapter, "the nation" and "the state," though usually imbricated with each other, will be used as categorically distinct entities, respectively, as a changing imagined community (Anderson 1991) and as a changing governance apparatus (Hall 1986). These specific uses, and their implications for culture and border theories, will be examined throughout the chapter. Although this chapter reflects on the state of culture and the nation during the past two hundred years, it does not constitute in itself an exhaustive historical project. I wish mainly to point out some limitations and some new readings of these topics as they connect to issues raised throughout the book. Nonetheless, the analysis of the nation, culture, and the state will be presented here as a point of reference rooted in my discussion of both monarchy and empire in the U.S.-Mexico borderlands in Chapters 2 and 3.

3. "Deterritorializing" from "within" is a multilinear process and a complicated political project. It is multilinear because there are several fronts of struggle: late capitalism, the nation-state, contested communities, colonizer/colonized relations, theory itself, and the individual subject, among many others. It is a complicated political project because agents inhabit multiple locations, creating immediate re-territorializing. For instance, I write from diverse but interconnected positions: as a cultural anthropologist who did fieldwork among maquila (factory) workers and who was trained in American institutions; as a Mexican who spent his childhood and was born in Ciudad Juárez, Mexico, but who became Chicano *en el otro lado* (on the other side) while continuing his secondary and university schooling in Las Cruces, New Mexico. While living in Las Cruces, I visited Ciudad Juárez (my grandparents) every weekend until I was twenty-two years of age; thus, I am also a borderer (*fronterizo*) whose everyday experiences could be unpredictably located at the Mexico (Ciudad Juárez)/Texas (El Paso)/New Mexico (Las Cruces) borders. In spite of my multiple locations and possibilities, however, in this chapter I would like to reflect on why, as academics, we have come to think seriously about "culture" and "borders" to begin with and how these two concepts can help us better critique the many forms of

conquest that have impacted the working-class Mexican and indigenous communities considered in this book.

4. Foucault wrote that "the purpose of the present study [*The History of Sexuality*] is in fact to show how deployments of power are directly connected to the body" (1978, 151). These "deployments of power" overlap with the deployments of sexuality in the modern West. In Part Four, "Deployment of Sexuality," Foucault examines in detail the objectives, methods, domains, and periodizations through which power operated and dispersed itself from the late eighteenth century to the late nineteenth century in Europe (see 1978, 75–131). He also argues, as is well known nowadays, that power is omnipresent: "The omnipresence of power: not because it has the privilege of consolidating everything under its invisible unity, but because it is produced from one moment to the next, at every point, or rather in every relation from one point to another" (1978, 93).

5. Foucault wrote: "Law was not simply a weapon skillfully wielded by monarchs; it was the monarchic system's mode of manifestation and the form of its acceptability. In Western societies since the Middle Ages [and here we must include New Spain], the exercise of power has always been formulated in terms of law" (1978, 87). He adds, "One is attached to a certain image of power-law, of power-sovereignty, which was traced out by the theoreticians of right and the monarchic institution. *It is this image that we must break free of, that is, of the theoretical privilege of the law and sovereignty, if we wish to analyze power within the concrete and historical framework of its operation. We must construct an analytics of power that no longer takes law as a model and code*" (1978, 90; my emphasis).

6. Interestingly, in his analysis of the nation, Benedict Anderson uses the same periodization that Foucault used to examine the deployment of sexuality and E. P. Thompson used to examine class and industrial capitalism: the late 1700s and the nineteenth century. For the most part, Rosaldo limited himself to the twentieth century.

7. Edward Said's more elaborate response to Ania Loomba's question about how to combine Gramsci and Foucault is worth stating much more fully here, especially since it is analytically relevant to my own historico-theoretical argument in this book: "Once you've begun to circulate a bit in Gramsci, you realize that he is talking about very different situations at very different times, and that there is a danger of abstracting from the situation to a general theoretical term—which is almost impossible, I mean the danger is almost too great. Nevertheless, Gramsci, unlike Foucault, is working with an evolving political situation in which certain extremely important and radical experiments were taking place in the Turin factories in which he was involved, and from them he generalized periodically, I mean in a periodical form. You don't get that sense in Foucault; what you get instead is a sense of teleology where everything is tending toward the same end . . . The introduction of historical, what I would call a historical context, to Foucault is extremely important and worth doing" (Said 2002, 10).

8. In fact, Sherry Ortner organizes her highly influential essay on "practice theory" (1984) along such dialectics as system/action, structure/practice.

9. In Chapter 5, I showed how this double life of culture is manifested in the

electronics maquiladora through an analysis of how specific notions of laziness at the workplace reproduce ideologies of masculinity and machismo as well as the working-class experience.

10. Foucault associates this periodization—"1870"—with the production of the homosexual as "a personage, a past, a case history, and a childhood, in addition to being a type of life" (1978, 43). He adds, "We must not forget that the psychological, psychiatric, medical category of homosexuality was constituted from the moment it was characterized—Westphal's famous article of 1870 ["Archiv fur Neurologie"] on "contrary sexual relations" can stand as its date of birth. . . . The sodomite had been a temporary aberration; the homosexual was now a species" (Foucault 1978, 43).

11. As we have seen in the case of Mexico, the question of *mestizaje* as a national project emerged at the same time that the nation-state was trying to consolidate itself immediately after the Mexican Revolution of 1910–1920. Before the Mexican Revolution, especially immediately after independence, Mexico struggled with its monarchic legacy (with the exception of Benito Juárez's presidency, which coincided with and against the French invasion of the 1860s). In the context of world politics of the late nineteenth century, the Porfiriato (1877–1911) carried the seeds of exploitation that led to the Revolution, which in turn led to the production of the "state" identified by Gramsci in the 1930s (Gramsci himself was a contemporary of President Lázaro Cárdenas).

12. Also, while analyzing the work of literary theorist Kenneth Burke, Rosaldo wrote:

> Recent social thinkers [Giddens 1979; Ortner 1984] have updated Burke's style of analysis by identifying the interplay of "structure" and "agency" as a central issue in social theory. Most central for them, in other words, is the question of *how received structures shape human conduct, and how, in turn, human conduct alters received structures.* (1993, 104; my emphasis)

13. Of course, the self/"other" distinction has been both contested and problematized in most recent writings of culture and power.

14. In his experimental ethnography, *Dancing with the Devil,* José Limón applies the metaphor of war in ways I am suggesting here, but following Gramsci's "war of maneuver" and "war of position." In the following quotation, Limón uses the metaphor of war quite appropriately to depict the racial struggle between Mexicans and Anglos in South Texas: "For it is a basic premise and organizing metaphor for this essay that since the 1830's, the Mexicans of south Texas have been in a state of social war with the 'Anglo' dominant Other and their class allies. This has been at times a war of overt, massive proportions; at others, covert and sporadic; at still other moments, repressed and internalized as a war within the psyche, but always conditioned by an ongoing social struggle fought out of different battlefields" (1994, 16).

15. Also, feminist anthropologists were, and have been, at the forefront of this exciting anthropology produced in the late twentieth century (see especially the provocative and theoretically sophisticated volumes *Uncertain Terms* (1990), edited by

Faye Ginsburg and Anna Tsing, and *Women Writing Culture* (1995), edited by Ruth Behar and Deborah Gordon—two among many others).

16. For some very useful critiques of Benedict Anderson's *Imagined Communities*, the works of the following authors stand out: in Subaltern Studies, Chatterjee (1993) and Chakrabarty (2000); in Latin Americanist anthropology, Thurner (1997) and Lomnitz (2001). My own border reading of this text vis-à-vis *Culture and Truth* attempts to contribute to the necessary dialogue on two of the most important essays of late-twentieth-century U.S.-based scholarship (R. Rosaldo's and Anderson's).

17. The presence of hundreds of maquiladoras in Ciudad Juárez, as well as the fragmented life that they create, makes the working-class men and women part of the articulation of domination of both industrial and state capital; after all, the Mexican state, particularly in northern Chihuahua, has been mostly controlled by elite families, themselves industrial entrepreneurs.

18. Of course, this notion of culture as shared patterns of behavior still reigns in some quarters.

19. In *The Making of the English Working Class* (1966), E. P. Thompson examined the role of print "capitalism" in the radicalization of the working and middle classes in England during the early nineteenth century. This kind of radicalization, through print, has not occurred in Ciudad Juárez, although in his *Terror of the Machine* (1997), Devon Peña briefly documented a few such historical moments in the early 1980s.

20. As we also saw in Chapter 2, this imagined and practiced kingship led to the domination and conquest of Nueva España, Nueva Galicia, Nueva Vizcaya, and Nueva México.

21. See Chapter 2 for the encounters of conquest both Hernán Cortés and Juan de Oñate had with uncertain, unidentified groups of people, not yet "labeled" by the Europeans, on the coast of Mexico and in what came to be New Mexico.

22. One of the most important contributions of Renato Rosaldo's thinking is precisely his sensitivity to analysis of power as it is found in patterns and borderlands, chaos and order, subjectivity and objectivity, and culture and politics. None of these entities holds a monopoly on truth. This is Rosaldo's most important message regarding culture, identity, and power/knowledge.

23. I have also argued that if within anthropology such dialectics as "practice and structure" and "beliefs and action" do not explicitly appear in early anthropological debates about culture and the individual, the individual and society, the individual and social structure, or culture and the environment, it is because "practice," as a category of analysis, was suppressed due to its implication for political mobilizations on the part of colonized subjects, the working poor, and other subaltern subjects— the usual targets of anthropologists throughout most of the twentieth century.

Also, anthropologists have historically privileged such analytical domains as cognition, symbols, the environment, decision making, the superorganic, and personality, among many others, in trying to get to the cultural or the social in human beings. Yet, all these categories acquire meaning for academics only to the extent that they can explain or interpret people's beliefs and actions. Thus, we inevitably return to the "structure/practice" duality that, I argue, has constituted our dominant discourse on culture and power—so far.

Epilogue

1. In her book, *Cosecha de Mujeres* (2005), Diana Washington-Valdez presents and examines a slightly different version of the *informe,* or "report" (see pp. 214–217). Hers and González Rodríguez's are almost identical. After comparing both texts, it seems to me that the version published in *Norte de Ciudad Juárez* in 2003 is a bit more precise regarding a few details. I am deliberately leaving out names of people and places for reasons that concern what might ultimately be argued, sustained, or debated if the case were to go to a genuine international or binational court, which I hope it does, in the immediate future. I do not know if the report exists in English. What follows is my own translation of passages found in the *Norte* article.

2. Original text in Spanish in Washington-Valdez (2005, 237): "Ni un solo hombre ni un grupo son responsables de todos los crímenes de Juárez. Los sospechosos incluyen asesinos en serie, imitadores, pandilleros, narcotraficantes y un grupo de influyentes. Ninguno de los verdaderos asesinos de esta larga década de series de crímenes sexuales ha sido encarcelado. Mientras los criminales continúen en libertad, ninguna mujer estará segura en las calles de esta ciudad fronteriza. Ha sido claro que funcionarios corruptos han encubierto los crímenes y protegido a los asesinos. Debido a la complicidad oficial, las muertes significan crímenes de Estado, y son, de acuerdo con lo expresado por un funcionario del FBI, 'crímenes contra la humanidad'" (Washington-Valdez 2005, 237).

3. To be sure, I am not treating the femicides as "maquiladora killings" per se. I strongly agree with Rosa Linda Fregoso's warning and critique about the "myth of 'maquiladora killings.'" She wrote, quite convincingly: "Attributing the murders of women to processes of globalization has created the enduring myth of 'maquiladora killings,' one in which the killers are allegedly targeting maquiladora workers—a cliché that continues to this day. . . . As convincing as this narrative may be, there is ample evidence disputing the myth . . . especially in the research of independent journalists and academics in Mexico. A study conducted by Benítez et al. [1999] of murders between 1993 and 1998 identifies only 15 maquiladora workers out of 137 victims. Drawing from a larger sample—162 murdered women between 1993 and 1999—the research of Monárrez [2000] further corroborates the earlier figure of 15 maquiladora workers killed, citing additional occupations for the victims: students, housewives, sales clerks, sex workers, domestics, drug traffickers" (Fregoso 2003, 8). I highlighted the experiences of maquiladora workers because of the larger nature of this particular study.

Abu-Lughod, Lila
1991   "Writing against Culture." In *Recapturing Anthropology,* ed. Richard Fox, 137–162. Santa Fe, NM: SAR Press.
Aguirre, Elea A.
1993   "The Urban Form of El Paso del Norte: A Cluster Analysis." Master's thesis, Department of Sociology, University of Texas at El Paso.
Alarcón, Norma
1996   "Anzaldúa's *Frontera:* Inscribing Gynetics." In *Displacement, Diaspora, and Geographies of Identity,* ed. Smadar Lavie and Ted Swedenburg, 41–53. Durham: Duke University Press.
Alcázar de Velasco, Ángel
n.d.   *Historia del Templo de Nuestra Señora de Guadalupe.* University of Texas at El Paso (UTEP), Special Collections NH 5252 C5d4H.
Aldama, Arturo J.
2001   *Disrupting Savagism: Intersecting Chicana/o, Mexican Immigrant, and Native American Struggles in Self-Representation.* Durham: Duke University Press.
Alonso, Ana María
1995   *Thread of Blood: Colonialism, Revolution, and Gender on Mexico's Northern Frontier.* Tucson: University of Arizona Press.
Alonso, Ana María, and María Teresa Koreck
1988   "Silences: Hispanics, AIDS, and Sexual Practices." *Difference* 1:101–124.

Altamirano, Graziella, and Guadalupe Villa, eds.

1988a   *Chihuahua: Textos de su historia, 1824–1921.* Ciudad Juárez: Instituto de In-
         vestigaciones Dr. José María Luis Mora.

1988b   *Chihuahua, una historia compartida: 1824–1921.* Colección Historia General
         de Chihuahua. Ciudad Juárez: Gobierno del Estado de Chihuahua.

Alurista [Urista Heredia, Alberto Baltazar]

1989   "Myth, Identity, and Struggle in Three Chicano Novels: Aztlán-Anaya
         Mendez, and Acosta." In *Aztlán: Essays on the Chicano Homeland,* ed.
         Rudolfo A. Anaya and Francisco A. Lomelí, 219–229. Albuquerque: Uni-
         versity of New Mexico Press.

Alvarez, Robert R., Jr.

1995   "The Mexican-U.S. Border: The Making of an Anthropology of Border-
         lands." *Annual Review of Anthropology* 24:447–470.

Anaya, Rudolfo A.

1989   "Aztlán: A Homeland without Boundaries." In *Aztlán: Essays on the Chi-
         cano Homeland,* ed. Rudolfo A. Anaya and Francisco Lomelí, 230–241.
         Albuquerque: University of New Mexico Press.

Anderson, Benedict

1991   *Imagined Communities: Reflections on the Origin and Spread of National-
         ism.* Rev. ed. London: Verso.

Anderson, Perry

1968   "Components of the National Culture." *New Left Review* 1(50):1–34.

1980   *Arguments within English Marxism.* London: Verso.

Anzaldúa, Gloria

1987   *Borderlands/La Frontera: The New Mestiza.* San Francisco: Spinsters/Aunt
         Lute.

1989   "The Homeland, Aztlán/El Otro México." In *Aztlán: Essays on the Chicano
         Homeland,* ed. Rudolfo A. Anaya and Francisco A. Lomelí, 191–204. Albu-
         querque: University of New Mexico Press.

Arnold, Katherine

1977   "The Introduction of Poses to a Peruvian Brothel and Changing Images of
         Male and Female." In *The Anthropology of Body,* ed. John Blacking, 179–197.
         London: Academic Press.

Arreola, Daniel D., and James R. Curtis

1993   *The Mexican Border Cities: Landscape Anatomy and Place Personality.*
         Tucson: University of Arizona Press.

Balderas Domínguez, Jorge

2002   *Mujeres, antros y estigmas en la noche juarense.* Chihuahua, Mexico: Solar
         Colección.

Balderston, Daniel, and Donna J. Guy, eds.

1997   *Sex and Sexuality in Latin America.* New York: New York University Press.

Bancroft, Hubert Howe

1962   *History of Arizona and New Mexico.* Albuquerque: Horn and Wallace.
         (Orig. pub. 1889.)

Bannon, John Francis

1974   *The Spanish Borderlands Frontier, 1513–1821.* Albuquerque: University of New Mexico Press.

Barth, Frederik

1966   *Models of Social Organization.* Occasional Paper No. 23. London: Royal Anthropological Institute.

Bartra, Roger

1992   *The Cage of Melancholy: Identity and Metamorphosis in the Mexican Character.* Trans. Christopher J. Hall. New Brunswick, NJ: Rutgers University Press.

Basso, Keith

1981   "'Wise Words' of the Western Apache: Metaphor and Semantic Theory." In *Language, Culture, and Cognition: Anthropological Perspectives,* ed. R. W. Casson, 244–267. New York: Macmillan.

Behar, Ruth

1993   *Translated Woman: Crossing the Border with Esperanza's Story.* Boston: Beacon Press.

1995   "Writing in My Father's Name: A Diary of *Translated Woman*'s First Year." In *Women Writing Culture,* ed. Ruth Behar and Deborah A. Gordon, 65–82. Berkeley: University of California Press.

Behar, Ruth, and Deborah A. Gordon, eds.

1995   *Women Writing Culture.* Berkeley: University of California Press.

Bejarano, Cynthia L.

2002   "Las Super Madres de Latino América: Transforming Motherhood and Houseskirts by Challenging Violence in Juárez, Mexico; Argentina; and El Salvador." *Frontiers* 23(1):126–150.

2005   *"¿Qué Onda?": Urban Youth Cultures and Border Identity.* Tucson: University of Arizona Press.

Benedict, Ruth

1934   *Patterns of Culture.* Boston: Houghton Mifflin.

Benítez-Rojo, Antonio

1992   *The Repeating Island: The Caribbean and the Postmodern Perspective.* Trans. James E. Maranis. Durham: Duke University Press.

Berdahl, Daphne

1999   *Where the World Ended: Re-Unification and Identity in the German Borderland.* Berkeley: University of California Press.

Bhabha, Homi K.

1990   "Interrogating Identity: The Postcolonial Prerogative." In *Anatomy of Racism,* ed. David Theo Goldberg, 183–209. Minneapolis: University of Minnesota Press.

Boas, Franz

1940   *Race, Language, and Culture.* New York: Free Press. (Orig. pub. 1920.)

1963   *The Mind of Primitive Man.* New York: Collier Press. (Orig. pub. 1911.)

Bonfil Batalla, Guillermo

1996   *México Profundo: Reclaiming a Civilization.* Trans. Philip A. Dennis. Austin: University of Texas Press. (Orig. pub. 1987.)

Bonilla, Frank, et al.
1998   *Borderless Borders: U.S. Latinos, Latin Americans, and the Paradox of Inter-
          dependence.* Philadelphia: Temple University Press.
Borofsky, Robert, ed.
1994   *Assessing Cultural Anthropology.* New York: McGraw-Hill.
Bourdieu, Pierre
1977   *Outline of a Theory of Practice.* New York: Cambridge University Press.
          (Orig. pub. 1972.)
Brandes, Stanley
1980   *Metaphors of Masculinity: Sex and Status in Andalusian Folklore.* Philadel-
          phia: University of Pennsylvania Press.
1981   "Like Wounded Stags: Male Sexual Ideology in an Andalusian Town." In
          Sexual Meanings, ed. Sherry Ortner and Harriet Whitehead, 216–239. Cam-
          bridge: Cambridge University Press.
Brannon, Jeffrey, and G. William Lucker
1889   "The Impact of Mexico's Economic Crisis on the Demographic Compo-
          sition of the Maquiladora Labor Force." *Journal of Borderlands Studies*
          4:39–70.
Burden, Philip D.
1996   *The Mapping of North America: A List of Printed Maps 1511–1670.* London:
          Raleigh Publications.
Burton, Antoinette
2003   *Dwelling in the Archive: Women Writing House, Home, and History in Late
          Colonial India.* New York: Oxford University Press.
Buschman, Johann Karl Edvard
1998   "De los nombres de los lugares aztecas." In *Los nombres de México,* ed.
          Ignacio Guzmán Betancourt, 203–207. Mexico City: Miguel Angel Porrúa.
Bustamante, Jorge
1983   "Maquiladoras: A New Face of International Capitalism on Mexico's
          Northern Frontier." In *Women and the International Division of Labor,* ed.
          June Nash and María P. Fernández-Kelly, 224–256. Albany: State University
          of New York Press.

Carrillo, Héctor
2002   *The Night Is Young: Sexuality in Mexico in the Time of AIDS.* Chicago: Uni-
          versity of Chicago Press.
Carrillo, Jorge, and Alberto Hernández
1985   *Mujeres fronterizas en la industria maquiladora.* Mexico City: Consejo Na-
          cional de Fomento Educativo.
Castellanos, Alicia G.
1981   *Ciudad Juárez: La vida fronteriza.* Mexico City: Editorial Nuestro Tiempo.
Castillo, Debra A., and María Socorro Tabuenca Córdoba
2002   *Border Women: Writing from La Frontera.* Minneapolis: University of Min-
          nesota Press.

Catanzarite, Lisa M., and Myra H. Strober
1993   "The Gender Recomposition of the Maquiladora Workforce in Ciudad Juárez." *Industrial Relations* 32:133–147.
Chagnon, Napoleon
1992   *Yanomamo*. 4th ed. Fort Worth, TX: Harcourt Brace College Publishers.
Chakrabarty, Dipesh
1992   "Postcoloniality and the Artifice of History: Who Speaks for 'Indian Pasts'?" *Representations* 37:1–26.
2000   *Provincializing Europe: Postcolonial Thought and Historical Difference.* Princeton: Princeton University Press.
Chatterjee, Partha
1993   *The Nation and Its Fragments: Colonial and Postcolonial Histories.* Princeton: Princeton University Press.
Chávez, Armando B.
1991   *Historia de Ciudad Juárez, Chihuahua.* Mexico City: Editorial Pax México.
Chávez, John R.
1989   "Aztlán, Cíbola, and Frontier New Spain." In *Aztlán: Essays on the Chicano Homeland*, ed. Rudolfo A. Anaya and Francisco A. Lomelí, 49–71. Albuquerque: University of New Mexico Press.
Chavez, Leo R.
1998   *Shadowed Lives: Undocumented Immigrants in American Society.* Ft. Worth, TX: Harcourt, Brace, Jovanovich College Publishers. (Orig. pub. 1992.)
Christopherson, Susan
1982   "Family and Class in the New Industrial City." Ph.D. diss., Department of Geography. University of California at Berkeley.
"Ciudad Juárez, Chihuahua, 1999."
1999   Document. Ciudad Juárez, Mexico: Desarrollo Económico de Ciudad Juárez, A.C.
"Ciudad Juárez en cifras—1991: Estadísticas socioeconómicas básicas."
1991   Document. Ciudad Juárez, Mexico: Desarrollo Económico de Ciudad Juárez, A.C.
Clavigero, Francesco Saverio
1945   *Historia antigua de México.* Mexico City: Editorial Porrúa. (Orig. pub. 1784.)
Clendinnen, Inga
1987   *Ambivalent Conquest: Maya and Spaniard in Yucatan, 1517–1570.* Cambridge: Cambridge University Press.
Clifford, James
1986   "Introduction: Partial Truths." In *Writing Culture: The Poetics and Politics of Ethnography,* ed. James Clifford and George Marcus, 1–26. Berkeley: University of California Press.
Clifford, James, and George Marcus, eds.
1986   *Writing Culture: The Poetics and Politics of Ethnography.* Berkeley: University of California Press.

Cline, Howard
1972   "Ethnohistorical Regions of Middle America." In *Guide to Ethnohistori-
          cal Sources,* Part One, ed. Howard Cline, 166–183. Handbook of Middle
          American Indians Series. Austin: University of Texas Press.
Collier, George, with Elizabeth Lowery Quaratiello
1999   *Basta! Land and the Zapatista Rebellion in Chiapas.* 2nd ed. Oakland, CA:
          Food First Books.
Collier, Jane, and Michelle Z. Rosaldo
1981   "Politics and Gender in Simple Societies." In *Sexual Meanings,* ed. Sherry
          Ortner and Harriet Whitehead, 275–329. Cambridge: Cambridge Univer-
          sity Press.
Comaroff, John L.
1987   "Sui Genderis: Feminism, Kinship Theory, and Structural 'Domains.'" In
          Gender and Kinship: Essays toward a Unified Analysis, ed. Jane Fishburne
          Collier and Sylvia Junko Yanagisako, 53–85. Stanford: Stanford University
          Press.
Conway, George Robert Graham (G.R.G.)
1940   *Postrera voluntad y testamento de Hernando Cortés, Marqués del Valle.* In-
          troducción y notas por G.R.G. Conway. Mexico City: P. Robredo. (Orig.
          pub. 1939.)
Cooper, Frederick, and Ann Laura Stoler, eds.
1997   *Tensions of Empire: Colonial Cultures in a Bourgeois World.* Berkeley: Uni-
          versity of California Press.
Cortés, Hernán
1986   *Hernán Cortés: Letters from Mexico.* Trans. and ed. Anthony Pagden. New
          Haven: Yale University Press.
1994   *Hernán Cortés: Cartas de relación.* Mexico City: Editorial Porrúa.
Crocker, J. Christopher
1977   "My Brother the Parrot." In *The Social Use of Metaphor,* ed. J. David Sapir
          and J. Christopher Crocker, 164–192. Philadelphia: University of Pennsylva-
          nia Press.
Cruz, Juan Manuel
1993   "Clausuran cafetería de maquiladora pese a que la habían inspeccionado."
          Norte de Ciudad Juárez, May 26, 3B.
Cruz, Juan Manuel, and J. Martínez
1993   "Solicitarán cancelar las concesiones a cafetería." *Norte de Ciudad Juárez,*
          May 28, 5B.

De Genova, Nicholas
2005   *Working the Boundaries: Race, Space, and "Illegality" in Mexican Chicago.*
          Durham: Duke University Press.
De Genova, Nicholas, and Ana Y. Ramos-Zayas
2003   *Latino Crossings: Mexicans, Puerto Ricans, and the Politics of Race and Citi-
          zenship.* New York: Routledge.

Derrida, Jacques
1978   *Writing and Difference.* Trans. Alan Bass. Chicago: University of Chicago
        Press. (Orig. pub. 1966.)
Díaz del Castillo, Bernal
1956   *The Discovery and Conquest of Mexico, 1517–1521.* New York: Random House.
1963   *The Conquest of New Spain.* Trans. J. M. Cohen. New York: Penguin. (Orig.
        pub. 1568.)
Diccionario de la Lengua Española.
1992   Madrid: Real Academia Española.
di Leonardo, Micaela
1991   "Introduction: Gender, Culture, and Political Economy: Feminist Anthro-
        pology in Historical Perspective." In *Gender at the Crossroads of Knowledge:
        Feminist Anthropology in the Postmodern Era,* ed. Micaela di Leonardo,
        1–48. Berkeley: University of California Press.
Dore, Elizabeth, and Maxine Molyneux, eds.
2000   *Hidden Histories of Gender and the State in Latin America.* Durham: Duke
        University Press.
Dow, Pauline
1987   "Maids of El Paso." Master's thesis, Department of Sociology, University of
        Texas at El Paso.
Duara, Prasenjit, ed.
2004   *Decolonization: Perspectives from Now and Then.* New York: Routledge.
Dubois, Laurent
1995   "'Man's Darkest Hours': Maleness, Travel, and Anthropology." In *Women
        Writing Culture,* ed. Ruth Behar and Deborah A. Gordon, 306–321. Berke-
        ley: University of California Press.
Duncan, Dawn
2002   "A Flexible Foundation: Constructing a Postcolonial Dialogue." In *Relocat-
        ing Postcolonialism,* ed. David Theo Goldberg and Ato Quayson, 320–333.
        Malden, MA: Blackwell Publishing.
Durkheim, Emile
[1893] 1933   *The Division of Labor.* Trans. George Simpson. New York: Free Press.
[1912] 1965   *The Elementary Forms of the Religious Life.* Trans. J. W. Swain. New York:
        Random House.
Dutton, Bertha
1983   *American Indians of the Southwest.* Albuquerque: University of New
        Mexico Press.

Ebron, Paulla, and Anna Lowenhaupt Tsing
1995   "In Dialogue? Reading across Minority Discourses." In *Women Writing
        Culture,* ed. Ruth Behar and Deborah A. Gordon, 373–389. Berkeley: Uni-
        versity of California Press.
Ehrenreich, Barbara
1983   *The Hearts of Men: American Dreams and the Flight from Commitment.*
        New York: Anchor Press.

Elliot, J. H.

1986   "Introduction: Cortés, Velázquez, and Charles V." In *Hernán Cortés: Letters from Mexico,* trans. and ed. Anthony Pagden, xi–xxxvii. New Haven: Yale University Press.

Elson, Diane, and Ruth Pearson

1984   "The Subordination of Women and the Internationalization of Factory Production." In *Of Marriage and the Market: Women's Subordination Internationally and Its Lessons,* ed. Kate Young et al., 18–40. London: Routledge.

Encinias, Miguel, Alfred Rodríguez, and Joseph P. Sánchez, trans. and eds.

1992   *Historia de la Nueva México, 1610.* By Gaspar Pérez de Villagrá. Albuquerque: University of New Mexico Press.

Fernandez, James W.

1986   *Persuasions and Performances: The Play of Tropes in Culture.* Bloomington: Indiana University Press.

1991   *Beyond Metaphor: The Theory of Tropes in Anthropology.* Stanford, CA: Stanford University Press.

Fernández-Kelly, María Patricia

1983   *For We Are Sold, I and My People: Women and Industry in Mexico's Frontier.* Albany: State University of New York Press.

Flores, Juan

1993   *Divided Borders: Essays on Puerto Rican Identity.* Houston: Arte Público Press.

Flores, William V., and Rina Benmayor, eds.

1997   *Latino Cultural Citizenship: Claiming Identity, Space, and Rights.* Boston: Beacon Press.

Foucault, Michel

1970   *The Order of Things: An Archaeology of the Human Sciences.* New York: Pantheon Books.

1978   *The History of Sexuality, Vol. 1.* New York: Pantheon.

Fregoso, Rosa Linda

2003   *meXicana Encounters: The Making of Social Identities on the Borderlands.* Durham: Duke University Press.

Froebel, Folker, et al.

1980   *The New International Division of Labor.* Cambridge: Cambridge University Press.

Fuentes, Annette, and Barbara Ehrenreich

1983   *Women in the Global Factory.* New York: South End Press.

Fusco, Coco

1995   *English Is Broken Here: Notes on Cultural Fusion in the Americas.* New York: The New Press.

Galindo, Alejandro, dir.

1953   *Espaldas mojadas.* Mexican film.

García, Alma M., ed.
1997   *Chicana Feminist Thought: The Basic Historical Writings.* New York:
         Routledge.
García, Mario T.
1981   *Desert Immigrants: The Mexicans of El Paso, 1880–1920.* New Haven: Yale
         University Press.
García-Mason, Velma
1979   "Acoma Pueblo." In *Handbook of North American Indians, Vol. 9:
         Southwest,* ed. Alfonso Ortiz, 450–466. Washington, DC: Smithsonian
         Institution.
García Sáiz, María Concepción
1989   *The Castes: A Genre of Mexican Painting* [*Las castas mexicanas: Un género
         pictórico americano*]. Milan, Italy: Olivetti.
Geertz, Clifford
1973a   *The Interpretation of Cultures.* New York: Basic Books.
1973b   "Religion as a Cultural System." In *The Interpretation of Cultures,* 87–125.
         New York: Basic Books.
1973c   "Thick Description: Toward an Interpretive Theory of Culture." In *The
         Interpretation of Cultures,* 3–30. New York: Basic Books.
Gerhard, Peter
1972   "Colonial New Spain, 1519–1786: Historical Notes on the Evolution of
         Minor Political Jurisdictions." In *Guide to Ethnohistorical Sources, Part
         One,* ed. Howard Cline, 63–137. Handbook of Middle American Indians
         Series. Austin: University of Texas Press.
Giddens, Anthony
1979   *Central Problems in Social Theory: Action, Structure, and Contradiction in
         Social Analysis.* Berkeley: University of California Press.
Gilmore, David D.
1990   *Manhood in the Making: Cultural Concepts of Masculinity.* New Haven: Yale
         University Press.
Ginsburg, Faye
1997   "The 'Word-Made' Flesh: The Disembodiment of Gender in the Abortion
         Debate." In *Situated Lives,* ed. Louise Lamphere, Helena Ragone, and Patri-
         cia Zavella, 142–156. New York: Routledge.
Ginsburg, Faye, and Anna Lowenhaut Tsing, eds.
1990   *Uncertain Terms: Negotiating Gender in American Culture.* Boston: Beacon
         Press.
Goldberg, David Theo, and Ato Quayson, eds.
2002   *Relocating Postcolonialism.* Malden, MA: Blackwell Publishing.
González Obregón, Luis
1959   *México viejo: 1521–1821.* Mexico City: Editorial Patria.
González Rodríguez, Sergio
2002   *Huesos en el desierto.* Barcelona: Editorial Anagrama.
2003   "Los intocables." *Norte de Ciudad Juárez,* August 25, 5B.

Gordon, Deborah A.

1995   "Border Work: Feminist Ethnography and the Dissemination of Literacy."
        In *Women Writing Culture,* ed. Ruth Behar and Deborah A. Gordon, 373–
        389. Berkeley: University of California Press.

Gordon, Deborah A., and Ruth Behar, eds.

1995   *Women Writing Culture.* Berkeley: University of California Press.

Gramsci, Antonio

1971   *Selections from the Prison Notebooks.* Ed. and trans. Quintin Hoare and
        Geoffrey Nowell-Smith. New York: International Publishers.

1985   *Selections from Cultural Writings.* Ed. Geoffrey Nowell-Smith. Cambridge:
        Harvard University Press.

Gregory, Derek

2004   *The Colonial Present: Afghanistan, Palestine, and Iraq.* Malden, MA: Black-
        well Publishers.

Griswold del Castillo, Richard

1990   *The Treaty of Guadalupe Hidalgo: A Legacy of Conflict.* Norman: University
        of Oklahoma Press.

Grossberg, Lawrence

1996   "Identity and Cultural Studies—Is That All There Is?" In *Questions of
        Cultural Identity,* ed. Stuart Hall and Paul du Gay, 87–107. London: Sage
        Publications.

Gruzinski, Serge

2002   *The Mestizo Mind: The Intellectual Dynamics of Colonization and Globaliza-
        tion.* New York: Routledge.

Gupta, Akhil, and James Ferguson

1997   "Beyond 'Culture': Space, Identity, and the Politics of Difference." In *Cul-
        ture, Power, Place: Explorations in Critical Anthropology,* ed. Akhil Gupta
        and James Ferguson, 33–51. Durham: Duke University Press.

Gutiérrez, Ramón A.

1989   "Aztlán, Montezuma, and New Mexico: The Political Uses of Ameri-
        can Indian Mythology." In *Aztlán: Essays on the Chicano Homeland,* ed.
        Rudolfo A. Anaya and Francisco A. Lomelí, 172–190. Albuquerque: Univer-
        sity of New Mexico Press.

1991   *When Jesus Came, the Corn Mothers Went Away: Marriage, Sexuality, and
        Power in New Mexico, 1500–1846.* Stanford: Stanford University Press.

Gutmann, Matthew C.

1996   *The Meanings of Macho: Being a Man in Mexico City.* Berkeley: University
        of California Press.

2000   "A (Short) Cultural History of Mexican Machos and Hombres." In *Gender
        Matters: Rereading Michelle Z. Rosaldo,* ed. Alejandro Lugo and Bill Mau-
        rer, 160–184. Ann Arbor: University of Michigan Press.

Guzmán, Eulalia

1989   *Una visión crítica de la historia de la conquista de México-Tenochtitlán.*
        Mexico City: Universidad Autónoma de México, Instituto de Investigacio-
        nes Antropológicas.

Guzmán Betancourt, Ignacio, ed.
1998   *Los nombres de México.* Mexico City: Miguel Ángel Porrúa.

Hall, Stuart
1986   "Gramsci's Relevance for the Study of Race and Ethnicity." *Journal of Communication Inquiry* 10(2):5–27.
Haraway, Donna
1986   "Situated Knowledges: The Science Question in Feminism and the Privilege of Partial Perspective." *Feminist Studies* 14(3):575–599.
1991   *Simians, Cyborgs, and Women: The Reinvention of Nature.* New York: Routledge.
Hart, John Mason, ed.
1998   *Border Crossings: Mexican and Mexican-American Workers.* Wilmington, DE: SR Books.
Herdt, Gilbert H.
1981   *Guardians of the Flutes: Idioms of Masculinity.* New York: McGraw-Hill.
Hernández Palacios, Luis, and Juan Manuel Sandoval
1989   *Frontera norte: Chicanos, pachucos y cholos.* Zacatecas, Mexico: Ancien régime (Universidad Autónoma de Zacatecas).
Herzfeld, Michael
1985   *Poetics of Manhood: Contest and Identity in a Cretan Mountain Village.* Princeton: Princeton University Press.
Heyman, Josiah McC.
1991   *Life and Labor on the Border: Working People of Northeastern Sonora, Mexico, 1886–1986.* Tucson: University of Arizona Press.
1998   *Finding a Moral Heart for U.S. Immigration Policy: An Anthropological Perspective.* American Ethnological Society Monograph Series, No. 7. Arlington, VA: American Anthropological Association.
Hertzog, Carl, and Bud Newman
n.d.   *The Mission Nuestra Señora de Guadalupe del Paso.* University of Texas at El Paso, Special Collections.
Hill, Jane
1993   "Hasta La Vista, Baby: Anglo Spanish in the American Southwest." *Critique of Anthropology* 13(2):177–208.
Hill, Jane H., and K. C. Hill
1986   *Speaking Mexicano: Dynamics of Syncretic Language in Central Mexico.* Tucson: University of Arizona Press.
Hill, Sarah
2003   "Metaphoric Enrichment and Material Poverty: The Making of 'Colonias.'" In *Ethnography at the Border,* ed. Pablo Vila, 141–165. Minneapolis: University of Minnesota Press.
Hobbes, Thomas
[1642] 1958   *Leviathan.* New York: Liberal Arts Press.
Houser, Nicholas P.
1979   "Tigua Pueblo." In *Handbook of North American Indians, Vol. 9: Southwest,* ed. Alfonso Ortiz, 336–342. Washington, DC: Smithsonian Institution.

Humboldt, Alejandro
[1822] 1998   "Ensayo político sobre el reino de la Nueva España, 1808–1822." In *Los
               nombres de México,* ed. Ignacio Guzmán Betancourt, 199–201. Mexico City:
               Miguel Ángel Porrúa.
Huyssen, Andreas
1990   "Mapping Postmodernism." In *Feminism/Postmodernism,* ed. Linda Nich-
               olson, 267–271. New York: Routledge.

Iglesias, Norma
1985   *La flor más bella de la maquiladora: Historias de vida de la mujer obrera en
               Tijuana, B.C.N.* Mexico City: Secretaría de Educación Pública.

Jackson, Robert H., ed.
1998   *New Views of Borderlands History.* Albuquerque: University of New Mexico
               Press.
Julyan, Robert
1998   *The Place Names of New Mexico,* Rev. ed. Albuquerque: University of New
               Mexico Press.

Kearney, Michael
1991   "Borders and Boundaries of State and Self at the End of Empire." *Journal of
               Historical Sociology* 4(1):52–74.
1996   *Reconceptualizing the Peasantry: Anthropology in Global Perspective.* Boul-
               der: Westview Press.
Keesing, Roger
1994   "Theories of Culture Revisited." In *Assessing Cultural Anthropology,* ed.
               Robert Borofsky, 301–312. New York: McGraw-Hill.
Kelleher, William F., Jr.
2003   *Troubles in Ballybogoin: Memory and Identity in Northern Ireland.* Ann
               Arbor: University of Michigan Press.
Klor de Alva, Jorge
1992   Foreword to *The Broken Spears,* by Miguel León-Portilla. Boston: Beacon
               Press.
1995   "The Postcolonization of the (Latin) American Experience: A Reconsidera-
               tion of 'Colonialism,' 'Postcolonialism,' and 'Mestizaje.'" In *After Colonial-
               ism: Imperial Histories and Postcolonial Displacements,* ed. Gyan Prakash,
               241–275. Princeton: Princeton University Press.
Kopinak, Kathryn
1996   *Desert Capitalism: Maquiladoras in North America's Western Industrial Cor-
               ridor.* Tucson: University of Arizona Press.
Kuhn, Josh
1997   "Against Easy Listening: Audiotopic Readings and Transnational Sound-
               ings." In *Every-night Life: Culture and Dance in Latin/o America,* ed. Celeste
               Fraser Delgado and José Esteban Muñoz, 288–309. Durham: Duke Univer-
               sity Press.

Lakoff, George, and Mark Johnson
1980   "Conceptual Metaphor in Everyday Language." *The Journal of Philosophy*
        87(8):453–486.
Lamphere, Louise
1987   "Feminism and Anthropology: The Struggle to Reshape Our Thinking
        about Gender." In *The Impact of Feminist Research in the Academy,* ed.
        Christie Farnham, 67–77. Bloomington: Indiana University Press.
1993   "The Domestic Sphere of Women and the Public World of Men: The
        Strengths and Limitations of an Anthropological Dichotomy." In *Gender in
        Cross-Cultural Perspective,* ed. Caroline B. Brettell and Carolyn F. Sargent,
        67–77. Englewood, NJ: Prentice-Hall.
Lamphere, Louise, Helena Ragoné, and Patricia Zavella, eds.
1997   *Situated Lives: Gender and Culture in Everyday Life.* New York: Routledge.
Lancaster, Roger N.
1988   "Subject Honor and Object Shame: The Construction of Male Homosexu-
        ality and Stigma in Nicaragua." *Ethnology* 27(2):111–125.
1992   *Life Is Hard: Machismo, Danger, and the Intimacy of Power in Nicaragua.*
        Berkeley: University of California Press.
1997   "Guto's Performance: Notes on Transvestism of Everyday Life." In *Sex and
        Sexuality in Latin America,* ed. Daniel Balderston and Donna J. Guy, 9–32.
        New York: New York University Press.
Lavie, Smadar, and Ted Swedenburg
1996   *Displacement, Diaspora, and Geographies of Identity.* Durham: Duke Uni-
        versity Press.
Lavrin, Asunción, ed.
1989   *Sexuality and Marriage in Colonial Latin America.* Lincoln: University of
        Nebraska Press.
Leach, Edmund
1976   *Culture and Communication: The Logic by Which Symbols Are Connected.*
        Cambridge: Cambridge University Press.
Leacock, Eleanor
1981   *Myths of Male Dominance.* New York: Monthly Review Press.
León-Portilla, Miguel
1992   *The Broken Spears: The Aztec Account of the Conquest of Mexico.* Boston:
        Beacon Press. (Orig. pub. 1962.)
Lerma, Jorge
1990   "Los mandados." Recorded by Vicente Fernandez in *Vicente Fernández: 15
        Grandes Éxitos.* Miami, FL: CBS.
Lévi-Strauss, Claude
1966   *The Savage Mind.* Trans. George Weidenfeld and Nicolson Ltd. Chicago:
        University of Chicago Press.
Lewin, Ellen
1995   "Writing Lesbian Ethnography." In *Women Writing Culture,* ed. Ruth Behar
        and Deborah A. Gordon, 322–335. Berkeley: University of California Press.
2006   *Feminist Anthropology: A Reader.* New York: Routledge.

Lewis, Laura A.

2000   "Black, Black Indians, Afromexicans: The Dynamics of Race, Nation, and
        Identity in a Moreno Mexican Community (Guerrero)." *American Ethnolo-
        gist* 27(4):898–926.

2001   "Of Ships and Saints: History, Memory, and Place in the Making of Moreno
        Mexican Identity." *Cultural Anthropology* 16(1):62–82.

2004   "Modesty and Modernity: Photography, Race, and Representation on
        Mexico's Costa Chica (Guerrero)." *Identities: Global Studies in Culture and
        Power* 11(4):471–499.

Limón, Jose

1989   "Carne, Carnales, and the Carnivalesque: Bakhtinian Batos, Disorder, and
        Narrative Discourses." *American Ethnologist* 16:471–486.

1994   *Dancing with the Devil: Society and Cultural Poetics in Mexican-American
        South Texas.* Madison: University of Wisconsin Press.

Linne, Sigvald

1948   *El Valle y la Ciudad de México en 1550.* Stockholm, Sweden: Esselte.

Lipschutz, Alejandro

1944   *El indoamericanismo y el problema racial en las Américas.* Santiago, Chile:
        Editorial Nascimiento.

Lockhart, James

1992   *The Nahuas after the Conquest: A Social and Cultural History of the Indians
        of Central Mexico, Sixteenth through Eighteenth Centuries.* Stanford, CA:
        Stanford University Press.

Lomnitz, Claudio

2001   *Deep Mexico, Silent Mexico: An Anthropology of Nationalism.* Minneapolis:
        University of Minnesota Press.

Lugo, Alejandro

1987   "Maquiladoras, Gender, and Culture Change in Ciudad Juárez, Mexico."
        Unpublished preliminary report, Ibero-American Studies, University of
        Wisconsin at Madison.

1990   "Cultural Production and Reproduction in Ciudad Juárez, Mexico: Tropes
        at Play among Maquiladora Workers." *Cultural Anthropology* 5(3):173–196.

1995   "Fragmented Lives, Assembled Goods: A Study in Maquilas, Culture, and
        History at the Mexican Borderlands." Ph.D. diss., Department of Anthro-
        pology, Stanford University.

1997   "Reflections on Border Theory, Culture, and the Nation." In *Border Theory:
        The Limits of Cultural Politics,* ed. Scott Michaelsen and David E. Johnson,
        43–67. Minneapolis: University of Minnesota Press.

2000a   "Destabilizing the Masculine, Refocusing 'Gender': Men and the Aura
        of Authority in Michelle Z. Rosaldo's Work." In *Gender Matters: Reread-
        ing Michelle Z. Rosaldo,* ed. Alejandro Lugo and Bill Maurer, 54–89. Ann
        Arbor: University of Michigan Press.

2000b   "Theorizing Border Inspections." *Cultural Dynamics* 12(3):353–373.

2003   "Genders Matter: Women, Men, and the Production of Feminist Knowl-
        edge." In *Disciplines on the Line: Feminist Research on Spanish, Latin*

American, and U.S. Latina Women, ed. Anne J. Cruz, Rosilie Hernández-
Pecoraro, and Joyce Tolliver, 79–100. Newark, DE: Juan de la Cuesta Press.

Lugo, Alejandro, and Bill Maurer

2000   "The Legacy of Michelle Rosaldo: Politics and Gender in Modern Soci-
        eties." In *Gender Matters: Rereading Michelle Z. Rosaldo,* ed. Alejandro
        Lugo and Bill Maurer, 16–34. Ann Arbor: University of Michigan Press.

Lugo, Mario

1998   *Detén mis trémulas manos: Crónicas de suicidios.* Chihuahua, Mexico: Solar
        Colección.

Lutz, Catherine

1995   "The Gender of Theory." In *Women Writing Culture,* ed. Ruth Behar and
        Deborah A. Gordon, 249–266. Berkeley: University of California Press.

MacCormack, Carol, and Marilyn Strathern, eds.

1980   *Nature, Culture, and Gender.* Cambridge: Cambridge University Press.

MacKinnon, Catharine A.

1982   "Feminism, Marxism, Method, and the State: An Agenda for Theory."
        In *Feminist Critique: A Critique of Ideology,* ed. Nannerl O. Keohane,
        Michelle Z. Rosaldo, and Barbara C. Gelpi, 1–30. Chicago: University of
        Chicago Press.

Maciel, David R., and María Rosa García-Acevedo

1998   "The Celluloid Immigrant: The Narrative Films of Mexican Immigration."
        In *Culture across Borders: Mexican Immigration and Popular Culture,* ed.
        David R. Maciel and María Herrera-Sobek, 149–202. Tucson: University of
        Arizona Press.

Maciel, David R., and María Herrera-Sobek, eds.

1998   *Culture across Borders: Mexican Immigration and Popular Culture.* Tucson:
        University of Arizona Press.

Malinowski, Bronislaw

1944   *A Scientific Theory of Culture and Other Essays.* Chapel Hill: University of
        North Carolina Press.

Mallon, Florencia

1994   "The Promise and Dilemma of Subaltern Studies: Perspectives from Latin
        American History." *American Historical Review* 99(5):1491–1515.

Marcus, George E.

1986   "Contemporary Problems of Ethnography in the Modern World System."
        In *Writing Culture: The Poetics and Politics of Ethnography,* ed. James Clif-
        ford and George Marcus, 165–193. Berkeley: University of California Press.

1994   "After the Critique of Ethnography: Faith, Hope, and Charity, but the
        Greatest of These Is Charity." In *Assessing Cultural Anthropology,* ed. Robert
        Borofsky, 40–52. New York: McGraw-Hill.

Marcus, George, and Michael Fischer

1986   *Anthropology as Cultural Critique.* Chicago: University of Chicago Press.

Márquez Terrazas, Zacarías

1991   *Origen de la iglesia en Chihuahua.* Chihuahua: Editorial Camino.

Martín-Rodríguez, Manuel M.
1996   "The Global Border: Transnationalism and Cultural Hybridism in Alejan-
          dro Morales's 'The Rag Doll Plagues.'" In *Alejandro Morales: Fiction Past,
          Present, Future Perfect,* edited by José Antonio Gurpegui, 86–98. Tempe,
          AZ: Bilingual Review.
Martínez, Josefina
1993a   "Intoxicación en maquila." *Norte de Ciudad Juárez.* May 27, 9B.
1993b   "Se intoxican 30 obreros en Corcom." *Norte de Ciudad Juárez,* May 22, 4B.
Martínez, Josefina, and Juan Manuel Cruz
1993   "Culpan al mal manejo de los alimentos de las intoxicaciones masivas en
          las maquiladoras." *Norte de Ciudad Juárez,* May 29, 3B.
Martínez, José Luis, ed.
1990   *Documentos cortesianos.* Vol. 1–4. Mexico City: Fondo de Cultura
          Económica.
Martínez, Oscar
1978   *Border Boom Town: Ciudad Juárez since 1848.* Austin: University of Texas
          Press.
Mecham, J. Lloyd
1968   *Francisco de Ibarra and Nueva Vizcaya:* New York: Greenwood Press.
          (Orig. pub. 1927.)
Menchaca, Martha
1993   "Chicano Indianism: A Historical Account of Racial Repression in the
          United States." *American Ethnologist* 20(3):583–603.
Michaelsen, Scott, and David E. Johnson, eds.
1997   *Border Theory: The Limits of Cultural Politics.* Minneapolis: University of
          Minnesota Press.
Montoya, Rosario, Lessie Jo Frazier, and Janise Hurtig, eds.
2002   *Gender's Place: Feminist Anthropologies of Latin America.* New York:
          Palgrave Macmillan.
Mora, Pat
1984   *Chants.* Houston, TX: Arte Público Press.
Morales, Alejandro
1996   "Dynamic Identities in Heterotopia." In *Alejandro Morales: Fiction Past,
          Present, Future Perfect,* ed. José Antonio Gurpegui, 14–27. Tempe, AZ:
          Bilingual Review Press.
Moran, Rachel
2001   *Interracial Intimacy: The Regulation of Race and Romance.* Chicago: Uni-
          versity of Chicago Press.
Morner, Magnus
1967   *Race Mixture in the History of Latin America.* Boston: Little Brown.
Mortón, Carlos
1993   "Of Two Minds, of Two Worlds." *Vista* (Summer): N.p.

Nash, June
1983   "The Impact of the Changing International Division of Labor on Different
          Sectors of the Labor Force." In *Women, Men, and the International Division*

of Labor, ed. June Nash and María Patricia Fernández-Kelly, 3–38. Albany: State University of New York Press.

2001　*Mayan Visions: The Quest for Autonomy in an Age of Globalization.* New York: Routledge.

Nash, June, and María Patricia Fernández-Kelly, eds.

1983　*Women, Men, and the International Division of Labor.* Albany: State University of New York Press.

Newton, Judith, and Judith Stacey

1995　"Reflections on Studying Academic Men." In *Women Writing Culture,* ed. Ruth Behar and Deborah A. Gordon, 287–305. Berkeley: University of California Press.

Oboler, Suzanne

1995　*Ethnic Labels, Latino Lives: Identity and the Politics of (Re)Presentation in the United States.* Minneapolis: University of Minnesota Press.

Ohnuki-Tierney, Emiko

1987a　*The Monkey as Mirror: Symbolic Transformations in Japanese History and Ritual.* Princeton: Princeton University Press.

1987b　"Why Metaphor?" Paper presented in the Metaphor Theory in Anthropology session at the American Anthropological Association Meetings in Chicago.

1990　"The Ambivalent Self of the Contemporary Japanese." *Cultural Anthropology* 5(2):197–216.

O'Laughlin, Bridget

1974　"Mediation of Contradiction: Why Mbum Women Do Not Eat Chicken." In *Woman, Culture, and Society,* ed. Michelle Zimbalist Rosaldo and Louise Lamphere, 301–318. Stanford: Stanford University Press.

Olwig, Karen Fog, and Kirsten Hastrup, eds.

1997　*Siting Culture: The Shifting Anthropological Object.* New York: Routledge.

Ong, Aihwa

1987　*Spirits of Resistance and Capitalist Discipline: Factory Women in Malaysia.* Albany: State University of New York Press.

1995　"Women Out of China: Traveling Tales and Traveling Theories in Postcolonial Feminism." In *Women Writing Culture,* ed. Ruth Behar and Deborah A. Gordon, 350–372. Berkeley: University of California Press.

Opler, Morris E.

1983　"The Apachean Culture Pattern and Its Origins." In *Handbook of North American Indians, Vol. 10: Southwest,* ed. Alfonso Ortiz, 368–392. Washington, DC: Smithsonian Institution.

Orozco Orozco, Víctor

1992　*Las guerras indias en la historia de Chihuahua.* Ciudad Juárez: Universidad Autónoma de Ciudad Juárez—Instituto Chihuahuense de la Cultura.

Ortiz, Víctor

2003　"El Paso as an Eternal Yet Not Last Frontier." In *Ethnography at the Border,* ed. Pablo Vila, 236–250. Minneapolis: University of Minnesota Press.

Ortner, Sherry

1974   "Is Female to Male as Nature Is to Culture?" In *Woman, Culture, and So-ciety,* ed. Michelle Zimbalist Rosaldo and Louise Lamphere, 67–87. Stanford: Stanford University Press.

1984   "Theory in Anthropology since the Sixties." *Comparative Studies in Society and History* 26(1):126–166.

Pagden, Anthony

1986   "Translator's Introduction." In *Hernán Cortés: Letters from Mexico,* trans. and ed. Anthony Pagden, xxxix–lxvii. New Haven: Yale University Press.

Paredes, Américo

1958   *With His Pistol in His Hand: A Border Ballad and Its Hero.* Austin: University of Texas Press.

1968   "Folk Medicine and the Intercultural Jest." In *Spanish-Speaking People in the United States,* American Ethnological Society Proceedings of the 1968 Annual Spring Meeting, ed. June Helm, 104–119. Seattle: University of Washington Press.

Paz, Octavio

1985   *The Labyrinth of Solitude and Other Writings.* New York: Grove Press. (Orig. pub. 1961.)

Peña, Devon G.

1980   "Las Maquiladoras: Mexican Women and Class Struggle in the Border Industries." *Aztlán* 1(2):159–229.

1997   *The Terror of the Machine: Technology, Work, Gender, and Ecology on the U.S.-Mexico Border.* Austin: University of Texas Press.

Pérez Espino, José

1995   "Se intoxican 180 en RCA." *Diario de Juárez,* November 10, 1B.

Pérez-Firmat, Gustavo

1994   *Life on the Hyphen: The Cuban-American Way.* Austin: University of Texas Press.

Piña, Michael

1989   "The Archaic, Historical and Mythicized Dimensions of Aztlán." In *Aztlán: Essays on the Chicano Homeland,* ed. Rudolfo A. Anaya and Francisco A. Lomelí, 14–48. Albuquerque: University of New Mexico Press.

Portillo, Lourdes

2001   *Señorita Extraviada.* Documentary. New York: Distributed by Women Make Movies.

Prakash, Gyan

1990   "Writing Post-Orientalist Histories of the Third World: Perspectives from Indian Historiography." *Comparative Studies in Society and History* 32(2):383–408.

Radcliffe-Brown, A. R.

1952   *Structure and Function in Primitive Society.* New York: Free Press.

Rapp, Rayna

1997   "Constructing Amniocentesis: Maternal and Medical Discourses." In

Situated Lives, ed. Louise Lamphere, Helena Ragone, and Patricia Zavella, 128–141. New York: Routledge.

Reglamento interior del trabajo.

1980   Internal brochure distributed to workers at an automobile maquiladora, Ciudad Juárez, Mexico.

Reiter, Rayna

1975   "Men and Women in the South of France: Public and Private Domains." In *Toward an Anthropology of Women,* ed. Rayna Reiter, 252–282. New York: Monthly Review Press.

Richards, I. A.

1965   *The Philosophy of Rhetoric.* New York: Oxford University Press. (Orig. pub. 1936.)

Riva Palacio, Vicente

1888   *México a través de los siglos.* Vol. 1. Mexico City: Ballescá y Comp.

Robertson, Donald

1959   *Mexican Manuscript Painting of the Early Colonial Period: The Metropolitan Schools.* New Haven: Yale University Press.

Rodríguez, Ileana, ed.

2001   *The Latin American Subaltern Studies Reader.* Durham: Duke University Press.

Rodríguez, Victoria E., and Peter M. Ward

1992   *Policymaking, Politics, and Urban Governance in Chihuahua.* Austin: LBJ School of Public Affairs.

Romero, Mary

2003   "Nanny Diaries and Other Stories: Imagining Women's Labor in the Social Reproduction of American Families." *DePaul Law Review* 52(3):809–847.

2005   "Violation of Latino Civil Rights Resulting from INS and Local Police's Use of Race, Culture, and Class Profiling: The Case of the Chandler Roundup in Arizona." *Cleveland State Law Review* 52(1&2):75–96.

Rosaldo, Michelle Zimbalist

1974   "Woman, Culture, and Society: A Theoretical Overview." In *Woman, Culture, and Society,* ed. Michelle Zimbalist Rosaldo and Louise Lamphere, 17–42. Stanford: Stanford University Press.

1980   "The Use and Abuse of Anthropology: Reflections on Feminism and Cross-Cultural Understanding." *Signs* 5(3):389–417.

Rosaldo, Michelle Zimbalist, and Louise Lamphere, eds.

1974   *Woman, Culture, and Society.* Stanford: Stanford University Press.

Rosaldo, Renato

1980   *Ilongot Headhunting 1883–1974: A Study in Society and History.* Stanford: Stanford University Press.

1993   *Culture and Truth: The Remaking of Social Analysis.* Boston: Beacon Press. (Orig. pub. 1989.)

1997   "Cultural Citizenship, Inequality, and Multiculturalism." In *Latino Cultural Citizenship: Claiming Identity, Space, and Rights,* ed. William V. Flores and Rina Benmayor, 27–38. Boston: Beacon Press.

Rosaldo, Renato, and William Flores
1997   "Identity, Conflict, and Evolving Latino Communities: Cultural Citizenship
          in San Jose, California." In *Latino Cultural Citizenship: Claiming Identity,
          Space, and Rights,* ed. William V. Flores and Rina Benmayor, 57–96. Boston:
          Beacon Press.
Rouse, Roger
1996   "Mexican Migrants and the Space of Postmodernism." In *Between Two
          Worlds: Mexican Immigrants in the United States,* ed. David Gutiérrez, 247–
          263. Wilmington, DE: Scholarly Resources.
Ruiz, Vicki L., and Susan Tiano, eds.
1987   *Women on the U.S.-Mexico Border: Responses to Change.* Boston: Allen and
          Unwin.

Sacks, Karen
1974   "Engels Revisited: Women, the Organization of Production, and Private
          Property." In *Woman, Culture, and Society,* ed. Michelle Zimbalist Rosaldo
          and Louise Lamphere, 207–222. Stanford: Stanford University Press.
1979   *Sisters and Wives: The Past and the Future of Sexual Equality.* Westport, CT:
          Greenwood Press.
Sáenz, Benjamin Alire
1992   *Flowers for the Broken: Stories.* Seattle: Broken Moon Press.
Safa, Helen
1981   "Runaway Shops and Female Employment: The Search for Cheap Labor."
          Signs 7(2):418–433.
Sahlins, Marshall
1981   *Historical Metaphors and Mythical Realities: Structure in the Early History of
          the Sandwich Islands Kingdom.* Ann Arbor: University of Michigan Press.
1982   "Individual Experience and Cultural Order." In *The Social Sciences: Their
          Nature and Uses,* ed. William H. Krustel, 35–48. Chicago: University of Chi-
          cago Press.
1985   *Islands of History.* Chicago: University of Chicago Press.
2000   *Culture in Practice: Selected Essays.* New York: Zone Books.
Said, Edward
2002   "In Conversation with Neeladri Bhattacharya, Suvir Kaul, and Ania
          Loomba." In *Relocating Postcolonialism,* ed. David Theo Goldberg and Ato
          Quayson, 1–14. Malden, MA: Blackwell Publishing.
Saldívar, José David
1997   *Border Matters: Remapping American Cultural Studies.* Berkeley: University
          of California Press.
Salzinger, Leslie
2003   *Genders in Production.* Berkeley: University of California Press.
Sampson Vera Tudela, Elisa
2000   *Colonial Angels: Narratives of Gender and Spirituality in Mexico, 1580–1750.*
          Austin: University of Texas Press.

Sanday, Peggy Reeves, and Ruth Gallagher Goodenough, eds.

1990   *Beyond the Second Sex: New Directions in the Anthropology of Gender.* Philadelphia: University of Pennsylvania Press.

Sapir, J. David

1977   "The Anatomy of Metaphor." In *The Social Use of Metaphor,* ed. Christopher J. Crocker and J. David Sapir, 3–32. Philadelphia: University of Pennsylvania Press.

Scheffler, Harold W.

1991   "Sexism and Naturalism in the Study of Kinship." In *Gender at the Crossroads of Knowledge: Feminist Anthropology in the Postmodern Era,* ed. Micaela di Leonardo, 361–382. Berkeley: University of California Press.

Schirmer, Jennifer

1994   "The Claiming of Space and the Body Politic within National-Security States: The Plaza de Mayo Madres and the Greenham Common Women." In *Remapping Memory: The Politics of TimeSpace,* ed. Jonathan Boyarin, 185–220. Minneapolis: University of Minnesota Press.

Shapiro, Judith

1979   "Cross-Cultural Perspectives on Sexual Differentiation." In *Human Sexuality: A Comparative and Developmental Perspective,* ed. Herant Katchadourian, 269–308. Berkeley: University of California Press.

1987   "Men in Groups: A Reexamination of Patriliny in Lowland South America." In *Gender and Kinship: Essays toward a Unified Analysis,* ed. Jane F. Collier and Sylvia J. Yanagisako, 301–323. Stanford: Stanford University Press.

1991   "Transsexualism: Reflections on the Persistence of Gender and the Mutability of Sex." In *Body Guards: The Cultural Politics of Gender Ambiguity,* ed. Julia Epstein and Kristina Straubb, 248–279. New York: Routledge.

Singh, Amritjit, and Peter Schmidt, eds.

2000   *Postcolonial Theory and the United States: Race, Ethnicity, and Literature.* Jackson: University Press of Mississippi.

Sklair, Leslie

1989   *Assembling for Development: The Maquila Industry in Mexico and the United States.* San Diego: Center for U.S.-Mexican Studies.

Smith, Michael E.

1996   *The Aztecs.* Malden, MA: Blackwell Publishers.

Solano, Francisco de

1984   *Cedulario de Tierras: Compilación de legislación agraria colonial (1497–1820).* Mexico City: Universidad Nacional Autónoma de México.

Spicer, Edward H.

1962   *Cycles of Conquest.* Tucson: University of Arizona Press.

Spivak, Gayatri C.

1988   "Can the Subaltern Speak?" In *Marxism and the Interpretation of Culture,* ed. Cary Nelson and Lawrence Grossberg, 283–298. Urbana: University of Illinois Press.

Spyer, Patricia

1998   "Introduction." In *Border Fetishisms: Material Objects in Unstable Spaces*,
          ed. Patricia Spyer, 1–11. New York: Routledge.

Staudt, Kathleen

1986   "Economic Change and Ideological Lag in Households of Maquila Workers
          in Ciudad Juárez." In *The Social Ecology and Economic Development of
          Ciudad Juárez*, ed. Gay Young, 97–120. Boulder: Westview Press.

1998   *Free Trade? Informal Economies at the U.S.-Mexico Border*. Philadelphia:
          Temple University Press.

Staudt, Kathleen, and Irasema Coronado

2002   *Fronteras No Más: Toward Social Justice at the U.S.-Mexico Border*. New
          York: Palgrave Macmillan.

Stephen, Lynn

2002   *Zapata Lives!: Histories and Cultural Politics in Southern Mexico*. Berkeley:
          University of California Press.

Stoddard, Ellwyn

1987   *Maquila: Assembly Plants in Northern Mexico*. El Paso: Texas Western
          Press.

Stoler, Ann Laura

1991   "Carnal Knowledge and Imperial Power: Gender, Race, and Morality in
          Colonial Asia." In *Gender at the Crossroads of Knowledge: Feminist Anthro-
          pology in the Postmodern Era*, ed. Micaela di Leonardo, 51–101. Berkeley:
          University of California Press.

Strathern, Marilyn

1988   *The Gender of the Gift: Problems with Women and with Society in Melane-
          sia*. Berkeley: University of California Press.

Taussig, Michael

1987   *Shamanism, Colonialism, and the Wild Man: A Study in Terror and Healing*.
          Chicago: University of Chicago Press.

1998   "Crossing the Face." In *Border Fetishisms: Material Objects in Unstable
          Spaces*, ed. Patricia Spyer, 224–244. New York: Routledge.

Taylor, Lawrence J., and Maeve Hickey

2001   *Tunnel Kids*. Tucson: University of Arizona Press.

Tedlock, Barbara

1995   "Works and Wives: On the Sexual Division of Textual Labor." In *Women
          Writing Culture*, ed. Ruth Behar and Deborah A. Gordon, 267–286. Berke-
          ley: University of California Press.

Thompson, Edward P.

1966   *The Making of the English Working Class*. New York: Vintage Books.

Thurner, Mark

1997   *From Two Republics to One Divided: Contradictions of Postcolonial Nation-
          making in Andean Peru*. Durham: Duke University Press.

Tiano, Susan

1994   *Patriarchy on the Line: Labor, Gender, and Ideology in the Mexican Maquila-
          dora Industry*. Philadelphia: Temple University Press.

Timmons, W. H.
1990 *El Paso: A Borderlands History.* El Paso: Texas Western Press.
Torres-Saillant, Silvio
2002 "Problematic Paradigms: Racial Diversity and Corporate Identity in the Latino Community." In *Latinos Remaking America,* ed. Marcelo M. Suárez-Orozco and Mariela M. Páez, 435–455. Berkeley: University of California Press.
Trejo Delarbe, Raúl
1976 "The Mexican Labor Movement: 1917–1975." *Latin American Perspectives* Issue 8, Vol. 111, No. 1:133–153.
Trouillot, Michel-Rolph
2003 *Global Transformations: Anthropology and the Modern World.* New York: Palgrave Macmillan.
Turner, Terence
1987 "Tropes, Structures, and Operations: A Reinterpretation of the Assertion that 'We Are Araras.'" Paper presented at the symposium "Metaphor Theory in Anthropology," Chicago.
Twinam, Ann
1989 "Honor, Sexuality, and Illegitimacy in Colonial Spanish America." In *Sexuality and Marriage in Colonial Latin America,* ed. Asunción Lavrin, 118–155. Lincoln: University of Nebraska Press.

U.S. Congress
2005 *Border Protection, Antiterrorism, and Illegal Immigration Control Act of 2005.* House of Representatives Bill 4437, 109th U.S. Congress, Washington, DC.

Valdés-Villalva, Guillermina
1985 "New Policies and Strategies of Multinational Corporations during the Mexican National Crisis 1982–1983." In *The U.S. and Mexico: Borderland Development and the National Economies,* ed. Lay J. Gibson and Alfonso C. Rentería, 159–176. Boulder: Westview Press.
Valdivia, Angharad
2005 "Geographies of Latinidad: Deployments of Radical Hybridity in the Mainstream." In *Race, Identity, and Representation in Education,* 2nd ed., ed. Cameron McCarthy et al., 307–317. New York: Routledge.
Valeri, Valerio
1990 "Both Nature and Culture: Reflections on Menstrual and Parturitional Taboos in Huaulu (Seram)." In *Power and Difference: Gender in Island Southeast Asia,* ed. Jane M. Atkinson and Shelly Errington, 253–272. Stanford: Stanford University Press.
Vélez-Ibáñez, Carlos G.
1996 *Border Visions: Mexican Culture of the Southwest United States.* Tucson: University of Arizona Press.
2004 "Regions of Refuge in the United States: Issues, Problems, and Concerns for the Future of Mexican-Origin Populations in the United States."

[Malinowski Award Lecture, 2003] *Human Organization* 63(1):1–20. (Ernesto Galarza Applied Research Center Monograph Series No. 2, University of California, Riverside).

Vélez-Ibáñez, Carlos G., and Anna Sampao, eds.

2002   *Transnational Latina/o Communities: Politics, Processes, and Cultures.* Boulder: Rowman and Littlefield.

Vila, Pablo

2000   *Crossing Borders, Reinforcing Borders: Social Categories, Metaphors, and Narrative Identities on the U.S.-Mexico Frontier.* Austin: University of Texas Press.

————, ed.

2003   *Ethnography at the Border.* Minneapolis: University of Minnesota Press.

Washington-Valdez, Diana

2005   *Cosecha de Mujeres: Safari en el desierto mexicano.* Mexico City: Océano.

Weber, Max

1958   *The Protestant Ethic and the Spirit of Capitalism.* New York: Charles Scribner's Sons. (Orig. pub. 1920.)

1977   "'Objectivity' in Social Science and Social Policy." (Orig. pub. 1905.) In *Understanding and Social Inquiry,* ed. B. Dallmayr and T. McCarthy, 24–37. Notre Dame, IN: University of Notre Dame Press.

Webster's New Collegiate Dictionary.

1974   Springfield, MA: G. & C. Merriam Company.

White, Hayden

1973   *Metahistory: The Historical Imagination in Nineteenth-Century Europe.* Baltimore: Johns Hopkins University Press.

Williams, Raymond

1976   *Keywords: A Vocabulary of Culture and Society.* New York: Oxford University Press.

1979   *Politics and Letters: Interview with New Left Review.* New York: Schoken Books.

Williams, William Carlos

1954   *The Desert Music and Other Poems.* New York: Random House.

Willis, Paul

1977   *Learning to Labor: How Working-Class Kids Get Working-Class Jobs.* New York: Columbia University Press.

Wilson, Thomas W., and Hastings Donnan, eds.

1998   *Border Identities: Nation and State at International Frontiers.* Cambridge: Cambridge University Press.

Wolf, Eric R.

1958   "The Virgin of Guadalupe: A Mexican National Symbol." *Journal of American Folklore* 71(279):34–39.

1959   *Sons of the Shaking Earth: The People of Mexico and Guatemala — Their Land, History, and Culture.* Chicago: University of Chicago Press.

1982   *Europe and the People without History.* Berkeley: University of California Press.

Wright, Melissa

1998　"'Maquiladora Mestizas' and a Feminist Border Politics: Revisiting Anzaldúa." *Hypatia* 13(3):114–131.

Yanagisako, Sylvia, and Jane F. Collier

1987　"Toward a Unified Analysis of Gender and Kinship." In *Gender and Kinship: Essays toward a Unified Analysis,* ed. Jane Collier and Sylvia Yanagisako, 14–50. Stanford: Stanford University Press.

1994　"Gender and Kinship Reconsidered: Toward a Unified Analysis." In *Assessing Cultural Anthropology,* ed. Robert Borofsky, 190–201. New York: McGraw-Hill.

Young, Gay

1986　*The Social Ecology and Economic Development of Ciudad Juárez.* Boulder: Westview Press.

The author and the publisher gratefully acknowledge the permission granted to reproduce the following copyright material in this book:

Images of "La Rosa" and "La Calavera" are used by permission of Don Clemente, Inc., Images, registered at the Instituto Mexicano de la Propiedad, Querétaro, Mexico.

Map "The Entradas of Francisco de Ibarra" is used by permission of Duke University Press (originally published in *Francisco de Ibarra and Nueva Vizcaya* [1927], by J. Lloyd Mecham, p. 114).

Map (from 1660) by Pierre Duval, showing "R. de Nort" flowing from "Nueva Mexico" into "Mer verm e ille" (current Gulf of California), is used by permission of Philip Burden (originally published in *The Mapping of North America*, by Philip D. Burden, p. 454. Ricksmansworth, England: Raleigh Publications, 1996).

Portion from Giovanni Battista Nicolosi's map (Rome 1660) is used by permission of Philip Burden (originally published in *The Mapping of North America*, by Philip D. Burden, p. 454. Ricksmansworth, England: Raleigh Publications, 1996).

Portion of "North America" map, scale ca. 1:21, 250,000, by the Society for the Diffusion of Useful Knowledge, 1844. London: Chas. Knight and Co. Courtesy of the Map and Geography Library, University of Illinois at Urbana-Champaign.

Drawing from illustration "Incidents after the surrender of the Aztec" (originally published in *Broken Spears: The Aztec Account of the Conquest*, by Miguel León-Portilla, p. 143. Boston: Beacon Press, 1990).

Lyrics from song "Los Mandados," by Jorge Lerma, Peer Music de México, 1978.

Three Maps of Ciudad Juárez (Population by Zones, Socioeconomic Zones, and

Industrial Zones and Parks) used by permission and courtesy of Instituto Municipal de Investigación y Planeación, Ciudad Juárez, Chihuahua, Mexico (originally published in Ciudad Juárez, Chihuahua, 1999, in *Desarrollo Económico de Ciudad Juárez*, pp. 7, 17, and 21).

Poem "Mexican Maid," by Pat Mora is reprinted with permission from the publisher of *Chants* (Houston: Arte Público Press–University of Houston, 1985).

Materials reprinted in Chapter 5 from author's "Cultural Production and Reproduction: Tropes at Play among Maquiladora Workers in Ciudad Juárez, Mexico" (published in *Cultural Anthropology* 5, no. 2 [1990]: 173–196), courtesy of the American Anthropological Association.

Materials reprinted in Chapter 8 from author's "Destabilizing the Masculine, Refocusing 'Gender': Men and the Aura of Authority in Michelle Z. Rosaldo's Work" (published in *Gender Matters: Rereading Michelle Z. Rosaldo*, edited by Alejandro Lugo and Bill Maurer, 54–89 [Ann Arbor: University of Michigan Press, 2000]), courtesy of the University of Michigan Press.

Materials reprinted in Chapter 9 from author's "Reflections on Border Theory, Culture, and the Nation" (published in *Border Theory: The Limits of Cultural Politics*, edited by Scott Michaelsen and David Johnson, 43–67 [Minneapolis: University of Minnesota Press, 1997]), courtesy of the University of Minnesota Press.

A serious attempt has been made to trace all copyright holders in order to obtain permission. We would be grateful to be informed of any necessary corrections for future editions of this book.